Essentials of Functional Grammar

Trends in Linguistics

Studies and Monographs 38

Editor

Werner Winter

Mouton de Gruyter
Berlin · New York · Amsterdam

Essentials of Functional Grammar

A Structure-Neutral Theory of Movement, Control, and Anaphora

by

George M. Horn

Mouton de Gruyter
Berlin · New York · Amsterdam   1988

Mouton de Gruyter (formerly Mouton, The Hague)
is a Division of Walter de Gruyter & Co., Berlin.

Library of Congress Cataloging-in-Publication Data

Horn, George M.
  Essentials of functional grammar.

  (Trends in linguistics. Studies and monographs ; 38)
  Bibliography: p.
  Includes index.
  1. Grammar, Comparative and general. 2. Anaphora
  (Linguistics) I. Title. II. Series.
  P151.H57 1988 415 88-18947
  ISBN 0-8992-5348-2 (alk. paper)

Deutsche Bibliothek Cataloging-in-Publication Data

Horn, George M.:
Essentials of functional grammar : a structure-neutral theory of
movement, control, and anaphora / by George M. Horn. -
Berlin ; New York ; Amsterdam : Mouton de Gruyter, 1988
    (Trends in linguistics : Studies and monographs ; 38)
    ISBN 3-11-011286-8
    NE: Trends in linguistics / Studies and monographs

Printed on acid free paper.

Printing: Ratzlow-Druck, Berlin – Binding: Lüderitz & Bauer, Berlin. – Printed in
Germany.

Acknowledgments

I am grateful to the following people for their time and patience in assisting me with the data: Ola Horn (Polish), Anita van der Wal (Dutch), Melinda Meredith (Samoan), Nobuaki Nishioka (Japanese), and Kiyoharu Ono (Japanese). I, of course, take full responsibility for the accuracy of the data and the conclusions reached.

I also wish to thank Geraldine MacNeill and Peter Peterson for their help in editing and proof-reading. Special thanks are due to Joyce Bennett, who worked long hours typing the manuscript and assisting in the editing and revision. Her services have been invaluable.

INTRODUCTION

Lexical-Functional Grammar, Horn (1983a), is essentially a collection of analyses of various bodies of data which are formulated in a functional framework related to that of Bresnan et al., yet differing from it in certain significant respects. This basic approach, I believe, is correct, but the emphasis is on the mechanical properties of the rules of the model, and relatively little attention is given to higher-level generalizations.

Here, I develop a coherent theory of universal grammar (UG) along the same general lines. In this proposal, UG is composed of general rule schemata and related principles and parameters which together define, in effect, the notion "possible grammatical process." The major grammatical processes which I consider are what are traditionally labelled movement, control, and anaphora. Cross-language variation in each of these areas is a consequence of variation of the values of the relevant parameters.

On this level, the proposed theory can be more meaningfully compared with the Government and Binding (GB)Theory and the other variant of Lexical-Functional Theory in the context of the debate over the configurational/non-configurational distinction and the nature of the rules and principles which provide the best explanation of the behavior of languages of these two types. The most important specific innovations of this proposal are the following:

(a) The operations on F-structures discussed in Horn (1983a) are shown to be subcases of two generalized rule systems: the Argument Reduction System and the Generalized Co-Indexing System. The first includes the passivization process, certain other lexical and non-lexical processes which were discussed briefly, and object deletion. The Argument Reduction rules are roughly analogous to, but more general than, the Move NP subcase of the Move-α rule in the GB Theory. The remaining operations, the co-indexing rule, the Raqui rule, the reflexive/reciprocal rule, and the Gerundive/Infinitive Phrase Subject Interpretation Rule, are subcases of a single General Co-Indexing Rule, which is the analog of the control and anaphora rules of the GB theory, but, which again, applies to a rather wider domain.

(b) An S-structure/F-structure Interface Component has been added to UG. This contains rules and principles which mediate between the S-structure and F-structure levels. The role of grammatical functions, as well as the relationship between case and grammatical function is more clearly developed, and the Grammatical Relations Deletion Rule, whose sole function was a house-keeping one, is eliminated.

(c) The four universal F-structure types are replaced by a single canonical form. This, along with a small set of parameters, provides a definition of the notion "possible predicate."

(d) The constraints on the EA rule, which is the analog of wh-movement in the GB Theory, are generalized. The Noun Phrase Constraint (NPC) is shown to be a subcase of a more general Predicate Argument Constraint, which defines the conditions under which both NPs and APs are islands as well as those under which they are not. The NPGOC is eliminated. A set of parameters associated with the remaining two constraints defines the range of cross-language variation of the patterns of wh-movement.

Some knowledge of the material in Horn (1983a) will be helpful, but not essential to understanding this proposal.

TABLE OF CONTENTS

Chapter I

Preliminary Remarks

1. Universal Grammar

In formal terms, universal grammar (UG) consists of general rules and principles from which particular rules of grammar for particular languages are derivable by fixing the values of relevant parameters in permissible ways. An adequate theory of UG must be based on principles which restrict the class of grammars of natural languages in some meaningful way and parameters whose values vary within definable limits. In such a theory, the significant universal grammatical patterns and the observed range of variation within those patterns are a consequence of the interaction of these principles. Therefore, an adequate theory of UG, in effect, defines the notion "possible grammatical process."

On the syntactic level, the major grammatical processes fall into three categories: movement, control, and anaphora. We may think of movement as the process which relates sentence pairs, or S-structure pairs, S_1/S_2, in which some constituent X occurs in position A in S_1, and in position B in S_2. One example is the active/passive pair shown in (1.1):

(1.1) a. Brunhilda hated Smyth
      b. Smyth was hated by Brunhilda

Here, the constituent X is either *Smyth* or *Brunhilda*. In the former case, position A is object position and position B is subject position.

Alternatively, we may think of movement as the process which relates pairs of successive phrase markers, PM_1/PM_2, in which some constituent X occurs in position A in PM_1 and in position B in PM_2. This is illustrated below:

(1.2) a.   Brunhilda seemed to hate Smyth

b.

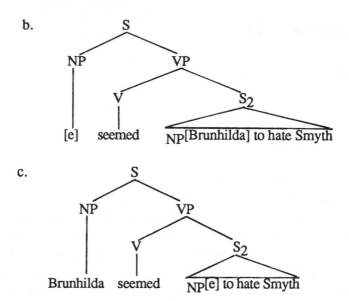

c.

Here, *Brunhilda* is constituent X, position A is the complement subject position in Structure b, and position B is the matrix subject position in Structure c.

Equivalently, we may define movement as the relation between S_1/S_2 pairs or PM_1/PM_2 pairs of this sort.

The control relation is the relation between a noun phrase (NP) antecedent in a phrase marker and an understood complement subject position, which contains no lexical material, elsewhere in the structure. This is illustrated by the following examples:

(1.3) a.   Hortense tried to eat termites
     b.   Hortense forced her dog to eat termites

In example (1.3a), *Hortense*, the subject of the verb *try*, is interpreted as the subject of the embedded verb *eat* also. *Hortense* is the controller of the phonologically empty subject position of *eat*. In some analyses, this position is not represented at any level of syntactic structure (see Brame 1976a,b and Bresnan 1978, for example), and in other analyses, it is represented at the D-structure and S-structure levels as PRO or its equivalent (see Chomsky 1981). Example (1.3b) is analyzed in the same way except that the object, *her dog,* is the controller.

The anaphora relation is the relation between an overt element, or anaphor, which is a member of a set that is designated in each language, and an NP antecedent elsewhere in the structure that it is obligatorily related to, as shown below:

(1.4)   Randolf saw himself in the mirror

Here, *himself* is the overt anaphor and *Randolf* is the antecedent.

The issue which I raise here does not concern the empirical adequacy of any of the current major theories, but rather the nature of the principles upon which an adequate theory of UG should be based. It is impossible to argue for or against a theory on purely empirical grounds. Any theory can be augmented to account for additional data. The criterion for evaluating theories is the rather more subtle one of relative plausibility.

There are two basic approaches to the construction of a theory of UG. The first is what we may call the structural approach and the second is what we may call the functional approach. The first approach begins with the assumption that structural configurations are primitive, and that the principles of UG are formulated, or defined, in terms of structural configurations. GB theory is built on this assumption. Although this theory has appeared in several significantly different and increasingly sophisticated versions over the last fifteen or so years, all of the versions share this characteristic.

The functional approach, in contrast, begins with the assumption that grammatical relations, or grammatical functions, are primitive, and are not derived from, or defined in terms of, syntactic configurations. The principles which interact to explain the patterns of movement, control, and anaphora are formulated in terms of grammatical function; that is, in terms of functions like subject and object. In this approach, structural configurations are also primitive, but the relation between structural configurations and grammatical relations or functions is quite different from that of the structural approach. Lexical Functional Grammar (LFG) is based on this assumption, and perhaps represents the extreme version of the functional approach.

In the next section, I look at the fundamental body of data which any theory of UG must explain, and in Section 3, I suggest that the functional approach is the more fruitful of the two for constructing a theory of UG. I close the chapter with a broad outline of the basic characteristics of the proposed theory, which is based on this approach and the major differences between it and the two most important current theories: GB theory and LFG.

2. Configurational and Non-Configurational Languages

Hale (1981) suggested that there are two major, structurally distinct, language types: configurational and non-configurational. Non-configurational languages are ones which have a certain set of properties which include relatively free word order, extensive case-marking systems, and discontinuous elements. He also claims that there is little or no evidence in such languages of NP movement. Most of the properties associated with the configurational/non-configurational distinction are relative at best. For example, there are probably no languages with completely free word order, or languages with no intra-clausal constituent structure. There are probably degrees of non-configurationality. There is also some disagreement over the configurationality or non-configurationality of a number of particular languages. These issues, however, are matters of detail, which need not concern us here. Some examples of non-configurational languages are Warlpiri (Hale 1981 and 1983), Guugu Yimidhirr, Japanese (Hale 1981), Icelandic (Andrews 1982), and Malayalam (Mohanan 1982.) Sentences in each of these languages, accompanied by their surface structures, are shown below:

(2.1) a. Wawirri kapi-rna   panti-rni yalumpu
          kangaroo AUX   spear-NONPAST that
          I will spear that kangaroo

b.

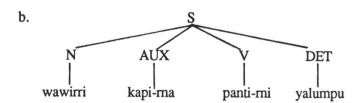

(2.2) a. Yarrga-ngun nambal dudaay-mani
        boy (ERG) rock (ABS) roll away-CAUSE-past
        The boy rolled the rock away

   b.

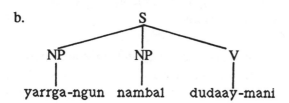

(2.3) a. Hanako ga piano o hii-ta
        Hanako (NOM) piano (ACC) play-PAST
        Hanako played the piano

   b.

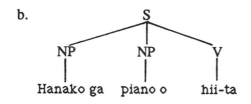

(2.4) a. Stulkan kyssti drengina
        the-girl (NOM) kiss-PAST-3rd person-sg the-boys (ACC)
        The girl kissed the boys

   b.

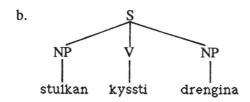

(2.5) a. Kuṭṭi aanaye kaṇṭu
        child (NOM) elephant (ACC) see-PAST
        The child saw the elephant

b.

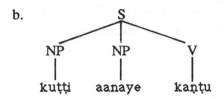

Although the differences among these languages are obvious even
from these few examples, the characteristic which they all share, and
which distinguishes them from configurational languages like English,
is the absence of various syntactic categories, in particular, the VP
category, at the surface structure level. It is claimed that this lack exists
at all levels of structure, and that their clausal structures are produced
by rules of the following type:

(2.6)   S --> X* V X*

In this rule schema, X* represents a string of zero or more [-V] lexical
categories or maximal projections, and S may be considered to be ∇.
The relative position of V in the string may vary from language to
language, and there may be other constraints on order. A comparison
of these examples and the English example in (2.7), shown with its
configurational surface structure, illustrates this contrast:

(2.7) a.   Matthew saw the elephant

b.

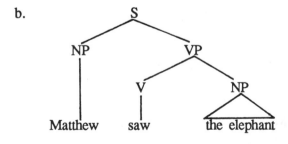

Of course the same sorts of variation in preferred word order, constituent categories, and so forth are observed within the configurational
language type. The crucial difference between structures which are
variants of the type in (2.7) and structures like (2.1b) to (2.5b) is the
structural subject/object asymmetry of the former structures and the

absence of this asymmetry in the latter.

These structural differences notwithstanding, essentially the same major grammatical patterns occur in both language types. Firstly, those patterns which are attributed to some movement process in configurational languages occur in non-configurational languages as well. Secondly, embedded complements of designated types, whose subject positions (however formally represented) are externally controlled, occur in both configurational and non-configurational languages. Finally, in both language types, anaphors in non-subject NPs are bound to subject NP antecedents, but anaphors in subject NPs cannot be bound to non-subject NP antecedents within the same clause. To illustrate the first point, consider the Japanese and Malayalam active/passive sentence pairs in (2.8) and (2.9), and the Icelandic sentences in (2.10):

(2.8)a. Naomi ga Seiji o ut-ta
         Naomi (NOM) Seiji (ACC) hit-PAST
         Naomi hit Seiji

   b. Seiji ga ut-are-ta
         Seiji (NOM) hit-PASSIVE-PAST
         Seiji was hit

(2.9)a. Kuṭṭi aanaye aaɾaaɟhiccu
         child (NOM) elephant (ACC) worship-PAST
         The child worshipped the elephant

   b. Aana aaɾaadhikkappeṭṭu
         elephant (NOM) worship-PASSIVE-PAST
         The elephant was worshipped

(2.10)a. Hann verðist ₛ[elska hana]
          He (NOM) seems [to-love her (ACC)]
          He seems to love her

   b. Skipstjórinn reyndist ₛ[vera fífl]
          the-captain (NOM) proved [to be a fool]
          The captain proved to be a fool

In Examples (2.8) and (2.9), the NPs which correspond to the subjects of the active sentences (in a.) are optional in the passive counterparts (in b). The location of these NPs when they occur is not important
to this discussion. In each case, the object NP in the active member of
the pair corresponds to the subject NP in the passive member of the pair.
This relation is identical to that between the members of English active/
passive pairs like (1.1) in this respect.

The sentences in (2.10) contain verbs that are members of the
analog of the English *seem* class. The S-structure subjects of these
verbs are interpreted as the subjects of the complements. This pattern is
identical to the pattern created by the rule of raising to subject position
(a subcase of the Move-α rule in the standard theory) in English,
illustrated in (1.2).

The following Icelandic and Malayalam sentences contain obligatorily controlled complements:

(2.11)a. Ég vonast til ₅[að mælast vel í kirkjunni]
I (NOM) hope to [to speak well in the church]
I hope to speak well in church

b. Þeir ákváðu ₅[að vitja Ólafs]
they (NOM) decided [to visit Olaf]
They decided to visit Olaf

c. Hún skipaði honum ₅[að fara]
She (NOM) ordered him (DAT) [to go]
She ordered him to go

(2.12) Ellaawarkkum [ɾaawile kuḷik'k'uṇṇatə] iṣṭamaaṇə
All (DAT)   [morning bathe-PRES-it] liking-be-PRES
Everyone likes bathing in the morning

These sentences contain control verbs which are the analogs of the
English *try/force* class. In each case, an NP argument of the matrix
predicate is also interpreted as the subject of the embedded predicate.
This pattern is identical to the English control pattern in (1.3), which is
attributable to PRO indexing in the standard theory.

The following Malayalam examples illustrate the bound anaphora pattern in that language:

(2.13)a. Raajaawə swaṇṭam bhaařyaye ṇulḷi
      king (NOM) self (POSS) wife (ACC) pinch-PAST
      The king pinched his own wife

    b. *Raajaawine swaṇṭam bhaařya ṇulḷi
      king (ACC) self (POSS) wife (NOM) pinch-PAST
      *His own wife pinched the king

In example (2.13a), the reflexive form *swaṇṭam* occurs in a non-subject NP and refers to the subject NP, *raajaawə*. In the ungrammatical example (2.13b), the reflexive form occurs in the subject NP *swaṇṭam bhaařya* and its antecedent is the object NP, *raajaawine*. This is functionally identical to the English pattern, which is shown in (2.14):

(2.14)a. The king pinched himself
    b. *Himself pinched the king

An adequate theory of UG must accommodate the configurational/non-configurational distinction in a natural way, and explain the differences between languages of these two types, which I have only mentioned in passing. More importantly, however, it must explain the occurrence of essentially the same major grammatical patterns of movement (defined as a relation between sentence/S-structure pairs or PM pairs), control, and anaphora in both configurational and non-configurational languages.

3. Structural and Functional Theories of UG

The standard, or GB, theory may be thought of as essentially a structural theory of subject/object asymmetry with respect to its principal relations, c-command and government. The categorial rules produce, and the various subtheories are designed to apply to, structures of the general type shown in (3.1):

(3.1)

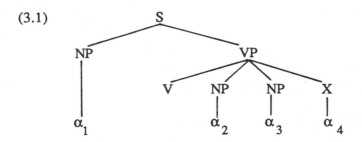

In this structure, X = non-NP constituent, complement S, etc.   The non-subject terms, α_2, α_3,   and α_4,   are c-commanded by the verb, V, and governed by this verb. In general, the heads of $\overline{X}$ constructions, which include VP and NP, govern their complements. The subject position, α_1, is not c-commanded or governed by the verb, primarily because VP is a maximal projection. So, in the core cases, elements of VP (complements of the verb) are always c-commanded and governed by the appropriate head of the construction, and subjects may or may not be governed. Potential governors of subjects include other elements of S, such as INFL, elements in COMP, and elements in the matrix VP in which a complement sentence is embedded.

Government, which is based, at least partially, on the c-command relation, is the central relation of the   Case theory, Theta theory, and Binding theory. This relation must exist between two elements, α and β, in order for α to assign case to β. Normally, verbs govern and assign case to their NP complements. They do not assign case to their subjects. Thus subject position may or may not be case-marked depending on other factors.   Similarly, verbs, as heads of $\overline{X}$ constructions, must directly assign a θ-role to each of their complements (which they govern.) They assign θ-roles indirectly to their subjects through the VP of which they are the head. Consequently, complement (non-subject) positions must be θ-marked, but subject positions may or may not be, depending upon other factors.

The Binding theory makes indirect use of the government relation. This plays a crucial role in the definition of binding category. Roughly speaking, a non-subject of the relevant type must be bound within a category that contains a subject (provided other conditions are satisfied), but the reverse is not necessarily true. That is, subjects need not be bound within categories that contain objects.   This correlates with the fact that subjects c-command objects, but not vice versa.

Finally, grammatical functions (GF) are defined on basic structures like (3.1). The GF subject is [NP,S], direct object is [NP,VP], and so forth. These grammatical functions appear in the lexical entries of predicates, and θ-roles, which are also specified in lexical entries, are assigned to terms in syntactic structures according to the grammatical functions which they bear.

This subject/object asymmetry, through the various subtheories, accounts for the patterns of movement, control, and anaphora. In simple sentences, NPs are always moved from some non-subject position to subject position. This is explained by the fact that NP movement must occur from a position which is not case-marked, but is assigned a θ-role, to a position that is case-marked, but is not assigned a θ-role. To account for the movement of objects in passive constructions, we must assume that passive morphology absorbs the case of a single complement of the verb, and that subjects escape this process because they are located outside of the complement structures (VPs) of verbs. In complex sentences, the subject of a tenseless complement S can be moved because this position need not be case-marked either.

So, NP movement, in general, requires that: (i) subject position, [NP,S], can escape θ-role assignment under certain circumstances; (ii) non-subjects such as [NP,VP], and subjects of complement sentences can escape case assignment under certain circumstances; (iii) objects, [NP,VP], must be assigned a θ-role; and (iv) θ-roles are assigned to constituents in syntactic structures according to the structurally defined GFs that they bear on the basis of information in the lexical entries of the appropriate items.

The explanation of NP movement is inextricably bound to the hierarchical structure type in (3.1) as is the explanation of the partial similarity of the distribution of overt anaphors and NP movement traces, and the explanation of the distribution of PRO. Traces can generally occur in object position, but can only occur in subject position under certain circumstances, and PRO, which must be ungoverned, can occur in subject position, but not in object positions. GB theory potentially provides a unified, principled explanation of these three syntactic phenomena for languages with basic structures like (3.1). In effect, it defines the notions of possible movement, possible controller/controlled position pair, and possible antecedent/anaphor pair, and satisfies the formal adequacy condition proposed in Section 1.

The syntactic structures of non-configurational languages, as we have seen, differ from structures like (3.1) in that they do not contain a VP configuration. Such syntactic structures obviously do not contain substructures that satisfy the definitions of GFs such as [NP,VP], and the central relations, c-command and government, generally hold of different constituents. In the absence of some additional factors or assumptions, the GB theory predicts that non- configurational languages display markedly different behavior in all three areas. Consider the following structure:

(3.2)

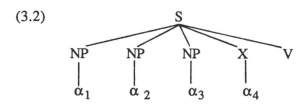

As in Structure (3.1), X represents any non-NP constituent. The explanation of subject/object asymmetry based on structures like (3.1) cannot be adapted to structures like (3.2) in any obvious way. In structures like (3.2), all the NPs, α_1, α_2, and α_3, are complements of the verb, V, and all are c-commanded and governed by the verb. This predicts that PRO cannot occur in any of these positions, and that there are no controlled complements in non-configurational languages analogous to English controlled complements with verbs like *force* and *try*. Moreover, both case-marking and θ-role assignment should be obligatory for all of the NPs, precluding the occurrence of NP traces, and predicting that the analogs of passive sentences and raising structures with verbs like *seem* do not occur in non-configurational languages. Alternatively, case absorption can, in theory, apply to any of the NPs, predicting the equally likely occurrence of passive-like analogs with morphological case patterns and thematic structures different than those in hierarchical languages, assuming that the θ-role problem can be overcome. Since none of the NPs in (3.2) occurs in a configuration that satisfies the definition of subject, [NP,S], or object, [NP,VP], the θ-role assignment rule, which applies to NPs according to the GFs that they bear, cannot apply correctly to this type of structure. Finally, since each of the NPs c-commands the others, each of them can be the antecedent of a bound anaphor in any of the others, predicting quite different patterns of anaphora in non-configurational languages.

To explain the similarities between configurational and non-configurational languages pointed out in Section 2, the GB theory, or any similar structural theory, must assume that all languages are configurational in some sense or at some level. In formal terms, there are two variants of this assumption:

(a) that there is a universal abstract structure, distinct from syntactic structure,that is hierarchical, and that those principles of the theory which explain the patterns of movement, control, and anaphora apply to this structure;

(b) that sentences in non-configurational languages have hierarchical D-structures which are converted to flat S-structures, or perhaps hierarchical S-structures that are converted to flat PF, by language-particular rules of various types.

Chomsky (1981) assumes (a). He claims that we may think of D-structures and S-structures as 'pairs (α, β), where α is a formal syntactic structure and β is a representation of associated GFs' and continues 'for [configurational languages], β is derived from α by abstraction from order, etc. For [non-configurational languages], α is a "flat" structure ... and β is essentially the same as the corresponding element in [hierarchical languages]' (p.132). Case theory and Binding theory crucially consider the element β of the pair in all languages, and the Projection Principle applies to the β-structure also. This means that the basic relations, c-command and government, are defined on β-structures. With this in mind, let us look at his analysis of Japanese active and passive sentences.

GFs are defined on β-structures, and therefore the GFs for Japanese are identical to English GFs. That is, subject is [NP,S], object is [NP,VP], and so forth. Lexical entries are essentially the same in Japanese and English, and θ-roles are assigned in the same way in both languages. The difference between Japanese and English is that the configurations that determine GFs are not represented in the α structures of the former. Consider the lexical entry for the Japanese verb *ut-* (hit) in (3.3) and the D-structure α/β pair in (3.4):

(3.3) [UT-: [NP,S] - θ_1, [NP,VP] - θ_2]

(3.4) a.   α-structure:

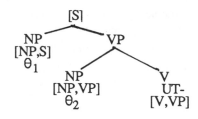

b.   β-structure:

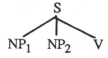

In the β-structure, the GFs [NP,S] and [NP,VP] are assigned to the appropriate NPs, and the θ-roles, θ_1 and θ_2, are assigned to the NPs on the basis of the information in the lexical entry. In the α-structure, neither NP_1 nor NP_2 satisfies the definition of the GFs in the lexical entry. Therefore, GFs are assigned to α-structures randomly in Japanese. Either GF in the lexical entry can be assigned to each of the NPs. Once the GFs have been assigned, θ-role assignment can proceed. No formal difficulties arise from random GF assignment since any misapplication such as assignment of both GFs to the same NP, or failure to assign a GF to an NP would result in a violation of the Theta Criterion. Ultimately, the NP assigned the GF [NP,S] receives nominative Case (GA), and the NP assigned the GF [NP,VP] receives objective Case (O). This produces the α S-structure shown below:

(3.5)

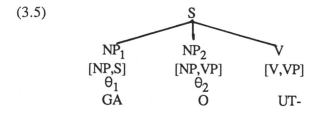

Thus active sentences like (2.7), above, are derived.

Japanese passives pattern analogously to English ones, as we have seen. That is, they contain a verb with passive morphology and a subject NP, with nominative Case, that is assigned the θ-role of the object of the corresponding active verb. The D-structure α/β pair of a passive sentence is shown in (3.6):

(3.6) a. α-structure:

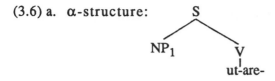

b. β-structure:

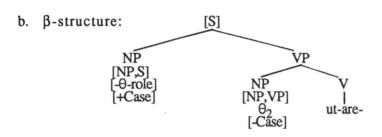

In the β-structure, the appropriate NPs are assigned the GFs [NP,S] and [NP,VP]. The passive verb *ut-are-* (and passive participles in general) directly assigns a θ-role, θ_2, to its NP complement in VP, but does not assign a θ-role to the subject NP, located outside of the VP. The passive morphology absorbs the Case of the NP complement in VP.

In the α-structure, random GF assignment can only assign the GF [NP,VP] to the lone NP, and not [NP,S], since the subject in the β-structure is not assigned a θ-role. This produces the following structure:

(3.7)

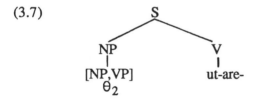

However, the NP with the GF [NP,VP], as we saw, is not assigned Case. Unlike analogous English passive structures, there is no place in (3.7) to move the NP so that it can be assigned Case. Consequently, the analog of Move α in non-configurational languages, which may be formulated as 'Assume a GF', applies to assign the NP a GF chain of the following form:

(3.8)   GF*, [NP,VP]

GF* must be a GF that lacks a θ-role and permits Case assignment to the

NP that bears it.   The only such GF in the β-structure is [NP,S].   Once this GF has been assigned, the NP ultimately receives nominative Case (GA).   The resulting   α S-structure is shown below:

(3.9)

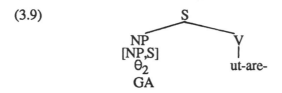

This accounts for the Japanese active/passive pattern and explains its similarity to the English pattern.

Since the major principles and subtheories apply to β-structures in derivations like these, it is easy to see how an explanation of the distribution of PRO and that of overt anaphors might be formulated for non-configurational languages, and how the theory might explain the similarity of configurational and non-configurational languages in all three areas.

My primary objection to the theory is its lack of relative plausibility. We must assume, for example, the existence of abstract lexical structures with vaguely defined arbitrary properties and functions. They are not necessarily isomorphic to the syntactic structures of a given language.   In fact, they appear to be either identical to their corresponding syntactic D-structures and S-structures, in which case they need play no role, or else they differ in various ways from their syntactic D-structure and S-structure correlates, in which case they assume the role of these syntactic structures, with respect to the applicability of the principles of the theory.   In configurational languages, for example, lexical and syntactic structures are identical at all levels, while in non-configurational languages they can differ both by the presence or absence of VP, as in (3.4), and in the number and labelling of NP arguments, as in (3.6).   In non-configurational VSO languages, lexical and syntactic structures, presumably, would also have to differ in the order of constituents that appear in them.

The addition of lexical structures of this sort to the theory raises questions about the status and function of categorial rules, and the relationship between lexical entries and syntactic structures.   It is not clear, for example, how the lexical structures are generated.   Chomsky claims that they are derived from α-structures in English, but this cannot be the case in Japanese. He also claims that D-structures (and thus S-structures) are projected from lexical structure. This is a trivial process for configurational languages, in which the relation between the two is quite simple, but it is more complex for non-configurational languages, in which the lexical entries must contain constituents that are not represented in the syntactic structures.

Chomsky suggests that the categorial rule for S, S --> NP INFL VP, is part of UG. This, of course, does not mean that it must be utilized by all languages. However, the introduction of lexical structures implies that this rule, or a functionally identical one, must be part of the grammar of languages that do not use it to generate syntactic structures. In any case, the lexical and syntactic rules of non-configurational languages must refer to the VP category, which does not occur in their syntactic structures.

Assumption (b) entails that the grammars of non-configurational languages contain a scrambling rule which breaks up VP structures to create flat sentence structures. In an analysis built on this assumption, the rules and principles of the various subtheories apply at some level of structure prior to the application of this rule, which most plausibly applies to S-structure to produce PF. This position has been argued in a number of places. See for example Williams (1984) and Emonds (1985). It is generally supported by syntactic evidence for the existence of a VP configuration at some more abstract level of structure, such as S-structure, in particular languages, most significantly ones with VSO word order, and necessarily flat sentence structure, at the level of PF. An example of such evidence is topicalization of VP in Breton (Williams 1984). The argument continues that the most elegant theory of UG is one in which VP is a universal S-structure category and this sort of analysis applies to all non-configurational languages. Any analysis, however, is as plausible as its consequences. The fact remains that a large number of non-configurational languages (such as Malayalam, Icelandic, Warlpiri, and possibly Samoan) offer no evidence of this sort for a VP configuration at any level. The analysis ignores, or seriously understates, the nature of the distinctions between these remaining languages as a class and the class of configurational languages that is quite readily attributable to this structural difference, and which is captured automatically by the distinction reflected in the PS rules in (3.10a and b) and the principles associated with each:

(3.10) a.   S --> X* V X*
      b.   S --> NP VP

What we have here is an argument over the membership of the non-configurational language class, and not necessarily an argument that non-configurationality is only a relatively superficial property of some languages.

   Moreover, and perhaps more importantly, the scrambling process itself is not a single rule which applies only in non-configurational languages or in the same way in all languages with non-configurational structures at the level of PF. It must be obligatory in some languages (such as Warlpiri and Icelandic), and optional, or quite late, after the application of other operations (such as Breton VP topicalization) in other languages. It must apply across the board to front verbs in strictly VSO languages like Samoan, leaving no reflex, but in more restricted environments in Modern Irish, also a VSO language, but probably not an underlyingly non-configurational one. Also this rule must perform quite different formal operations when it fronts the verb to produce a VSO structure from an SVO one, as in (3.11a) and when it breaks up the VP in an SVO language like Icelandic, as in (3.11b):

(3.11) a.

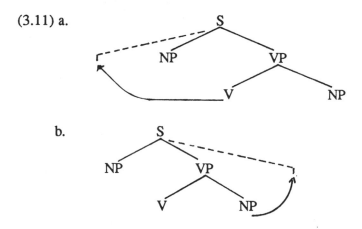

Furthermore, the scrambling process applies much more extensively in some languages (such as Warlpiri) than in others.

   So this process is a sort of *deus ex machina,* on which there are no well-defined constraints, and this kind of analysis is virtually unfalsifiable, hence not particularly enlightening. We see, then, that under neither assumption (a) nor assumption (b) does the GB Theory accommodate the configurational/non-configurational distinction in an elegant way.

Lexical Functional Grammar (LFG) is based on the functional approach. In this model, grammatical functions such as SUBJ, OBJ, OBJ2 (second object), and XCOMP (controlled complement, where X = V, N, A) are primitives, which are assigned to categories in syntactic structures. The lexical entries of predicates contain their lexical forms, which specify the grammatical functions of the NP arguments that occur with them, and their predicate argument structures, which specify the semantic relations borne by these NP arguments. This is shown for the predicate *eat,* whose lexical entry contains the following structures:

(3.12) a.   EAT((SUBJ)(OBJ))
       b.   EAT (arg 1   arg 2)
                   α   β

Structure (3.12a) is the lexical form of *eat.* It indicates that *eat* occurs in syntactic structures with a subject (SUBJ) and an object (OBJ). Structure (3.12b) is the predicate argument structure. It indicates that *eat* is a two-argument predicate whose first argument bears the semantic relation α and whose second argument bears the semantic relation β. The values of α and β are unimportant to the present discussion. The rules of the grammar provide sentences with a syntactic structure, the C-structure, which is roughly analogous to PF in the standard theory, and a functional structure, as shown for the sentence in (3.13):

(3.13)   The dog ate snails

The C-structure of this sentence appears in (3.14):

(3.14)

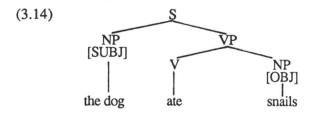

In English, the NP immediately dominated by S is the subject, SUBJ, and the NP daughter of VP is the object, OBJ. These grammatical functions are assigned to the arguments in the predicate argument structure of EAT as shown in (3.15):

(3.15)   (SUBJ)   (OBJ)
                            | |
        EAT   arg 1   arg 2
                         α β

Ignoring extraneous details, the lexical items which bear the surface grammatical functions are associated with the proper arguments and semantic relations in the F-structure of the sentence:

(3.16) $\begin{bmatrix} \text{SUBJ:} & \text{the dog} \\ \text{OBJ:} & \text{snails} \\ \text{PRED:} & \text{EAT (SUBJ)(OBJ)} \\ & \phantom{\text{EAT }}\alpha \beta \end{bmatrix}$

Grammatical processes are formulated in terms of grammatical functions rather than syntactic structure. Consider the passive sentence in (3.17):

(3.17)   The snails were eaten by the dog

The passivization process is formulated as a lexical rule. This rule, for English, excluding the associated morphological change, is shown in (3.18):

(3.18)   SUBJ --> Ø/(BY OBJ)
         OBJ   --> SUBJ

It applies to the lexical form of *eat* to create the lexical form of the passive participle *eaten,* which specifies that this form occurs in syntactic structures with NPs that bear the grammatical functions (BY OBJ) and (SUBJ), as shown in (3.19a), below. The predicate argument structure of *eaten* appears in (3.19b):

(3.19) a. EAT((Ø/BY OBJ)(SUBJ))

     b. EAT (arg 1   arg 2)
                α   β

The symbol Ø in (3.19a) indicates that the (BY OBJ) function need not be present in the syntactic structures which contain *eaten*.

The C-structure of example (3.17) is the following:

(3.20)

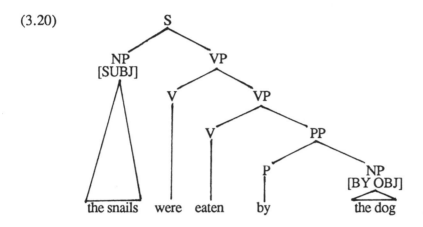

The C-structure grammatical functions are assigned to the arguments in (3.19b) as shown below:

(3.21)   (BY OBJ)   (SUBJ)

    EAT   arg 1   arg 2

The F-structure of (3.17), again ignoring details, is the following:

(3.22)   ⎡ SUBJ: the snails   ⎤
           | BY OBJ: the dog |
           | PRED: EAT (BY OBJ)(SUBJ) |
                             α   β
           ⎣   ⎦

This accounts for the active/passive relation.

Control processes are also formulated in terms of grammatical function. The choice of the controller of the embedded complements of obligatory control verbs is determined by a generalization which Bresnan calls the Lexical Rule of Functional Control. This is stated informally below:

(3.23)   The XCOMP of a lexical form is functionally controlled by
the OBJ2 if there is one, otherwise by the OBJ if there is
one, otherwise by the SUBJ.

The controlled element is the SUBJ function of embedded complements
with the function XCOMP.

Consider the following sentences:

(3.24) a.   Matilda tried to eat kangaroo stew
b.   Matilda forced Bruce to eat kangaroo stew

The lexical forms of verbs like *force* and *try* specify that they occur
with controlled complements, VCOMP, and the controller of the complement is identified in the lexical entry of each verb. This is shown in
(3.25):

(3.25)a.   TRY((SUBJ)(VCOMP))
SUBJ = VCOMP SUBJ

b.   FORCE((SUBJ)(OBJ)(VCOMP))
OBJ = VCOMP SUBJ

The C-structures of (3.24a and b) appear in (3.26a and b), respectively:

(3.26) a.

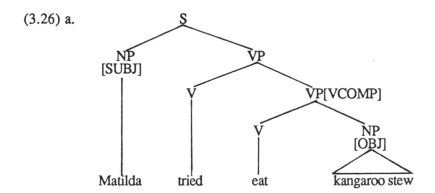

b.

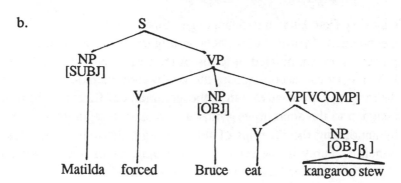

The F-structures of these examples, in which the lexical forms of both predicates are combined, are something like the following:

(3.27) a.

$$
\begin{bmatrix}
\text{SUBJ:} & \text{Matilda}_i \\
\text{PRED}_1: & \underset{\alpha}{\text{TRY}((\text{SUBJ})(\text{VCOMP})} \\
\\
\text{VCOMP:} & \begin{array}{ll} \text{SUBJ:} & \text{PRO}_i \\ \text{PRED}_2: & \underset{\alpha \quad \beta}{\text{EAT}((\text{SUBJ})(\text{OBJ}))} \\ \text{OBJ :} & \text{kangaroo stew} \end{array}
\end{bmatrix}
$$

b.

$$
\begin{bmatrix}
\text{SUBJ:} & \text{Matilda} \\
\text{PRED}_1: & \underset{\alpha \quad \beta}{\text{FORCE}((\text{SUBJ})(\text{OBJ})(\text{VCOMP}))} \\
\\
\text{OBJ:} & \text{Bruce}_i \\
\text{VCOMP:} & \begin{array}{ll} \text{SUBJ:} & \text{PRO}_i \\ \text{PRED}_2: & \underset{\alpha \quad \beta}{\text{EAT}((\text{SUBJ})(\text{OBJ}))} \\ \text{OBJ}_\beta : & \text{kangaroo stew} \end{array}
\end{bmatrix}
$$

In these structures, the appropriate controller is associated with the VCOMP SUBJ position, PRO, by an index, i.

The anaphora relation, like the movement and control processes, can be formulated in terms of grammatical functions in a straightforward way. I will not, however, discuss this.

In this theory, only the grammatical functions themselves, and not syntactic configurations, are universal. Grammatical functions may be assigned to NPs (and other categories) in syntactic configurations which may vary from language to language. Since grammatical functions are independent of particular syntactic configurations, and the grammatical processes are formulated in terms of the former and not the latter, the LFG theory can accommodate the configurational/non-configuational distinction quite easily. Once the grammatical functions have been assigned to the appropriate syntactic structure categories, presumably by annotating the PS rules of the language, the remaining rules and principles apply in the same way to languages of both major types. Consider examples (2.4a) and (2.8a), repeated below:

(2.4) a.   Stulkan kyssti drengina
(2.8) a.   Naomi ga Seiji o ut-ta

The lexical forms and predicate argument structures of these verbs appear in (3.28) and (3.29):

(3.28) a.   KYSSTA((SUBJ)(OBJ))
       b.   KYSSTA(arg 1   arg 2)
                       α   β

(3.29) a.   UT-((SUBJ)(OBJ))
       b.   UT-(arg 1   arg 2)
                   α   β

The C-structures of these examples are shown in (3.30), below. The grammatical functions SUBJ and OBJ are assigned to Japanese and Icelandic structures as indicated:

(3.30) a.

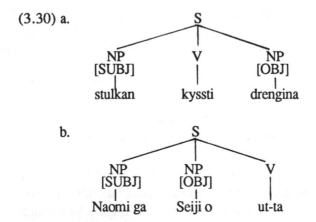

       b.

The F-structures of these examples are derived as above. These structures are shown in (3.31):

(3.31) a.
$$\begin{bmatrix} \text{SUBJ:} & \text{stulkan} \\ \text{OBJ:} & \text{drengina} \\ \text{PRED:} & \text{KYSSTI((SUBJ)(OBJ))} \\ & \quad\quad\quad\;\; \alpha \quad\;\; \beta \end{bmatrix}$$

b.
$$\begin{bmatrix} \text{SUBJ:} & \text{Naomi ga} \\ \text{OBJ:} & \text{Seiji o} \\ \text{PRED:} & \text{UT-TA((SUBJ)(OBJ))} \\ & \quad\quad\quad\;\; \alpha \quad\;\; \beta \end{bmatrix}$$

The passivization process in Japanese is functionally identical to that in English. The universal lexical passive rule in the LFG Theory is the following:

(3.32) a.   SUBJ --> Ø/OBL
     b.   OBJ --> SUBJ

Part a of this rule reflects the fact that languages vary in their treatment of the demoted subject if it is not deleted. In English, as we saw, it becomes the BY OBJ. In Japanese, and other languages, it becomes INSTR, and appears as an NP with special case marking. OBL (oblique) is the cover symbol for this set of grammatical functions.

Consider example (2.8b), repeated below:

(2.8) b.   Seiji ga ut-are-ta

The passive rule applies to the lexical form of the active verb *ut-* to create the lexical form of the passive verb *ut-are-*. This latter form appears in (3.33a), along with the predicate argument structure of *ut-are-* in (3.33b):

(3.33) a.   UT-ARE-((Ø/INSTR)(SUBJ))
     b.   UT-ARE- (arg 1   arg 2)
                      α β

The C-structure of (2.8b) is shown in (3.34):

(3.34)

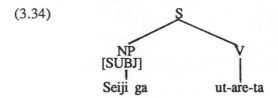

The C-structure grammatical function is assigned to the appropriate argument in (3.33b) as shown below:

(3.35)   (∅)   (SUBJ)
                          | |
         UT-ARE-   arg 1   arg 2
                        α   β

The F-structure of this example appears in (3.36):

(3.36) $\begin{bmatrix} \text{SUBJ:} & \text{Seiji ga} \\ \text{PRED:} & \text{UT-ARE-TA((∅)(SUBJ))} \\ & \quad\quad\quad\ \alpha\ \ \ \beta \end{bmatrix}$

This accounts for the active/passive relation in Japanese.

It is easy to see that the theory accounts for the universality of control patterns. Consider the Icelandic example in (2.11c), repeated below:

(2.11) c. Hún skipaði honum ₛ[að fara]

The lexical entry of the verb contains its lexical form and identifies the controller of its complement, as shown in (3.37):

(3.37)   SKIPA((SUBJ)(OBJ)(VCOMP))
          OBJ = VCOMP SUBJ

The C-structure of this example is the following:

(3.38)

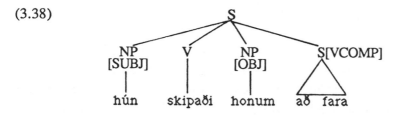

The derivation of the F-structure of this example is identical to the derivations of the F-structures of its English analogs in (3.24). This F-structure is shown in (3.39):

(3.39)

$$
\begin{bmatrix}
\text{SUBJ:} & \text{hún} \\
\text{PRED}_1: & \text{SKIPA}((\underset{\alpha}{\text{SUBJ}})(\underset{\beta}{\text{OBJ}})(\text{VCOMP})) \\
\\
\text{OBJ:} & \text{honum}_i \\
\text{VCOMP:} & \text{SUBJ: PRO}_i \\
& \text{PRED}_2: \quad \text{FARA}(\underset{\alpha}{\text{SUBJ}})
\end{bmatrix}
$$

The object, OBJ, of PRED_1 is associated with the VCOMP SUBJ, PRO, as shown. This sort of analysis extends to the analogs of English raising verbs in sentences like (1.2) as well.

In spite of the universal applicability of its rules and principles, the LFG Theory, in its present form, has certain shortcomings. Perhaps the most serious weakness of this theory is that it does not adequately constrain the notion 'possible grammatical process' in any particularly insightful way. The following hypothetical lexical rules are no more or less complex than the lexical passive rule in (3.32):

(3.40) a. SUBJ --> OBJ
      b. OBJ   --> Ø/OBL

(3.41) a. SUBJ --> OBJ2
      b. OBJ2 --> SUBJ

The rule in (3.40) produces the analog of movement from subject position to object position in the standard theory. It can apply to the lexical form of a verb like *eat* to create the following lexical form, of a theoretically possible verb *Eat* :

(3.42)   EAT((OBJ)(Ø/OBL))

This verb would occur in hypothetical examples something like (3.43a) in languages whose sentences do not require overt subjects, and (3.43b), with a dummy subject (represented here as *it*), in languages whose sentences require overt subjects:

(3.43) a.   Ate steak
      b.   It ate steak

The C-structures of these sentences are the following:

(3.44) a.

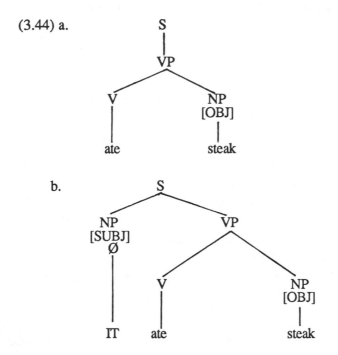

The C-structure grammatical functions are associated with the appropriate arguments in the predicate argument structure of *Eat,* as shown below:

(3.45)   (OBJ)   (SUBJ/Ø)
            | |
   Eat   arg 1   arg 2
          α   β

The F-structure of these examples is something like (3.46), ignoring the details associated with dummy elements like IT:

(3.46)
$$
\begin{bmatrix}
\text{(SUBJ:} & \text{IT)} \\
\text{OBJ:} & \text{steak} \\
\text{PRED:} & \text{Eat((OBJ)(Ø))} \\
& \alpha
\end{bmatrix}
$$

The predicate *Eat* is a sort of 'reverse' impersonal verb. The structures in (3.44), which have no lexical subjects, are similar to the impersonal structures in languages like Polish. However, in both examples in (3.43), *steak,* the C-structure object, is assigned the semantic relation α, which is borne by the subject of the transitive verb *eat*. Variants of this type, of two-argument verbs, and associated sentences like (3.43), do not appear to occur in any language.

The second rule produces the analog of movement of the subject of three-argument verbs like *give* to the second object, or OBJ2, position, and the movement of the OBJ2 NP to subject position. This rule can apply to the lexical form of *give*, shown in (3.47a), to produce the lexical form in (3.47b):

(3.47) a.   GIVE((SUBJ)(OBJ2)(OBJ))
      b.   GIVE((OBJ2)(SUBJ)(OBJ))

This theoretically possible variant of the verb *give* would occur in hypothetical examples like the following, shown with its C-structure:

(3.48) a.   A book gave Jason Alfred

    b.

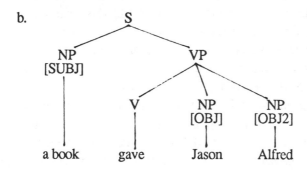

The C-structure grammatical functions are associated with the arguments in the predicate argument structure of *give* as shown in (3.49):

(3.49)   (OBJ2)   (SUBJ)   (OBJ)
                    | | |
       GIVE   arg 1   arg 2   arg 3
                 source   theme   goal

The F-structure of this example appears in (3.50):

(3.50)   ⎡ SUBJ: a book   ⎤
          ⎢ OBJ: Jason   ⎥
          ⎢ OBJ2:   Alfred   ⎥
          ⎢ PRED: GIVE((OBJ2)(SUBJ)(OBJ))   ⎥
          ⎣   source theme goal   ⎦

In Example (3.48a), the subject, *a book,* is interpreted as the **theme** and *Alfred,* the second object, is interpreted as the **source**. Variants of this type, of three-argument verbs, and associated sentences like (3.48a) with such an interpretation do not seem to occur in any language.

We see, then, that there is no explanation in the theory for the fact that the analog of movement from direct object position to subject position is a virtually universal process, while the reverse process, the analog of movement from subject position to direct object position or indirect object position is never (or at best extremely rarely) observed.

Let us turn now to the control relation. The VCOMP SUBJ position is simply designated to be the controlled position in the complements of obligatory control verbs like *force* and *try.* These are cases of what Bresnan calls functional control. There is no principled reason why some other grammatical function, say VCOMP OBJ, cannot be obligatorily controlled by arguments of verbs of this type. Yet this pattern is not observed in any language. The choice of the controller of XCOMP controlled complements is, as we saw earlier, dictated by the Lexical Rule of Functional Control in (3.23). This rule utilizes a rather odd hierarchy of grammatical functions which neither follows from anything in the theory nor applies to any other body of data. There appears to be no reason why SUBJ cannot generally be the controller regardless of the presence of an OBJ and/or OBJ2; ·or why OBJ cannot generally be the controller regardless of the presence of an OBJ2.

There is no particularly interesting explanation for the fact that (3.23), and not some other generalization, describes the existing unmarked situation.

Grammatical functions in the LFG theory serve to mediate between syntactic structures and predicate argument structures in the production of F-structures, and are distinct from either structural configurations or conventional case systems, both of which instantiate grammatical relations. The addition of grammatical functions of this sort to the theory introduces a certain level of redundancy. This, in itself, is not necessarily a serious weakness, but the GF system is a quite powerful mechanism, and is not a particularly welcome addition to UG. (Williams 1984 argues that universal primitive GFs are unnecessary, although his motivation and the context of his arguments are quite different from my own.)

The LFG theory fails to define the notions 'possible movement' (or its analog), 'possible controller', or 'possible controlled position', in any principled way. Consequently, it does not satisfy the formal adequacy criterion proposed in Section 1.

So a comparison of the GB theory and the LFG theory reveals that the former is preferable on purely theoretical grounds, but entails a rather inelegant treatment of the configurational/non-configurational language distinction; while the latter is rather less elegant on purely theoretical grounds, but accommodates the configuration/non-configurational language distinction in a much more satisfactory way, suggesting that this is the better of the two approaches overall. What is required then is a theory which combines the advantages of each of these approaches. The theory which I propose here may be thought of as the product of an attempt to reconcile these two positions.

4. The Proposed Theory

My goal is to demonstrate that it is feasible to formulate a structure-neutral theory of UG; that is, one which is equally applicable to configurational and non-configurational languages as independent types, avoiding the need for assumption (a) or (b); and which satisfies the formal adequacy criterion as defined in Section 1.

UG is organized into subcomponents, or systems of rules, principles, and parameters. These systems produce the patterns of movement, control, and anaphora, and define the limits of language-particular variation in each area. There are two significant levels of structure:

(a) S-structure

(b) Derived F-structure

S-structure is produced by the categorial rules, lexical insertion rules, the analog of the wh-movement rule (when applicable), and optional scrambling rules, whose effects are directly observable. It is roughly analogous to PF in the standard theory, and to C-structure in the LFG theory. S-structure types may vary from language to language, within limits imposed by the X-bar theory.

Derived F-structures have some of the properties and functions of logical form in the standard theory, and F-structures in the LFG theory. Antecedents and anaphors are co-indexed at this level, control relations are explicit, variables are bound to wh-operators, and semantic relations are assigned to appropriate arguments of predicates.   F-structure types are universal. They are formally somewhat different from F-structures in the LFG theory.   They consist of simple or complex ordered predicate/argument structures, to which various non-lexical indexing operations apply.

F-structures are paired with the S-structures of sentences by interface rules. These rules apply to both configurational and non-configurational structures in accordance with correlation statements which are based on primitive Grammatical Relations Indicators (GRIs). GRIs, however, differ from the GFs of the LFG theory. They are not separate entities (like SUBJ, OBJ, and OBJ2), and they do not comprise a universal set. Rather, they manifest themselves in different ways in different languages (within certain limits), as structural configurations, ordered constituent sequences, and/or morphological indicators of various sorts including nominal case markers. They differ in much the same way from GFs in the standard theory, which are defined on universal structural configurations.

In this theory, the rules of the grammar of a language, L_x, produce a well-formed S-structure and well-formed derived F-structure for all grammatical sentences in the language. The rules and principles which govern movement, control, and anaphora are analogous to the Move-α rule, the PRO indexing rule, the anaphor binding rule, and the various principles which govern these in the standard theory. However, they are F-level operations and principles and, as such, they are not formulated in terms of syntactic configurations, in contrast to the Standard theory, or GRIs, in contrast to the LFG theory. In this way, the proposed theory explains the universality of the patterns associated with these three grammatical processes. Other aspects of syntactic behavior are governed by S-structure-level and lexical-level factors. More specific differences between the proposed theory on the one hand, and the standard theory and LFG theory on the other, will become evident in the next four chapters, and need not be discussed at this point.

Chapter II

Basic Concepts

1. Overview

In the proposed theory, the syntactic component of UG is organized into a categorial component (some version of the X-bar theory), a lexical component, and the four rule systems shown in (1.1):

(1.1) a.   The S-structure/F-structure Interface System
     b.   The Generalized Co-Indexing System
     c.   The Generalized Argument Reduction System
     d.   The E-A System

These systems are clusters of rules, principles, and parameters. The rules of the S-structure/F-structure Interface (SFI) System apply in all derivations to relate the S-structures of sentences and the F-structures of the predicates that occur in them. The Generalized Co-Indexing System contains the analogs of control rules of various sorts and raising rules. The Generalized Argument Reduction System contains the analog of the NP movement rule in the standard theory, and the E-A System contains the analog of the wh-movement rule in earlier theories. These last three systems are discussed at length in Chapters III, IV, and V, respectively

The rules of the categorial component, the lexical insertion rules, scrambling rules in certain cases, and the E-A rule where appropriate apply to produce the S-structures of sentences. The F-structures of sentences are derived from their S-structures by the general rules of the SFI System and the relevant rules of the appropriate systems in (1.1b and c), which apply to the basic F-structures of their predicates, or more accurately, to the bare Predicate/Argument (PRED/ARG) structures of these predicates (as discussed below.)

The canonical form of basic F-structures is shown in (1.2):

(1.2)   PRED   [...ARG$_n$...]

The term PRED represents the predicate. Predicates can be verbs [+V], nouns [+N], adjectives [+A], and prepositions [+P], as well as phrasal constructions. The term [...ARG$_n$...] represents the argument structure of the predicate. Argument structures contain one, two, or three NP[θ] arguments, as well as arguments of other categories. NP[θ] arguments are ones to which the predicate assigns a semantic relation (SR). SRs in the proposed theory differ from standard theory θ-roles in that the former are only assigned to NP arguments, and not to arguments of other categories, such as complement sentences, S, or prepositional phrases, PP. I will assume that it is possible to formulate some adequate set of SRs, perhaps along the lines of Jackendoff (1972) and later proposals. However, since no non-lexical operation on F-structures is sensitive to particular values of SRs, I will not pursue this question. I will simply adopt the convention of labelling SRs as α, β, and ɣ. A more detailed basic F-structure is shown below:

(1.3)   PRED   1-NP[α]   2-NP[β]   ...X...

Here, ...X... represents either a third NP[θ] argument, which is represented as 3-NP[ɣ], or a non-θ argument. There are three types of non-θ arguments. These are shown in (1.4):

(1.4) a.   S
      b.   PP
      c.   [(NP*)XP]

There is no F-component analog of the categorial component. That is, there are no rules which generate basic F-structures. Rather, these appear in the lexical entries of predicates as PRED/Argument Structure complexes of the form shown in (1.3). The different subclasses of predicates have basic F-structures that are variants of this general type with different combinations of PRED and argument categories.

The predicates *hit* and *believe*, which occur in examples like (1.5), have the basic F-structures shown in (1.6):

(1.5) a.   Murry$_i$ hit Murgatroyd$_j$

    b.   Nobody$_i$ believed that Murry$_j$ hit Murgatroyd$_k$

(1.6) a.   HIT   1-NP[α]   2-NP[β]
       b.   BELIEVE   1-NP[α] S

The predicate HIT has two NP[θ] arguments, while the predicate BELIEVE, in this sense, has a single NP[θ] argument and a non-θ argument of category S.   The SR α of the first NP[θ] argument of HIT does not necessarily have the same value as the SR α of the NP[θ] argument of BELIEVE. Here, and throughout the book, unless otherwise stated, I adopt the convention of labelling SRs as α, β, γ, according to their linear order within the argument structure of a single predicate.

    The rules of the categorial component and the lexical insertion rules apply to produce the D-structures of the examples in (1.5). Since no relevant S-level rules apply in these cases, their S-structures and D-structures are isomorphic. The S-structures are shown in (1.7):[1]

(1.7) a.

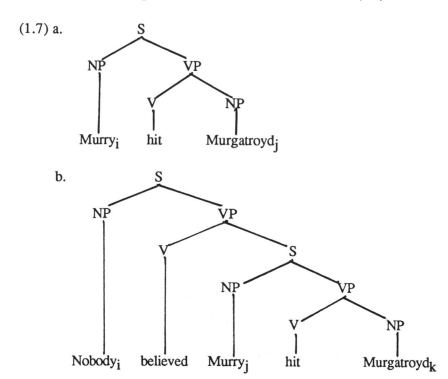

The F-structure of example (1.5a) is derived from the bare PRED/ ARG structure of the predicate HIT, which is shown below:

(1.8)   HIT   1-NP   2-NP

The rules of the SFI System apply to (1.8). These are the Index Insertion Rule, which relates S-structures to PRED/ARG structures, and the Semantic Relations Assignment (SRA) Rule. These rules are formulated in (1.9) and (1.10):

(1.9)   The Index Insertion Rule: Into each NP argument position of the PRED/ARG structure, insert the index of the S-structure NP correlate of that argument.

(1.10)   The Semantic Relations Assignment Rule: Assign the semantic relations, α, β, γ, to x-NP arguments in the PRED/ARG structure in the order in which these appear in the basic F-structure of the relevant PRED.

For English, the S-structure correlate of the 1-NP argument is the NP immediately dominated by S in structures like (1.7a and b). The S-structure correlate of the 2-NP argument is the NP immediately dominated by VP in structures like these. The application of the rules in (1.9) and (1.10) to the structure in (1.8) produces the following:

(1.11)   HIT $\text{NP}^{[i]}_{\alpha}$ $\text{NP}^{[j]}_{\beta}$

This is the derived F-structure of example (1.5a).

Example (1.5b) is a complex sentence which contains two predicates, *believe* and *hit*. To derive the F-structures of such examples, the basic F-structure, or more accurately, the bare PRED/ARG structure, of the predicate in the subordinate clause is inserted into the appropriate non-θ position, in this case, S, in the PRED/ARG structure of the predicate in the main clause. This operation produces the structure in (1.12):

(1.12)   BELIEVE   1-NP   [HIT   1-NP   2-NP]

The Index Insertion rule and the SRA rule apply separately to the argument structure of each predicate to produce the complex derived F-structure of (1.5b), which is shown below:

(1.13)   BELIEVE $\underset{\alpha}{NP^{[i]}}$ [HIT $\underset{\alpha}{NP^{[j]}}$ $\underset{\beta}{NP^{[k]}}$]]

Well-formed (complex) derived F-structures like (1.11) and (1.13) are the basis for the interpretation of sentences. These are F-structures that satisfy the following condition:

(1.14)   <u>Well-formedness Condition (WFC) I</u>: Each NP argument in the argument structure of the PRED must be assigned a single index and a single SR.

It is easy to see that the F-structures in (1.11) and (1.13) satisfy this condition.

In the proposed theory, there are two significant levels of structure: S-structure and derived F-structure. No movement or deletion rules apply to phrase structures, apart from optional scrambling rules in some languages. In S-structures, but not D-structures, certain anaphoric relations between empty categories and wh-constituents, and between pronouns and antecedents under certain circumstances, are represented. Certain syntactic well-formedness conditions are also checked at this level.[2]

The well-formedness condition in (1.14) applies to the level of derived F-structure. The determination of grammaticality, ambiguity, and synonymy (of sentence pairs) is made at this level. Grammatical sentences are ones from whose S-structures a well-formed (complex) derived F-structure can be produced, and ungrammatical sentences are ones from whose S-structures no well-formed (complex) derived F-structure can be produced. Ambiguous sentences are ones for which a well-formed (complex) derived F-structure corresponding to each interpretation can be produced, and synonymous sentences are ones which have equivalent derived F-structures. See Horn (1983a) for a more extensive discussion of these points. Examples of each are discussed below where relevant.

A basic assumption of the theory is that argument structures are linearly ordered. Consequently, the NP[θ] arguments can be distinguished from one another on the basis of their position in the argument structure. I will adopt the convention of labelling them as 1-NP, 2-NP, and 3-NP, but it should be understood that this is merely a convenient notational device, and it has no theoretical significance.

Because argument structures are ordered, the concept of distance, or perhaps more accurately, relative distance, as it relates to two or more F-structure constituents, can be defined. Thus in the F-structure in (1.13), above, the $_{NP}[j]$ argument is closer to the $_{NP}[k]$ argument than the $_{NP}[i]$ argument is. The significance of this concept of relative distance will become apparent in the discussion of control in Chapter III.

In Sections 2 and 3, I discuss predicate types and argument types in more detail. I demonstrate how the notion "possible predicate" is defined in the theory, and how language variation in this area is accounted for. In Section 4, I look at different types of complex sentences and introduce an additional method of combining basic PRED/ARG structures into complex ones. In Section 5, I examine the role of grammatical relations in the theory as these relate to S-structure/F-structure correlates and the application of the Index Insertion rule. Parameters which account for the relevant aspects of language variation are proposed. The most important points of the chapter are summarized in Section 6, and the role of F-structures in subcategorization is discussed.

2. Basic F-Structure Components: Predicates

Predicates may be defined as elements whose basic F-structures contain one or more NP arguments, to which they assign SRs (with certain exceptions which are discussed below). There are two categories of predicates: simple and complex.

Simple predicates are individual lexical items, which may consist of more than one morpheme, and in many cases are quite complex on the morphological level. However, on the syntactic level, they are units, of category [+V], [+N], [+A], and [+P].[3] Constructions containing examples of each category are shown below, along with their derived F-structures:

(2.1) a.   Murry$_i$ kissed [+V] Mary$_j$
KISS $_{NP[i]}$ $_{NP[j]}$
       α β

b.   They$_j$ elected Murgatroyd$_j$ president [+N]
... [PRESIDENT $_{NP[j]}$]
                  α

c.   Everyone$_i$ considered Murry$_j$ tall [+A]
... [TALL $_{NP[j]}$]
            α

d.   The army's$_i$ destruction [+N] of the village$_j$
... DESTRUCTION $_{NP[i]}$ $_{NP[j]}$
                     α β

e.   in the city$_i$
IN $_{NP[i]}$
      α

Regardless of the syntactic category of the predicate, the derived F-
structures of all of these constructions are produced in the same way: by
the application of the Index Insertion and SRA rules (and other
operations) to the bare PRED/ARG structure of the relevant predicate.[4]

Complex predicates, in contrast, are phrasal constructions of various
sorts at the S-structure level of category $\bar{V}$. $\bar{V}$ predicates occur in S-
structure configurations like that in (2.2), below:

(2.2)

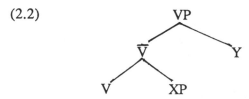

The initial constituent of $\bar{V}$ is a predicate of category [+V]. The
second constituent is a phrase of category NP or AP, to which severe
selectional restrictions often apply, or a particle, PRT. Y is the complement of the $\bar{V}$ predicate.

The F-structure representation of $\bar{V}$ predicates is shown in (2.3):

(2.3)   [PRED XP^c] ...ARG$_n$...

XP^c is the F-structure correlate of the XP sister of V in $\bar{V}$ in the
relevant S-structure. XP^c terms are arguments of the verbal head of
the $\bar{V}$ predicate (the lefthand element, PRED, in (2.3).) When XP^c =

NP^c, it may or may not bear an SR, θ, depending on the degree to which the PRED/XP expression is fixed.

A large class of $\bar{V}$ predicates consists of semi-productive idioms of various sorts. Some examples are shown below:

(2.4) a.   Fred$_i$ took advantage$_j$ of Murry$_k$
       b.   Everyone$_i$ took umbrage$_j$ at Murgatroyd's remarks$_k$
       c.   The FBI$_i$ kept tabs$_j$ on Stein$_k$

These examples have S-structures like the following, shown for (2.4a):

(2.5)

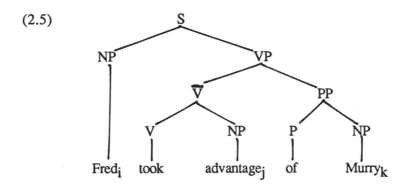

The basic F-structures of predicates of this sort, which appear in the lexical entries of the verbs *take*, *keep*, and so forth, in their idiomatic senses, are of the form shown in (2.6):

(2.6)   [VERB NP^c[ζ]] 1-NP[θ] ...X...

Here, NP^c represents a relatively limited set of NP arguments that can appear with each verb in expressions of this sort. These are probably listed in the lexical entries of the idiomatic verbs. These NP^c arguments are NP[θ] arguments which are indexed at the S-structure and F-structure levels. They bear SRs which I have represented as ζ.

The derived F-structure of example (2.4a) is produced from the bare PRED/ARG structure of the predicate, *take NP^c of*, shown in (2.7):

(2.7)   [TAKE NP^c] 1-NP 2-NP

The Index Insertion rule and the SRA rule apply to this structure to produce the F-structure of example (2.4a). This appears in (2.8), below:[5]

(2.8)   [TAKE $\underset{\zeta}{NP^{c[j]}}$ $\underset{\alpha}{NP^{[i]}}$ $\underset{\beta}{NP^{[k]}}$

The derived F-structures of the other examples in (2.4) are produced in the same way.

Additional examples of $\overline{V}$ predicates are shown in (2.9), below:

(2.9) a.   Chung wrote a book about Nguyen
      b.   Zoe took a picture of Gryff
      c.   Wolfgang drank a quart of milk

The predicates *write a book*, *take a picture*, and *drink a quart* have basic F-structures like that in (2.6), above.[6] In these examples, however, the [VERB NP^C] units are not as frozen as their counterparts in the idioms in (2.4). Verbs like *write*, *drink* (and *eat* in examples like *Clyde ate a loaf of bread*) have non-idiomatic interpretations and occur with a wider range of NP^C elements than do verbs like *take* and *keep* in idiomatic expressions of the type represented in (2.4). Therefore the permissible NP^C arguments are not specified in the lexical entries of the former verbs. However, predicates like those in (2.9) and ones like those in (2.5) share certain properties, and the $\overline{V}$ analysis provides the basis for an explanation of these similarities, which are discussed briefly at the end of this section. We may, in fact, imagine a continuum on which all of these expressions may be located, with the more strongly frozen ones (like the examples in (2.4)) at one end, and the less frozen ones (like the examples in (2.9)) at the other.[7]

The NP^C arguments of the predicates in (2.9) are also NP[θ] arguments, and I will continue to represent the SR borne by such arguments as ζ. As NP[θ] arguments, the NP^C arguments are indexed at both the S-structure and F-structure levels.

The S-structures of the examples in (2.9), in the relevant sense, are shown below:

(2.10) a.

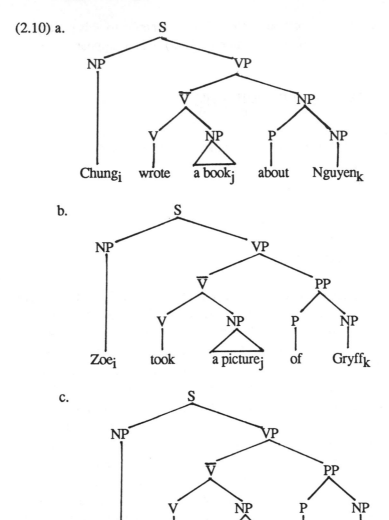

The basic F-structures of these predicates are shown in (2.11):

(2.11) a.   [WRITE $NP^c[\zeta]$] $1\text{-}NP[\alpha]$ PP_{about}
    b.   [TAKE $NP^c[\zeta]$] $1\text{-}NP[\alpha]$ PP_{of}
    c.   [DRINK $NP^c[\zeta]$] $1\text{-}NP[\alpha]$ PP_{of}

These appear in the lexical entries of *write, take,* and *drink* (as alternate F-structures.) The derived F-structures of the examples in (2.9) are produced from the following bare PRED/ARG structures:

(2.12) a.   [WRITE NP^C] 1-NP [ABOUT 1-NP]
    b.   [TAKE NP^C] 1-NP [OF 1-NP]
    c.   [DRINK NP^C] 1-NP [OF 1-NP]

These structures are formed by combining the basic PRED/ARG structure of the $\bar{V}$ predicate in each case with that of the appropriate preposition. The Index Insertion rule and the SRA rule apply in the normal way to produce the derived F-structures of (2.9), which are shown in (2.13):

(2.13) a.   [WRITE NP[j]] NP[i] [ABOUT NP[k]]
                        ς α α
    b.   [TAKE NP[j]] NP[i] [OF NP[k]]
                      ς α α
    c.   [DRINK NP[j]] NP[i] [OF NP[k]]
                        ς α α

The following examples contain $\bar{\bar{V}}$ predicates that represent one extreme of the continuum alluded to above. These are completely frozen idiomatic expressions:

(2.14) a.   Ferdinand$_i$ kicked the bucket
    b.   Boguslav$_i$ flew the coop

These predicates, *kick the bucket* and *fly the coop*, consist of a verbal lefthand element, and an NP element, the S-structure correlate of the NP^C argument. However, in contrast to the examples in (2.4) and (2.9), there is no choice of NP^C expressions. Nor are the meanings of these idioms in any sense composed of the meanings of their constituents. The basic F-structures of these predicates are shown in (2.15):

(2.15) a.   [KICK NP^c[THE BUCKET]] 1-NP[α]
    b.   [FLY NP^c[THE COOP]] 1-NP[α]

Here, the NP^C arguments are not NP[θ] arguments, and are not indexed at either the S-structure level or the F-structure level.

The S-structures of examples (2.14a and b) are shown below:

(2.16) a.

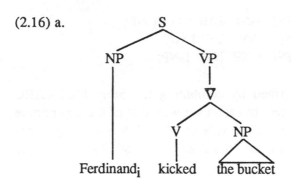

Ferdinand$_i$ kicked   the bucket

b.

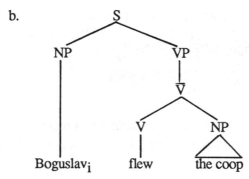

Boguslav$_i$ flew   the coop

The derived F-structures of these examples are produced from the PRED/ARG structures in (2.17):

(2.17)a. [KICK $_{NP}$c[THE BUCKET]] 1-NP
    b. [FLY $_{NP}$c[THE COOP]] 1-NP

The Index Insertion rule and the SRA rule apply to (2.17) to produce (2.18):

(2.18)a. [KICK $_{NP}$c[THE BUCKET]] $_{NP[i]}$
                                        α
    b. [FLY $_{NP}$c[THE COOP]] $_{NP[i]}$
                                    α

A fourth subclass of $\overline{V}$ predicates consists of ones whose verbal element is the copular verb BE and whose XP^c argument is a noun or adjective, and which appear in examples like the following:

(2.19) a. Claude$_i$ is tall
     b. Attila$_i$ was nasty
     c. Enid$_i$ was a man

In these examples, the adjectives *tall* and *nasty* function as predicate adjectives and the noun *a man* functions as a predicate noun. In English, predicate adjectives and nouns, which are not [+V] (that is, are not true verbs), cannot occur in the S-structure positions occupied by verbs, and, in main clauses, must therefore occur as an argument of BE in a complex predicate.[8]

These complex predicates differ from the ones in (2.4) and (2.9) in degree of productivity and in the function of the XP^C arguments. The basic F-structure of BE as the head of $\widetilde{V}$ predicates is shown in (2.20):

(2.20) [BE XP^C] 1-NP[θ] ...X...

In contrast with (2.9), when $XP^C = NP^C$, the NP^C is not an NP[θ] argument and is not indexed. Instead, the basic F-structure of the predicate noun or adjective is combined with that of BE.

The predicate adjectives *tall* and *nasty* and the predicate noun *man* have the basic F-structures shown in (2.21):

(2.21) a. TALL   1-NP[α]
     b. NASTY 1-NP[α]
     c. MAN   1-NP[α]

These appear in their lexical entries.[9]

The S-structures of the examples in (2.19), which are identical to their D-structures, are the following:

(2.22) a.

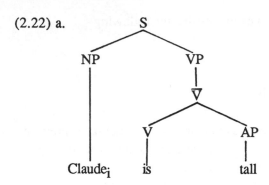

b.

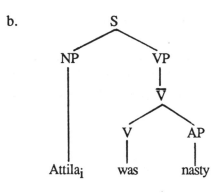

c.

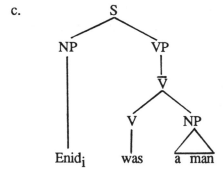

The derived F-structures of the examples in (2.19) are produced from the bare PRED/ARG structures shown below:

(2.23) a.   [BE [TALL]]   1-NP
    b.   [BE [NASTY]] 1-NP
    c.   [BE [MAN]]   1-NP

The Index Insertion rule and the SRA rule apply to these structures to produce the F- structures shown in (2.24):

(2.24) a. [BE [TALL]]   NP[i]
                                    α

　　　b. [BE [NASTY]]   NP[i]
                                    α

　　　c. [BE [MAN]]   NP[i]
                                    α

Some predicate adjectives and nouns have basic F-structures that contain two arguments, as well as the single-argument F-structures like the ones above. Two examples are the adjective *nasty* and the noun *president*, in sentences like the following:

(2.25) a. Attila$_i$ was nasty to his mother$_j$
　　　b. Zoe$_i$ was president of the sorority$_j$

The basic F-structures of *nasty* and *president* in these senses are shown in (2.26):

(2.26) a. NASTY   1-NP[α]   PP
　　　b. PRESIDENT   1-NP[α]   PP

The S-structures of the examples in (2.25) are the following, in which the $\bar{V}$ predicate occurs with a PP complement (whose head is the preposition *to* with *nasty* and *of* with *president*):

(2.27) a.

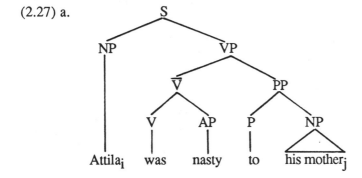

b.

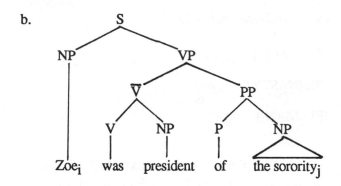

The derived F-structures of examples (2.25a and b) are produced from the following PRED/ARG structures, which are formed, as above, by combining the PRED/ARG structure of BE in each case with those of the appropriate predicate noun or adjective, and preposition:

(2.28) a.   [BE [NASTY]] 1-NP [TO   1-NP]
    b.   [BE [PRESIDENT]] 1-NP [OF 1-NP]

The Index Insertion rule and the SRA rule apply to these structures to produce the structures in (2.29):

(2.29) a.   [BE [NASTY]] $_{NP[i]}$ [TO $_{NP[j]}$]
                            α α
    b.   [BE [PRESIDENT]] $_{NP[i]}$ [OF $_{NP[j]}$]
                                 α α

(Note that the SR of the first (and only) NP[θ] argument of each predicate in these structures is labelled α following the convention established above. This does not imply that the SR of BE NASTY or BE PRESIDENT has the same value as the SR of TO or OF.) The structures in (2.29) are the derived F-structures of examples (2.25a and b). The predicate adjective TALL, unlike NASTY and PRESIDENT, has only a single-argument basic F-structure like the one in (2.21a).

The maximal projections of [-V] heads can function as predicate XPs, the XP^c arguments of complex predicates, in examples like the following:

(2.30) a.   Nelson$_i$ is tall for a ballplayer$_j$
     b.   Cerise$_i$ was beautiful for a redhead$_j$
     c.   That$_i$ was a bastard of a math test$_j$

In examples (2.30a and b), the APs *tall for a ballplayer* and *beautiful for a redhead*, function as XP^c arguments of complex predicates. In example (2.30c), the NP, *a bastard of a math test*, has the same function. Predicate XPs all have basic F-structures that contain a single NP[θ] argument, of the type shown below:

(2.31)   [XP] 1-NP[α]

The predicate XP is composed of the head, X, and the F-level representation of the complement of X in XP.

The S-structures of the examples in (2.30) are shown in (2.32):[10]

(2.32) a.

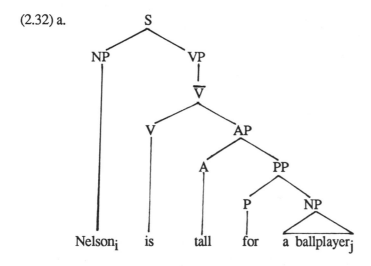

b.

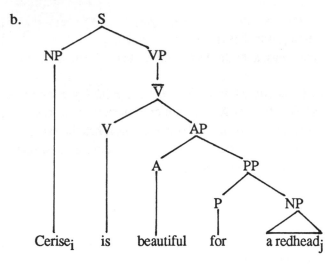

c.

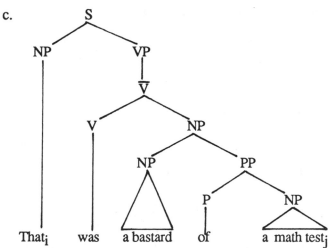

In main clauses, predicate XPs, as [-V] constituents, must also occur in
S-structures like these with the verb *be* . The derived F-structures of
these examples are produced from the following bare PRED/ARG constructions:

(2.33) a.   [BE [TALL[FOR 1-NP]]] 1-NP
       b.   [BE [BEAUTIFUL[FOR 1-NP]]] 1-NP
       c.   [BE [BASTARD[OF 1-NP]]] 1-NP

These are formed by combining the basic F-structure of BE, which is the head of the $\bar{V}$ predicate in each case, and the F-level representation of the predicate XP, which is the XP^C argument of the $\bar{V}$ predicate. The F-level representations of the predicate XPs are formed by combining the representations of the adjectives TALL and BEAUTIFUL and the noun BASTARD with the basic F-structures of the prepositions, FOR and OF, respectively. No new operations are required here. These are simply more complex examples of the general $\bar{V}$ predicate type.

The Index Insertion rule and the SRA rule apply to the structures in (2.33) to produce the following derived F-structures for (2.30a, b, and c), respectively.

(2.34) a. [BE [TALL [FOR $\underset{\alpha}{NP^{[j]}}$]]] $\underset{\alpha}{NP^{[i]}}$

    b. [BE [BEAUTIFUL [FOR $\underset{\alpha}{NP^{[j]}}$]]] $\underset{\alpha}{NP^{[i]}}$

    c. [BE [BASTARD [OF $\underset{\alpha}{NP^{[j]}}$]]] $\underset{\alpha}{NP^{[i]}}$

The predicate XP generalization applies to all constructions with [-V] heads. That is, any NP or AP may have this function, in which case its basic F-structure is of the form shown in (2.31). As we saw earlier, some predicate adjectives and predicate nouns, like *nasty* and *president*, have two-argument basic F-structures, and others, like *tall* and *beautiful*, do not. The analysis predicts that two F-structures can be derived for sentences containing predicate nouns and adjectives like the former: one in which the head, X, is the XP^C argument of a complex predicate, and one in which the XP of which it is head functions as the XP^C argument of a complex predicate. The former case was discussed above for examples (2.25). Their derived F-structures appear in (2.29).

In the second case, the entire AP of (2.25a) and the entire NP of (2.25b) function as XP^C arguments of complex predicates. These examples are repeated below:

(2.25) a. Attila$_i$ was nasty to his mother$_j$
      b. Zoe$_i$ was president of the sorority$_j$

The predicate XP-F-structures of these examples, which are parallel in structure to (2.34), are shown in (2.35):

(2.35) a.   [BE [NASTY [TO $_{NP[j]}$]]] $_{NP[i]}$
                              α   α
       b.   [BE [PRESIDENT [OF $_{NP[j]}$]]] $_{NP[i]}$
                                 α   α

Therefore, the analysis explains the ambiguity of examples like (2.25), which is subtle, but nevertheless exists. These contrast with examples like (2.30), which are not ambiguous. The adjectives *tall* and *beautiful* have only single-argument basic F-structures, and consequently, only derived F-structures like (2.34) can be produced for the examples in (2.30).[11] In Chapter V, I will demonstrate that the wh-movement analog disambiguates examples like (2.25) and does not apply to the AP and NP complements of examples like (2.30)· This analysis provides the basis for an explanation of those facts.

The predicate XP generalization also applies to prepositional phrases since these are constructions with [-V] heads. The following example contains a PP which functions as a predicate XP:

(2.36)   Salvador$_i$ is in the room$_j$

The S-structure of this example is shown in (2.37):

(2.37)

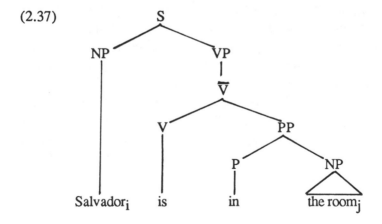

The derived F-structure of (2.36) is produced from the PRED/ARG structure in (2.38), below, which is formed by inserting the F-level representation of the PP, which is also the PRED/ARG structure of the preposition IN, into the XP^c position in the PRED/ARG structure of BE:

(2.38)   [BE [IN 1-NP]] 1-NP

The Index Insertion rule and the SRA rule apply to produce the derived F-structure of the example. This appears in (2.39):

(2.39)   [BE [IN NP[j]]]   NP[i]
                      α α

Finally, examples like the following contain $\tilde{V}$ predicates of a slightly different type:

(2.40) a.   Philena$_i$ looked up the number$_j$
       b.   Chen$_i$ burned down the apartment building$_j$

Here, the predicates are the verb/particle combinations *look up* and *burn down*. Their basic F-structures are shown in (2.41):

(2.41) a.   [LOOK UP] 1-NP[α] 2-NP[β]
       b.   [BURN DOWN] S 1-NP[α] 2-NP[β]

In these F-structures, the $\tilde{V}$ predicate is of the form: [VERB PRT]. The VERB/PRT combinations are fixed expressions (similar to the completely frozen idioms in (2.14) in this respect.)   The derived F-structures of the examples in (2.40) are produced from the relevant bare PRED/ARG structures by the application of the Index Insertion rule and the SRA rule. These are shown in (2.42), below:

(2.42) a.   [LOOK UP]   NP[i]   NP[j]
                          α β
       b.   [BURN DOWN] NP[i] NP[j]
                          α β

We see, then, that the class of $\tilde{V}$ predicates comprises four subtypes:
(a)   semi-productive idioms (*take advantage of*, *keep tabs on*, and so forth), and completely frozen idioms (*kick the bucket*, *fly the coop*);
(b)   expressions that we might label "quasi-idioms" (*take a picture of*, *write a book about*, *drink a quart of*);
(c)   expressions consisting of the verb *be* and a predicate noun or

adjective (*be tall, be nasty, be president , be a man*), or a predicate
XP (*be [tall for a ballplayer], be [a bastard of a math test]*);
(d)   verb/particle combinations (*burn down, look up*).

$\bar{V}$ predicates have basic F-structures of the general type shown in
(2.43):

(2.43)   [PRED XP^C]   1-NP[α]   ...X...

The complex predicate itself consists of a [+V] head, the lefthand
element labelled PRED in (2.43), and an XP^C element. The XP^C
element is an internal argument of the PRED and not a predicate itself.
The 1-NP[α] argument and the other arguments (represented as ...X...
in (2.43)) are arguments of the complex predicate as a whole, and
external arguments of the head of the complex predicate, PRED. The
XP^C elements in (2.43) can be NPs or APs, as in examples (2.30), in
which case they have internal structures of the form: [X[COMP]], as
shown in (2.33) and (2.34). The [-V] X heads of these constructions,
TALL, BEAUTIFUL, and BASTARD, are not themselves predicates
since they have no NP arguments of their own within the [XP] construction. (In these examples they have only PP complements. They can
have S complements also.) In contrast, if the XP^C element is a PP, as in
Structure (2.39), its head X, the preposition, is a predicate since it has an
internal NP argument.

Predicate adjectives and nouns, and predicate XPs, also function as
predicates in the complements of certain verbs. Examples of this were
shown in (2.1b and c). These are discussed in the next section.

The analysis, as briefly mentioned above, provides the basis for
explaining both the syntactic behavior of expressions like (a) and the
parallel behavior in certain respects of predicates of subtypes (a) and
(b). These are discussed at some length in Horn (1983a), and I do not
wish to repeat that discussion in its entirety. A brief synopsis of its main
points, however, is called for here.

As regards the first point, the $\bar{V}$ analysis allows us to account for the
occurrence of passive sentences like (2.44a and b), and the non-
occurrence of ones like (2.44c and d):

(2.44) a.   Advantage was taken of Jason
       b.   Tabs were kept on Murphy

    c. *Advantage of Jason was taken (by everyone)
    d. *Tabs on Murphy were kept (by the FBI)

This pattern is a consequence of the fact that such idioms have structures like (2.5), above, in which the S-structure correlate of the NP^c argument and the PP are not sisters in a single higher-level constituent, and F-structures like (2.6) which reflect this fact.

    Passive sentences like (2.44a and b) also contrast with ones like the following:

(2.45) a. *The bucket was kicked by Aaron
     b. *The coop was flown by Jeroboam

(These sentences are, of course, grammatical in their somewhat odd literal interpretations.) This contrast is a consequence of the fact that the NP^c arguments in the F-structures of the expressions in (2.44) are NP[θ] arguments, while those in the F-structures of completely frozen expressions like the ones in (2.45) are not. The S-structure and derived F-structure of (2.44a) are shown in (2.46):

(2.46) a.

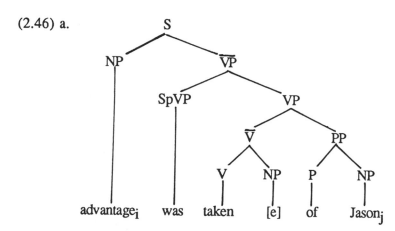

  b.   SpVP[BE][TAKEN] NP$^{[i]}_\zeta$ NP$^{[j]}_\beta$

The derived F-structure in (2.46b) is produced from the bare PRED/ARG structure of the expression *take advantage of* in (2.7) by the application of the Index Insertion rule, the SRA rule, and the

argument reduction operation which is discussed in Chapter IV. The SR
ζ is reassigned by this operation to the indexed 1-NP[θ] argument.
The important point here is that this is a well-formed F-structure.

The S-structure of example (2.45a) must be something like that
shown below:

(2.47)

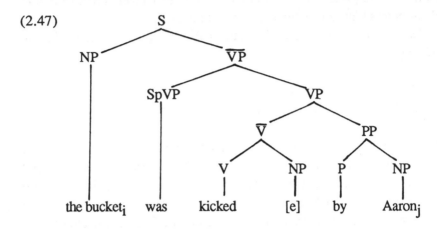

However, because the NP^C argument in the F-structure of the expression
kick the bucket is not an NP[θ] argument, and bears no SR, no SR is
available for reassignment to the $_{NP}$[i] argument in the following
derived F-structure whose source is the PRED/ARG structure of
(2.15a):

(2.48) $_{SpVP}$[BE][KICKED] $_{NP}$[i] [BY $_{NP}$[j]]
                                                  α

This structure violates the well-formedness condition in (1.14), ac-
counting for the ungrammaticality of example (2.45a). The ungrammaticality of (2.45b) is explained in the same way.

The parallel behavior of predicates of subtypes (a) and (b) relates
primarily to two areas: the oddness of examples produced by the application of wh-movement to the S-structure correlate of the NP^C argument; and the rather severe selectional restrictions on the S-structure
correlates of NP^C arguments. The following examples illustrate the
first area:

(2.49) a. ?*What did Ezra$_i$ take of Alyse$_j$ [advantage]
     b.   *What did the FBI$_i$ keep on Murphy$_j$ [tabs]

(2.50) a. ?*What did Ferdinand$_i$ take of Orion$_j$ [a photograph]
     b. ?*What did Murry$_i$ drink of that wine$_j$ [a quart]
     c. ?What did Salazar$_i$ write about Allah$_j$ [a book]

(Example (2.50c) is relatively more acceptable than the other examples. A possible explanation for this is suggested in footnote 13.)

Whatever the nature of the constraints on wh-movement turns out to be, the $\overline{V}$ analysis provides the basis of a unified structure-based or function-based analysis of these, since both types of expression have the same sorts of S- and F-structures.

The derived F-structures of (2.49) and (2.50) are shown in (2.51) and (2.52), respectively:

(2.51) a. $(\text{WHAT}_k)[[\text{TAKE } \text{NP}[x_k]]_\zeta \quad \text{NP}[i]_\alpha \quad \text{NP}[j]_\beta]$

     b. $(\text{WHAT}_k)[[\text{KEEP } \text{NP}[x_k]]_\zeta \quad \text{NP}[i]_\alpha \quad \text{NP}[j]_\beta]$

(2.52) a. $(\text{WHAT}_k)[[\text{TAKE } \text{NP}[x_k]]_\zeta \quad \text{NP}[i]_\alpha \quad \text{PP}[\text{OF } \text{NP}[j]]_\alpha]$

     b. $(\text{WHAT}_k)[[\text{DRINK } \text{NP}[x_k]]_\zeta \quad \text{NP}[i]_\alpha \quad \text{PP}[\text{OF } \text{NP}[j]]_\alpha]$

     c. $(\text{WHAT}_k)[[\text{WRITE } \text{NP}[x_k]]_\zeta \quad \text{NP}[i]_\alpha \quad \text{PP}[\text{ABOUT } \text{NP}[j]]_\alpha]$

(The operations involved in the derivation of such F-structures are discussed in Chapter V.)

The second area of parallel behavior, the existence of severe selectional restrictions on the S-structure correlate of the NP^c argument, is illustrated in the following examples:

(2.53) a. ?*Rolf$_i$ took that advantage of Mork$_j$
     b. ?*The CIA$_i$ kept the FBI's tabs on Murphy$_j$

(2.54)   ?Aaron$_i$ drank $\left\{ \begin{array}{l} \text{those} \\ \text{Attila's} \end{array} \right\}$ quarts of wine$_j$

The examples in (2.53) contain type (a) expressions, and example (2.54) is a type (b) expression. For reasons that are discussed in footnote 13, the applicability of these selectional restrictions to many type (b) expressions only manifests itself clearly in wh-questions like the following:

(2.55) a. ?*What did Ono$_i$ drink that glass bottle of
      b. ?*Who did Norris$_i$ take those large pictures of
      c. ?*What did Alyce$_i$ write that leatherbound book about

Selectional restrictions of this type are a consequence of what are probably rather complex semantic properties of these expressions, and are not uniform for all members of both types of expression.[12] However, in all cases, they seem to restrict the range of determiners that can occur with the NP elements, excluding ones like *that* in (2.53a), *the FBI's* in (2.53b), *those* in (2.54), and so on. The important point here, however, is that these restrictions can all be stated on the same type of S-structure and F-structure if all of these expressions are analyzed as $\overline{V}$ predicates, and a unified account of these selectional restrictions is possible in this analysis.[13] The relevance of the $\overline{V}$ analysis to other areas is discussed in Chapters III and V.

3. Basic F-Structure Components: Arguments

The argument structures of predicates, as we saw in Section 1, can contain one, two, or three NP[θ] arguments, as well as various types of non-θ arguments. These latter types are arguments to which the predicate does not assign an SR. Two general types of non-θ argument can occur in the basic F-structures of predicates: uncontrolled complements and controlled complements.

Uncontrolled complements are the F-structure correlates of embedded S and PP constituents in S-structures. These occur in examples like the following:

(3.1) a. Morrison$_i$ believed [that the Post-Würmian deglaciation$_j$
         began in 9000 BC]
      b. Elan$_i$ would prefer $_S$[for Jezebel$_j$ to kiss rattlesnakes$_k$]

(3.2) a. Jonah$_i$ walked $_{PP}$[to England$_j$]
    b. Moreau$_i$ put the fossil$_j$ $_{PP}$[in the case$_k$]
    c. Obadiah$_i$ gave a pyx$_j$ $_{PP}$[to the priest$_k$]

The examples in (3.1) contain complement sentences, which may be *that*-clauses or tenseless *for-to* clauses. The verbs *believe* and *prefer* have the basic F-structures shown in (3.3):[14]

(3.3) a. BELIEVE   1-NP[α]   S
    b. PREFER   1-NP[α]   S

The S-structures of these examples are shown below:

(3.4) a.

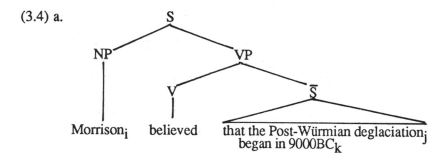

Morrison$_i$ believed   that the Post-Würmian deglaciation$_j$ began in 9000BC$_k$

    b.

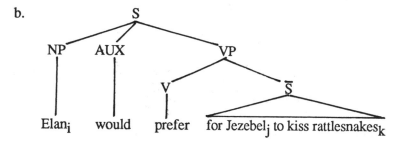

Elan$_i$ would   prefer   for Jezebel$_j$ to kiss rattlesnakes$_k$

(The assignment of the category AUX rather than some other category to *would* in (3.4b) does not affect this analysis.)

The F-structures of (3.1) are derived from the bare PRED/ARG constructions in (3.5):

(3.5) a. BELIEVE 1-NP [BEGIN 1-NP [IN 1-NP]]
    b. PREFER 1-NP [KISS 1-NP 2-NP]

Structure (3.5a) is produced by inserting the PRED/ARG structure of BEGIN into the S-argument position of the predicate BELIEVE. The PRED/ARG structure of IN is attached as an adverbial to the PRED/ARG structure of BEGIN. Structure (3.5b) is produced by inserting the PRED/ARG structure of KISS into the S-argument position of the PRED/ARG structure of PREFER.

The Index Insertion rule and the SRA rule apply to the PRED/ARG structure of each predicate separately to produce the derived F-structures in (3.6):

(3.6) a.   BELIEVE $NP[i]$ [BEGIN $NP[j]$ [IN $NP[k]$]]
$\qquad\qquad\quad \alpha \qquad\qquad\quad \alpha \qquad\quad \alpha$

$\quad$ b.   PREFER $NP[i]$ [KISS $NP[j]$ $NP[k]$]]
$\qquad\qquad\quad \alpha \qquad\qquad \alpha \qquad \beta$

The examples in (3.2) contain embedded prepositional phrases. In these examples, the prepositions, *to* in (3.2a and c), and *in* in (3.2b), function as predicates, and assign an SR to lone NP[θ] arguments. So the embedded prepositional phrases are functionally analogous to the embedded sentences in (3.1). The basic F-structures of the verbs *walk*, *put*, and *give* (which correspond to the S-structures of these examples) are shown in (3.7):

(3.7) a.   WALK $1\text{-}NP[\alpha]$ PP
$\quad$ b.   PUT $1\text{-}NP[\alpha]$ $2\text{-}NP[\beta]$ PP
$\quad$ c.   GIVE $1\text{-}NP[\alpha]$ $2\text{-}NP[\beta]$ PP

The S-structures of (3.2) are shown in (3.8), below:

(3.8) a.

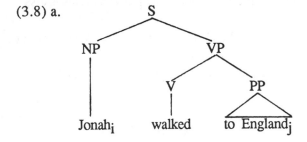

b.

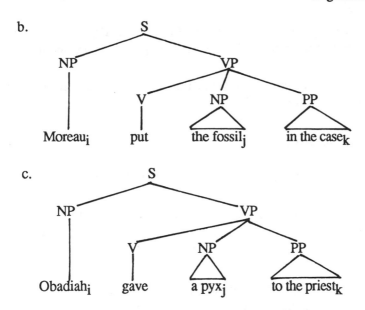

c.

The F-structures of these examples are derived from the bare PRED/ARG structures in (3.9), which have been constructed by inserting the PRED/ARG structure of the appropriate preposition into the PP-argument position in the basic PRED/ARG structure of the verb:

(3.9) a. WALK 1-NP [TO 1-NP]
    b. PUT 1-NP 2-NP [IN 1-NP]
    c. GIVE 1-NP 2-NP [TO 1-NP]

The Index Insertion rule and the SRA rule apply in the normal way to produce the derived F-structures shown in (3.10):

(3.10) a. WALK $\text{NP}^{[i]}_\alpha$ [TO $\text{NP}^{[j]}_\alpha$]
    b. PUT $\text{NP}^{[i]}_\alpha$ $\text{NP}^{[j]}_\beta$ [IN $\text{NP}^{[k]}_\alpha$]
    c. GIVE $\text{NP}^{[i]}_\alpha$ $\text{NP}^{[j]}_\beta$ [TO $\text{NP}^{[k]}_\alpha$]

Both S complements in examples like (3.1) and PP complements in examples like (3.2) are uncontrolled in the sense that none of the NP[θ] arguments of the predicates in these complements are (or must be) anaphorically related to an NP[θ] argument of some external predicate.

In the F-structures of these examples, (3.6) and (3.10), above, the NP[θ] arguments of the embedded verbs and prepositions are independently indexed and assigned SRs.

The general F-level representation of controlled complements is shown in (3.11), below:

(3.11)   [(NP*)XP]

The NP* term is the controller of the complement, and the XP term is the controlled predicate structure.

The classical cases of controlled complements in English are sentences which contain so-called "equi" and "raising" verbs. Some examples are the following:

(3.12) a. Yuri_i believed Zoe_j to have kissed Seneca_k
       b. Scipio_i forced Boguslav_j to kiss the serpent_k

The verb *believe* in example (3.12a) is the archetypal raising verb, and the verb *force* in example (3.12b) is the archetypal equi-NP-deletion verb, or control verb. In the standard theory, an NP argument of the latter verb type controls an embedded PRO subject of a complement sentence.

In the proposed theory, following Brame (1976a,b) and Bresnan (1978), examples like (3.12a and b) have (D- and) S-structures like the following:

(3.13) a.

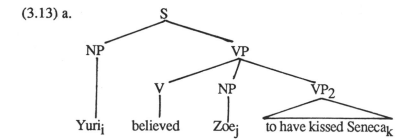

b.

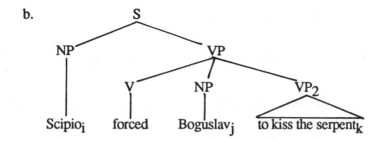

These structures are identical down to the category level.

The basic F-structures of *believe* and *force* are shown in (3.14), below:

(3.14) a. BELIEVE 1-NP[α] [(NP*)VP]
       b. FORCE 1-NP[α] 2-NP[β] [(NP*)VP]

In these structures, the XP component of the controlled complement is VP. Raising verbs like *believe* and control verbs like *force* are distinguished from one another at the level of F-structure. The basic F-structure of BELIEVE, in (3.14a), contains a single NP[θ] argument. That of FORCE, in (3.14b), contains two NP[θ] arguments.

The embedded VP constituent, VP_2, in each of the structures in (3.13) is the S-structure correlate of the controlled complement argument in the basic F-structure of the relevant predicate. The F-structure of example (3.12a) is derived from the following bare PRED/ARG structure:

(3.15)   BELIEVE 1-NP [(NP*)[KISS 1-NP 2-NP]]

This structure is produced in the usual way by embedding the PRED/ARG structure of KISS in the VP-argument position in the controlled complement argument of the PRED/ARG structure of BELIEVE.

First, the Index Insertion rule must apply to this structure. The S-structure correlate of the 1-NP argument is the NP[i] constituent in (3.13a), as we would expect. The S-structure correlate of the NP* argument is the NP[j] constituent. The 1-NP argument of the embedded predicate KISS has no S-structure correlate. The S-structure correlate of the 2-NP argument of KISS is the NP[k] constituent, again, following the general pattern for English. The Index Insertion rule and the SRA rule apply to (3.15) to produce the following:

(3.16)   BELIEVE $\text{NP}[i]$ $[(\text{NP*}[j])[\text{KISS NP NP}[k]]]$
$\qquad\qquad\quad\ \alpha\qquad\qquad\qquad\qquad\quad \alpha\ \ \ \beta$

At this point, an addditional operation must apply to (3.16) to assign
the index j to the initial NP argument of KISS. This operation is the
analog of the raising rule (in this case, raising to object position), and
was referred to as Raqui in Horn (1983a). A first pass at its formulation
is shown in (3.17):

(3.17)   <u>Raqui</u>
$\qquad\qquad$ $(\text{NP*}[i])$ PRED   NP
$\qquad\qquad\qquad 1\qquad\quad 2\qquad\ \ 3 \Longrightarrow \emptyset\quad 2\ \ \text{NP}[i]$

(In Chapter III, I will demonstrate that this rule is actually a subcase of a
general co-indexing operation.)

The Raqui rule applies to (3.16) to produce the derived F-structure
of (3.12a), which is shown in (3.18):

(3.18)   BELIEVE $\text{NP}[i]$ $[\text{KISS NP}[j]\ \text{NP}[k]]$
$\qquad\qquad\qquad\quad \alpha\qquad\qquad\quad \alpha\qquad \beta$

The F-structure of example (3.12b) is derived from the following
PRED/ARG structure:

(3.19)   FORCE 1-NP 2-NP [(NP*)[KISS 1-NP 2-NP]]

This structure is produced, as above, by inserting the PRED/ARG
structure of KISS into the VP-argument position in the controlled complement argument of the PRED/ARG structure of the higher predicate,
in this case, FORCE.

The S-structure correlates of the 1-NP and 2-NP arguments in (3.19)
are the $\text{NP}[i]$ constituent and the $\text{NP}[j]$ constituent, respectively, in
(3.13b), again, following the general pattern for English. The S-
structure correlate of the 2-NP argument of KISS is the $\text{NP}[k]$ constituent in (3.13b). As was the case with the previous example, there is no
S-structure correlate of the 1-NP argument of KISS. In contrast with
the previous example, however, there is also no S-structure correlate of

the NP* argument. The Index Insertion rule and the SRA rule apply to (3.19) to produce the following:

(3.20)   FORCE $NP^{[i]}_\alpha$ $NP^{[j]}_\beta$ [(NP*)[KISS NP_α $NP^{[k]}_\beta$]]]

Now a rule must apply to assign an index to the NP* argument so that the Raqui rule, in turn, can assign this index to the initial NP argument of KISS. Following Horn (1983a), I will refer to this rule as the Co-indexing rule. A first pass at its formulation appears in (3.21), below:

(3.21):   The Co-indexing Rule:
$NP^{[i]}$ X   (NP*)
  1   2   3   ===> 1   2   ($NP*^{[i]}$)

(I will demonstrate in Chapter III that this rule is also a subcase of the general co-indexing operation referred to above.)

The Co-indexing rule must apply in Structure (3.20) to assign the index j of the second NP[θ] argument of FORCE to the NP* argument. The application of the rule in this way produces the structure shown in (3.22):

(3.22)   FORCE $NP^{[i]}_\alpha$ $NP^{[j]}_\beta$ [($NP*^{[j]}$)[KISS NP_α $NP^{[k]}_\beta$]]]

Now, the Raqui rule can apply to produce the derived F-structure of example (3.12b), which is shown below:

(3.23)   FORCE $NP^{[i]}_\alpha$ $NP^{[j]}_\beta$ [KISS $NP^{[j]}_\alpha$ $NP^{[k]}_\beta$]]]

Earlier we saw that raising verbs like *believe* and control verbs like *force* differed in the number of NP[θ] arguments that appear in their basic F-structures. (Compare Structure (3.14a) with Structure (3.14b).) A more significant difference between these predicate types concerns the NP* element of the controlled complement in their basic F-structures.

For raising verbs, the NP* element has an S-structure indexed NP correlate. For *believe*, this was the NP_2 constituent, the NP dominated

by VP, or direct object, in more familiar terms. In this respect, the NP*
argument behaves like an x-NP argument, except, of course, that it is
assigned no SR. Although I have not stated it explicitly up to this point, I
have assumed that x-NP[θ] arguments have a feature, [+GR], which
identifies them as the F-structure correlates of S-structure NP constituents. (The term GR is an abbreviation for "Grammatical Relation".
The nature and role of Grammatical Relations are discussed in Section 5
of this chapter.)   In keeping with this assumption, the NP* argument in
the basic F-structures of raising verbs   like *believe* has the feature
[+GR].   A more accurate representation of the basic F-structure of
believe is shown below:

(3.24)   BELIEVE   1-NP[α]   [(NP*[+GR])VP]

For control verbs, the NP* element has no S-structure indexed NP
correlate, as we have seen. Generally, F-structure constituents that have
no S-structure correlates are ones that do not have the feature [+GR], or,
equivalently, ones that have the feature [-GR]. If we consider this to be
the unmarked case, then the basic F-structures of verbs of this class are
represented as shown for *force* in (3.14b). This structure is repeated
below, so that it may be compared with (3.24):

(3.14) b.   FORCE   1-NP[α]   2-NP[β]   [(NP*)VP]

The structure shown in (3.25), below, is a generalized representation
of the basic F-structure-type of both control and raising verbs, which
contains a controlled complement argument like the one in (3.11):

(3.25)   PRED   1-NP[α]   ...   [(NP*)XP]

We can now think of the feature [GR] as a parameter whose value, when
applied to the NP* element of the F-structure representation of contolled complements can be either [+], for raising verbs, or [-] for equi-
NP-deletion verbs. Because NP* arguments are not NP[θ] arguments of
verbs, the unmarked case is the one in which they do not have the feature
[+GR] and have no S-structure NP correlate. Consequently, we may
think of the basic F-structures of raising verbs as being more highly
marked than those of control verbs. This markedness correlates with

the fact that the control process, however formulated, is more wide-spread than the raising process (at least the raising to object position subcase of this process). It is not unusual for a language to have control predicates, but no raising predicates like *believe*. This situation, in fact, occurs in most of the Indo-European languages. For these languages, the value of the [GR] parameter for NP* arguments can only be [-] under certain conditions. See Horn (1985b) for more discussion and examples. The [GR] parameter with its set of possible values defines the notion "possible controlled complement type" (and consequently, partially defines the notion "possible predicate type"). Moreover, by constraining the value that can be assigned to this parameter for any particular language, we can account for the cross-language distribution of raising and control predicates, and hence the cross-language distribution of these processes.

Now consider the following examples:

(3.26) a.   Wilson$_i$ seemed to have halitosis$_j$
  b.   Melissa$_i$ appeared to like Wragge$_j$

(3.27) a.   Kinderhook$_i$ tried to hit Sneed$_j$
  b.   Blakely$_i$ attempted to set a record$_j$

The verbs *seem* and *appear* are analyzed as raising verbs, like *believe*, in most earlier analyses. However, unlike *believe*, these verbs occur in structures which the raised NP is in subject position. Similarly, the verbs *try* and *attempt* are analyzed as control verbs, like *force*, but unlike this verb, they occur in structures in which their subjects are the controllers of the embedded predicate-subject positions.

In the proposed theory, the (D- and) S-structures of the examples in (3.26) are the ones shown in (3.28):

(3.28) a.

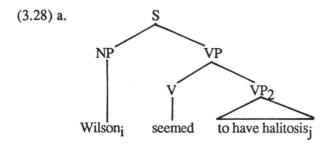

b.

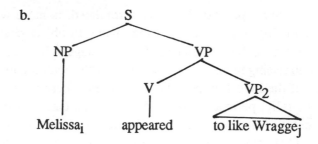

These structures are analogous to the one in (3.13a) containing the verb *believe* .

The basic F-structures of *seem* and *appear* (in the relevant sense) are shown in (3.29):

(3.29) a.   SEEM   [(NP*[+GR])VP]
      b.   APPEAR   [(NP*[+GR])VP]

The derived F-structures of the examples in (3.26) are produced from the following PRED/ARG constructions:

(3.30) a.   SEEM   [(NP*[+GR])[HAVE 1-NP 2-NP]]
      b.   APPEAR   [(NP*[+GR])[LIKE 1-NP 2-NP]]

These constructions are formed in the normal way by inserting the basic PRED/ARG structure of the embedded predicate in VP_2 into the VP-argument position in the controlled complement argument of the PRED/ARG structure of the higher verb.

For Structure (3.30a), the S-structure correlate of the NP* argument is the $_{NP}[i]$ constituent, the S-structure correlate of the 2-NP argument of HAVE is the $_{NP}[j]$ constituent, and the 1-NP argument of HAVE has no S-structure correlate.   The Index Insertion rule and the SRA rule apply to this structure to produce the following:

(3.31)   SEEM   [($_{NP*}$[i])[HAVE NP NP[j]]]
                                    α   β

The Raqui rule can now apply to (3.31) to produce the derived F-structure of example (3.26a), shown below:

(3.32)   SEEM [HAVE NP[i] NP[j]]
                        α   β

The derived F-structure of example (3.26b) is produced from the PRED/ARG construction in (3.30b), in the same way, by the application of the Index Insertion rule, the SRA rule, and the Raqui rule. This F-structure is shown in (3.33):

(3.33)   APPEAR [LIKE NP[i] NP[j]]
                          α   β

The (D- and) S-structures of the examples in (3.27) are shown below:

(3.34) a.

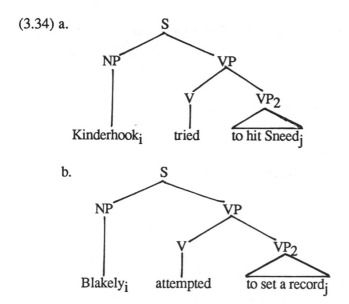

  b.

The basic F-structures of *try* and *attempt* are the following:

(3.35) a. TRY   1-NP[α]   [(NP*)VP]
       b. ATTEMPT 1-NP[α]   [(NP*)VP]

The derived F-structures of these examples are produced from the PRED/ARG structures shown in (3.35), which are constructed in the normal way:

(3.36) a. TRY 1-NP [(NP*)[HIT 1-NP 2-NP]]
     b. ATTEMPT 1-NP [(NP*)[SET 1-NP 2-NP]]

In these structures, the NP* arguments do not have the feature [+GR], and have no S-structure correlates. In (3.36a), the S-structure correlate of the 1-NP argument of TRY is the $_{NP}$[i] constituent in (3.34a), the S-structure correlate of the 2-NP argument of HIT is the $_{NP}$[j] constituent, and the 1-NP argument of HIT has no S-structure correlate.   The Index Insertion rule applies to (3.36a) to produce the following:

(3.37)   TRY $_{NP}$[i] [(NP*)[HIT NP $_{NP}$[j]]]
             α   α   β

The Co-indexing rule in (3.21) and the Raqui rule in (3.17) apply to this structure to produce the derived F-structure of example (3.27a). This is shown in (3.38):

(3.38)   TRY $_{NP}$[i] [HIT $_{NP}$[i] $_{NP}$[j]]
             α   α   β

The derived F-structure of example (3.27b) is produced in the same way from (3.36b). This structure is shown in (3.39):

(3.39)   ATTEMPT $_{NP}$[i] [SET $_{NP}$[i] $_{NP}$[j]]
                α   α   β

The predicates *seem* and *appear* differ from *believe* in that the basic F-structures of the former contain no NP[θ] argument, while that of the latter contains a single NP[θ] argument. Compare (3.29) with (3.24). Similarly, the basic F-structures of *try* and *attempt* differ from that of *force* in that the former contain a single NP[θ] argument while the latter contains two NP[θ] arguments. Compare (3.35) and (3.14b).

We can distinguish verbs like *seem* and *appear*, which are associated with the analog of raising to subject position in the proposed theory, from verbs like *believe*, which are associated with the analog of raising to object position, by the number of NP[θ] arguments that appear in their basic F-structures. This number may be thought of as a value of what we might call the θ-Argument parameter. For verbs like *believe*, which have basic F-structures like (3.24), the value of this parameter is

1. For verbs like *seem* and *appear*, which have the basic F-structures shown in (3.29), the value of this parameter is ∅.

The θ-Argument parameter may be applied to distinguish verbs like *try* and *attempt*, whose subjects are the controllers of PRO in the standard theory, from verbs like *force*, whose objects have this function. For the former, whose basic F-structures appear in (3.35), the value of this parameter is 1, and for the latter, whose basic F-structure appears in (3.14b), the value of this parameter is 2. The θ-Argument parameter, with a suitably constrained set of potential values, defines the notion "possible raising analog subtype" (that is, analog of raising to subject position or raising to object position), and "possible control subtype" (subject controller or object controller). So this parameter, like the [GR] parameter, provides the theory with a mechanism to partially define the notion "possible predicate type."

Again, by constraining the maximum value that can be assigned to this parameter for any particular language, we can account for the cross-language distribution of predicate types. For example, there are languages in which the analog in this theory of raising to subject position, but not raising to object position occurs. Two such languages are Polish and Dutch. In Polish, examples like (3.40a) are grammatical, but ones like (3.40b) are not:

(3.40) a.   Jan wydawał się być zadowolony
            Jan (NOM) seemed REFLEX be [-finite] glad
            Jan seemed to be glad

       b.   *Jan wierzył Marii mówić prawdę
            Jan (NOM) believed Maria (DAT) speak [-finite] truth(ACC)
            Jan believed Maria to have spoken the truth

In Dutch, the pattern is the same, as illustrated by the following examples:

(3.41) a.   Jan bleek Mary te mogen
            Jan appeared Mary to like
            Jan appeared to like Mary

b. *Jan geloofde Bill Mary te kussen
   Jan believed Bill Mary to kiss
   Jan believed Bill to have kissed Mary

We can account for these facts, as well as the distinction between these languages and English in this respect, by assigning a maximum value of $\emptyset$ to the θ-Argument parameter for the former, and a maximum value of $\underline{1}$ to the θ-Argument parameter for the latter, for raising predicates, whose basic F-structures contain controlled complements of the form: [(NP*[+GR])XP]. A maximum value of $\underline{1}$, in the absence of conditions stating otherwise, implies a possible value of $\emptyset$. This predicts that if the analog of raising to object position occurs in a language, then the analog of raising to subject position also occurs. However, since a value of $\emptyset$ does not imply a value of $\underline{1}$, the reverse is not necessarily true. This prediction appears to be correct.[15]

Next, consider the following examples:

(3.42) a.   Zofia$_i$ considered Horatio$_j$ a man
       b.   Poles$_i$ consider the zloty$_j$ worthless
       c.   They$_i$ elected Ferdinand$_j$ president

In these examples, the verb *consider* occurs with an NP complement in (3.42a) and an AP complement in (3.42b). The verb *elect* in (3.42c). occurs with an NP complement. These complements are functionally analogous to the controlled VP complements in the examples discussed previously. The basic F-structures of these predicates are shown in (3.43) and (3.44), below:

(3.43) a.   CONSIDER   1-NP[α]   [(NP*[+GR])NP]
       b.   CONSIDER   1-NP[α]   [(NP*[+GR])AP]

(3.44)   ELECT   1-NP[α]   2-NP[β]   [(NP*)NP]

The S-structures of the examples in (3.42a and b) are the following:

(3.45) a.

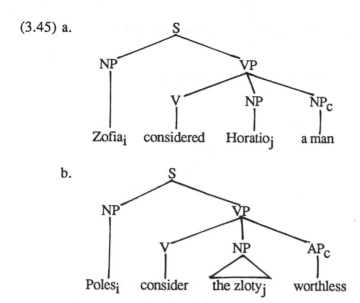

b.

In Structure (3.45a), the term NP_C represents the NP complement, and in Structure (3.45b), the term AP_C represents the AP complement.

The F-structures of these examples are derived from the following bare PRED/ARG structures:

(3.46) a. CONSIDER 1-NP [(NP*[+GR])[MAN 1-NP]]
      b. CONSIDER 1-NP [(NP*[+GR])[WORTHLESS 1-NP]]

These structures are produced by inserting the basic PRED/ARG structure of the [+N] predicate MAN and that of the [+A] predicate WORTHLESS into the NP-argument position and the AP-argument position, respectively, in the controlled complement arguments in the PRED/ARG structures of CONSIDER.

The S-structure correlate of the 1-NP argument in each case is the NP[i] constituent in the appropriate structure, and the S-structure correlate of the NP*[+GR] argument is the NP[j] constituent in each case. The Index Insertion rule, SRA rule, and Raqui rule apply to (3.46) to produce the following derived F-structures:

(3.47) a. CONSIDER NP[i] [MAN NP[j]]
                     α   α

b.   CONSIDER $_{NP}[i]$ [WORTHLESS $_{NP}[j]]$
                  α α

The S-structure of (3.42c) is shown in (3.48):

(3.48)

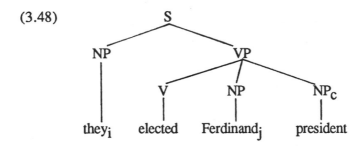

    The F-structure of this example is derived from the bare PRED/ARG structure in (3.49), below, which is constructed by inserting the basic PRED/ARG structure of the [+N] predicate *president* into the NP argument position in the controlled complement argument of the verb ELECT:

(3.49)   ELECT 1-NP 2-NP [(NP*)[PRESIDENT 1-NP]]

The S-structure correlates of the 1-NP and 2-NP arguments of ELECT are the $_{NP}[i]$ constituent and the $_{NP}[j]$ constituent, respectively. The NP* argument of ELECT does not have the feature [+GR], and it has no S-structure correlate. The Index Insertion rule, SRA rule, Co-indexing rule, and Raqui rule apply to (3.49) to produce the derived F-structure of (3.42c), which is shown in (3.50):

(3.50)   ELECT $_{NP}[i]$ $_{NP}[j]$ [PRESIDENT $_{NP}[j]]$
                    α β α

    We see, then, that the verb *consider* is analogous to verbs like *believe*, and the verb *elect* is analogous to verbs like *force*. Compare the basic F-structures of *consider* in (3.43) with that of *believe* in (3.24); and compare the basic F-structure of *elect* in (3.44) with that of *force* in (3.14b). The only significant difference between these predicates and *believe* and *force* is the category of the XP controlled complement.

    A third parameter, which I will refer to as the XP Category parameter, can be formulated to account for this difference. The possible values of the XP parameter are VP, NP, AP, and PP, (expressed as matrices of suitable category features in the context of some version of X-bar theory). The value of this parameter varies for particular predicates in a language. For English, the value of the XP parameter for *believe* and *force* is [+VP], the value of the XP parameter for *consider* is [+NP] or [+AP], and the value of the XP parameter for *elect* is [+NP]. By fixing the values of this parameter for each predicate class, we can account for the distribution of the different categories of controlled complements within a language.

The value of the XP Category parameter for individual predicates can vary from language to language. This means that the translational analogs of predicates can occur with complements of different categories in different languages. The Polish example in (3.51), which contains the verb *zmuszić* (force), illustrates such a contrast:

(3.51) Jan zmusził Marka do uderzenia Marii
   Jan (NOM) forced Marek (ACC) to hitting (GEN) Maria
   (GEN)
   Jan forced Marek to hit Maria

The verb *zmuszić* in examples like this occurs with a [+NP] controlled complement. The basic F-structure of this verb is shown in (3.52):

(3.52) ZMUSZIĆ 1-NP[α] 2-NP[β] [(NP*)NP]

If we compare this F-structure with that of *force* in (3.14b), we see that they are the same general type, and that they differ only in the value of the XP parameter. By fixing the permissible values of the XP parameter for the predicates of different languages, we can account for the cross-language distribution of controlled complements of the various categories. (I return to this example below.)

Now consider the following examples:

(3.53) a. Catlyn$_i$ considered Breen$_j$ tall for a gnome$_k$
   b. They$_i$ elected Randolf$_j$ president of the club$_k$

As mentioned at the end of Section 2, the maximal projections of [-V] heads can also function as predicates. Example (3.53a) contains an AP complement of the form [A PP]. Example (3.53b) contains an NP complement of the form [N PP]. In (3.53a), the entire AP functions as the predicate of the embedded complement. The derived F-structure of this example is produced from a PRED/ARG structure in which the single-argument PRED/ARG structure of the AP predicate, of the form shown in (2.31), is inserted into the AP argument position in the controlled complement argument of CONSIDER. This structure, after the application of the Index Insertion rule, the SRA rule, and the Raqui rule, is the following:

(3.54)   CONSIDER $\underset{\alpha}{\text{NP[i]}}$ [[TALL[FOR $\underset{\alpha}{\text{NP[k]}}$]] $\underset{\alpha}{\text{NP[j]}}$]

(Following the convention established at the beginning of the chapter, the SRs, α, of each predicate in this structure are not necessarily identical.) Example (3.53a), with this derived F-structure, is analogous to example (2.30a), whose derived F-structure is shown in (2.35a).

The predicate *president*, as we saw earlier, has two basic F-structures: one which contains a lone NP[θ] argument and one which contains an NP[θ] argument and a PP argument. Consequently, example (3.53b) has the two derived F-structures shown in (3.55):

(3.55) a.   ELECT $\underset{\alpha}{\text{NP[i]}}$ $\underset{\beta}{\text{NP[j]}}$ [PRESIDENT $\underset{\alpha}{\text{NP[j]}}$ [OF $\underset{\alpha}{\text{NP[k]}}$]]

   b.   ELECT $\underset{\alpha}{\text{NP[i]}}$ $\underset{\beta}{\text{NP[j]}}$ [[PRESIDENT[OF $\underset{\alpha}{\text{NP[k]}}$]] $\underset{\alpha}{\text{NP[j]}}$]]

The F-structure in (3.55a) contains the two-argument F-structure of *president*. Here *president* functions as the [+N] predicate of the controlled complement as in (3.50). Example (3.53b), in this sense, is analogous to (2.25b) with the derived F-structure in (2.29b). The F-structure in (3.55b) is the XP predicate F-structure, in which the entire NP, *president of the club*, functions as the predicate of the controlled complement. This structure is produced from a PRED/ARG structure in which the single-argument PRED/ARG structure of the NP predicate is inserted into the NP argument position in the controlled complement argument of ELECT. Example (3.53b), in this sense, is analogous to (2.25b) with the derived F-structure in (2.35b).

In the following example, a PP functions as the XP predicate of a controlled complement:

(3.56)   Gnorman$_i$ wanted gnomes$_j$ in his garden$_k$

The S-structure of this example is shown in (3.57):

(3.57)

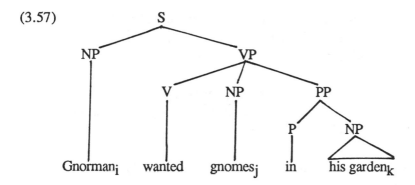

The basic F-structure of the verb *want* in this sense appears in (3.58):

(3.58)   WANT 1-NP[α] [(NP*[+GR])PP]

The derived F-structure of this sentence is produced from the following PRED/ARG structure, which is formed by inserting the single-argument PRED/ARG structure of the PP predicate into the PP argument position in the controlled complement argument of WANT:

(3.59)   WANT 1-NP [(NP*[+GR])[[IN 1-NP] 1-NP]]

The Index Insertion rule, SRA rule, and Raqui rule apply in the normal way to derive the structure in (3.60):

(3.60)   WANT $_{NP}$[i] [[IN $_{NP}$[k]] $_{NP}$[j]]
                        α α α

This example is analogous to (2.36) with the derived F-structure in (2.39).[16]

Once the three parameters associated with them are fixed, the same principles and operations apply to controlled complements in all languages. I will close this section with some illustrative examples. First, consider the following Polish sentences:

(3.61)a. Jan$_i$ zmusił Marka$_j$ do uderzenia Marii$_k$
Jan (NOM) forced Marek (ACC) to hitting (GEN) Maria
(GEN)
Jan forced Marek to hit Maria

b. Tadeusz$_i$ nauczył niedźwiedzia$_j$ tańczyć
Tadeusz (NOM) taught bear (ACC) (to) dance
Tadeusz taught the bear to dance

c. Oni$_i$ wybrali Bolesława$_j$ prezydentem
They (NOM) elected Boleslaw (ACC) president (INSTR)
They elected Boleslaw president

These sentences have the S-structures shown in (3.62):

(3.62) a.

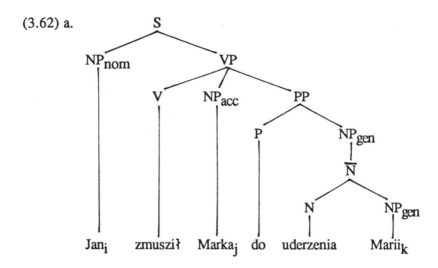

b.

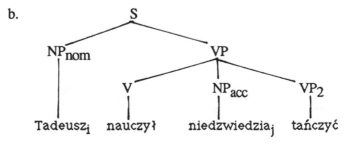

c.

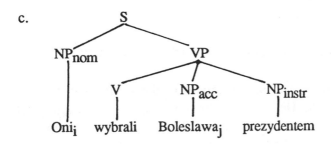

The basic F-structures of the verbs *zmuszić, nauczyć*, and *wybrać* are shown in (3.63):

(3.63)a. ZMUSZIĆ   1-NP[α]   2-NP[β]   [(NP*)NP]
    b. NAUCZYĆ   1-NP[α]   2-NP[β]   [(NP*)VP]
    c. WYBRAĆ   1-NP[α]   2-NP[β]   [(NP*)NP]

These are control predicates of the same type as the English verb *force*.

The derived F-structure of (3.56a) is produced from the following PRED/ARG structure:

(3.64)   ZMUSZIĆ 1-NP 2-NP [(NP*)[UDERZENIE 1-NP 2-NP]]

This structure is formed by embedding the PRED/ARG structure of the nominal UDERZENIE into the NP position in the controlled complement of the PRED/ARG structure of ZMUSZIĆ.[17] In accordance with the general pattern for Polish, the S-structure correlates of the 1-NP and 2-NP arguments of ZMUSZIĆ are the NPnom[i] constituent and the NPacc[j] constituent, respectively, in Structure (3.62a). The S-structure correlate of the NP argument of UDERZENIE is the NPgen[k] constituent in this structure. The NP* argument and the 1-NP argument of UDERZENIE have no S-structure correlates. The Index Insertion rule, the SRA rule, the Co-indexing rule, and the Raqui rule apply in the normal fashion to (3.64) to produce the derived F-structure of this example, which is shown in (3.65):

(3.65)   ZMUSZIĆ NP[i] NP[j] [UDERZENIE NP[j] NP[k]]
                   α   β   α   β

The derived F-structure of (3.61b) is produced from the PRED/ARG structure shown below:

(3.66)   NAUCZYĆ 1-NP 2-NP [(NP*)[TAŃCZYĆ 1-NP]]

As above, the S-structure correlates of the 1-NP argument and 2-NP argument of NAUCZYĆ are the $NP_{nom}[i]$ and the $NP_{acc}[j]$ constituents, respectively, in Structure (3.62b). The NP* argument and the 1-NP argument of TAŃCZYĆ do not have S-structure correlates. The Index Insertion rule, the SRA rule, the Co-indexing rule and the Raqui rule apply to (3.66) to produce (3.67):

(3.67)   NAUCZYĆ $\underset{\alpha}{NP[i]}$ $\underset{\beta}{NP[j]}$ [TAŃCZYĆ $\underset{\alpha}{NP[j]}$]

The derived F-structure of (3.61c) is produced in the same way. This structure is shown in (3.68):

(3.68)   WYBRAĆ $\underset{\alpha}{NP[i]}$ $\underset{\beta}{NP[j]}$ [PREZYDENT $\underset{\alpha}{NP[j]}$]

The following Dutch sentence contains a control verb in that language:

(3.69)   Jan$_i$ dwong Van Horn$_j$ Cecelia$_k$ te kussen
          Jan forced Van Horn Cecelia to kiss
          Jan forced Van Horn to kiss Cecelia

The S-structure of this sentence is shown in (3.70):

(3.70)

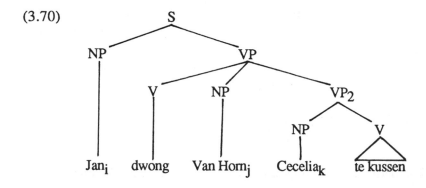

The basic F-structure of the predicate DWINGEN is shown in (3.71):

(3.71)   DWINGEN   1-NP[α]   2-NP[β]   [(NP*)VP]

The derived F-structure of this example is produced from the following PRED/ARG structure:

(3.72)   DWINGEN   1-NP   2-NP   [(NP*)[KUSSEN   1-NP   2-NP]]

Following the general pattern for Dutch, the S-structure correlates of the 1-NP argument and 2-NP argument of DWINGEN are the NP[i] constituent and the NP[j] constituent, respectively. The S-structure correlate of the 2-NP argument of KUSSEN is the NP[k] constituent. The NP* argument and the 1-NP argument of KUSSEN have no S-structure correlates. The Index Insertion rule, the SRA rule, the Co-indexing rule, and the Raqui rule apply to (3.72) in the normal way to produce the following structure:

(3.73)   DWINGEN $\underset{\alpha}{NP[i]}$ $\underset{\beta}{NP[j]}$ [KUSSEN $\underset{\alpha}{NP[j]}$ $\underset{\beta}{NP[k]}$]]

The example in (3.74a), below, is a Japanese sentence. Example (3.74b) is a Samoan sentence. Both of these sentences contain control verbs:

(3.74) a.   Taroo wa$_i$ Hanako o$_j$ baka da (to) omotte-ita
             Taroo (NOM) Hanako (ACC) fool is thinking was
             Taro thought Hanako to be a fool

       b.   Na fosi e Ioane$_i$ Mele$_j$ e ave le taavale$_k$
             TENSE force (SUBJ) Ioane   Mele TENSE drive   the car
             Ioane forced Mele to drive the car

The verb *omotte* in (3.74a) is the same type of predicate as *believe* in English. The S-structure of this example is shown in (3.75):

(3.75)

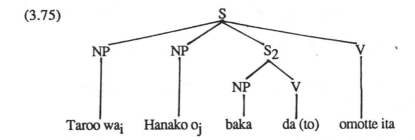

In non-configurational languages, which have structures like the one in (3.75) that contain no VP constituent, S may be analyzed as the maximal projection of V (with certain reservations). Consequently, the S-structure correlates of controlled complements with [+V] heads are embedded S (=V^n) constituents. The controlled complement in (3.75) is S_2.

The basic F-structure of OMOTTE is shown in (3.76):

(3.76)   OMOTTE 1-NP[α] [(NP*[+GR])S]

For the controlled complement in this structure, XP = S. The derived F-structure of example (3.74a) is produced from the PRED/ARG structure in (3.77), which is formed in the normal way:

(3.77)   OMOTTE 1-NP [(NP*[+GR])[[DA [BAKA]] 1-NP]

Following the general pattern for Japanese, the S-structure correlate of the 1-NP argument of OMOTTE is the NP[i] constituent in (3.75). The S-structure correlate of the NP*[+GR] argument is the NP[j] constituent. The 1-NP argument of DA BAKA has no S-structure correlate. The Index Insertion rule, the SRA rule, and the Raqui rule apply to (3.77) to produce the F-structure of the example, which is shown below:

(3.78)   OMOTTE NP[i] [[DA [BAKA]] NP[j]]
$\quad\quad\quad\quad\quad\quad\;$ α $\quad\quad\quad\quad\quad\quad\quad\;$ α

The S-structure of example (3.74b) is the following:

(3.79)

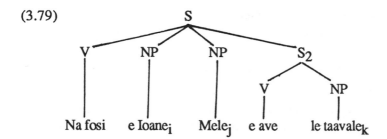

The verb *fosi* in this example is the same type of predicate as the English verb *force*. Its basic F-structure is shown in (3.80):

(3.80)   FOSI   1-NP[α]   2-NP[β]   [(NP*)S]

Again, in the controlled complement argument, XP=S. The derived F-structure of (3.74b) is produced from the PRED/ARG structure in (3.81):

(3.81)   FOSI 1-NP 2-NP [(NP*)[AVE 1-NP 2-NP]]

Following the general pattern for Samoan, the S-structure correlates of the 1-NP and 2-NP arguments of FOSI are the $_{NP}[i]$ and $_{NP}[j]$ constituents, respectively, and the S-structure correlate of the 2-NP argument of AVE is the $_{NP}[k]$ constituent. The NP* argument and the 1-NP argument of AVE have no S-structure correlates. The Index Insertion rule, the SRA rule, the Co-indexing rule, and the Raqui rule apply to produce the derived F-structure of the example, which is shown in (3.82):

(3.82)   FOSI $_{NP}[i]$ $_{NP}[j]$ [AVE $_{NP}[j]$ $_{NP}[k]$]
         $\quad\quad\quad$ α $\quad$ β $\quad\quad\quad\quad$ α $\quad$ β

Samoan and Japanese sentences like the following, whose embedded S complements contain an overt subject, are ungrammatical:

(3.83) a. *Taroo wa$_i$ Hanako o$_j$ Kioji ga$_k$ baka da (to) omotte-ita
         Taro (NOM) Hanako (ACC) Kioji (NOM) fool was thinking
         was
         Taro thought Hanako Kioji to be a fool

b. *Na fosi e Ioane$_i$ Mele$_j$ e ave e Pili$_k$ le taavale$_m$
TENSE force (SUBJ) Ioane Mele TENSE drive (SUBJ) Pili
the car
Ioane forced Mele Pili to drive the car

The derived F-structures of these examples must be produced from the PRED/ARG structures in (3.77) and (3.81), respectively. However, in these cases, the 1-NP arguments of the embedded predicates DA BAKA and AVE have S-structure correlates: the $_{NP}$[k] constituents. Consequently, the application of the Index Insertion rule and the SRA rule to the appropriate PRED/ARG structures produces the following:

(3.84) a.   OMOTTE $_{NP}$[i]   [($_{NP*}$[j])[DA BAKA] $_{NP}$[k]]]
                         α   α

b.   FOSI $_{NP}$[i] $_{NP}$[j]   [($_{NP*}$)[AVE $_{NP}$[k] $_{NP}$[m]]]
                    α   β   α   β

The Co-indexing rule can apply to (3.84b) to produce the following:

(3.85)   FOSI $_{NP}$[i] $_{NP}$[j]   [($_{NP*}$[j])[AVE $_{NP}$[k] $_{NP}$[m]]]
                        α   β   α   β

However, the Raqui rule cannot apply to either Structure (3.84a) or (3.85). Both of these structures contain an indexed NP argument, $_{NP*}$[j], which does not bear an SR. Therefore they violate the well-formedness condition in (1.14). This explains the ungrammaticality of the examples in (3.83).

We see, then, that the theory of controlled complementation formulated here applies to all languages which contain the relevant predicate types. Sentences containing controlled complements in the various languages are functionally identical. The same predicate types occur in all of these languages, and the same operations apply to produce the derived F-structures of sentences that contain them.

These sentences, however, conform to the general morphological and syntactic patterns of the particular language, and we can observe variation here which falls into two general types: (a) structural variation and (b) categorial variation. Let us look at these in turn.

Some languages, like English, Dutch, and Polish, have hierarchical sentential S-structures, and others like Japanese and Samoan, have flat sentential S-structures. Moreover, a comparison of Dutch and English, and of Japanese and Samoan, indicates that there is variation within each general structural type. The Phrase Structure rules of a language determine its structural type, and these can vary from language to language (within the constraints imposed by the X-bar theory.) This accounts for structural variation. As a consequence of this structural variation, the correlation patterns of S-structure NP constituents and F-structure NP arguments differ (within limits) from language to language, or perhaps more accurately, from language type to language type. (This is discussed in more detail in Section 5.)

We can also observe variation of the second type. That is, variation in the distribution of the categories of the S-structure correlates of controlled complements. Polish verbs like *zmuszić*, in examples like (3.61a), occur with NP complements (in prepositional phrases), and contrast in this respect with their English counterparts, like *force*, which occur with VP complements. The range of permissible values of the XP parameter for a language in general or (as in this case) for particular verb classes in a language determines this distribution. The range of values of this parameter can vary from language to language. This accounts for the categorial variation observed here.

In the proposed theory, then, we can account for the sort of variation observed here by fixing the values of the XP parameter and the parameters involved in the definition of specific PS grammars; and at the same time, we can explain why essentially the same patterns of controlled complementation seem to occur in all languages. (I look at these patterns in more detail in Chapter III.) Moreover, the proposed theory applies equally to configurational and non-configurational languages, and does not require the assumption that hierarchical structure is universal at some level. So the theory does not require either α/β structure pairs or a mechanism for converting hierarchical structure to flat structure.

4. Building Complex F-structures

The various types of arguments that were discussed in Section 3 were ones that can occur in basic F-structures. These included uncontrolled complements, S and PP, and controlled complements, [(NP*)XP], both of which can occupy the rightmost argument position in basic F-structures which contain one or two NP[θ] arguments. In this section, I will look at sentences that contain elements whose F-structure correlates do not appear in the basic F-structures of the relevant predicates. The derived F-structures of such sentences are composed of the basic F-structures of their predicates and the F-structure representations of these additional elements, which are either embedded in NP[θ] argument positions or other positions in the basic F-structure, or adjoined to the basic F-structure.

Consider the following examples of the first case:

(4.1) a.   Shaving$_j$ was hard for Horace$_i$

b.   Horace$_i$ thought that shaving$_k$ would disturb Melissa$_j$

c.   Penelope$_i$ realized that to shave$_j$ was necessary

The S-structures of these examples are shown below:

(4.2) a.

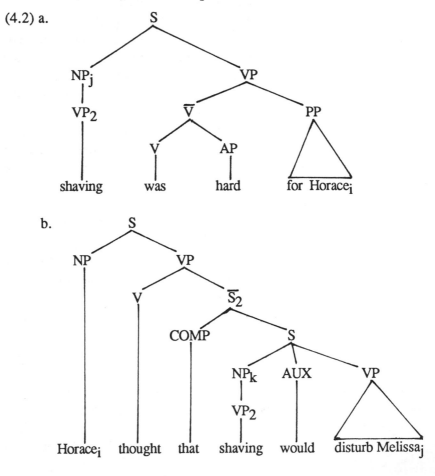

c.

(Details of these structures not relevant to the present discussion have been omitted.)

In each of these structures, a VP (VP$_2$) is embedded in the subject NP position of some predicate: *be hard* in (4.2a), *disturb* in (4.2b), and *be necessary* in (4.2c). The constructions in (4.2a and b) are probably the VP elements of POSS-ING constructions. These are discussed in Horn (1975). The embedded verbal constructions in such examples are not obligatorily controlled. That is, each sentence has two interpretations, one in which the understood subject of the verbal construction is the referent of the NP[i] constituent (or the NP[j] constituent in (4.2b), and one in which the subject of the verbal construction is understood as having indefinite reference. The F-structure correlates of these constructions are therefore not obligatorily controlled complements of the type discussed in the last section.

The basic F-structures of the matrix predicates in these examples, *be hard, think, disturb, realize,* and *be necessary,* are shown below:

(4.3) a. [BE [HARD]]   1-NP[α]
   b. THINK   1-NP[α]   S
   c. DISTURB   1-NP[α]   2-NP[β]
   d. REALIZE   1-NP[α]   S
   e. [BE [NECESSARY]]   1-NP[α]

The predicates in (4.3a and e) are complex predicates and are formed as discussed in Section 2. Strictly speaking, these are not basic F-structures, but this does not affect the present discussion.

The basic F-structure of the verb *shave*, which appears in each of the embedded VPs is shown in (4.4a), and that of the preposition *for*, which appears in example (4.1a), is shown in (4.4b):

(4.4) a.   SHAVE   1-NP[α]
      b.   FOR   1-NP[α]

The derived F-structure of example (4.1a) is produced from the following bare PRED/ARG structure:

(4.5)   [BE [HARD]] $_{NP}$[VP] [FOR 1-NP]

In this structure, the F-level representation of the embedded VP, VP$_2$, in Structure (4.2a) has been inserted into the 1-NP argument position of the predicate [BE HARD], and the PRED/ARG structure of FOR has been embedded in that of [BE HARD]. The PRED/ARG structure of SHAVING (which is identical to that of SHAVE in (4.4a) is embedded in the 1-NP argument position of the complex predicate [BE HARD]. This produces (4.6), below:

(4.6)   [BE [HARD]] $_{NP}$[SHAVING 1-NP] [FOR 1-NP]

The Index Insertion rule and the SRA rule apply to (4.6) to produce the following:

(4.7)   [BE [HARD]] $_{NP}$[SHAVING NP]$_j$ [FOR $_{NP}$[i]]
                        α α α

The 1-NP argument of SHAVING has no S-structure correlate. A general co-indexing operation, which is discussed in the next chapter, applies to co-index the NP argument of SHAVING and the $_{NP}$[i] argument. This produces a derived F-structure for (4.1a). This structure is shown in (4.8):[18]

(4.8)   [BE [HARD]] $_{NP}$[SHAVING $_{NP}$[i]]$_j$ [FOR $_{NP}$[i]]
                        α α α

The derived F-structures of examples (4.1b and c) are produced from the PRED/ARG structures in (4.9a and b), respectively:

(4.9) a. THINK 1-NP [DISTURB $_{NP}$[SHAVING 1-NP] 2-NP]

b. REALIZE 1-NP [[BE [NECESSARY]] $_{NP}$[SHAVE 1-NP]]

In (4.9a), the PRED/ARG structure of SHAVING has been embedded in the 1-NP argument position of DISTURB, and in (4.9b), the PRED/ARG structure of SHAVE has been embedded in the 1-NP argument position of [BE NECESSARY]. The Index Insertion rule, the SRA rule, and the co-indexing process introduced above apply to produce the derived F-structures shown in (4.10):

(4.10) a. THINK $_{NP}$[i] [DISTURB $_{NP}$[SHAVING $_{NP}$[i]]$_k$ $_{NP}$[j]]
$\quad\quad\quad\quad\alpha\quad\quad\quad\quad\quad\alpha\quad\quad\quad\quad\alpha\quad\quad\quad\beta$

b. REALIZE $_{NP}$[i] [[BE [NECESSARY]] $_{NP}$[SHAVE $_{NP}$[i]]$_j$]
$\quad\quad\quad\quad\alpha\quad\quad\quad\quad\quad\quad\quad\quad\quad\alpha\quad\quad\quad\alpha$

The embedding procedure that applies in these derivations is essentially the same as that which applies to sentences containing uncontrolled and controlled complements like those discussed in Section 3. In all cases, the basic PRED/ARG structure of an embedded predicate in an S-structure VP (or S or PP) is inserted into an F-structure VP (or S or PP) argument position. In the former cases, the basic F-structures of the higher predicates contain S, PP, or VP arguments (in [(NP*)VP] controlled complement arguments), while in these cases, the VP arguments are embedded in NP[θ] argument positions of the higher predicates. After this has been accomplished, the same operations apply to produce the derived F-structures of the examples.

Now consider the following examples:

(4.11) a. Jesse$_i$ gave Zelma$_j$ the letter$_k$ unopened

b. Matilda$_i$ served the meat$_j$ raw

c. Smyth$_i$ carried Zelma$_j$ naked (through the town)

d. Matthew$_i$ entered a boy and left a man

These examples contain the S-structure correlates of controlled complements. In (4.11a, b, and c), these are the adjectives *unopened*, *raw*, and *naked*, and in (4.11d) the NPs *a boy* and *a man* have this function. These complements are not obligatory arguments of the matrix predicates, whose basic F-structures are shown in (4.12):

(4.12) a.   GIVE   1-NP[α]   2-NP[β]   3-NP[γ]
      b.   SERVE   1-NP[α]   2-NP[β]
      c.   CARRY   1-NP[α]   2-NP[β]
      d.   ENTER   1-NP[α]
      e.   LEAVE   1-NP[α]

The S-structures of examples (4.11a and b) are shown below:

(4.13) a.

b.

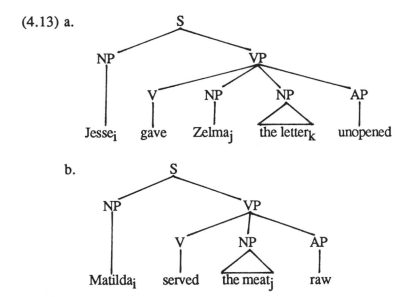

These S-structures are similar to those of sentences containing control verbs like *consider* and *elect*. In both cases, the S-structure correlates of controlled XP complements appear in the VP of the matrix verb, and in neither case do the complements occupy positions that are correlates of NP[θ] argument positions of the matrix verbs.

The derived F-structures of these examples are produced from the PRED/ARG structures shown in (4.14):

(4.14) a.   GIVE   1-NP   2-NP   3-NP   [(NP*)AP]
      b.   SERVE   1-NP   2-NP   [(NP*)AP]

These structures are formed by embedding the F-structure representation of the controlled complement in each case in the basic F-structure of the relevant predicate. Now, the basic F-structures of the predicates *unopened* and *raw* are inserted into the AP position in each controlled complement to produce the following:

(4.15) a.   GIVE 1-NP 2-NP 3-NP [(NP*)[UNOPENED 1-NP]]
       b.   SERVE 1-NP 2-NP [(NP*)[RAW 1-NP]]

The relevant operations apply to these structures in the normal way. The Index Insertion rule and the SRA rule apply to produce the structures shown in (4.16):

(4.16) a.   GIVE $\text{NP}^{[i]}_{\alpha}$ $\text{NP}^{[j]}_{\beta}$ $\text{NP}^{[k]}_{\gamma}$ [(NP*)[UNOPENED $\text{NP}^{]}_{\alpha}$]]
       b.   SERVE $\text{NP}^{[i]}_{\alpha}$ $\text{NP}^{[j]}_{\beta}$ [(NP*)[RAW $\text{NP}^{]}_{\alpha}$]]

The NP* arguments and the NP arguments of UNOPENED and RAW have no S-structure correlates. In this regard, these complements are the same type as the complements of control verbs like *force* and *elect*. The Co-indexing rule and the Raqui rule apply to these structures to produce the derived F-structures, which appear below:

(4.17) a.   GIVE $\text{NP}^{[i]}_{\alpha}$ $\text{NP}^{[j]}_{\beta}$ $\text{NP}^{[k]}_{\gamma}$ [UNOPENED $\text{NP}^{[k]}_{\alpha}$]]
       b.   SERVE $\text{NP}^{[i]}_{\alpha}$ $\text{NP}^{[j]}_{\beta}$ [RAW $\text{NP}^{[j]}_{\alpha}$]]

The derived F-structures of the remaining examples in (4.11) are produced in the same way. These are shown in (4.18), below:

(4.18) a.   CARRY $\text{NP}^{[i]}_{\alpha}$ $\text{NP}^{[j]}_{\beta}$ [NAKED $\text{NP}^{[j]}_{\alpha}$]]
       b.   [ENTER $\text{NP}^{[i]}_{\alpha}$ [[A BOY] $\text{NP}^{[i]}_{\alpha}$]]] & [LEAVE $\text{NP}^{[i]}_{\alpha}$
            [[A MAN] $\text{NP}^{[i]}_{\alpha}$]]]

The following examples also contain S-structure correlates of controlled XP complements of various categories:

(4.19) a.   Heathcliffe$_i$ served the meat$_j$ naked
      b.   Horace$_i$ did everything$_j$ to sit on the throne$_k$
      c.   Efraim$_i$ spotted Senta$_j$, walking down the corridor$_k$

As above, the matrix verbs in these sentences have basic F-structures that do not contain controlled complement arguments. The structure of *serve* appears in (4.12b), and the structures of *do* and *spot* are shown below:

(4.20) a.   DO   1-NP[α]   2-NP[β]
      b.   SPOT   1-NP[α]   2-NP[β]

The S-structures of the examples in (4.19) are shown in (4.21):

(4.21) a.

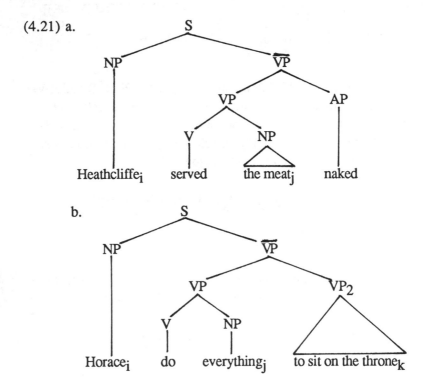

c.

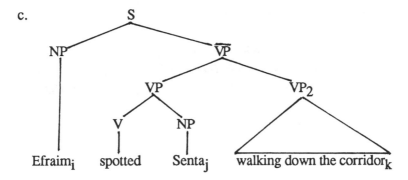

These structures contrast with the ones in (4.13a). Here, the S-structure correlates of the controlled complements, AP in (4.21a) and VP$_2$ in (4.21b and c), are sisters of VP in a higher constituent that I have labelled $\overline{\text{VP}}$. (Whether these are analyzed as daughters of $\overline{\text{VP}}$ or of S is of no importance here.)[19] Evidence of this sort of structural difference between examples like (4.19) and ones like (4.11) is the contrast between the sentences in (4.22) and (4.23), below:

(4.22) a.   Naked, Heathcliffe$_i$ served the meat$_j$
     b.   To sit on the throne$_k$, Horace$_i$ did everything$_j$
     c.   Walking down the corridor$_k$, Efraim$_i$ spotted Senta$_j$

(4.23) a.   *Unopened, Jesse$_i$ gave Zelma$_j$ the letter$_k$
     b. ?*Raw, Matilda$_i$ served the meat$_j$
     c. ?*A boy, Matthew$_i$ entered ...

The derived F-structures of the examples in (4.19) are produced from the following PRED/ARG structures:

(4.24) a.   [SERVE 1-NP 2-NP][(NP*)AP]
     b.   [DO 1-NP 2-NP][(NP*)VP]
     c.   [SPOT 1-NP 2-NP][(NP*)VP]

These structures are formed by adjoining the F-structure representation of the controlled complement to the basic PRED/ARG structure of the matrix predicate in each case. As before, the basic F-structures of the predicates *naked*, *sit*, and *walking*, and those of *on* and *down*, are inserted into the appropriate AP or VP position in (4.24) in the normal way to produce the following:

(4.25) a. [SERVE 1-NP 2-NP][(NP*)[NAKED 1-NP]]
    b. [DO 1-NP 2-NP][(NP*)[SIT 1-NP [ON 1-NP]]]
    c. [SPOT 1-NP 2-NP][(NP*)[WALKING 1-NP [DOWN1-NP]]]

The Index Insertion rule and the SRA rule apply to produce the structures in (4.26):

(4.26) a. [SERVE $\underset{\alpha}{NP[i]}$ $\underset{\beta}{NP[j]}$][(NP*)[NAKED $\underset{\alpha}{NP}$]]
    b. [DO $\underset{\alpha}{NP[i]}$ $\underset{\beta}{NP[j]}$][(NP*)[SIT $\underset{\alpha}{NP}$ [ON $\underset{\alpha}{NP[k]}$]]]
    c. [SPOT $\underset{\alpha}{NP[i]}$ $\underset{\beta}{NP[j]}$][(NP*)[WALKING $\underset{\alpha}{NP}$ [DOWN $\underset{\alpha}{NP[k]}$]]]

A subcase of the Co-indexing rule, which is discussed in Chapter III, and the Raqui rule apply to produce the derived F-structures shown in (4.27):

(4.27) a. [SERVE $\underset{\alpha}{NP[i]}$ $\underset{\beta}{NP[j]}$][NAKED $\underset{\alpha}{NP[i]}$]]
    b. [DO $\underset{\alpha}{NP[i]}$ $\underset{\beta}{NP[j]}$][SIT $\underset{\alpha}{NP[i]}$ [ON $\underset{\alpha}{NP[k]}$]]
    c. [SPOT $\underset{\alpha}{NP[i]}$ $\underset{\beta}{NP[j]}$][WALKING $\underset{\alpha}{NP[i]}$ [DOWN $\underset{\alpha}{NP[k]}$]]

Examples like (4.11c), repeated below, and the following are ambiguous:

(4.11) b. Smyth$_i$ carried Zelma$_j$ naked (through the town$_k$)

(4.28)   Frome$_i$ marched his concubines$_j$ through the streets$_k$ naked

These examples have two interpretations: one in which the object NP, NP[j], is the controller of the complement, and one in which the subject NP, NP[i], is the controller of the complement. We can account for this quite easily by assigning these sentences either S-structures like (4.13)

or ones like (4.21). As a result, two derived F-structures can be produced for them, one like the structures in (4.17) and (4.18), and one like the structures in (4.27). The first is associated with the first interpretation above, and the second is associated with the second interpretation. This is discussed at more length in Chapter III.

Controlled complements like these occur in other languages. The following Polish sentences illustrate this:

(4.29)a.　Bolesław$_i$ podał kapustę$_j$ na surowo
　　　　　Boleslaw (NOM) served cabbage (ACC) on raw
　　　　　Boleslaw served the cabbage raw

　　　b.　Jadwiga$_i$ podała obiad$_j$ nago
　　　　　Jadwiga (NOM) served dinner (ACC) naked
　　　　　Jadwiga served dinner naked

These examples have S-structures like the following:

(4.30) a.

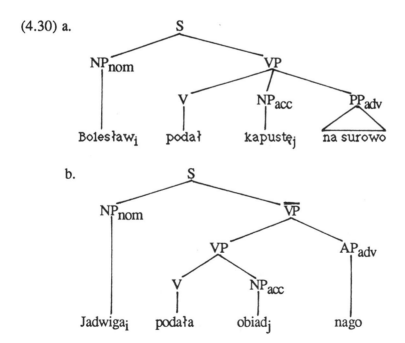

b.

The S-structure correlate of the controlled complement in (4.30a) is a PP consisting of the preposition *na* and an invariant form of the adjective *surowo* (raw). The one in (4.30b) is an AP which contains the same type of invariant form of the adjective *nago*. Such invariant forms of adjectives function as adverbials in Polish, and I have labelled the PP constituent in (4.30a) and the AP constituent in (4.30b) accordingly for clarity (adv = adverbial.) These labels have no theoretical significance.

The derived F-structures of (4.29) are produced from the following PRED/ARG structures:

(4.31) a. PODAĆ 1-NP 2-NP [(NP*)AP]
       b. [PODAĆ 1-NP 2-NP] [(NP*)AP]

In these structures, the F-structure representations of the controlled complements are combined with the basic F-structure of the verb *podać*, as previously discussed. The basic F-structures of *surowo* and *nago* are inserted into the appropriate AP positions in (4.31) to produce (4.32):

(4.32) a. PODAĆ 1-NP 2-NP [(NP*)[SUROWO 1-NP]]
       b. [PODAĆ 1-NP 2-NP][(NP*)[NAGO 1-NP]]

The Index Insertion rule, the SRA rule, the Co-indexing rule, and the Raqui rule apply to these structures in the normal way to produce the derived F-structures shown in (4.33):[20]

(4.33) a. PODAĆ NP[i] NP[j] [SUROWO NP[j]]
                    α β α
       b. [PODAĆ NP[i] NP[j]][NAGO NP[i]]
                     α β α

The derivation of the F-structures of sentences which contain complements embedded in S-structure NP positions and of sentences which contain complements embedded in other positions with non-control verbs involves only the two combinatory procedures discussed here: embedding in NP[θ] or non-NP positions in basic F-structures, and adjunction to basic F-structures. The various operations on F-structures apply as they do in all derivations.[21]

The English sentences that contain constructions like these, such as (4.11) and (4.19), and their Polish counterparts in (4.29), are functionally identical. The differences between them are basically differences of the same sort that was observed in the discussion of complements with control verbs in Section 3. Polish and English are quite similar structurally (both are hierarchical languages with SVO word order). Consequently, the differences observed here are primarily due to the fact that controlled complements have different S-structure correlates in each language (as we have seen above). These include constructions of the form [na XP] and lone adverbial forms like *nago* for Polish, and lone adjective and noun constituents, as well as bare VP constructions, in English. These are additional examples of cross-language variation in the values of the XP parameter and the patterns of correlation between S-structure constituents and F-structure arguments that we would expect to occur.

5. The S-structure/F-structure Interface

Here, I examine the principles and conditions of the S-structure/F-structure Interface (SFI) System which govern the application of the Index Insertion rule. This rule functions as the link between the S-structure level and the F-structure level in derivations, as we have seen. It applies to insert the indices of S-structure NP constituents into the proper F-structure NP argument positions, which I have represented as 1-NP, 2-NP, and 3-NP in the argument structures of predicates. NP constituents in S-structures are identified and distinguished from one another by the grammatical relations (GR) that they bear, or more accurately, by what we may call the GR indicators (GRI) that are associated with them. GRIs are morpho-syntactic features of S-structure NP constituents such as the structural configurations that they occur in, their position in ordered sequences of elements, affixes (of certain types) that are attached to their head nouns and/or other constituents, or independent elements that occur in them. Affixes and independent elements associated with other S-structure constituents can also function as GRIs. GRIs of the first and second types are inherent features of NPs as members of more complex constructs (PS Markers), and are not assigned to them by any rule. Affixes and independent elements that function as GRIs are freely introduced by the appropriate WFRs or categorial rules and lexical insertion rules.

F-structure NP arguments which have the feature [+GR] are associated with S-structure NP constituents by statements which identify the S-structure correlate of each NP argument by its GRI. These correlation statements vary from language to language, or from language type to language type, depending on how GRIs are instantiated in the particular language. I will first look at structural, or configurational, GRIs and then at morphological and lexical GRIs of various sorts and at serial, or ordinal, GRIs insofar as these types of GRIs must be determined independently of structural configurations.

Consider the following English sentences:

(5.1) a.   Froom$_i$ disliked Smyth$_j$
      b.   Phylicia$_i$ gave Alicia$_j$ the buttonhook$_k$

The verbs in these sentences have the basic F-structures shown below:

(5.2) a.   DISLIKE   1-NP[α]   2-NP[β]
      b.   GIVE   1-NP[α]   2-NP[β]   3-NP[γ]

The S-structures of (5.1a and b) are shown in (5.3a and b), respectively:

(5.3) a.

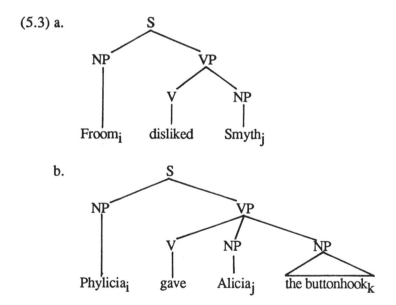

    b.

These structures are typical English sentential structures. The NPs that are traditionally designated as their subjects and those that are traditionally designated as their objects are identified and distinguished from each other by their positions in phrase structures like these.   GRIs

in English are structural configurations, and we may think of the traditional grammatical functions, subject and object, as names of the relevant
configurations. The subject NP, $_{NP}[i]$ in each case, is the sister of VP
and the daughter of S. The object NP in Structure (a), $_{NP}[j]$, is the sister
of V and the daughter of VP. In Structure (b), there are two object NPs,
$_{NP}[j]$ and $_{NP}[k]$, both of which are sisters of V and daughters of VP.

To derive the F-structures of the examples in (5.1), the $_{NP}[i]$ constituent in each S-structure must be associated with the 1-NP argument
in the relevant F-structure in (5.2), the $_{NP}[j]$ constituent in each S-
structure must be associated with the 2-NP argument of the relevant
F-structure, and the $_{NP}[k]$ constituent in (5.3b) must be associated with
the 3-NP argument in (5.2b). This information is contained in correlation statements like the following:

(5.4) a.   The S-structure correlate of the 1-NP argument is the NP in
           the configuration: $_S$[NP VP].

      b.   The S-structure correlate of the 2-NP argument is the NP in
           the configuration: $_{VP}$[V NP X].

      c.   The S-structure correlate of the 3-NP argument is the
           rightmost NP in the configuration: $_{VP}$[V NP NP].

In accordance with these correlation statements, the Index Insertion
rule, along with the SRA rule, applies to the PRED/ARG structures in
(5.5) to produce the structures in (5.6):

(5.5) a.   DISLIKE 1-NP 2-NP
      b.   GIVE 1-NP 2-NP 3-NP

(5.6) a.   DISLIKE $_{NP}[i]$ $_{NP}[j]$
                      α β
      b.   GIVE $_{NP}[i]$ $_{NP}[j]$ $_{NP}[k]$
                   α β γ

The correlation statements in (5.4) must be modified slightly to
accommodate the full range of relevant English data. Consider the following sentences:

(5.7) a. Wulf$_i$ depended on Rolf$_j$
    b. Ran$_i$ took advantage$_j$ of Retief$_k$
    c. Beelzebub$_i$ believed Balthazar$_j$ to have sinned
    d. Balthazar$_i$ seemed to sin

The S-structure of (5.7a) is shown in (5.8):

(5.8)

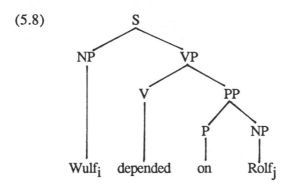

Here, the verb *depend* occurs with a prepositional phrase, *on Rolf$_i$*.
However, at the F-structure level, this verb has two NP[θ] arguments.
Its basic F-structure is shown below:

(5.9)   [DEPEND ON] 1-NP[α] 2-NP[β]

The derived F-structure of example (5.7a) is produced from the
PRED/ARG structure in (5.10):

(5.10)   [DEPEND ON] 1-NP 2-NP

The $_{NP}$[i] constituent in (5.8) must be associated with the 1-NP argument in (5.10) and the $_{NP}$[j] constituent, which is the object of the
preposition *on*, must be associated with the 2-NP argument. The correlation statement in (5.4a) applies to the $_{NP}$[i] constituent and the 1-NP
argument, as in the previous examples. However, the correlation statement in (5.4b) does not apply to the NP object of *on*. A subcase of
(5.4b) is required for certain verbs, such as *depend*. This is formulated
in (5.11):

(5.11)   The S-structure correlate of the 2-NP argument for verbs of
Class X is the NP in the configuration: $_{VP}[V _{PP}[P \ NP]]$.

The Class X in this statement must be specified. Verbs in this class are
atypical, but by no means unusual. Additional examples are verbs like
speak (about), *look (at)*, and so forth, as well as complex predicates like
take advantage, as we saw in Section 3.

   The Index Insertion rule, in accordance with (5.11), applies, along
with the SRA rule, to (5.10) to produce the derived F-structure in
(5.12):

(5.12)   [DEPEND ON] $_{NP}[i] \ _{NP}[j]$
                          α β

   The S-structure of example (5.7b) is shown in (5.13), below:

(5.13)

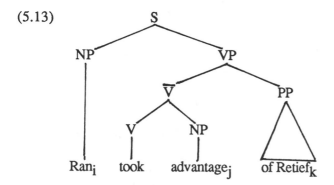

The derived F-structure of this example is produced from the following
PRED/ARG structure:

(5.14)   [TAKE NP^C] 1-NP 2-NP

Here, the $_{NP}[i]$ constituent in (5.13) must be associated with the 1-NP
argument in (5.14), the $_{NP}[j]$ constituent must be associated with the
NP^C argument, and the $_{NP}[k]$ constituent must be associated with the
2-NP argument. The correlation statement in (5.4a) properly associates
the $_{NP}[i]$ constituent and the 1-NP argument. However, in (5.13), the
$_{NP}[j]$ constituent is the sister of V in $\bar{V}$, and the $_{NP}[k]$ constituent
is contained in a PP that is the sister of $\bar{V}$ in VP. Therefore, neither the

correlation statement in (5.4b) nor that in (5.11) applies. To associate the $_{NP[j]}$ constituent and the NP^c constituent, the following correlation statement is required:

(5.15)   The S-structure correlate of the NP^c argument is the NP in the configuration: $_\nabla[V\ NP]$.

Now, to accommodate both VP structures that contain non-complex predicates, V, in examples like (5.1) and (5.7a, c, and d), and VP structures that contain complex predicates, $\bar{V}$, in examples like (5.7b), the correlation statements in (5.4b and c). and (5.11) must be modified as shown below:

(5.16) a.   The S-structure correlate of the 2-NP argument is the NP in the configuration:

$$_{VP}[V^{(1)}\ NP\ X]$$

   b.   The S-structure correlate of the 3-NP argument is the right-most NP in the configuration:

$$_{VP}[V^{(1)}\ NP\ NP]$$

   c.   The S-structure correlate of the 2-NP argument for verbs of Class X is the NP in the configuration:

$$_{VP}[V^{(1)}\ _{PP}[P\ NP]]$$

This relatively minor modification consists of accommodating the possibility of an optional extra level of structure of the X-bar category, V^n. Here, $V^{(1)}$ represents either V^0 (that is, V) or V^1 (that is, $\bar{V}$).

   Now, the Index Insertion rule can apply to the PRED/ARG structure in (5.14), along with the SRA rule, to produce the derived F-structure of example (5.7b). This structure is shown in (5.17):

(5.17) $[TAKE\ _{NP^c[j]}]\ _{NP[i]}\ _{NP[k]}$
          $\quad\quad\quad\quad\quad\zeta\quad\quad\alpha\quad\beta$

Finally, consider examples (5.7c and d), whose S-structures appear in (5.18a and b), respectively:

(5.18) a.

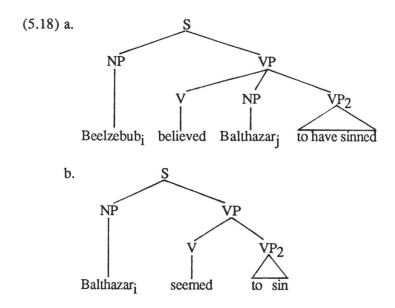

b.

The derived F-structures of these examples are produced from the following PRED/ARG structures:

(5.19) a. BELIEVE 1-NP [(NP*[+GR])[SIN 1-NP]]
      b. SEEM [(NP*[+GR])[SIN 1-NP]]

The $_{NP}[i]$ constituent in (5.18a) must be associated with the 1-NP argument in (5.19a), and the $_{NP}[j]$ constituent in (5.18a) must be associated with the NP*[+GR] argument in (5.19a). Similarly, the $_{NP}[i]$ constituent in (5.18b) must be associated with the NP*[+GR] argument in (5.19b). The correlation statements as formulated above apply correctly to these structures. In the F-structure of BELIEVE, the NP*[+GR] argument is the second NP argument in the predicate structure, and in the F-structure of SEEM, the NP*[+GR] argument is the first NP argument in the predicate structure. By definition, then, these are, in effect, the 2-NP argument of (5.19a) and the 1-NP argument of (5.19b). (Remember that the labels 1-NP, 2-NP, and 3-NP are only labels of convenience, and have no theoretical significance.) Consequently, the Index Insertion rule, the SRA rule, and the Raqui rule apply in the normal way to the structures in (5.19) to produce the derived F-structures shown below:

(5.20) a. BELIEVE $\underset{\alpha}{\text{NP}[i]}$ [SIN $\underset{\alpha}{\text{NP}[j]}$]

     b. SEEM [SIN $\underset{\alpha}{\text{NP}[i]}$]

For the sake of clarity, I repeat the final formulations of the struct-ure-based correlation statements for English:

(5.21) a. The S-structure correlate of the 1-NP argument is the NP in the configuration: $_S$[NP VP]

     b. (1) The S-structure correlate of the 2-NP argument is the NP in the configuration:

$$_{VP}[V^{(1)} NP X]$$

        (2) The S-structure correlate of the 2-NP argument for verbs of Class X is the NP in the configuration:

$$_{VP}[V^{(1)} _{PP}[P NP]]$$

     c. The S-structure correlate of the 3-NP argument is the right-most NP in the configuration:

$$_{VP}[V^{(1)} NP NP]$$

     d. The S-structure correlate of the NP^C argument is the NP in the configuration:

$$\overline{V}[V NP]$$

The precise formulation of these statements depends on the version of X-bar theory adopted and on the PS grammar determined by that theory as it applies to the particular language, in this case, English.

A final correlation statement is required to associate S-structure NP constituents that are the objects of prepositions with the NP[θ] arguments in the basic F-structures of the prepositions. This statement is formulated in (5.22):

(5.22)   The S-structure correlate of the NP[θ] argument of a prepo-
         sition (when the preposition functions as a predicate) is
         the NP in the configuration:

$$_{PP}[P \quad NP]$$

The other configurational languages are similar to English (except
for details which need not concern us here.) Consider the following
Polish sentences:

(5.23) a.   Stanisław$_i$ widział Basię$_j$
            Stanislaw (NOM) saw Basia (ACC)
            Stanislaw saw Basia

      b.   Jacek$_i$ dał książkę$_j$ Adamowi$_k$
           Jacek (NOM) gave book (ACC) Adam (DAT)
           Jacek gave Adam a book

The S-structures of these examples are the following:

(5.24) a.

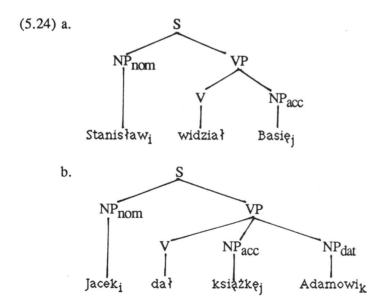

b.

The basic F-structures of the verbs *widzieć* and *dać* are shown in
(5.25):

(5.25) a. WIDZIEĆ 1-NP[α] 2-NP[β]
     b. DAĆ 1-NP[α] 2-NP[β] 3-NP[ɣ]

The derived F-structures of these examples are produced from the following PRED/ARG structures:

(5.26) a. WIDZIEĆ 1-NP 2-NP
     b. DAĆ 1-NP 2-NP 3-NP

The $_{NP}$[i] constituents in Structures (5.24a and b). must be associated with the 1-NP arguments of each predicate; the $_{NP}$[j] constituent in each S-structure must be associated with the 2-NP argument of each predicate; and the $_{NP}$[k] constituent in (5.24b) must be associated with the 3-NP argument of DAĆ in (5.26b). The 1-NP correlation statement for Polish is virtually identical to that for English. This statement is formulated in (5.27):

(5.27)   The S-structure correlate of the 1-NP argument is the NP in the configuration: $_S$[NP   VP].

Alternatively, the S-structure correlate of the 1-NP argument is the NP marked for nominative case in this configuration. I return to this point below. The 2-NP and 3-NP correlation statements for Polish differ in detail from their counterparts for English. In Polish sentences like (5.23b), word order is relatively free, and the following variant also occurs:

(5.28)   Jacek$_i$ dał Adamowi$_k$ książkę$_j$
     Jacek (NOM) gave Adam (DAT) book (ACC)
     Jacek gave Adam a book

To allow for such variants, the relevant correlation statements must be formulated as shown in (5.29):

(5.29) a. The S-structure correlate of the 2-NP argument is the NP$_{acc}$ in the configuration:
        $_{VP}$[X, V, Y, NP$_{acc}$, Z]

b. The S-structure correlate of the 3-NP argument is the NP_{dat} in the configuration:

$$_{VP}[\ X, \ V, \ Y, \ NP_{dat}, \ Z \ ]$$

The Index Insertion rule applies to the structures in (5.26), in accordance with these correlation statements, along with the SRA rule, to produce the derived F-structures of examples (5.23). These are shown below:

(5.30) a. WIDZIEĆ $NP[i] \ NP[j]$
$\alpha \qquad \beta$

b. DAĆ $NP[i] \ NP[j] \ NP[k]$
$\qquad \alpha \qquad \beta \qquad \gamma$

The correlation statements in (5.29) apply regardless of the order of the NP_{acc} and NP_{dat} constituents in the S-structure. Therefore, a derived F-structure, for example (5.28), which is identical to that of example (5.23b), can be produced.[22]

Let us turn now to Japanese and Samoan sentences like those in (5.31) and (5.32), respectively:

(5.31) a. Taroo ga$_i$ piano o$_j$ hii-ta
Taro (NOM) piano (ACC) play-PAST
Taro played the piano

b. Hanako ga$_i$ Taroo o$_j$ nagutte-iru
Hanako (NOM) Taro (ACC) hitting-is
Hanako is hitting Taro

(5.32) a. Na fofoe e Ioane$_i$ le fai$_j$
TENSE peel (SUBJ) Ioane the banana
Ioane peeled the banana

b. Na faitau e Mele$_i$ le tusi$_j$
TENSE read (SUBJ) Mele the book
Mele read the book

The Japanese examples in (5.31) have the S-structures shown in (5.33):

(5.33) a.

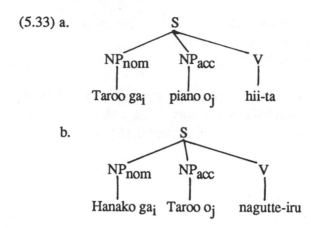

b.

These non-configurational sentential structures contrast with structures like (5.18) and (5.24), above.

The verbs *hii-* and *nagutte-* have the basic F-structures shown in (5.34a and b):

(5.34) a.   HII-   1-NP[α]   2-NP[β]
      b.   NAGUTTE-   1-NP[α]   2-NP[β]

The derived F-structures of the sentences in (5.31) are produced from the following PRED/ARG structures:

(5.35) a.   HII-TA   1-NP   2-NP
      b.   NAGUTTE-IRU   1-NP   2-NP

In both cases, the $_{NP}$[i] constituents in Structures (5.33) must be associated with the 1-NP arguments of the appropriate predicates in (5.35), and the $_{NP}$[j] constituents in (5.33) must be associated with the 2-NP arguments of the appropriate predicates in (5.35). In Structures (5.33), however, both NP constituents are sisters of V. Therefore, they must be distinguished in some other way (either by their linear ordering or by their case markers, *ga* and *o*). The relevant correlation statements for Japanese are formulated as shown in (5.36):

(5.36) a.   The S-structure correlate of the 1-NP argument is the
         NP$_{NOM}$ in the configuration:
            S[NP$_{NOM}$, NP$_X$, Y, V]

b. The S-structure correlate of the 2-NP argument is the NP$_{ACC}$ in the configuration:

$$_S[NP_X , NP_{ACC} , Y , V]$$

(In these statements, Y is a variable, NOM = *ga*, and ACC = *o*.)

The SRA rule and the Index Insertion rule can apply, in accordance with these correlation statements, to the PRED/ARG structures in (5.35) to produce the derived F-structures in (5.37):

(5.37) a. HII-TA NP[i] NP[j]
$\quad\quad\quad\quad\quad\quad\quad\quad \alpha \quad\ \beta$

b. NAGUTTE-IRU NP[i] NP[j]
$\quad\quad\quad\quad\quad\quad\quad\quad\quad\quad \alpha \quad\ \beta$

The Samoan examples in (5.32) have the S-structures shown in (5.38a and b), respectively:

(5.38) a.

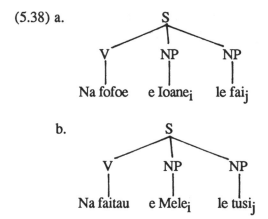

b.

These structures are of the same general type as the Japanese structures in (5.33). The primary difference between them is the order of the constituents.

The basic F-structures of the verbs *fofoe* and *faitau* are shown in (5.39), and the derived F-structures of these sentences are produced from the PRED/ARG structures in (5.40):

(5.39) a. FOFOE   1-NP[α]   2-NP[β]

b. FAITAU   1-NP[α]   2-NP[β]

(5.40) a.   NA FOFOE   1-NP   2-NP
       b.   NA FAITAU   1-NP   2-NP

In each case, the $_{NP}[i]$ constituent in the S-structure in (5.38) must be associated with the 1-NP argument of the relevant predicate and the $_{NP}[j]$ constituent in the S-structure must be associated with the 2-NP argument of the relevant predicate. In these S-structures, as in (5.33), both NP constituents are sisters of V, and must be distinguished in some other way, either by their order in the structure or by their case marking. (The particle *e* marks the subject of a transitive sentence in Samoan.) The following correlation statements apply to Samoan:

(5.41) a.   The S-structure correlate of the 1-NP argument is the leftmost NP (or the NP preceded by the particle *e*) in the configuration: $_S[V$ e NP X].

       b.   The S-structure correlate of the 2-NP argument is the rightmost NP in the configuration: $_S[V$ NP NP].

It is easy to see that the Index Insertion rule can apply correctly to the PRED/ARG structures in (5.40). This rule and the SRA rule produce the following derived F-structures:

(5.42) a.   NA FOFOE $_{NP}[i]$ $_{NP}[j]$
                            α β
       b.   NA FAITAU $_{NP}[i]$ $_{NP}[j]$
                            α β

If we compare configurational languages like English and Polish on the one hand with non-configurational languages like Japanese and Samoan on the other, certain universal structural generalizations can be made about the correlation statements in both language types. Consider the following generalized S-structures:

(5.43) a.

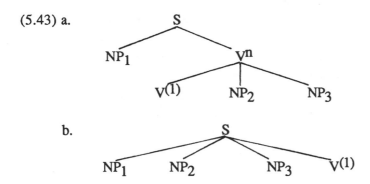

b.

Here, I am only concerned with hierarchical structure, not linear order. In Structure (a), V^n is the maximal projection of V. In both structures, NP_1, NP_2, and NP_3 are the S-structure correlates of 1-NP, 2-NP, and 3-NP arguments, respectively. A comparison of these structures reveals the following patterns:

(5.44) a.   The S-structure correlate of the 1-NP argument is the NP sister of V^n, where V^n is the maximal projection of V (i.e. of V^0) that has NP sisters.

   b.   The S-structure correlates of the 2-NP and 3-NP arguments are NP sisters of $V^{(1)}$.

The difference between configurational and non-configurational languages is that in the former, V^n is not $V^{(1)}$, while in the latter, these are identical.

   However, as we have seen, these structural generalizations are not sufficient to distinguish the S-structure correlates of 2-NP arguments from the S-structure correlates of 3-NP arguments in hierarchical structures like (5.43a), nor are they sufficient to distinguish the S-structure correlates of 1-NP arguments, 2-NP arguments, and 3-NP arguments from one another in non-configurational structures like (5.43b). In addition to structure, the correlation statements for the various languages require case and/or word order. The English 3-NP correlation statement in (5.21c) refers to linear order. The Polish 2-NP and 3-NP correlation statements in (5.29) refer to case-marking, as do the Japanese 1-NP and 2-NP correlation statements in (5.36). The Samoan 1-NP and 2-NP correlation statements, like those in (5.41), may be formulated to refer to either order or case-marking (or both). The best formulation is an empirical issue that I will not discuss here.

We can account for the universal S-structure constituent/F-structure argument correlations by incorporating the correlation statements in (5.44) into UG. The variation among languages of the sort observed here can be attributed to variation in case marking systems and word order conventions, which must be specified for each language in language-particular correlation statements.   These are shown below for English, Polish, Japanese, and Samoan:[23]

(5.45)   *English:* The S-structure correlate of the 3-NP argument is the rightmost NP in the sequence: [...NP...NP...].

(5.46)   *Polish:*
　　(a)   The S-structure correlate of the 1-NP argument is the NP marked for nominative case.
　　(b)   The S-structure correlate of the 2-NP argument is the NP marked for accusative case.
　　(c)   The S-structure correlate of the 3-NP argument is the NP marked for dative case.

(5.47)   *Japanese:*
　　(a)   The S-structure correlate of the 1-NP argument is the NP marked for nominative case.
　　(b)   The S-structure correlate of the 2-NP argument is the NP marked for accusative case.
　　(c)   The S-structure correlate of the 3-NP argument is the NP marked for dative case.

(5.48)   *Samoan:*
　　(a)   The S-structure correlate of the 1-NP argument is the leftmost NP in the sequence: [...NP   NP...].
　　(b)   The S-structure correlate of the 2-NP argument is the rightmost NP in the sequence: [...NP   NP...].

None of these statements refer to structure. The universal correlation statement in (5.44b), along with the appropriate PS grammar for each language, specifies that English and Polish S-structure correlates of 2-NP and 3-NP arguments are located in VP. Consequently, this need not be restated in (5.45) and (5.46).[24] Similarly, both of the universal correlation statements in (5.44), along with the appropriate PS grammars, specify the structural positions of the Japanese and Samoan S-structure correlates of 1-NP, 2-NP, and 3-NP arguments, and these need not be stated in (5.47) or (5.48).

Both the universal structural correlation statements and the language particular case/word order correlation statements must be satisfied in any derivation. However, situations arise when either the universal statements or the language-particular statements are neutralized. In these cases, the remaining statements (of either type) assume the primary role in determining how the Index Insertion rule applies. Let us look at an example of each situation.

The first situation is one in which the universal structural correlation statements are effectively neutralized. This situation can occur in languages which have relatively free word order, which may be viewed as the result of a scrambling process whose formulation need not concern us here. Polish is such a language. The sentences in (5.49), below, are variants, with the same interpretation:

(5.49) a. Wiesław$_i$ czytał ksiązkę$_j$
            Wieslaw (NOM) read book (ACC)
            Wieslaw read the book

   b. Ksiązkę$_j$ Wiesław$_i$ czytał
        book (ACC) Wieslaw (NOM) read
        Wieslaw read the book

   c. Czytał Wiesław$_i$ ksiązkę$_j$
        read Wieslaw (NOM) book (ACC)
        Wieslaw read the book

The verb czytać has the basic F-structure shown in (5.50):

(5.50)   CZYTAĆ 1-NP[α] 2-NP[β]

The derived F-structures of all the examples in (5.49) are produced from the PRED/ARG structure shown in (5.51):

(5.51)   CZYTAĆ 1-NP 2-NP

The S-structure of example (5.49a) is shown below:

(5.52)

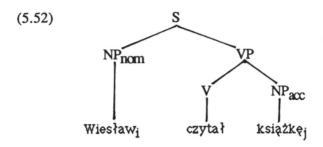

The universal structural correlation statements in (5.44) apply to associate the $_{NP}[i]$ constituent in this structure with the 1-NP argument of CZYTAĆ in (5.51) and the $_{NP}[j]$ constituent in this structure with the 2-NP argument of CZYTAĆ in (5.51). The Index Insertion rule and the SRA rule apply to produce the derived F-structure of (5.49a), which is shown below:

(5.53)   CZYTAĆ $_{NP}[i] \atop \alpha$ $_{NP}[j] \atop \beta$

The S-structures of examples (5.49b and c) are shown in (5.54a and b), respectively:

(5.54) a.

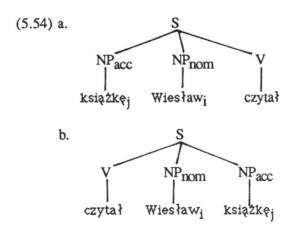

The scrambling process which produces structures like these destroys the hierarchical structure which is characteristic of Polish sentences like (5.49a) above. The correlation statements in (5.44) are neutralized for these structures in the sense that both the 1-NP correlation statement in (5.44a) and the 2-NP correlation statement in (5.44b) apply to each of the NP constituents in Structures (5.54a) and (5.54b) (as is generally the case for flat structures). In this situation, the correlation statements in (5.46a and b), which are based on case marking, apply to associate the NP[i] constituents in Structures (5.54a and b), which are marked for nominative case, with the 1-NP argument of CZYTAĆ in (5.51), and to associate the NP[j] constituents in Structures (5.54a and b), which are marked for accusative case, with the 2-NP argument of CZYTAĆ in (5.51). The Index Insertion rule and the SRA rule apply to produce the F-structure for these examples, which is identical to that of (5.49a). This structure is shown in (5.55):

(5.55)   CZYTAĆ NP[i] NP[j]
                      α β

This accounts for the synonmy of the examples in (5.49).

I turn now to an example of the second situation. It is not uncommon in languages that have case marking systems for sentences to occur in which the case markers, for any of a number of reasons that need not concern us here, either provide no information on S-structure/F-structure correlations of the sort that we are considering here, or conflicting information. These are examples of what we might call case neutralization. A Polish example of this is shown in (5.56), below:

(5.56)   Ciekawość$_i$ (niekiedy) strach$_j$ przezwycięży
           Curiosity (NOM/ACC) (sometimes) fear (NOM/ACC)
               overcome
           Curiosity (sometimes) overcomes fear

For some Polish noun classes, the nominative and accusative forms are identical. *Ciekawość* and *strach* are both members of such a class. The S-structure of this example is shown in (5.57):

(5.57)

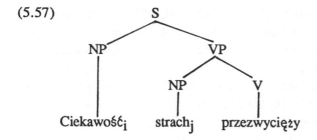

The basic F-structure of the verb *przezwyciężyć* is shown in (5.58):

(5.58)   PRZEZWYCIĘŻYĆ   1-NP[α]   2-NP[β]

The derived F-structure of this sentence is produced from the bare PRED/ARG structure shown below:

(5.59)   PRZEZWYCIĘŻYĆ   1-NP   2-NP

   The strongly favored interpretation of this sentence is the one in which *ciekawość* is the subject and *strach* is the object. This means that *ciekawość*, the $NP[i]$ constituent in (5.57), must be associated with the 1-NP argument of the predicate in (5.59), and *strach*, the $NP[j]$ constituent in (5.57), must be associated with the 2-NP argument of the predicate in (5.59). However, the Polish 1-NP correlation statement in (5.46a) and 2-NP correlation statement in (5.46b), which are based on case marking, each apply to both of the NP constituents in (5.57). In this situation, the universal structural correlation statements in (5.44) apply to associate *ciekawość*, the sister of V^n, with the 1-NP argument of PRZEZWYCIĘZYC, and *strach* , the sister of $V^{(1)}$, with the 2-NP argument of PRZEZWYCIĘZYC. The Index Insertion rule and the SRA rule apply to (5.59) to produce the derived F-structure of (5.56), which is shown in (5.60):

(5.60)   PRZEZWYCIĘŻYĆ $NP[i] \atop \alpha$ $NP[j] \atop \beta$

Unlike the examples in (5.49) above, the following sentence, in which the NPs *ciekawość* and *strach* have been reordered, and the sentence in (5.56), are not variants with the same interpretation:

(5.61)   Strach$_i$ (niekiedy) ciekawość$_j$ przezwycięży
       fear (NOM/ACC)   (sometimes)   curiosity (NOM/ACC)
        overcome
       Fear (sometimes) overcomes curiosity

The strongly favored interpretation of this example is the one in which the subject is *strach$_i$* and the object is *ciekawość$_j$*. The S-structure of this sentence is shown in (5.62):

(5.62)

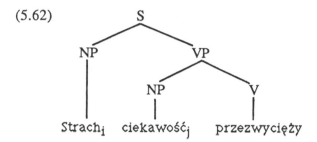

The derived F-structure of this example is produced from the PRED/ ARG structure in (5.59), above. As before, only the universal structural correlation statements apply to the S-structure in (5.62). In this case, *strach* is the $_{NP}[i]$ constituent, which is the sister of V^n and is associated with the 1-NP argument of the predicate, and *ciekawość* is the $_{NP}[j]$ constituent, which is the sister of $V^{(1)}$ and is associated with the 2-NP argument of the predicate. The Index Insertion rule and the SRA rule apply to (5.59) to produce the F-structure of (5.61), which appears in (5.63):

(5.63)   PRZEZWYCIĘŻYĆ $\underset{\alpha}{_{NP}[i]}$ $\underset{\beta}{_{NP}[j]}$

This accounts for the contrast between (5.56) and (5.61).

We have seen in this section that Grammatical Relation Indicators (GRI) serve to identify the S-structure correlates of the NP arguments of predicates, and to distinguish these from one another. They fall into three general types: structural configurations, morpho-syntactic markers, and positions in ordered sequences. The first type is universal. That is, all languages seem to utilize some form of syntactic phrase structure. The third type is also universal (insofar as there appear to be no languages with completely free word order). The second type, however, may or may not occur in any given language.

Case markers are a widely occurring subcategory of the second type of GRI. These are associated with S-structure NP constituents, and may be thought of as features assigned to NPs.[25] They may be realized as affixes attached to head nouns and/or other constituents of the NP, in Polish and languages of this general type, or they may be realized as particles that occur in NPs, in languages like Japanese and Samoan.

Case markers, or features that are ultimately realized as case markers, are freely introduced into D-structures by the rules of the categorial component (PS rules and lexical insertion rules). General principles preclude derivations that involve S-structures with "improper" case markers. To see this more clearly, consider the following Polish sentence and S-structure:

(5.64)   Książkę$_j$ czytała Małgorzata$_i$
         book (ACC) read Malgorzata (NOM)
         Malgorzata read the book

(5.65)

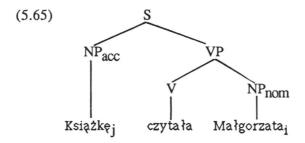

The S-structure in (5.65) can be produced either by freely inserting NPs with nominative and accusative case markers (or features of NPs that are ultimately realized as the nominative and accusative case markers) into the appropriate D-structure, or by applying the scrambling process discussed earlier to permute the NP$_{nom}$ and NP$_{acc}$ constituents in the appropriate D-structure. In this S-structure, the NP$_{acc}$ constituent is the sister of V^n, and is therefore the S-structure correlate of the 1-NP argument of the predicate CZYTAĆ, according to the universal correlation statement in (5.44a). However, this contradicts the language-particular correlation statement for Polish in (5.46b). Moreover, the NP$_{nom}$ constituent is the sister of V$^{(1)}$, which is not identical to V^n here, and according to the universal correlation state- ment in (5.44b), it is the S-structure correlate of the 2-NP argument of CZYTAĆ.   However, this contradicts the language-particular correlation statement in (5.46a). Consequently, the derivation involving this S-structure violates the condition proposed earlier that both the universal and language-particular correlation statements must be satisfied.   This S-structure contrasts with the S-structures in (5.54), above, which are also produced by the scrambling process. The derivations involving these structures, as we have seen, do not violate the universal or the language-particular correlation statements for Polish.   Consequently, no constraints on the introduction of case markers, or on the application of the scrambling process, which is quite productive in Polish, are required by the theory to prevent the construction of S-structures like (5.65).[26]

In some languages, morpho-syntactic markers occur which are associated with S-structure constituents other than NPs. An example of this is Mohawk verb affixation. Consider the following sentences:

(5.66) a.   Ieksá:'a$_i$ wahonwá:ienhte' raksá:'a$_j$
female-child TENSE-female subject/male object-hit male-child
The girl hit the boy

   b.   Raksá:'a$_i$ wahshakó:ienhte' ieksá:'a$_j$
male-child TENSE-male subject/female object-hit female-child
The boy hit the girl

In Mohawk, nouns are marked for gender, and verbs occur with affixes that indicate the gender of the subject and that of the object. In these examples, -ksá.a means "child" and occurs with either the masculine (M) prefix, ra-, or the feminine (F) prefix, ie-. The verbal affix -honwa- in example (5.66a) indicates that the subject is feminine and the object is masculine. The verbal affix -hshako- in (5.66b) indicates that the subject is masculine and the object is feminine. It is easy to see that the verb affixes in conjunction with the nominal gender affixes function as GRIs for Mohawk. We can formulate the following language-particular correlation statements for this language:

(5.67) a.   The S-structure correlate of the 1-NP argument is the NP
marked for Gender X in the string:
$$[..., \ _V[...AF_{XY}...], ...]$$

b.   The S-structure correlate of the 2-NP argument is the NP
marked for Gender Y in the string:
$$[..., \ _V[...AF_{XY}...], ...]$$

In these statements, AF_{XY} represents the verbal affix which indicates
the gender of the subject, X, and that of the object, Y.   The commas in
the strings indicate that these are unordered. (The gender system of
Mohawk must also be specified, but its particular organization and
content is not important to the present discussion.)

These correlation statements are analogous to the Polish and Japanese
correlation statements in (5.46) and (5.47), which are based on case
marking.   The basic F-structure of the verb *-ienhte'* (hit) is shown in
(5.68):

(5.68)   -IENHTE'   1-NP[α]   2-NP[β]

The derived F-structures of the sentences in (5.66a and b) are produced
from the PRED/ARG structures in (5.69a and b), respectively:

(5.69) a.   WAHONWÁ:IENHTE'   1-NP   2-NP
      b.   WAHSHAKÓ:IENHTE'   1-NP   2-NP

In example (5.66a), the verbal affix *-honwa-* is AF_{XY}, where X = F
and Y = M. The correlation statements in (5.67) associate the $_{NP}[i]$
constituent, which occurs with the F gender affix, with the 1-NP
argument of the predicate in (5.69a) and the $_{NP}[j]$ constituent, which
occurs with the M gender affix, with the 2-NP argument of the predicate
in (5.69a). The Index Insertion rule and the SRA rule apply to (5.69a)
to produce the derived F-structure for (5.66a), which is shown in
(5.70):

(5.70)   WAHONWÁ:IENHTE' $_{NP}[i]$ $_{NP}[j]$
                            α β

In example (5.66b), the verbal affix, AF_{XY}, is *-hshako-*, and in this case, $X = M$ and $Y = F$.   Consequently, the correlation statements associate the NP[i] constituent in this sentence, which occurs with the M gender affix, and the 1-NP argument of the predicate in (5.69b), and the NP[j] constituent, which occurs with the F gender affix, with the 2-NP argument of the predicate in (5.69b). The Index Insertion rule and the SRA rule apply to (5.69b) to produce the derived F-structure of (5.66b), which is shown below:

(5.71)   WAHSHAKÓ:IENHTE'   NP[i]   NP[j]
$\qquad\qquad\qquad\qquad\qquad\quad \alpha \qquad \beta$

In examples like these, word order is quite free. The following sentence is a variant of (5.66b) with the same interpretation:

(5.72)   Ieksá:'a$_j$ wahshakó:ienhte' raksá:'a$_i$
female-child TENSE-male subject/female object-hit male-child
The boy hit the girl

Here, the S-structure order of the NP constituents has been changed. The derived F-structure of this example is produced from the PRED/ARG structure in (5.69b). The correlation statements in (5.67) associate the NP[i] constituent in (5.72) with the 1-NP argument of the , and the NP[j] constituent with the 2-NP argument of the predicate. The Index Insertion rule and the SRA rule apply to produce the F-structure in (5.73), below, which is identical to the derived F- structure in (5.71):

(5.73)   WAHSHAKÓ:IENHTE'   NP[i]   NP[j]
$\qquad\qquad\qquad\qquad\qquad\quad \alpha \qquad \beta$

This accounts for the synonymy of examples like (5.66b) and (5.72).[27]

We may think of GRIs as the basic units of the S-structure/F-structure Interface (SFI) System of UG. This component contains the principles and rules discussed in this section, which are summarized below:

(5.74) a.   The universal correlation statements formulated in terms of configurational GRIs in (5.44)

b.   A generalized correlation statement formulated in terms of morpho-syntactic markers and/or ordinal GRIs

c.   The Index Insertion rule and the SRA rule

The manner in which the type (a) correlation statements apply to a language depends on its general sentential structure type, which is determined by its phrase structure grammar.[28]

Type (b) correlation statements are of the form shown in (5.75):

(5.75)   The S-structure correlate of the x-NP argument is the NP identified by GRI_x

Here, GRI_x is the appropriate morpho-syntactic marker or ordinal GRI. Ordinal GRIs are designated positions, NP_x, in ordered sequences of NPs of the form: [...NP...NP...NP...] and fall into a single general type or category.   Morpho-syntactic markers, on the other hand, fall into one of a small number of possible subcategories, as we have seen. Perhaps these are limited to NP markers and verb markers. So there is parametric variation of two sorts associated with type (b) correlation statements. Firstly, the types of morpho-syntactic markers (if any) that occur in a language must be specified in the grammar of that language. These markers are members of case systems in languages like Polish and Japanese, or systems of other types in languages like Mohawk. Secondly, the individual morpho-syntactic and/or ordinal GRIs of the language must be associated with particular x-NP arguments in type (b) correlation statements for that language, as shown in (5.45) to (5.48) for English, Polish, Japanese, and Samoan, and in (5.67) for Mohawk. These statements are all derived from the general statement in (5.75) by fixing the values of these parameters.[29]

The Index Insertion rule applies in accordance with the type (a) and type (b) correlation statements of the language. Therefore, differences in the inventory and nature of the GRIs of particular languages partially account for variation in relative freedom of word order and other permissible S-structure patterns from language to language, or from language type to language type. The Index Insertion rule is reformulated as shown below:

(5.76)   Insert the indices of the S-structure NP constituents into the proper argument positions of the PRED/ARG structure in accordance with the correlation statements of the language.

Non-NP arguments of predicates, of course, also have S-structure correlates. In general, the S-structure correlates of non-NP arguments, such as controlled and uncontrolled complements, in the basic F-structures of predicates are daughters of V^n. In hierarchical languages, these occupy the position designated as X in structures like (5.77):

(5.77)

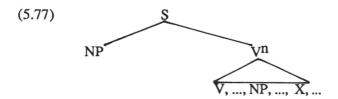

In the sentential structures of non-configurational languages, these occupy the position designated as X in structures like the following:

(5.78)

$$S \ (= V^n)$$
$$\overline{V, ..., NP, ..., X, ...}$$

(The commas in (5.77) and (5.78) indicate that order is not important here.)

6. Summary and Concluding Remarks

UG is organized into a categorial component (some version of the X-bar theory), a lexical component (which specifies the form of lexical entries and contains lexical rules of various sorts), and the four components listed in (6.1), below:

(6.1) a.   The SFI System
     b.   The Generalized Co-Indexing System
     c.   The Generalized Argument Reduction System
     d.   The E-A System

These components consist of rules of various sorts, general principles that govern the application of these rules, and parameters relevant to these rules, whose values must be fixed for particular languages. Only the SFI system has been discussed at any length.

The lexical entries of simple and complex predicates, of various S-structure categories, contain one or more basic F-structures of the form shown below:[30]

(6.2)   PRED [...ARG$_n$...]

Here, [...ARG$_n$...] represents the argument structure of the predicate. Argument structures are ordered and consist of one or more NP arguments, to which the predicates assign semantic relations (with certain exceptions). They may also contain non-NP arguments of various sorts, but they contain a maximum of three terms which have S-structure correlates. The canonical form of basic F-structures is shown below:

(6.3)
$$\text{PRED} \quad \text{1-NP}[\alpha] \quad \text{2-NP}[\beta] \left\{ \begin{array}{l} \text{3-NP}[\gamma] \\ \text{S} \\ \text{PP} \\ [(\text{NP*})\text{XP}] \end{array} \right\}$$

There are three parameters associated with the canonical form in (6.3): the [GR] Parameter, the θ-Argument Parameter, and the XP Category Parameter. These parameters, along with their possible values, appear in (6.4):

(6.4) a.   [GR] Parameter: The value of the feature [GR] of NP* arguments is [+] or [-].

   b. θ-Argument Parameter: The number of NP[θ] arguments that can appear in basic F-structures with controlled complements is $\emptyset$, 1, or 2.

   c.   XP Category Parameter: The category of XP in [(NP*)XP] arguments is VP, NP, AP, PP.

The notion "possible basic F-structure" can be defined in the theory as a structure like (6.3) in which permissible combinations of values of these parameters appear. The combinations shown in the following table are the result of varying the values of the [GR] Parameter and the θ-Argument Parameter independently:

(6.5)

		[GR] Parameter	
		+	–
θ-Argument Parameter		Ø (a)	*Ø (d)
		1 (b)	1 (e)
		*2 (c)	2 (f)

Predicates of types (a), (b), (e), and (f) occur. Examples of these appear in (6.6), with generalized basic F-structures:

(6.6) (a) PRED [(NP*[+GR])VP]: *seem, appear*
　　　(b) PRED 1-NP[α] [(NP*[+GR])VP]: *believe*
　　　(e) PRED 1-NP[α] [(NP*)VP]: *try*
　　　(f) PRED 1-NP[α] 2-NP[β] [(NP*)VP]: *force*

Type (d) predicates do not occur. These have basic F-structures like the following:

(6.7)　PRED [(NP*)VP]

The NP* argument, here, has no S-structure correlate. Moreover, there is no NP argument in this structure that has an S-structure correlate. Consequently, this argument cannot be assigned an index, either directly by the Index Insertion rule or indirectly by the co-indexing rule. Therefore no well-formed derived F-structure can be produced from structures like (6.7). This explains the non- occurrence of predicates of this type.

　　Type (c) predicates have basic F-structures like the following:

(6.8)　PRED 1-NP[α] 2-NP[β] [(NP*[+GR])XP]

This structure contrasts with the basic F-structures of verbs like *force* and *believe* in that it contains four terms which have S-structure correlates. These are the 1-NP argument, the 2-NP argument, the NP*[+GR] argument and the controlled complement XP constituent. It violates the three-term length condition, and this accounts for the non-occurrence of predicates of this type.

The combinations shown below are the result of varying the XP Category Parameter independently of the other two. These are subtypes of (a), (b), (e), and (f) in (6.6):

(6.9) (a)   PRED   [(NP*[+GR]) $\{^{NP}_{AP}\}$]:

  appear as in: *He appeared foolish/an arrogant man*

  (b)   PRED   1-NP[α]   [(NP*[+GR] $\left\{^{AP}_{NP}_{PP}\right\}$] :

  consider as in *We considered him a fool/foolish*
  want as in: *Gnorman wanted gnomes in his garden*

  (e)   PRED   1-NP[α]   [(NP*) $\{^{AP}_{NP}\}$]:

  become as in: *He became angry/president to intimidate his enemies*

  (f)   PRED   1-NP[α]   2-NP[β]   [(NP*) $\{^{NP}_{AP}\}$]:

  elect as in: *They elected him president*
  make as in: *We made him angry*

We see here that by defining the notion "possible basic F-structure", the theory, in effect, defines the notion "possible predicate". Each of these predicate types, however, may or may not occur in any particular language. Constraints on the assignment of certain values to the relevant parameters, or certain combinations of values to two or more of the relevant parameters, determine the types and distribution of the predicates that occur in a given language. Cross-language variation in this area is due to differences in these constraints from language to language.   Limitations of this sort on the range of permissible values of the parameters must be specified for each language.

For example,   raising verbs of the English *believe* class do not occur in many of the Indo-European languages. Thus, as we saw earlier, Polish and Dutch sentences like the following are ungrammatical:

(6.10)   *Jan wierzył Marii mówić prawdę
         Jan (NOM) believed Maria (DAT) speak [-finite] truth (ACC)
         Jan believed Maria to have spoken the truth

(6.11)   *Jan geloofde Bill Mary te kussen
         Jan believed Bill Mary to kiss
         Jan believed Bill to have kissed Mary

The non-occurrence of predicates like the ones in these examples is a consequence of a condition that, for these languages, when the value of the [GR] Parameter is [+], the value of the θ-Argument parameter must be Ø.

The Polish verb *zmuszić* (force) occurs with an NP controlled complement, in contrast to its English counterpart. The reason for this is that for Polish verbs of this class, the value of the XP parameter is NP, while for English verbs of this class, the value of the XP parameter is VP.[31]

Derivations in the proposed framework are organized as shown in the following diagram:

(6.12)   D-structure
              ↓
          S-structure
              ↓
          PRED/ARG structure
              ↓
          Derived F-structure

The rules of the categorial component and the lexical insertion rules apply to produce the D-structure. S-structures are derived from D-structures by the application of a general indexing operation, the E-A rule under the proper circumstances, and scrambling rules, again, under the proper circumstances. The general indexing operation applies to assign an index to each lexical NP in the structure so that it can be identified by the correlation statements. These indices have no other function.[32]   The E-A rule is the analog in this theory of the wh-movement rule, and applies to structures that contain wh-expressions and variables.   (See Chapter V.)   Scrambling operations apply option- ally in some languages. Some Polish examples were discussed in Section 5.

Bare PRED/ARG structures are produced from the basic F-structures of the predicates that occur in the S-structures. The rules of the S-structure/F-structure Interface Component, the Index Insertion rule and the SRA rule, as formulated in (5.76) and (1.10), respectively, apply to insert the indices of the S-structure NP constituents into the proper argument positions in the PRED/ARG structure, and to assign SRs to these arguments (where required.) These rules, in effect, relate PRED/ARG structures to S-structures.

S-structure NPs which are not assigned an index by the general indexing operation are not represented in PRED/ARG structures. There are two situations in which an S-structure NP is not indexed. These are shown in the following examples:

(6.13) a.   Reginald$_i$ kissed Luigi

b.

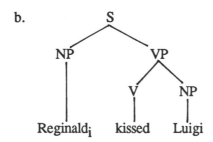

(6.14) a.   *Mowery$_i$ saw

b.

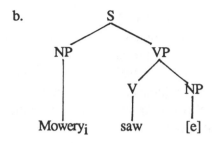

In example (6.13), the NP *Luigi* is not indexed, and consequently, no index is available for insertion into the 2-NP argument position in the PRED/ARG structure of KISS.   The S-structure of Example (6.14) contains a single lexical NP. The object NP contains no lexical material (as indicated by the symbol [e]) and cannot be indexed. The PRED/ARG structures of these sentences, after the application of the Index Insertion rule and the SRA rule, appear in (6.15a and b), respectively:

(6.15) a.   KISS $NP[i]$
$\qquad\qquad\qquad \alpha$

   b.   SEE $NP[i]$
$\qquad\qquad\qquad \alpha$

I return to these structures below. The properties of other types of S-structures which contain $NP[e]$ constituents are discussed in Chapter IV.

   NP arguments which do not have correlates in the relevant S-structures appear in PRED/ARG structures and are subsequently assigned indices by the F-level co-indexing rules. These NP arguments are the 1-NP arguments of predicates in XP complements, whose S-structure correlates are subjectless VP constructions (and subjectless constructions of other categories), and the NP*[-GR] arguments in the controlled complement arguments of verbs like *force*.

   Derived F-structures are produced from indexed PRED/ARG structures by the application of the appropriate rules of the Co-Indexing System and the Argument Reduction System. Tentative formulations of co-indexing rules appeared in (3.17) and (3.21). These rules both apply to PRED/ARG structures that contain controlled complements of the form: [(NP*)XP]. They are subcases of a general co-indexing rule which is the analog of the various control rules and raising rules in earlier theories. (See Chapter III.) The rules of the Argument Reduction system are the analogs in this theory of certain cases of NP movement in the standard theory. (See Chapter IV.)

There are two significant levels of structure: S-structure and Derived F-structure. Those aspects of the interpretation of sentences that involve the scope of various sorts of adverbials and negation are determined at the S-structure level. Pronominal co-indexing may be checked at this level. Finally, GRIs are checked for inconsistencies at this level, to eliminate structures like (5.65) above.

The general well-formedness condition, WFC I, formulated in (1.13), and the various conditions and constraints of the Co-Indexing System and the E-A System apply at the level of derived F-structure, and grammaticality is determined at this level. Grammatical sentences are ones for which a well-formed derived F-structure can be produced, and ungrammatical sentences are ones for which no well-formed derived F-structure can be produced. Some examples of this have been discussed. Others will be discussed in the remaining chapters where appropriate. Since no further operations apply to them, the structures in (6.15) are the derived F-structures of examples (6.13a) and (6.14a). Although they are well-formed, each contains only a single indexed NP argument, and is therefore the basis for only a partial interpretation, since KISS and SEE are two-argument predicates. Example (6.13a) is grammatical because a well-formed two-argument derived F-structure can be produced for it if the NP constituents in Structure (6.13b) are each assigned an index.

Those aspects of the interpretation of sentences that are associated with the meanings of individual lexical items and the semantic relations borne by the NP arguments of predicates are produced from derived F-structures. Ambiguity and synonymy are also determined at this level. An ambiguous sentence is one for which two or more well-formed derived F-structures can be produced, and two (or more) sentences are synonymous if equivalent well-formed derived F-structures can be derived from their S-structures. An example of the first case is shown in (6.16):

(6.16) $Finch_i$ read the $manuscript_j$ in the $attic_k$

This sentence has an interpretation in which the location of the activity is the attic, and one in which the particular book is the one that is, or was, in the attic. The sentence can be assigned two S-structures. The one in

(6.17a) corresponds to the first interpretation and the one in (6.17b) corresponds to the second interpretation:

(6.17) a.

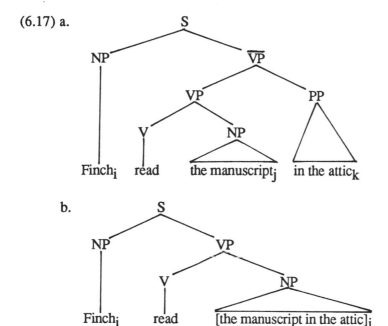

b.

A well-formed derived F-structure can be produced from each of these S-structures. These are shown below:

(6.18) a.   [READ NP[i] NP[j]][IN NP[k]]
                     α   β   α
        b.   READ NP[i] NP[j]
                     α   β

This accounts for the ambiguity of (6.16).

The two sentences in (6.19) are synonymous, at least in the relevant respects:

(6.19) a.   Murphy$_i$ slew O'Brian$_j$
        b.   O'Brian$_j$ was slain by Murphy$_i$

The derived F-structure of (6.19a) is shown in (6.20):

(6.20)   SLAY $\underset{\alpha}{NP^{[i]}}$ $\underset{\beta}{NP^{[j]}}$

The derived F-structure of (6.19b) is produced by the rules of the Argument Reduction System. This F-structure is shown in (6.21):

(6.21) $S_PVP[BE][SEEN]$ $\underset{\beta}{NP^{[j]}}$ $[BY$ $\underset{\alpha}{NP^{[i]}}]$

The structures in (6.20) and (6.21) contain the same predicate (*see/seen*) and the same indexed NP arguments (*Murphy*$_i$ and *O'Brian*$_j$). These arguments bear the same semantic relation in each structure. The SR of *Murphy*$_i$ is α, in both cases, and the SR of *O'Brian*$_j$ is β in both cases. These structures are therefore equivalent (in the relevant respects) and this accounts for the (partial) synonymy of the examples in (6.19).[33]

I will close the chapter with a brief discussion of subcategorization. Explicit subcategorization statements are not required in the theory. Instead, correlation statements interact with basic F-structures to explain the oddness of examples in which subcategorization restrictions are violated. This can best be seen by looking at specific examples. Consider the following sentences, each of which is shown with its S-structure:

(6.22) a.   ?*Joachim$_i$ put the clothes$_j$

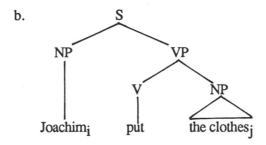

b.

(6.23) a.   ?*Jason$_i$ gave Persephone$_j$

b.

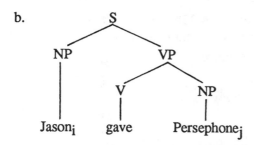

Jason$_i$ gave   Persephone$_j$

(6.24) a. ?*Jules$_i$ went Claudette$_j$

b.

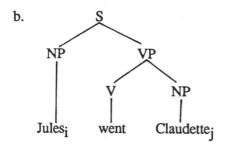

Jules$_i$ went   Claudette$_j$

The derived F-structure of example (6.22a) is produced from the bare PRED/ARG structure shown in (6.25):

(6.25)   PUT 1-NP 2-NP PP

In S-structure (6.22b), however, there is no S-structure correlate of the PP argument of PUT. Consequently, only the derived F-structure shown in (6.26) can be produced for this sentence:

(6.26)   PUT NP[i] NP[j]
                 α   β

As a result, the sentence has only a partial interpretation, which accounts for its oddness.

The same explanation applies to (6.23a). The derived F-structure of this example is produced from the PRED/ARG structure shown in (6.27):

(6.27)   GIVE 1-NP 2-NP 3-NP

However, in the S-structure in (6.23b), there is no S-structure correlate of the 3-NP argument of GIVE. Only the derived F-structure in (6.28) can be produced for this sentence:

(6.28)   GIVE $\underset{\alpha}{NP^{[i]}}$ $\underset{\beta}{NP^{[j]}}$

As above, the sentence has only a partial interpretation, and this accounts for its oddness or ungrammaticality.

The situation with example (6.24) is slightly different. The derived F-structure of this sentence is produced from the PRED/ARG structure shown in (6.29):

(6.29)   GO 1-NP

The S-structure in (6.24b) contains an NP constituent, $Claudette_j$, which has no F-structure correlate in (6.29). The only derived F-structure that can be produced for this example is the one shown in (6.30):

(6.30)   GO $\underset{\alpha}{NP^{[i]}}$

Therefore the $NP^{[j]}$ constituent in the S-structure does not appear in the derived F-structure, and cannot be assigned a SR by the predicate GO. Consequently, the S-structure contains a lexical NP that cannot be interpreted, an "extra" NP of sorts. This accounts for the ungrammaticality of example (6.24).

Now consider the following examples, which are assigned the S-structures shown:

(6.31)a. ?*Jeremiah$_i$ saw tomorrow$_{ADV}$

b.

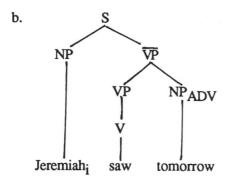

(6.32) a. Obadiah$_i$ put his yarmulka$_j$ in the closet$_k$

b.

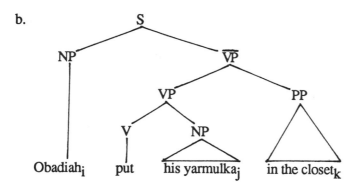

The S-structure of example (6.31a), which is shown in (6.31b), contains an adverbial expression, *tomorrow*$_{ADV}$, which is the sister of VP. As discussed in Section 4, the F-level representations of such constituents are adjoined to the basic PRED/ARG structure of the relevant predicate. Therefore, the derived F-structure of this example is produced from the following PRED/ARG structure:

(6.33)   [SEE 1-NP 2-NP][NP$_{ADV}$]

The S-structure correlate of the 1-NP argument of SEE is the NP$[i]$ constituent in (6.31b). However, the 2-NP argument of SEE has no S-structure correlate.   The only derived F-structure that can be produced from (6.33) is the following:

(6.34)   [SEE NP$[i]$][$_\alpha$NP$_{ADV}$ [TOMORROW]]

Consequently, example (6.31a), like examples (6.22a) and (6.23a) above, has only a partial interpretation, which accounts for its ungrammaticality.[34]

In Structure (6.32b) of example (6.32a), the PP *in the closet* is also a sister of VP, and its F-level representation is adjoined to the PRED/ARG structure of PUT. The derived F-structure of (6.32a) is produced from the following PRED/ARG structure:

(6.35)   [PUT 1-NP 2-NP PP][IN 1-NP]

The S-structure correlate of the 1-NP argument of PUT is the $_{NP}[i]$ constituent in (6.32b), the S-structure correlate of the 2-NP argument of PUT is the $_{NP}[j]$ constituent in (6.32b), and the S-structure correlate of the 1-NP argument of IN is the $_{NP}[k]$ constituent in (6.32b). The PP argument of PUT has no S-structure correlate. The general correlation statement for non-NP arguments discussed in Section 5 states that these are daughters of V^n, and there is no PP constituent in (6.32b) that satisfies this criterion.[35] The only derived F-structure that can be produced for this sentence is the one in (6.36), below:

(6.36)   [PUT $_{NP}[i]$ $_{NP}[j]$][IN $_{NP}[k]$]]
                  α   β   α

This F-structure, apart from the adjunct, is identical in form to (6.26), above, and it forms the basis for the same sort of partial interpretation as that of example (6.22a). Example (6.32a), however, is grammatical and fully interpretable because it can be assigned the S-structure shown in (6.37), below, and the derived F-structure shown in (6.38) can be produced for it:

(6.37)

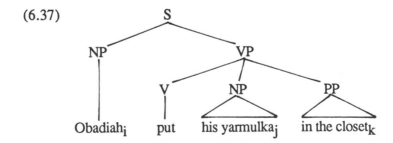

(6.38)   PUT $_{NP[i]}$ $_{NP[j]}$ [IN $_{NP[k]]}$
              α β α

Subcategorization violations involving case marking can be constructed for languages like Polish and are accounted for in an analogous way. Consider the following sentences, shown with their S- structures:

(6.39) a. *Jan$_i$ dał książkę$_j$ Bolesława$_k$
           Jan (NOM) gave book (ACC) Boleslaw (ACC)
           Jan gave Boleslaw a book

b.

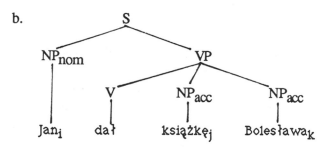

(6.40) a. *Tadeusz$_i$ pilnował skarb$_j$
           Tadeusz (NOM) guarded treasure (ACC)
           Tadeusz guarded the treasure

b.

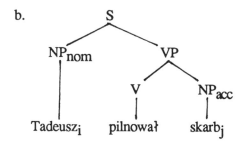

The derived F-structure of (6.39a) is produced from the PRED/ARG structure in (6.41):

(6.41)   DAĆ 1-NP 2-NP 3-NP

The S-structure correlate of the 1-NP argument of DAĆ is the $_{NP[i]}$ constituent in the S-structure in (6.39b). However, both the universal structural correlation statement in (5.44b) and the correlation statement based on case marking for Polish in (5.46b) apply to either of the NP constituents marked for accusative case, $_{NP}[j]$ or $_{NP}[k]$, to associate them with the 2-NP argument of DAĆ. There is no S-structure correlate of the 3-NP argument of DAĆ in this S-structure. Consequently, the only derived F-structures that can be produced for this example are the ones in (6.42):

(6.42) a.   DAĆ $\underset{\alpha}{_{NP}[i]}$ $\underset{\beta}{_{NP}[j]}$

  b.   DAĆ $\underset{\alpha}{_{NP}[i]}$ $\underset{\beta}{_{NP}[k]}$

Therefore example (6.39a) has only a partial interpretation. Moreover, in each case, the S-structure contains a lexical NP, either $_{NP}[k]$ or $_{NP}[j]$, which does not appear in the derived F-structure, and cannot be interpreted. These factors account for the ungrammaticality of this sentence.

The situation is similar for example (6.40a). Its derived F-structure is produced from the PRED/ARG structure shown in (6.43):

(6.43)   PILNOWAĆ 1-NP 2-NP

The S-structure correlate of the 1-NP argument of PILNOWAĆ is the $_{NP}[i]$ constituent in (6.40b). The S-structure correlate of the 2-NP argument of PILNOWAĆ, however, is marked for genitive case, not accusative case. (This must be specified for the verb *pilnować* and other verbs of this class.) Therefore there is no S-structure correlate of the 2-NP argument of PILNOWAĆ in the S-structure in (6.40b). Consequently, the only derived F-structure that can be produced for this example is the one shown in (6.44):

(6.44)   PILNOWAĆ $\underset{\alpha}{_{NP}[i]}$

As in the previous case, example (6.40a) can be only partially interpreted, and it contains an NP constituent, $_{NP}[j]$, which does not appear in the derived F-structure. This accounts for the ungrammaticality of this sentence.

This concludes the discussion of the basic principles of the proposed theory. In the next three chapters, I will examine the rules, principles and parameters associated with the three remaining components of UG: the Generalized Co-Indexing System, the Generalized Argument Reduction System, and the E-A System. These systems account for the universal patterns of control and anaphora, bounded movement (and deletion), and unbounded movement.

NOTES

1. Although I assume that the categorial component of UG is some form of the X-bar theory, I will continue to use abbreviated S-structures with conventional labels like (1.7) and (1.8), which contain only sufficient information for the relevant discussion. Because the theory is structure-neutral in the sense proposed in Chapter I, the details of S-structures (or phrase structure in general) are unimportant to most of the discussions in this and subsequent chapters.

2. These relate to the distribution of grammatical relations indicators such as case affixes, as discussed in Section 5.

3. I will continue to use these informal labels rather than feature complexes like those which appear in, or are implicit in, discussions of the standard theory, such as Chomsky (1981).

4. The additional operations that apply to produce the derived F-structures in (2.1b and c) are discussed in Section 3 of this chapter, and in Chapter III. Of course, nouns do not always function as predicates. In example (i), the noun man_i is the NP[α] argument of the predicate JUMP:

(i)   The man_i jumped over the cliff

5. The S-structure correlate of the 2-NP argument of this predicate is the NP object of the preposition *of*. A rather large number of predicates of different types and categories have NP objects of prepositions as the S-structure correlates of their 2-NP[β] arguments. Two examples are shown below with their derived F-structures:

(i) a. $Everyone_i$ depended on $Smoot_j$

    b.   [DEPEND ON] $\underset{\alpha}{NP[i]}$ $\underset{\beta}{NP[j]}$

(ii) a. Nobody$_i$ talks about Sneed$_j$

    b. [TALK ABOUT] NP[i] NP[j]
                                α   β

Such predicates are exceptions to the general correlation patterns of English, and must be marked as discussed in Section 5. Evidence for this sort of analysis is discusssed in Horn (1983a), following Bresnan (1982b).

An alternative representation of the basic F-structures of those idioms of the VERB NP^C type which have two NP[θ] arguments is one in which the preposition, P, is represented, as shown below:

(iii)   [VERB NP^C[ζ] P] 1-NP[α] ...X...

The basic F-structure of *take advantage of*, following this pattern, is shown in (iv):

(iv)   [TAKE NP^C[ζ] OF] 1-NP[α] 2-NP[β]

I will continue to use the representation in (2.6) for all idioms of the VERB NP^C type.

6. The verbs *write, drink,* and so forth, in examples like these also occur as non-complex predicates in transitive S-structures like the following:

(i)

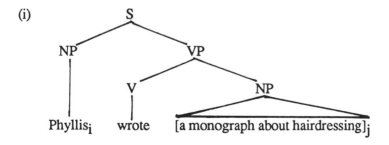

See footnote 13.

7. The idiomatic verbs *take, keep,* and *make,* in expressions like *take advantage of, take umbrage at, make progress on, make headway on,*

keep tabs on, keep track of, and so forth, occur with a relatively small number of NP^C arguments. In contrast, verbs like *write* and *drink* (whose meanings in $\overline{V}$ predicates are not idiomatic) occur with a much wider range of NP^C arguments. Degree of frozenness, then, at least partially correlates with the transparency of the meaning of the lefthand element and the range of possible NP^C elements.

8. This restriction on predicate nouns and predicate adjectives is not universal. It does not, for example, apply in Samoan. Consider the following examples:

(i) E aulelei le tama$_i$
     TENSE handsome the boy
     The boy is handsome

(ii) E manaia isi fale$_i$
     TENSE lovely some houses
     Some houses are lovely

(iii) E lanu mumu le fua a Samoa$_i$
     TENSE color red the flag of Samoa
     The flag of Samoa is red

In examples (i) and (ii), the adjectives *aulelei* and *manaia* function as predicates, and in example (iii), the noun phrase, *lanu mumu* has this function. There is no analog of the verb *be*, and these sentences conform to the general intransitive pattern in Samoan in all respects. The derived F-structures of these sentences are shown in (iv):

(iv) a.   [E AULELEI] NP[i]
                        α
     b.   [E MANAIA] NP[i]
                        α
     c.   [E LANU MUMU] NP[i]
                        α

The adjectives occur in normal adjectival position in NPs in examples like the following:

(v) a. Na faatau e Ioane le fale manaia
TENSE sell (SUBJ) Ioane the house lovely
Ioane sold the lovely house

   b. Na po e Mele le tama aulelei
TENSE hit (SUBJ) Mele the boy handsome
Mele hit the handsome boy

The derived F-structures in (iv) are analogous to the derived F-structures of sentences containing nouns and adjectives as the predicates of controlled complements which are discussed in Section 3, and illustrated in (2.1b and c), above.

9. In the unmarked case, non-verbal predicates (i.e predicate nouns and predicate adjectives) have single-argument basic F-structures like the ones in (2.21).

10. The precise internal structure of the predicate APs and NP in Structures (2.32a, b, and c) is not important to the present discussion.

11. For sentences containing single-argument predicate adjectives like TALL without a complement, the predicate adjective case and the predicate AP case yield equivalent derived F-structures. Consider the following example:

(i)   Horatio$_i$ is tall

Here, AP = A, *tall*. The only derived F-structure that can be produced for this example is the following:

(ii)   [BE [TALL]] $\underset{\alpha}{\text{NP[i]}}$

12. Various selected premodifiers can occur in the semi-productive idiomatic expressions, as illustrated in (i):

(i) a. The FBI kept close tabs on Murry
   b. Everyone took unfair advantage of Mork

The same is true of the type (b) expressions in (ii):

(ii) a.   Aaron drank a large bottle of wine
     b.   Rudolf took a color picture of Murphy

These differences, however, are only differences in degree of severity, and do not contradict the observation in the text.

13. Two factors operate to obscure the similarities between type (a) and type (b) predicates, as well as those among type (a) predicates themselves. Firstly, the verb/NP sequences that appear in type (b) predicates can also be analyzed (in most cases) as non—$\bar{V}$ [V NP] con- structions. Thus the examples in (i) have S-structures like those in (ii) as well as $\bar{V}$ S-structures like the ones in the text:

(i) a.   Salazar$_i$ wrote a book about politics$_j$
    b.   Attila$_i$ drank a quart of wine$_j$
    c.   Norris$_i$ took a picture of Chung$_i$
    d.   Nicephor$_i$ ate a loaf of bread$_j$

(ii) a.

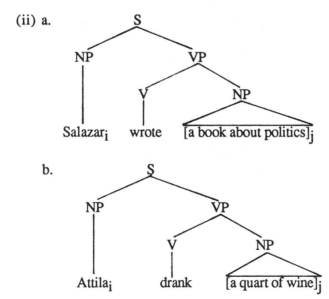

    b.

c.

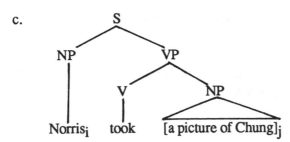

d.

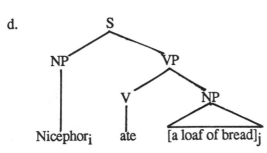

These are transitive VP structures, whose interpretations differ, however slightly in some cases, from those associated with the ∇ structures. The verbs in these examples have basic F-structures like the one shown in (iii):

(iii)   VERB   1-NP[α]   2-NP[β]

The derived F-structure of example (1a) is the following:

(iv)   WRITE   NP[i]   NP[j]
                    α   β

The other examples in (i) have analogous derived F-structures.

This analysis explains the grammaticality of examples like (v). These contrast with the ungrammatical sentences in (2.44c and d), which are repeated here:

(v) a.   [A book about politics]$_i$ was written (by Salazar$_j$)
    b.   [A quart of wine]$_i$ was drunk (by Attila$_j$)
    c.   [A picture of Chung]$_i$ was taken (by Norris$_j$)
    d.   [A loaf of bread]$_i$ was eaten (by Nicephor$_j$)

(2.44) c. *Advantage of Jason was taken (by everyone)
      d. *Tabs on Murphy were kept (by the FBI)

The examples in (v) have S-structures and derived F-structures like the following (for example (v a)):

(vi) a.

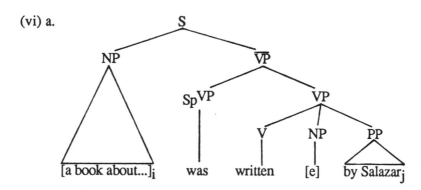

[a book about...]$_i$ was   written   [e]   by Salazar$_j$

(vii) SpVP[BE]WRITTEN NP$_{\beta}^{[i]}$ [BY NP$_{\alpha}^{[j]}$]

F-structures like (vii) are produced from bare PRED/ARG structures of F-structures of the type shown in (iii) by operations that are discussed in Chapter IV. Examples like (3.44), as we have seen, do not have structures like these.

The two-structure analysis also explains the grammaticality of the statement counterparts of the wh-questions of (2.55), shown in (viii) and the (marginal) acceptability of example (2.54), repeated below:

(viii) a. ?Ono$_i$ drank [that glass bottle of wine]$_j$
      b. Norris$_i$ took [those large pictures of Chung]$_j$
      c. Alyce$_i$ wrote [that leatherbound book about politics]$_j$

(2.54) ?Aaron$_i$ drank [those quarts of wine]$_j$

These sentences can all be assigned S-structures like the ones in (ii), and F-structures like the one in (iv) can be derived from them. The oddness of (viii a) and (2.54)) is due to the fact that wine, but not bottles or quarts, can be drunk. However, the latter interpretation is imposed by the non $-\overline{V}$ S-structure and associated F-structure.

A constraint on the application of the wh-movement analog interacts with the two-structure analysis of these expressions to isolate the reason for the ungrammaticality of the wh-questions in (2.55). The constraint, which is discussed at length in Chapter V, prevents the application of the wh-movement analog into NPs under certain circumstances. This rule can, however, apply to sentences containing $\bar{V}$ predicates, as shown by the grammaticality of examples like the following, which contain type (a) predicates:

(ix) a.   Who did everyone take advantage of
     b.   Whose remarks did the audience take umbrage at
     c.   Which ones did the FBI keep track of

Wh-questions like the following, which contain type (b) predicates, are also grammatical:

(x) a.   What did Ono$_i$ drink a bottle$_j$ of
    b.   Who did Norris$_i$ take a picture$_j$ of
    c.   What did Alyce$_i$ write a book$_j$ about

Because of the constraint on the wh-movement analog, the only S-structures that examples like these can have are $\bar{V}$ ones, and not one like (ii) above. Consequently, the VERB/NP sequences must be $\bar{V}$ predicates and these examples have derived F-structures like the following:

(xi) a. $(\text{WHAT}_k)[[\text{DRINK }_{NP}c_{[j]}]\ _{NP}[i]\ [\text{OF }_{NP}[x_k]]\ ]$
                                         α α

     b. $(\text{WHO}_k)[[\text{TAKE }_{NP}c_{[j]}]\ _{NP}[i]\ [\text{OF }_{NP}[x_k]]\ ]$
                                         α α

     c. $(\text{WHAT}_k)[[\text{WRITE }_{NP}c_{[j]}]\ _{NP}[i]\ [\text{ABOUT }_{NP}[x_k]]\ ]$
                                         α α

The contrast between these examples and the ungrammatical ones in (2.55), then, must be due to the fact that the latter violate selectional restrictions of some sort on $\bar{V}$ predicates, and consequently can only be derived from structures like (ii), in violation of the constraint.

The second obscuring factor is that some $\bar{V}$ predicates of type (a) have basic F-structures which contain two NP[θ] arguments, and others have basic F-structures that contain a single NP[θ] argument and a PP argument. These F-structure types are shown in (xii):

(xii) a. [VERB   NP^C[ζ]]   1-NP[α]   2-NP[β]
    b. [VERB   NP^C[ζ]]   1-NP[α]   PP

As we saw earlier, predicates like *take advantage of* have basic F-structures like (xii a). The same is true of the predicate *keep tabs on*. Predicates like *take umbrage at* and *make headway on*, in contrast, have basic F-structures like (xii b). Examples containing each predicate type are shown below, with their derived F-structures:

(xiii) a. Alison$_i$ took advantage$_j$ of Chung$_k$
       [TAKE   NP^C[j]]   NP[i]   NP[k]
                ζ   α   β
    b. The FBI$_i$ kept tabs$_j$ on Norris$_k$
       [KEEP   NP^C[j]]   NP[i]   NP[k]
                ζ   α   β

(xiv) a. Everyone$_i$ took umbrage$_j$ at Horace's remarks$_k$
       [TAKE   NP^C[j]]   NP[i]   [AT   NP[k]]
                ζ   α   α
    b. The team$_i$ made headway$_j$ on that problem$_k$
       [MAKE   NP^C[j]]   NP[i]   [ON   NP[k]]
                ζ   α   α

This accounts for the contrast between examples like (xv) and (xvi):

(xv) a. Chung$_i$ was taken advantage$_j$ of
    b. Norris$_i$ was kept tabs$_j$ on

(xvi) a. *Horace's remarks$_i$ were taken umbrage$_j$ at
    b. *That problem$_i$ was made headway$_j$ on

As we will see in Chapter IV, the passive analog is an operation that can apply to F-structures that contain two NP[θ] arguments, like (xii a), but not to F-structures that contain only a single NP[θ] argument, like the one in (xii b). The derived F-structures of the examples in (xv) are shown in (xvii), and those of (xvi) are shown in (xviii):

(xvii) a. $_{Sp}VP[BE][TAKEN]\ _{NP}c[j]]\ _{NP}[i]$
                                        ς   β

b. $_{Sp}VP[BE][KEPT]\ _{NP}c[j]]\ _{NP}[i]$
                                   ς   β

(xviii) a. $_{Sp}VP[BE][TAKEN]\ _{NP}c[j]]\ _{NP}[i]\ [AT\ ]$
                                          ς

b. $_{Sp}VP[BE][MADE]\ _{NP}c[j]]\ _{NP}[i]\ [ON\ ]$
                                      ς

In Structures (xvii), the SR β of the 2-NP argument in the basic F-structure of the predicate has been assigned to the $_{NP}[i]$ argument. These structures are well-formed. The basic F-structures of the predicates in (xviii), however, contain no 2-NP argument whose SR can be reassigned to the $_{NP}[i]$ argument. Therefore, these arguments bear no SR, and the F-structures are not well-formed. Consequently, the examples in (xv) are grammatical, and those in (xvi) are not.

The type of basic F-structure that a predicate has must be specified in its lexical entry. $\overline{V}$ predicates like *write a book about, take a picture of, drink a quart of*, and so forth, have basic F-structures like (xii b). This accounts for the ungrammaticality of examples like the following:

(xvix) a.   *Murphy was written a book about
       b.   *Zoe was taken a picture of
       c.   *That wine was drunk a quart of

It seems that no type (b) predicate has a basic F-structure like (xii a). I have no explanation for this. It may relate to the fact that these expressions are not frozen to the extent that type (a) predicates are. This, however, does not account for the fact that some, but not all, type (a) predicates have such F-structures.

Finally, let us look again at examples like (2.50c), repeated below:

(2.50) c.   ?What did Salazar$_i$ write about Allah$_j$

It was noted above that this example is relatively more acceptable than (2.50a and b). We have seen that VERB/NP sequences like *write NP about* can be analyzed as $\overline{V}$ predicates or as transitive verb/direct object constructions. The verb *write* also occurs in examples like the following:

(xx)   a.   Bulawi$_i$ wrote about politics$_j$
       b.   Bulawi$_i$ wrote books$_j$

These examples show that *write* occurs with a lone prepositional phrase, as well as with a lone NP direct object. The verb *write* may, in fact, occur in S-structures like the following:

(xxi)

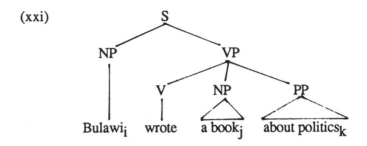

The derived F-structure of this example is shown in (xxii):

(xxii)   WRITE NP[i] NP[j] [ABOUT NP[k]]
                  α   β   α

This analysis provides a potential source for grammatical wh-questions like (2.50c).

14.   In general, predicates can have more than one basic F-structure. The verbs *believe* and *prefer* are no exception. See footnote 30.

15.   Similarly, a maximum value of 2 for this parameter implies all values less than 2 (1 or Ø). The value of the θ-argument parameter for control verbs like *force* is 2, and that for control verbs like *try* is 1. (A value of Ø is not possible for control verbs for reasons that are discussed in Section 6.) The theory therefore predicts that if a language has control verbs with object controllers (θ-Argument Parameter = 2), then that language has control verbs with subject controllers (θ-Argument Parameter = 1), but that the occurrence in a language of verbs with subject controllers does not necessarily imply the occurrence in that language of verbs with object controllers.

16.   Prepositions require a complement (the NP object) within the PP.

Therefore, they cannot function as [+P] X predicates of controlled complements. Instead, they only function as [+P] predicates of PPs, in examples like the following:

(i) a. They$_i$ helped Matilda$_j$ to her chair$_k$
 b. The admiral$_i$ welcomed Reagan$_j$ aboard the aircraft carrier$_k$
 c. The club members$_i$ elected Hildebrand$_j$ to the presidency$_k$

In these examples, the PPs are the S-structure correlates of uncontrolled complements. The derived F-structures of these examples are shown in (ii):

(ii) a. HELP $\underset{\alpha}{NP^{[i]}}$ $\underset{\beta}{NP^{[j]}}$ [TO $\underset{\alpha}{NP^{[k]}}$]]
 b. WELCOME $\underset{\alpha}{NP^{[i]}}$ $\underset{\beta}{NP^{[j]}}$ [ABOARD $\underset{\alpha}{NP^{[k]}}$]]
 c. ELECT $\underset{\alpha}{NP^{[i]}}$ $\underset{\beta}{NP^{[j]}}$ [TO $\underset{\alpha}{NP^{[k]}}$]]

The PP in each case functions as a directional adverbial. These examples are analogous in this respect to the following, shown with its derived F-structure:

(iii) a. We$_i$ sent Smoot$_j$ to Sydney$_k$

 b. SEND $\underset{\alpha}{NP^{[i]}}$ $\underset{\beta}{NP^{[j]}}$ [TO $\underset{\alpha}{NP^{[k]}}$]]

In the following example, the preposition functions as the [+P] predicate of a PP, which is itself the XP^c argument of a complex V ($\bar{V}$) predicate of the type discussed in Section 2:

(iv) Everyone$_i$ considered Jensen$_j$ to be in his prime$_k$

Here, *consider* occurs with a VP complement [*to be in his prime*]. The derived F-structure of this example is shown in (v):

(v) CONSIDER $\underset{\alpha}{NP^{[i]}}$ [[BE [IN $\underset{\alpha}{NP^{[k]}}$]] $\underset{\alpha}{NP^{[j]}}$]

17. The S-structure correlate of this argument of *zmuszić* is the object of the preposition *do*. In this respect, *zmuszić* is similar to verbs like *depend*. Both have arguments whose S-structure correlates are the objects of prepositions. (These are the controlled complement argument of ZMUSZIĆ and the 2-NP[θ] argument of DEPEND).

18. If this co-indexing operation does not apply, then the 1-NP argument of SHAVING is assigned the feature [+INDEF]. The resulting derived F-structure is shown in (i):

(i)   [BE [HARD]] NP[SHAVING NP[+INDEF]]ⱼ [FOR NP[i]]
                      α   α   α

By convention, 1-NP arguments that have no S-structure correlate and are not assigned the index of some other NP argument in the F-structure are assigned the feature [+INDEF], and are ultimately interpreted as having indefinite reference.

19. Andrews (1982b) argues that sentential adverbials are VP internal as shown in (4.21), but contrast with VP adverbials in structures like (4.13). His analysis of the internal structure of these constructions is rather different than the one proposed here.

20. The adverbial expression, *na surowo* is a prepositional phrase at the level of S-structure, as shown in (4.30). Its F-structure correlate is the controlled complement structure shown in (i):

(i)   [(NP*)AP]

Here, the object of the preposition *na* is the S-structure correlate of the AP argument. This expression is parallel, in this sense, to controlled complements of verbs like *zmuszić*. The difference between them is that adjuncts of the form [*na* X] are independent lexical items and are not arguments in the basic F-structures of control predicates. Adjuncts of this type are analogous to English adjuncts of the form [*as* XP] in sentences like (ii):

(ii)   The court condemned O'Malley as a criminal

21. The analogs of structures like (4.13) and (4.21) in non-configurational languages are structures something like (i) and (ii), respectively:

(i)

$$S (=V^n)$$

NP, ..., ...X..., ..., V

(ii)

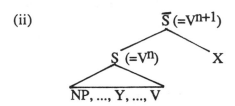

$$\bar{S} (=V^{n+1})$$

$$S (=V^n) \qquad X$$

NP, ..., Y, ..., V

In these structures, the label X represents the various sorts of controlled complements discussed in this section. (The commas indicate that order is not important here.)

22. The S-structure correlates of the 2-NP arguments of certain predicates in Polish are NPs marked for other than the accusative case. Some examples of this are shown in (i):

(i) a.   Jan pilnował skarbu
           Jan (NOM) guarded treasure (GEN)
           Jan guarded the treasure

   b.   Jan zaufał temu przyjacielowi
           Jan (NOM) trusted that friend (DAT)
           Jan trusted that friend

   c.   Imperialiści zagrozili pokojowi
           Imperialists (NOM) threatened peace (DAT)
           The imperialists threatened the peace

   d.   Jan pogardzał Markiem
           Jan (NOM) despised Mark (INSTR)
           Jan despised Mark

e.   Jan kierował tym samochodem
Jan (NOM) drove that car (INSTR)
Jan drove that car

These predicates all have basic F-structures like the following:

(ii)   PRED   1-NP[α]   2-NP[β]

They occur in sentences of the same types as two-argument predicates whose S-structure 2-NP correlates are NPs marked for accusative case. (See Horn (1983a and b).) Consequently, the subcase of the Polish 2-NP correlation statement shown below is required:

(iii)   The S-structure correlate of the 2-NP argument for verbs of Class X is the NP_y in the configuration:
$$_{VP}[\, X, V, Y, NP_y, Z\,]$$

Here, y represents the case affix, which must be specified for each verb or verb class, X. For example, y = DAT, for verbs of Class A (*zaufać, zagrozić, ...*); y = INSTR for verbs of Class B (*pogardzać, kierować, ...*); and so forth.

This situation, in which NP constituents with various oblique case markers are the S-structure correlates of the 2-NP arguments of designated predicates is parallel to the situation in English in which NP objects of prepositions (NP_p) are the S-structure correlates of the 2-NP arguments of designated predicates. In fact, the correlation statement in (iii), above, is analogous to the English correlation statement in (5.21b)(2). This parallelism is due to the fact that prepositions in English sentences, in their non-predicate function (with verbs whose 2-NP S-structure correlates are NP_p) have the same function as case markers in Polish. Both are morpho-syntactic GRIs which identify the arguments of predicates.

An additional correlation statement that identifies the S-structure correlate of the object of a preposition is also required for Polish. This is formulated in (iv):

(iv)   The S-structure correlate of the NP[θ] argument of a preposition (when the preposition functions as a predicate) is the NP in the configuration: $_{PP}[P\ NP]$.

This statement is identical to the one for English in (5.22).

23. The terms nominative, accusative, and dative, as used here, are cover terms meant to apply to any case system. The choice of particular sets of labels has no theoretical significance, and I have chosen conventional ones.

24. I do not rule out the possibility of language-particular structural correlation statements.

25. But note that if abstract case features are assigned to NPs, and these features are distinct from the affixes that realize them, then case neutralization would be impossible. The features would always be available to the correlation statements and hence to the Index Insertion rule. Consequently, some other explanation of the case neutralization data discussed here is required by any theory that assumes universal abstract case features of this sort.

26. Due to the limited role of case in this theory, nothing is gained by adopting a case assignment rule, governed by the verb or other predicate, as in the standard theory, rather than case correlation statements for 2-NP and 3-NP arguments like (5.46) and (5.47), even for marked verbs like the ones discussed in footnote 22.

27. The situation here is parallel to the Polish one involving examples like (5.49) which was discussed earlier. A second variant of (5.66b) is the following:

(i)   Wahshakó:ienhte' raksá:'a$_i$ ieksá:'a$_j$
      TENSE-male subject/female object-hit male-child female-child
      The boy hit the girl

It is easy to see that this example has the same derived F-structure as (5.66b) and (5.72). In these cases, in both Polish and Mohawk, correlation statements based on the same general type of GRI (morphosyntactic markers) are operating.

Like the Polish correlation statements based on case marking, these Mohawk correlation statements are neutralized in certain situations. Consider the following example:

(ii)   Kor$_i$ wahó:ienhte' Sak$_j$
       Kor TENSE-masculine subject/masculine object-hit Sak
       Kor hit Sak

In this example, *Kor* and *Sak* are men's names and are both masculine. The verbal affix, AF_{XY}, here, is AF_{MM}, *-ho-*, in example (ii). The derived F-structure of this example is produced from the following PRED/ARG structure:

(iii)   WAHÓ:IENHTE' 1-NP 2-NP

The preferred interpretation of this sentence is the one in which *Kor* is the subject and *Sak* is the object. However, the correlation statements in (5.67) each apply to both NP constituents in (ii). In this situation, correlation statements based on structure, or perhaps word order associate the $NP[i]$ constituent, which is the leftmost NP in (ii), with the 1-NP argument of the predicate in (iii), and the $NP[j]$ constituent, which is the rightmost one in (ii), with the 2-NP argument of the predicate in (iii). The Index Insertion rule and the SRA rule apply to produce the derived F-structure in (iv):

(iv)   WAHÓ:IENHTE' $\underset{\alpha}{NP[i]}$ $\underset{\beta}{NP[j]}$

The following example, in which the order of the NP constituents has been changed, contrasts with (ii):

(v)   Sak$_j$ wahó:ienhte' Kor$_i$
      Sak TENSE-masculine subject/masculine object-hit Kor
      Sak hit Kor

The preferred interpretation for this sentence is the one in which the subject is *Sak* and the object is *Kor*. The derived F-structure of (v) is produced from the PRED/ARG structure in (iii). The correlation state-

ments based on structure or word order apply as above to associate the
$NP[j]$ constituent in (v), which is the leftmost NP constituent, with the
1-NP argument of the predicate, and the $NP[i]$ constituent in (v), which
is the rightmost NP constituent, with the 2-NP argument of the predicate. The Index Insertion rule and the SRA rule apply to (iii) to produce the following derived F-structure for (v):

(vi)   WAHÓ:IENHTE' $\underset{\alpha}{NP[j]}$ $\underset{\beta}{NP[i]}$

This accounts for the difference in meaning of examples (ii) and (v).
This situation is parallel to the case neutralization situation in Polish discussed earlier, as we would expect, since both are cases of GRI neutralization of virtually the same type.

28. The statement in (5.44b) actually applies to all predicates, and not to
verbs [V] alone. Therefore a trivial modification to this effect of the
formulation in the text is required. It follows from Statement (5.44b),
appropriately generalized, and the relevant PS Rules, that the S-
structure correlate of the $NP[\theta]$ argument of a preposition which
functions as a predicate is the sister of P^0, the preposition itself, in the
PP, and that the S-structure correlates of NP^C arguments are sisters of
V^0 in $\bar{V}$. Consequently, reference to structure can be removed from
the English and Polish correlation statements which appear in (5.22) and
(iv), footnote 22, and the English correlation statement for NP^C arguments in (5.15) and (5.21d). The former need not appear as special
statements in the grammars of English, Polish or any other language,
and the latter can be replaced by a statement which associates NP^C
arguments with the heads of $\bar{V}$ structures.

29. The English 2-NP/NP_p correlation statement for designated predicates, which appears in (5.11) and (5.21b)(2); and the Polish
2-NP/$NP_{oblique}$ correlation statement for designated predicates, which
appears in (iii), footnote 22, are special cases of the general correlation
statement in (5.75). With the abstraction of the structural statements in
(5.44), these statements, like (5.45)-(5.48), need not refer to structural
configurations, and may be reformulated as shown below:

(i)   English: The S-structure correlate of the 2-NP argument for verbs of Class X is the NP_p of the preposition Y.

(ii)   Polish: The S-structure correlate of the 2-NP argument for verbs of Class X is the NP marked for Case y.

In the English statement, Y is the preposition selected by the verb.

30.   It is quite common for predicates to have more than one basic F-structure. For example, the verb *believe*, which occurs in sentences like (i) has the basic F-structures shown in (ii):

(i)   a. Nobody$_i$ believed the story$_j$
       b. Yeats$_i$ believed that a rough beast was slouching towards Bethlehem to be born
       c. Muggleston$_i$ believed Martha$_j$ to have committed adultery$_k$

(ii)   a. BELIEVE   1-NP[α]   2-NP[β]
       b. BELIEVE   1-NP[α]   S
       c. BELIEVE   1-NP[α]   [(NP*[+GR])VP]

The F-structures in (ii) correspond to the sentence patterns in (i). Similarly, the verb *give* occurs in sentences like (iii), and has the basic F-structures shown in (iv):

(iii) a. Snyder$_i$ gave Ferdinand$_j$ a box of candy$_k$
       b. Snyder$_i$ gave a box of candy$_j$ to Ferdinand$_k$

(iv)   a. GIVE   1-NP[α]   2-NP[β]   3-NP[ζ]
       b. GIVE   1-NP[α]   2-NP[β]   PP

(The SR ɣ in (iv a) is identical to the SR β in (iv b) for verbs of this class.)

In contrast, the verb *donate* occurs in sentences like (iii b), but not ones like (iii a). Thus (v a) is ungrammatical:

(v) a. *Snyder$_i$ donated the nunnery$_j$ a box of candy$_k$
    b. Snyder$_i$ donated a box of candy$_j$ to the nunnery$_k$

Donate, unlike *give* (except in the sense of *donate*), also occurs in sentences like the following:

(vi)   Snyder$_i$ donated a box of candy$_j$

Donate has the basic F-structures shown in (vii):

(vii) a.   DONATE   1-NP[α]   2-NP[β]   PP
     b.   DONATE   1-NP[α]   2-NP[β]

This accounts for the difference between *give* and *donate*.

31. The absence in a language of controlled complements of one or more of the S-structure categories, NP, AP, VP, can be explained as a consequence of a general condition that the XP parameter in that language cannot have a particular value or values x, where x = NP, VP, or AP. (There may be an implicational hierarchy of values to the effect that if a language has controlled complements of category XP then it has controlled complements of category YP, but not vice versa. I will not explore this issue.)

32. No constraints on the general indexing operation are required. Consider the following example:

(i)   Mowery$_i$ saw Remmel$_i$

In this example, both NP constituents have been assigned the same index. The derived F-structure of this example is therefore the one shown in (ii):

(ii)   SEE   NP[i]   NP[i]
             α β

This F-structure is equivalent to (iii), below:

(iii)   SEE   NP[i]
               $\alpha\beta$

This structure violates WFC I. Example (i), however, is grammatical because a well-formed derived F-structure can be produced for it if the NP constituents are assigned discrete indices.

33. Other aspects of meaning are not represented in these derived F-structures. F-structures, as the basis for the interpretation of sentences, may contain additional information pertinent to other aspects of meaning than the ones that I consider here. Alternatively, other aspects of the meaning of sentences may derive from other sources, such as S-structure. I leave these questions open.

34. Example (6.31a) also has a nonsensical literal interpretation. The source of this interpretation is the S-structure shown below, which can be assigned to this sentence:

(i)

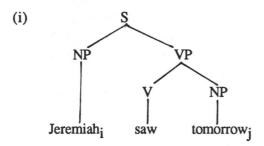

The derived F-structure of the sentence with this S-structure is produced from the PRED/ARG structure shown in (ii):

(ii)   SEE 1-NP 2-NP

Here, the S-structure correlate of the 1-NP argument of SEE is the $NP[i]$ constituent in (i) and the S-structure correlate of the 2-NP argument of SEE is the $NP[j]$ constituent in (i). The Index Insertion rule and the SRA rule apply to (ii) to produce (iii), below, which forms the basis for the intended interpretation:

(iii)   SEE $NP[i] \atop \alpha$ $NP[j] \atop \beta$

35. Some elaboration of this point is called for. Adjuncts, whose F-level representations do not occur in the basic F-structures of predi-

cates, occupy positions outside V^n in structures like the following (in which X represents the adjunct):

(i) a.

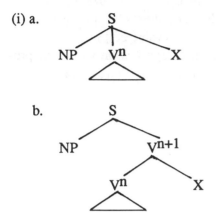

b.

These are both hierarchical structures, and either analysis of the location of adjuncts is possible. If the first is assumed, then the generalization suggested at the end of Section 5 is sufficient to distinguish non-NP arguments of predicates from adjuncts. In the (i b) structure, however, the maximal projection of V is V^{n+1}. Therefore, if the second analysis is assumed, as in the discussion of example (6.32), then this generalization must be modified to the effect that the non-NP arguments of predicates are daughters of V^2 (or some other suitably designated value of $\underline{n}$.) This appears to be a matter of detail, and the question of choosing one or the other of these structures is independent of the issues that I am examining here.

As suggested in footnote 21, the location of adjuncts like the ones in these examples in non-configurational structures is the position designated as X in (ii):

(ii)

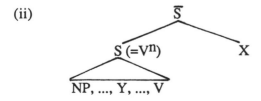

This situation is parallel to that of hierarchical languages. If S ($=V^n$) is the maximal projection of V in Structure (ii), then X is not a daughter of

V^n. The generalization at the end of Section 5 is sufficient to distinguish non-NP arguments of predicates from adjuncts. However, if $\overline{S} = V^{n+1}$, and is the maximal projection of V, then the generalization must be modified to the effect that non-NP arguments of predicates are daughters of V^2 (or some suitably designated value of $\underline{n}$.)

We see, then, that the account of subcategorization violations proposed in the text extends to non-configurational languages as well.

Chapter III

The Co-Indexing System: A Reanalysis of Control and Bound Anaphora

1. Introduction

General definitions of the control and anaphora relations, as S-structure level relations, were suggested in Chapter I. These relations can be redefined on the level of derived F-structure as shown in (1.1) and (1.2):

(1.1) The Control Relation: The relation between an antecedent $NP[i]$ argument and a target NP argument elsewhere in the (complex) derived F-structure which must be co-indexed with the antecedent

(1.2) The Anaphora Relation: The relation between an antecedent $NP[i]$ argument and a designated argument with the feature [+ANAPHOR] elsewhere in the derived F-structure which must be co-indexed with it

An adequate theory of UG, at a minimum, should specify the constraints on possible controllers (antecedents) and possible controlled elements (targets), and contain general principles which dictate the choice of controller from several NP arguments in the F-structure by defining the necessary structural and/or functional relationship between controllers and controlled elements.

There are two major subcategories of the control relation: the short-range control relation and the long-range control relation. The short-range control relation is the relation between an antecedent and target which are located in the argument structure of a single predicate, or in adjacent argument structures. The following examples, shown with their derived F-structures, illustrate this subcategory:

(1.3) a.   Malcolm$_i$ forced Ayn$_j$ to kiss the Blarney Stone$_k$

   b.   FORCE $NP^{[i]}_\alpha$ $NP^{[j]}_\beta$ [KISS $NP^{[j]}_\alpha$ $NP^{[k]}_\beta$]]

(1.4) a.   Malcolm$_i$ tried to kiss the Blarney Stone$_j$

   b.   TRY $NP^{[i]}_\alpha$ [KISS $NP^{[i]}_\alpha$ $NP^{[j]}_\beta$]]

In Structure (1.3b), the $NP^{[j]}$ argument of FORCE is the antecedent or controller and the $NP^{[j]}$ argument of KISS is the target (controlled element.) In Structure (1.4b), the $NP^{[i]}$ argument of TRY is the antecedent or controller and the $NP^{[i]}$ argument of KISS is the target.

   The long-range control relation involves (potentially) more distantly separated antecedents and targets, in examples like the following, also shown with its derived F-structure:

(1.5) a.   Shaving himself$_i$ was hard for Fromberg$_i$

   b.   [BE [HARD]] $NP[SHAVING$ $NP^{[i]}_\alpha$ $NP[REFLEX_i]]_\beta]]_j$ [FOR
        $NP^{[i]}]]_\alpha$

In Structure (1.5b), the antecedent of the long-range control relation is the $NP^{[i]}$ argument of the predicate FOR and the target is the NP [i] argument of the predicate SHAVING.

   I propose in this chapter that the Generalized Co-Indexing System of UG, which consists of a single co-indexing operation and associated general principles, comprises a unified theory of control. It applies to the short-range control relation, and accounts for the behavior of verbs like *try* and *force* in examples like (1.3) and (1.4), as well as to the long-range control relation in examples like (1.5). The co-indexing operation and general principles extend in a natural way to account for the behavior of verbs like *believe,* which occur in examples like the following:

(1.6) a.   Melvin$_i$ believed Dano$_j$ to have hidden the manuscript$_k$
   b.   BELIEVE $_{NP[i]}$ [HIDE $_{NP[j]}$ NP[k]]]
                  α α β

In the derived F-structures of sentences that contain verbs of this class, such as (1.6b), the control relation is not explicit.

Finally, the rules and principles of this system extend to the anaphora relation involving overt anaphors (reflexives and reciprocals), and provide the basis for an account of disjoint reference patterns. The Generalized Co-Indexing System accounts for the universal patterns of control and anaphora, which are observed in languages regardless of their differences on the S-structure and other levels.

Basic short-range control verbs like *try* and *force*, as well as verbs like *believe*, are discussed in Section 2. Here, I formulate a first approximation of the General Co-indexing rule. The remaining extensions of the analysis are the subject of Sections 3 and 4. In Section 5, the various co-indexing operations are shown to be subcases of a single general co-indexing rule. The most important points of the the chapter are summarized in Section 6.

2. The Short-Range Control Relation

Short-range (obligatory) control verbs are members of the class of predicates whose basic F-structures contain a controlled complement argument of the form shown in (2.1):

(2.1)   [(NP*)XP]

The properties of such arguments were discussed at some length in Chapter II. The NP* argument is the external controller of the embedded XP complement, and the value of XP is VP, NP, AP, or PP depending on the particular predicate. The NP* argument has the feature [-GR], and has no S-structure correlate. The paradigm cases of obligatory control in English are illustrated by the examples in (2.2) - (2.7), shown with their S-structures:

(2.2) a.   Jethro$_i$ tried to skin a lizard$_j$

b.

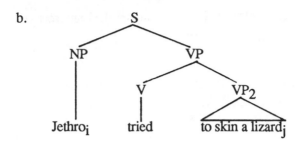

(2.3) a. Kelly$_i$ forced Cynthia$_j$ to commit unnatural acts$_k$

b.

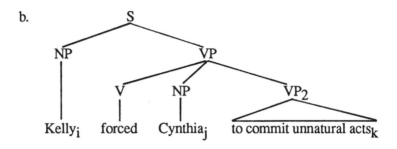

(2.4) a. Roth$_i$ made Gertrude$_j$ angry

b.

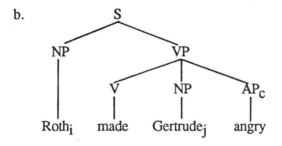

(2.5) a. Roth$_i$ made Gertrude$_j$ a virtuous woman

b.

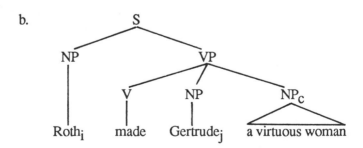

(2.6) a.   Mavis$_i$ {told / asked}   Fiona$_j$ to leave

b.
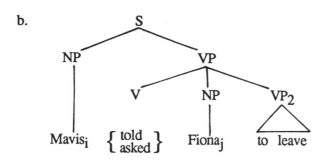

(2.7) a.   The members$_i$ elected Bertram$_j$ president

b.
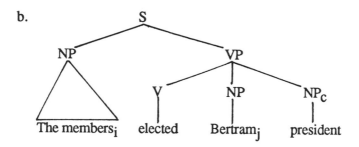

The main verbs in these sentences occur with controlled complements of various S-structure categories. They have basic F-structures of the type shown in (2.8):

(2.8)   PRED   1-NP[α] ...   [(NP*)XP]

(In this structure, ... may or may not contain a 2-NP[β] argument.) The PRED/ARG structures for examples (2.2a), (2.3a), and (2.4a) appear in (2.9a, b, and c), respectively:

(2.9) a.   TRY   1-NP [(NP*)[SKIN 1-NP 2-NP]]
       b.   FORCE   1-NP 2-NP [(NP*)[COMMIT 1-NP 2-NP]]
       c.   MAKE   1-NP 2-NP [(NP*)[ANGRY 1-NP]]

The index insertion rule and the SRA rule apply to the structures in (2.9) to produce the structures in (2.10), below:

(2.10) a.   TRY   NP[i]   [(NP*) [SKIN   NP   NP[j]]]
                       α   α   β

    b.   FORCE NP[i] NP[j] [(NP*)[COMMIT   NP   NP[k]]]
                             α   β   α   β

    c.   MAKE NP[i] NP[j] [(NP*)[ANGRY   NP]]
                           α   β   α

At this point, two operations apply. These are the Co-indexing rule and the Raqui rule. These rules are repeated here as (2.11) and (2.12):

(2.11)   <u>The Co-Indexing Rule</u>:

    NP[i]   X   (NP*)
     1   2   3   ===>   1   2   (NP*[i])

(2.12)   <u>The Raqui Rule</u>:

    (NP*[i])   PRED   NP
     1   2   3   ===>   ∅   2   NP[i]

The Co-indexing rule applies to (2.10a) to co-index the NP[i] argument of TRY and the NP* argument. This rule applies to (2.10b and c) to co-index the NP[j] argument of FORCE and MAKE, respectively, and the NP* argument. The Raqui rule then applies to produce the derived F-structures of (2.2a), (2.3a), and (2.4a), which are shown below:

(2.13) a.   TRY NP[i] [SKIN NP[i] NP[j]]
                      α   α   β

    b.   FORCE   NP[i] NP[j] [COMMIT NP[j] NP[k]]
                              α   β   α   β

    c.   MAKE   NP[i] NP[j] [ANGRY NP[j]]
                            α   β   α

The derived F-structures of the examples in (2.5a), (2.6a), and (2.7a) are produced in the same way.

    The antecedent of the NP* argument in (2.10a) is the initial (only) NP argument of the predicate TRY, while in (2.10b and c), the antecedents of the NP* arguments are the NP[j] arguments of the respective predicates FORCE and MAKE. In all cases, the antecedent is the closest NP argument to the NP* argument. This brings to mind the

Minimal Distance Principle (MDP), which was first proposed by Rosenbaum (1967 & 1970), who noticed that the NP which controlled the syntactic rule of equi-NP deletion in the then prevailing framework was the one closest to the deletion target in the syntactic structure. This principle governed the choice of controller in what were considered to be the "normal" cases. These were sentences containing verbs like *try, force, ask, tell,* and so forth, in sentences like (2.2a), (2.3a), and (2.6a), above.

An analog of this principle can be formulated as a condition on the Co-Indexing operation in (2.11). This appears in (2.14):

(2.14)   The F-structure Minimal Distance Principle (FMDP):   NP* arguments are co-indexed with the closest NP argument of the matrix predicate in (complex) PRED/ARG structures.

The FMDP, as formulated here, chooses the antecedent NP argument of the NP* argument in the PRED/ARG structures of examples like the ones in (2.2a), (2.3a), and (2.6a), which contain controlled VP complements (the "classical" control verbs), as well as examples like (2.4), (2.5), and (2.7), which contain controlled complements of other categories. We see, then, how the choice of antecedent from among several NP arguments in the structure is determined. Let us now consider the constraints on externally controlled positions (target positions).

Only the initial NP argument of the predicate of a controlled complement can be externally controlled. Thus there are no predicates like *force* or *try,* say *force** and *try**, which occur with complements whose objects are controlled by some argument of the matrix predicate. Consider the following sentences, which contain such hypothetical predicates:

(2.15) a.   Jardine$_i$ forced* Brandt$_j$ to visit
       b.   Brandt$_i$ tried* to visit

Example (2.15a) cannot mean that Jardine forced Brandt to have someone visit him (Brandt), nor can (2.15b) mean that Brandt tried to get someone to visit him.

The non-existence of such predicate types follows automatically from the FMDP, suitably reformulated, and the fact that the Raqui rule is also a co-indexing rule. All PRED/ARG structures which contain externally contolled complements are of the following form after the application of the Co-Indexing rule:

(2.16) $PRED_i \ldots NP[i] \ldots [(_{NP*}[i])[PRED_2 \; NP_a \; NP_b \ldots]]$

The FMDP dictatates that only the NP_a argument of $PRED_2$, and not the NP_b argument, in structures like (2.16), can be co-indexed with the $NP*[i]$ argument. As a consequence, non-initial NP arguments of controlled complements are never externally controlled.[1] The FMDP as reformulated in (2.17), below, applies to both the Co-Indexing rule and the Raqui rule:

(2.17)   <u>FMDP2:</u> In complex PRED/ARG structures, co-indexing rules must involve the antecedent/target pair relevant to the operation whose members, φ and ψ, are least distantly separated.

The FMDP analysis extends without modification to sentences like the following, shown with their S-structures:

(2.18) a. $Jesse_i$ gave $Zelma_j$ the $letter_k$ unopened

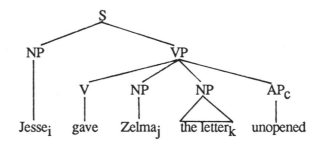

b. $Danton_i$ served the goanna $stew_j$ cold

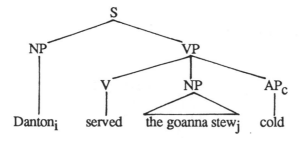

c. Smyth$_i$ carried Zelma$_j$ naked (through the town)

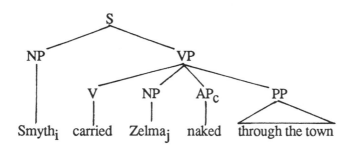

The verbs *give, serve,* and *carry* are not obligatory control verbs, and their basic F-structures do not contain controlled complement arguments. The derived F-structures of these examples are produced from PRED/ARG structures which are constructed by embedding the F-structure representation of the optional controlled complement in the PRED/ARG structure of the matrix predicate.[2] These structures are shown in (2.19), after the application of the Index Insertion rule and the SRA rule:

(2.19) a. GIVE   NP[i] NP[j] NP[k] [(NP*)[UNOPENED NP]]
                   α   β   γ   α
       b. SERVE   NP[i] NP[j] [(NP*)[COLD NP]]
                   α   β   α
       c. CARRY   NP[i] NP[j] [(NP*)[NAKED NP]]
                   α   β   α

The Co-Indexing rule must apply in (2.19a) to co-index the NP* argument and the NP[k] argument of GIVE, and it must apply in (2.19b and c) to co-index the NP* argument and the NP[j] arguments of SERVE and CARRY, respectively. In all cases, these are the closest NP arguments to the NP* argument, and the FMDP correctly predicts that these, and not the other NP arguments of the predicates, are the antecedents. The Raqui rule then applies to produce the derived F-structures of these examples, which appear in (2.20), below:

(2.20) a.   GIVE $\text{NP}^{[i]}_{\alpha}$ $\text{NP}^{[j]}_{\beta}$ $\text{NP}^{[k]}_{\gamma}$ [UNOPENED $\text{NP}^{[k]}_{\alpha}$]

   b.   SERVE $\text{NP}^{[i]}_{\alpha}$ $\text{NP}^{[j]}_{\beta}$ [COLD $\text{NP}^{[j]}_{\alpha}$]

   c.   CARRY $\text{NP}^{[i]}_{\alpha}$ $\text{NP}^{[j]}_{\beta}$ [NAKED $\text{NP}^{[j]}_{\alpha}$]

Finally, the FMDP analysis explains the behavior (in the relevant respects) of verbs like *seem* and *believe* in examples like the following:

(2.21) a.   Manfred$_i$ seemed to like Katrina$_j$
   b.   Nora$_i$ believed Percival$_j$ to be a pervert

As we saw in the last chapter, *believe* and *seem* differ from *force* and *try* in that the NP* argument in the basic F-structures of the former is assigned the feature [+GR], and has an S-structure correlate.   The S-structures of these sentences are shown in (2.22), below:

(2.22) a.

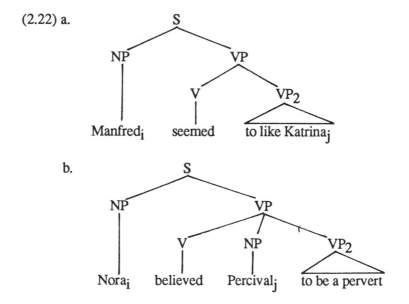

The derived F-structures of (2.21) are produced from the PRED/ARG structures in (2.23), shown after the application of the index insertion rule and the SRA rule:

(2.23)a.   SEEM   [$(_{NP*}[i])$[LIKE   NP   NP[j]]]
                            α β

b.   BELIEVE   NP[i]   [$(_{NP*}[j])$[[BE[PERVERT]]   NP]]
                      α α

The Raqui rule applies in each case to co-index the NP* argument and the NP argument of the embedded predicate. The resulting derived F-structures are shown in (2.24):

(2.24)a.   SEEM   [LIKE NP[i]   NP[j]]
                              α β

b.   BELIEVE   NP[i]   [[BE[PERVERT]]   NP[j]]
                        α α

The theory automatically accounts for the fact that the S-structure NP objects of verbs like *believe* and *seem* are interpreted as the subjects of the controlled complements, and not as non-subjects of these complements. That is, examples like the following do not have interpretations in which *Fiorella* is the object of the verb *visit* :

(2.25) a.   Whitsen$_i$ believed Fiorella$_j$ to have visited
       b.   Fiorella$_i$ seemed to visit

Example (2.25a) cannot mean that Whitsen believed someone to have visited Fiorella, and (2.25b) cannot mean that it seemed that someone visited Fiorella. The PRED/ARG structures of these examples, after the application of the index insertion rule and the SRA rule, and prior to the application of the Raqui rule, are shown in (2.26):

(2.26) a.   BELIEVE   NP[i]   [$(_{NP*}[j])$[VISIT   NP$_a$ NP$_b$]]
                              α α β

b.   SEEM   [$(_{NP*}[i])$[VISIT   NP$_a$ NP$_b$]]
                                              α β

As above, the Raqui rule can co-index the NP* argument and the closest NP argument of the complement predicate VISIT, that is, only with the NP$_a$ argument in each structure.   Consequently, in each case, *Fiorella* can only be interpreted as the subject of *visit*.

We see, then, that the same operation, the Raqui rule, applies to control verbs like *force* and *try*, and to verbs like *seem* and *believe*. This rule and the Co-indexing Rule are both, in fact, co-indexing operations, and both are constrained by the FMDP2, as formulated in (2.17). Consequently, these two rules can be combined and reformulated as a single general co-indexing rule. This rule is shown in (2.27):

(2.27)   <u>General Co-indexing Rule (GCR)</u>: In the PRED/ARG structure: [... φ... ψ...], co-index φ and ψ, and optionally delete φ.

In this rule, φ is the indexed NP antecedent and ψ is the unindexed NP target.

No constraints other than FMDP2 need to be placed on this rule as it applies to the cases discussed so far. In the co-indexing subcase, the antecedent φ is an NP[θ] argument of the predicate, and the target, ψ, is the unindexed NP* argument. (See, for example, Structures (2.10a and b).) In the Raqui subcase, the antecedent, φ, is the indexed NP* argument and the target, ψ, is the unindexed initial NP argument of the embedded predicate. Now let us reconsider example (2.3a), repeated below with its PRED/ARG structure after the application of the index insertion rule and the SRA rule:

(2.3) a.   Kelly$_i$ forced Cynthia$_j$ to commit unnatural acts$_k$

(2.10) b.   FORCE NP[i] NP[j] [(NP*)[COMMIT NP NP[k]]]
$\qquad\qquad\quad \alpha \quad \beta \qquad\qquad\qquad\quad \alpha \quad \beta$

For the co-indexing subcase of the GCR, the FMDP2 dictates that the antecedent, φ, is NP[j] of FORCE. The GCR applies to (2.10b) to produce the following:

(2.28)   FORCE NP[I] NP[j] [(NP*[j])[COMMIT NP NP[k]]]
$\qquad\qquad\quad \alpha \quad \beta \qquad\qquad\qquad\quad\quad \alpha \quad \beta$

If φ is deleted, then the predicate FORCE in the derived F-structure of the example will have no NP[j][β] argument, and consequently cannot be the basis of a complete interpretation of this sentence. However, an adequate derived F-structure for this sentence is produced if this optional deletion rule does not apply, so it need not be blocked in this case.

Now, for the Raqui subcase of the GCR, the antecedent, φ, is the $NP*[j]$ argument, and the FMDP2 dictates that the target is the initial NP argument of COMMIT. The GCR applies to (2.28) to produce the following:

(2.29)   FORCE $NP[i]$ $NP[j]$ $[(NP*[j])[COMMIT$ $NP[j]$ $NP[k]]]$
              α β α β

If the optional deletion of the φ argument does not take place, the resulting derived F-structure will be (2.29), above. However, this structure violates WFC I because it contains an indexed NP argument, $NP*[j]$. which is not assigned an SR. If the deletion process occurs, the well-formed derived F-structure shown below is produced, so the deletion process need not be obligatory here:

(2.30)   FORCE $NP[i]$ $NP[j]$ $[COMMIT$ $NP[j]$ $NP[k]]$
              α β α β

If the Co-indexing subcase of the GCR fails to apply to a structure like (2.10b), then the resulting derived F-structure will contain an NP argument, NP*, which is not indexed and does not bear an SR, again in violation of WFC I.   Similarly, if the Co-indexing subcase of the GCR applies and the Raqui subcase fails to apply, the resulting derived F-structure will contain an indexed NP argument, $NP*[j]$, that does not bear an SR (and an unindexed 1-NP argument of COMMIT that bears an SR.)   However, since a well-formed F-structure can be derived from (2.10b), neither subcase of the GCR need be obligatory. Hence, no constraints on applicability are required for this rule.

Although the FMDP is the primary condition which determines the choice of the antecedent from among several possible antecedents, and defines possible target (controlled) positions as well, there are additional constraints on possible antecedents themselves. These are rather complex. Working in their respective frameworks, Bresnan (1982d) lists some lexical restrictions on the controllers of embedded complements, and Chomsky (1981) suggests that θ-roles, pragmatic conditions, and/or semantic properties of verbs, as well as the possible requirement that the controller of an embedded complement be an element of the clausal argument structure of the matrix predicate, are all constraining factors. We can borrow, at least in spirit, from these observations and formulate the following constraints on possible controllers, that is, on possible antecedents, φ, of φ/ψ pairs co-indexed by the GCR:

(2.31) If the target, ψ, is the NP* argument of a controlled complement of the form [(NP*)XP] embedded in the PRED/ ARG structure of a predicate, $PRED_X$, then:
>   (a) the antecedent, φ, must be an NP argument of $PRED_X$;
>   (b) for predicates of Class X, the antecedent, φ, is the NP argument of the predicate that bears the designated SR, θ_X.

These conditions should be regarded as first approximations only, which are perhaps necessary, but certainly not sufficient. Some version of these (or rather, their analogs) is required by any adequate theory of control.

The condition in (2.31a) dictates that either the 1-NP argument, 2-NP argument or 3-NP argument of predicates like those in the examples discussed above is a possible antecedent of the NP* argument of a controlled complement. This condition distinguishes those examples and the examples in (2.32), below, from the examples in (2.33):

(2.32) a. Hermann$_i$ decided on the house$_j$ unpainted
>   b. Axelrod$_i$ took advantage$_k$ of the female prisoners$_j$ naked
>   c. Keyser$_i$ depended on Postal$_j$ to know the answers$_k$

(2.33) a. *Aethelbert$_i$ gave the manuscript$_j$ to Boris$_k$ naked
>   b. *Johannes$_i$ walked into the house$_j$ unlocked

In each of the examples in (2.32), the S-structure $_{NP}$[j] constituent can be interpreted as the controller of the optional controlled complement. In (2.33a), however, the optional controlled complement *naked* can only be controlled by the $_{NP}$[i] or the $_{NP}$[j] constituent, and not by the $_{NP}$[k] constituent, *Boris*. Similarly, in (2.33b), the controller of the complement *unlocked* cannot be the $_{NP}$[j] constituent *the house*. If the $_{NP}$[i] constituent *Johannes* is the controller of *unlocked,* the sentence has an odd interpretation, and this accounts for its unacceptability.

The predicates, $PRED_X$ of the examples in (2.32), are *decide on, take advantage of,* and *depend on.*   The basic F-structures of these predicates are shown in (2.34):

(2.34) a.   [DECIDE ON]   1-NP[α]   2-NP[β]
     b.   [TAKE NP^c[ζ]]   1-NP[α]   2-NP[β]
     c.   [DEPEND ON]   1-NP[α]   2-NP[β]

These predicates all have two (external) NP[θ] arguments.   The S-structure correlate of the 2-NP[β] argument, in each case, is the object of a preposition, NP$_j$. The derived F-structures of the examples in (2.32) are produced from the PRED/ARG structures in (2.35a, b, and c), shown after the application of the index insertion rule and the SRA rule:

(2.35) a.   [DECIDE ON]   NP[i]   NP[j]   [(NP*)[UNPAINTED   NP]]
                      α   β   α
     b.   [TAKE   NP^c[k]]   NP[i]   NP[j]   [(NP*)[NAKED   NP]]
                   ζ   α   β   α
     c.   [DEPEND ON]   NP[i]   NP[j]   [(NP*)[KNOW   NP   NP[k]]]
                      α   β   α   β

In these structures, both the NP[i] argument and the NP[j] argument are possible antecedents since they satisfy constraint (2.31a). The FMDP chooses the closest argument to the NP* target, and the Co-indexing and Raqui subcases of the GCR apply as discussed to produce the derived F-structures of these examples. These are shown below:

(2.36) a.   [DECIDE ON]   NP[i]   NP[j]   [UNPAINTED   NP[j]]
                      α   β   α
     b.   [TAKE   NP^c[k]]   NP[i]   NP[j]   [NAKED   NP[j]]
                   ζ   α   β   α
     c.   [DEPEND ON]   NP[i]   NP[j]   [KNOW   NP[j]   NP[k]]
                      α   β   α   β

The PRED$_x$ of (2.33a) is GIVE and that of (2.33b) is WALK. The basic F-structures of these predicates are shown in (2.37), below:

(2.37) a.   GIVE   1-NP[α]   2-NP[β]   PP
     b.   WALK   1-NP[α]

The derived F-structures of the examples in (2.33) are produced from the following PRED/ARG structures, shown after the application of the Index Insertion rule and the SRA rule:

(2.38) a.   GIVE $\text{NP}[i]$ $\text{NP}[j]$ [TO $\text{NP}[k]$]   [(NP*)[NAKED NP]]
         α β α α

       b.   WALK $\text{NP}[i]$ [INTO $\text{NP}[j]$]   [(NP*)[UNLOCKED NP]]
         α α α

In Structure (2.38a), NP_k is an an argument of TO, not GIVE, and in Structure (2.38b), NP_j is an argument of INTO, not WALK. Therefore, in (2.38a), only the $\text{NP}[i]$ argument and the $\text{NP}[j]$ argument of GIVE are possible antecedents, and in (2.38b), only the $\text{NP}[i]$ argument of WALK is a possible antecedent. The FMDP chooses the $\text{NP}[j]$ argument in (2.38a) as the antecedent and the lone $\text{NP}[i]$ argument in (2.38b) as the antecedent. The application of both of the subcases of the GCR produces the derived F-structures of these examples, which are shown below:

(2.39) a.   GIVE $\text{NP}[i]$ $\text{NP}[j]$ [TO $\text{NP}[k]$]   [NAKED $\text{NP}[j]$]
         α β α α

       b.   WALK $\text{NP}[i]$ [INTO $\text{NP}[j]$]   [UNLOCKED $\text{NP}[i]$]
         α α α

The structure in (2.39a) is the basis for an odd interpretation of (2.33a) in which the letter is naked. This example is acceptable, however, with the interpretation that Aethelbert is naked. This interpretation derives from another possible F-structure for this sentence, which is discussed below. The structure in (2.39b) is the basis for the odd interpretation of (2.33b) mentioned above in which Johannes is unlocked. This accounts for the oddness of (2.33b) and the difference between (2.32) and (2.33).

The constraint in (2.31b) applies to a well-known and much-discussed class of apparent exceptions to the FMDP, two examples of which are shown in (2.40):

(2.40) a. Thor_i promised Agnes_j to leave
       b. Davis_i made Mavis_j a good husband

The basic F-structures of the verbs *promise* and *make* (in the intended sense) are shown in (2.41):

(2.41) a.   PROMISE   1-NP[α]   2-NP[β]   [(NP*)VP]

   b.   MAKE   1-NP[α]   2-NP[β]   [(NP*)NP]

The PRED/ARG structures of the examples in (2.40), after the application of the index insertion rule and the SRA rule, are (2.42a and b), respectively:

(2.42) a.   PROMISE   NP[i] NP[j] [(NP*)[LEAVE NP]]
                         α β α

   b.   MAKE   NP[i] NP[j] [(NP*)[[GOOD HUSBAND] NP]]
                   α β α

In both of these structures, the NP[j] argument is an argument of the matrix predicate, and is the closest argument to the target NP* argument. Yet the NP[i] argument, in each case, must be the antecedent φ for the Co-indexing subcase of the GCR. *Promise* and *make* in this sense are subject to the constraint in (2.31b). The controller of the complement of these verbs must be designated as the NP argument that bears a particular specified SR, say θ_p for *promise* and θ_m for *make*. In both cases, this is the SR borne by their 1-NP arguments (represented as α in (2.41) and (2.42) above.) Therefore, their 2-NP arguments cannot be the antecedents of the NP* arguments of their complements. The NP[i] arguments in (2.42a and b) are the only possible antecedents, and are therefore the closest possible antecedents. The C o-indexing and Raqui subcases of the GCR apply to (2.42) to produce the derived F-structures of the examples in (2.40). These are shown in (2.43), below:[3]

(2.43) a.   PROMISE   NP[i] NP[j] [LEAVE NP[i]]
                         α β α

   b.   MAKE   NP[i] NP[j] [[GOOD HUSBAND] NP[i]]
                   α β α

Examples like (2.33a), repeated below, and the following are also exceptions to the FMDP:

(2.33) a.   ?Aethelbert$_i$ gave the manuscript$_j$ to Boris$_k$ naked

(2.44) a.   Sebastian$_i$ served the koalaburgers$_j$ naked
   b.   Efraim$_i$ spotted Senta$_j$ walking down the corridor$_k$
   c.   Ferguson$_i$ arrested transgressors$_j$ as a part-time policeman

These examples also contain optional controlled complements of various syntactic categories. In all cases, the subject of the matrix predicate, the NP[i] constituent, can be interpreted as the controller of the complement. For pragmatic reasons, this is the only plausible interpretation of (2.33a) and (2.44a) since manuscripts and koalaburgers are not often thought of as being naked.

As we saw in Chapter II, optional controlled complements can occur in S-structures embedded in the VP of the matrix predicate (as in the S-structures of examples (2.18) above) or adjoined to the VP of the matrix predicate.   Examples (2.33a) and (2.44) with the interpretations in which the NP[i] constituent is the controller of the complement have the latter type of S-structure.[4] The S-structures of these examples are shown below:

(2.45) a.

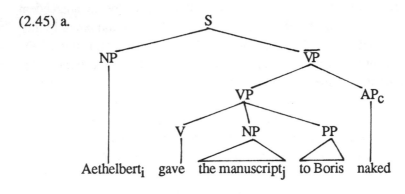

b.

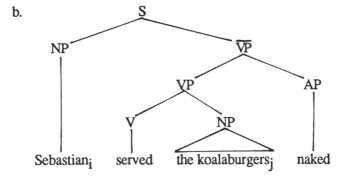

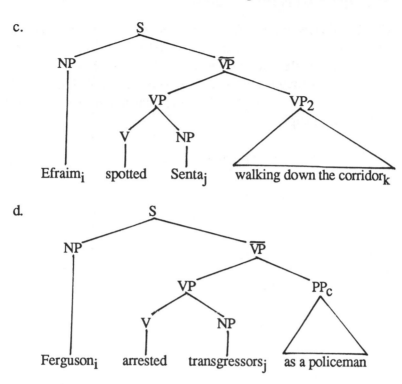

The derived F-structures of these sentences are produced from the PRED/ARG structures in (2.46) below, shown after the application of the index insertion rule and the SRA rule:

(2.46) a. [GIVE $_{NP[i]}$ $_{NP[j]}$ [TO $_{NP[k]}$]][(NP*)[NAKED NP]]
                   α   β   α   α

   b. [SERVE $_{NP[i]}$ $_{NP[j]}$][(NP*)[NAKED NP]]
                     α   β   α

   c. [SPOT $_{NP[i]}$ $_{NP[j]}$][(NP*)[WALKING NP [DOWN
                   α   β   α
       $_{NP[k]}$]]]
           α

   d. [ARREST $_{NP[i]}$ $_{NP[j]}$][(NP*)[POLICEMAN NP]]
                     α   β   α

In these structures, the F-structure representations of the controlled complements are adjoined to the PRED/ARG structures of the matrix predicates. In all cases, both the $_{NP[i]}$ argument and the $_{NP[j]}$ argument of the matrix predicate are possible antecedents of the NP* argument in the absence of constraints to prevent this. The FMDP, as formulated in

(2.17), chooses the $_{NP}[j]$ argument as the antecedent. However, in (2.33a) and (2.44), as we saw, the $_{NP}[i]$ argument must be the antecedent for the relevant interpretations. The choice of the antecedent in PRED/ARG structures like (2.46), which contrast with the PRED/ARG structures of the examples discussed earlier, is determined by the following principle:

(2.47)   <u>The Default Principle</u>: If the target ψ is the NP* argument of a controlled complement of the form [(NP*)XP] which is adjoined to the PRED/ARG structure of a predicate, $PRED_x$, then the antecedent ϕ is the 1-NP argument of $PRED_x$.

The co-indexing and Raqui subcases of the GCR apply to the structures in (2.46) in accordance with the Default Principle to produce the derived F-structures of (2.33a) and (2.44). These appear in (2.48), below:

(2.48) a.   [GIVE $_{NP}[i]$ $_{NP}[j]$ [TO $_{NP}[k]$]][NAKED $_{NP}[i]$]
$\qquad\qquad\;\; \alpha \qquad \beta \qquad\quad \alpha \qquad\qquad\quad \alpha$

   b.   [SERVE $_{NP}[i]$ $_{NP}[j]$][NAKED $_{NP}[i]$]
$\qquad\qquad\quad\; \alpha \qquad \beta \qquad\qquad\quad \alpha$

   c.   [SPOT $_{NP}[i]$ $_{NP}[j]$][WALKING $_{NP}[i]$ [DOWN $_{NP}[k]$]]
$\qquad\qquad\;\; \alpha \qquad \beta \qquad\qquad\quad \alpha \qquad\qquad\;\; \alpha$

   d.   [ARREST $_{NP}[i]$ $_{NP}[j]$][POLICEMAN $_{NP}[i]$]
$\qquad\qquad\;\; \alpha \qquad \beta \qquad\qquad\qquad\;\; \alpha$

The FMDP, then, applies without exception to determine the choice of antecedent when the controlled complement is embedded in the PRED/ARG structure of the matrix predicate in structures like (2.10), (2.19), (2.23), (2.35), and (2.38). It applies regardless of whether the controlled complement is an obligatory argument in the basic F-structure of the predicate (with verbs like *try* and *force*) or an optional argument in the complex PRED/ARG structure of a sentence that contains a non-control verb (like *give, serve,* and *carry*). The Default Principle applies to those PRED/ARG structures like (2.46), in which the controlled complement is not embedded in the PRED/ARG structure of the matrix predicate.

Examples like (2.18), (2.32), (2.33), and (2.44) can be assigned S-structures like the ones in (2.18), or S-structures like the ones in (2.45). Consequently, either derived F-structures like (2.20) and (2.36) or derived F-structures like (2.48) can be produced for them. This accounts for the real or potential ambiguity of such sentences, disregarding the pragmatic factors alluded to above.

3. Bound Anaphora

The analysis extends naturally to account for the behavior of overt anaphors (reflexives and reciprocals). Consider the following sentences:

(3.1) a.   Archibald$_i$ hated himself

    b.   Those basset hounds$_i$ disliked each other

I assume here that the general indexing operation discussed in Chapter II does not apply to overt anaphors. Consequently, these do not have indices at the level of S-structure. However, S-structure NPs with the feature [+ANAPHOR], which I adopt as a cover symbol for [+REFLEX] and [+RECIPROCAL], are represented in PRED/ARG structures. The examples in (3.1) have the following PRED/ARG structures, after the application of the Index Insertion rule and the SRA rule:

(3.2) a.   HATE   NP[i]   NP[+REFLEX]
               α β

    b.   DISLIKE   NP[i]   NP[+RECIPROCAL]
                  α β

Overt anaphors must be co-indexed with some other NP argument in the PRED/ARG structure. The operation that does this can be formulated as shown in (3.3):

(3.3)   <u>Reflexive/Reciprocal Co-Indexing</u>:
     NP[i] ... NP[+ANAPHOR]
       1   2   ===>   1   NP[+ANAPHOR$_i$]

From a formal viewpoint, ignoring details, this rule, like the Co-indexing rule and Raqui rule, is a subcase of the GCR as formulated in (2.27). Here, the target ψ is an NP with the feature [+ANAPHOR]. Consequently, unless otherwise stipulated, the FMDP applies to it. Examples like (3.4), however, suggest that some such stipulation is required:

(3.4) a.   Mahoney$_i$ told Mallone$_j$ about himself

    b.   The Simpsons$_i$ told their friends$_j$ about each other

The PRED/ARG structures of these examples, after the application of the Index Insertion rule and the SRA rule, are the following:

(3.5) a.   TELL $NP[i]$ $NP[j]$ [ABOUT $NP[+REFLEX]$]]
                    α β α

   b.   TELL $NP[i]$ $NP[j]$ [ABOUT $NP[+RECIPROCAL]$]]
                    α β α

In example (3.4a), the reflexive *himself* can refer to either *Mallone* or *Mahoney*, and in (3.4b), the reciprocal form *each other* can refer to either *The Simpsons* or *their friends*. This means that either the $NP[i]$ argument or the $NP[j]$ argument in the PRED/ARG structures in (3.5) can be the antecedent of the [+ANAPHOR] argument. The FMDP can be slightly modified to apply to this subcase of the GCR as shown below:

(3.6)   If the target, ψ, is an NP argument with the feature [+ANAPHOR], then the antecedent, φ is the closest indexed NP argument in the PRED/ARG structure, or the closest indexed 1-NP argument (subject) of the relevant predicate.

The reflexive/reciprocal subcase of the GCR applies in accordance with (3.6) to the structures in (3.5) to produce the structures in (3.7) and (3.8) below:

(3.7) a.   TELL $NP[i]$ $NP[j]$ [ABOUT $NP[+REFLEX_j]$]]
                    α β α

   b.   TELL $NP[i]$ $NP[j]$ [ABOUT $NP[+REFLEX_i]$]]
                    α β α

(3.8) a.   TELL $NP[i]$ $NP[j]$ [ABOUT $NP[+RECIPROCAL_j]$]]
                    α β α

   b.   TELL $NP[i]$ $NP[j]$ [ABOUT $NP[+RECIPROCAL_i]$]]
                    α β α

The structures in (3.7) are the derived F-structures of example (3.4a). In (3.7a), the [+REFLEX] NP argument of the predicate ABOUT is co-indexed with the closest indexed NP argument, the $NP[j]$ argument of TELL. In (3.7b), the [+REFLEX] NP argument is co-indexed with the 1-NP argument of TELL, $NP[i]$. The structures in (3.8) are the derived F-structures of example (3.4b). In (3.8a), the [+RECIPROCAL] NP argument of the predicate ABOUT is co-indexed with the closest indexed NP, the $_{NP}[j]$ argument of TELL, and in (3.8b), it is co-indexed with the 1-NP argument of TELL, $_{NP}[i]$. This accounts for the ambiguity of these examples.

In some languages, [+ANAPHOR] arguments can only refer to the subject of the sentence, suggesting that there is parametric variation associated with the subcase of the FMDP in (3.6) above. Polish is such a language. The Polish counterparts of the examples in (3.4) are unambiguous. These appear in (3.9):

(3.9) a. Jacek$_i$ powiedział Włodzimierzowi$_j$ o sobie
   Jacek (NOM) told Włodzimierz (DAT) about himself (LOC)
   Jacek told Włodzimierz about himself

   b. ?Jacek$_i$ spytał Adama$_j$ o siebie
   Jacek (NOM) asked Adam (ACC) about himself (ACC)
   ?Jacek asked Adam about himself

   c. Przyjaciele$_i$ nigdy nie rozmawiają z wrogami$_j$ o sobie
   Friends (NOM) never not talk with enemies (LOC) about each other (LOC)
   Friends never talk with enemies about each other

In example (3.9a), *sobie* can only refer to *Jacek*; in example (3.9b), *siebie* can only refer to *Jacek*, and in (3.9c), *sobie* can only refer to *przyjaciele*. Example (3.9b) is odd for the same reason that its English translational equivalent is odd with the interpretation in which *himself* refers to *Jacek*.

These examples have the following PRED/ARG structures after the application of the index insertion rule and the SRA rule:

(3.10) a. POWIEDZIEĆ $_{NP}[i]$ $_{NP}[j]$ [O $_{NP}$[+REFLEX]]
                        α   β   α
      b. SPYTAĆ $_{NP}[i]$ $_{NP}[j]$ [O $_{NP}$[+REFLEX]]
                    α   β   α
      c. ROZMAWIAĆ $_{NP}[i]$ [Z $_{NP}[j]$] [O $_{NP}$[+REFLEX]]
                        α   α   α

In these structures, the [+REFLEX] argument must be co-indexed with the $_{NP}[i]$ argument. This is the closest indexed 1-NP argument, or subject, of the relevant predicate. So, in Polish and languages of this type, the first member of the disjunction in (3.6) is inapplicable. The subcase of the FMDP which applies to languages of this type appears in (3.11):

(3.11)   If the target ψ is an NP argument with the feature [+ANAPHOR], then the antecedent φ is the closest indexed 1-NP argument (subject) of the relevant predicate.

The reflexive/reciprocal subcase of the GCR applies in accordance with (3.11) to the structures in (3.10) to produce the derived F-structures of the examples in (3.9). These are shown in (3.12), below:

(3.12) a.   POWIEDZIEĆ $\text{NP}^{[i]}$ $\text{NP}^{[j]}$ [O $\text{NP}^{[+\text{REFLEX}_i]}$]]
$\quad\quad\quad\quad\quad\quad\quad\quad\alpha\quad\quad\beta\quad\quad\quad\quad\alpha$

b.   SPYTAĆ $\text{NP}^{[i]}$ $\text{NP}^{[j]}$ [O $\text{NP}^{[+\text{REFLEX}_i]}$]]
$\quad\quad\quad\quad\quad\alpha\quad\quad\beta\quad\quad\quad\alpha$

c.   ROZMAWIAĆ $\text{NP}^{[i]}$ [Z $\text{NP}^{[j]}$]] [O $\text{NP}^{[+\text{REFLEX}_i]}$]]
$\quad\quad\quad\quad\quad\quad\quad\alpha\quad\quad\quad\alpha\quad\quad\quad\quad\alpha$

The statements in (3.6) and (3.11) are special exceptions to the general FMDP as formulated in (2.17). The situations in which the closest indexed NP argument is the antecedent of the [+ANAPHOR] argument follow from the general statement of the FMDP. Such a situation is illustrated by the English examples in (3.4) with the derived F-structures in (3.7a) and (3.8a). Therefore, the condition peculiar to bound anaphors can be extracted from the conditions in (3.6) and (3.11). This appears in (3.13):

(3.13)   If the target ψ is an NP argument with the feature [+ANAPHOR], then the antecedent φ is the 1-NP argument of the relevant predicate - optionally in languages of type X and obligatorily in languages of type Y.

English must be designated as a language of type X, and Polish must be designated as a language of type Y. If the special exception in (3.13) does not apply, then the general FMDP applies. If (3.13) applies, and the structure contains more than one indexed 1-NP argument, the FMDP chooses the closest one to the target as the antecedent. This is discussed later in the section.

The special condition in (3.13) is one of two conditions pertaining to bound anaphors that are required by the theory. The GCR,
along with this condition, the general FMDP, and the second condition,
which is discussed below, explains the distribution and interpretation of
reflexive and reciprocal NP constituents.

We have seen how the reflexive/reciprocal subcase of the GCR
applies to examples like (3.1) and (3.4) above. Now, consider the examples in (3.14) below:

(3.14) a.   Hortense$_i$ believed herself to be intelligent
       b.   Delilah$_i$ seemed to dislike herself
       c.   Kmak$_i$ forced Kowalski$_j$ to shave himself

The PRED/ARG structure of (3.14a), after the application of the
index insertion rule and the SRA rule, is shown in (3.15):

(3.15)   BELIEVE $_{NP[i]}$ [($_{NP*}$[+REFLEX]) [[BE[INTELLIGENT]]
         α
         NP]]
         α

The reflexive subcase of the GCR applies to co-index the [+REFLEX]
argument and its antecedent, which is the 1-NP argument of BELIEVE
(the closest indexed NP to the target.) This produces the structure in
(3.16):

(3.16)   BELIEVE $_{NP[i]}$ [($_{NP*}$[+REFLEX$_i$]) [[BE [INTELLIGENT]]
         α
         NP]]
         α

The Raqui subcase of the GCR applies to this structure to co-index the
NP argument of [BE[INTELLIGENT]], which is the closest possible
target, and the NP* argument, and the NP* argument is deleted. The resulting F-structure is shown in (3.17):

(3.17)   BELIEVE $_{NP[i]}$ [[BE[INTELLIGENT]] $_{NP}$[+REFLEX$_i$]]
         α α

This is the derived F-structure of example (3.14a).[5]

The PRED/ARG structure of example (3.14b) after the application of
the index insertion rule and the SRA rule appears in (3.18), below:

(3.18)   SEEM [($_{NP^*}$[i])[DISLIKE NP $_\alpha$ NP$_\beta$[+REFLEX]]]

The Raqui subcase of the GCR applies to co-index the NP* argument and the 1-NP argument of DISLIKE, which is the closest possible target. The NP* argument is then deleted. This produces the following structure:

(3.19)   SEEM [DISLIKE NP$_\alpha$[i] NP$_\beta$[+REFLEX]]

Now the application of the reflexive subcase of the GCR is straightforward. The NP[i] argument of DISLIKE is the closest possible antecedent. The resulting derived F-structure of example (3.14b) is shown in (3.20), below:

(3.20)   SEEM [DISLIKE NP$_\alpha$[i] NP$_\beta$[+REFLEX$_i$]]

Finally, the PRED/ARG structure of example (3.14c) after the application of the index insertion rule and the SRA rule is shown in (3.21):

(3.21)   FORCE NP$_\alpha$[i] NP$_\beta$[j] [(NP*)[SHAVE NP$_\alpha$ NP$_\beta$[+REFLEX]]]

The co-indexing subcase of the GCR applies to this structure in accordance with the FMDP to co-index the NP* argument and the NP[j] argument of FORCE, and the Raqui subcase of the GCR applies to co-index the NP* argument and the 1-NP argument of SHAVE, which is the closest possible target, and delete the NP* argument. This produces the structure in (3.22), below:

(3.22)   FORCE NP$_\alpha$[i] NP$_\beta$[j] [SHAVE NP$_\alpha$[j] NP$_\beta$[+REFLEX]]

Now the reflexive subcase of the GCR applies to co-index the [+REFLEX] argument and the NP[j] argument of SHAVE, which is the closest NP argument in the PRED/ARG structure. This produces the derived F-structure of (3.14c), which appears below:

(3.23)   FORCE $_{NP[i]}$ $_{NP[j]}$ [SHAVE $_{NP[j]}$ $_{NP[+REFLEX_j]}$]]
                 α β α β

For languages like Polish, as we saw earlier, the condition in (3.13) is obligatory. With this in mind, consider the following sentence:

(3.24)   Zbigniew$_i$ nauczył niedźwiedzia$_j$ szczypać się w łapęk
         Zbigniew (NOM) taught bear (ACC) (to) pinch self on paw
         (ACC)
         Zigniew taught the bear to pinch itself on the paw

The PRED/ARG structure of this example, after the application of the index insertion rule and the SRA rule, is the following:

(3.25)   NAUCZYĆ $_{NP[i]}$ $_{NP[j]}$ [(NP*) [SZCZYPAĆ NP
                 α β α

$_{NP[+REFLEX]}$ [W $_{NP[k]}$]]]]
   β α

The co-indexing and Raqui subcases of the GCR apply to this structure to produce the structure in (3.26), below:

(3.26)   NAUCZYĆ $_{NP[i]}$ $_{NP[j]}$ [SZCZYPAĆ $_{NP[j]}$ $_{NP[+REFLEX]}$
                 α β α β
         [W $_{NP[k]}$]]]
              α

Now, in accordance with (3.13), the 1-NP argument of NAUCZYĆ, $_{NP[i]}$, and the 1-NP argument of SZCZYPAĆ, $_{NP[j]}$, are possible antecedents of the [+REFLEX] NP argument. The FMDP chooses the closest one, the $_{NP[j]}$ argument of SZCZYPAĆ. The reflexive subcase of the GCR applies to the structure in (3.26) to produce the derived F-structure of example (3.24), which is shown below:

(3.27)   NAUCZYĆ $_{NP[i]}$ $_{NP[j]}$ [SZCZYPAĆ $_{NP[j]}$ $_{NP[+REFLEX_j]}$]
                 α β α β
         [W $_{NP[k]}$]]]
              α

Now consider the following ungrammatical examples:

(3.28) a. *Himself saw Greystoke$_i$
　　　b. *Hortense$_i$ believed that herself was intelligent
　　　c. *Alycia$_i$ believed the frogs$_j$ to like herself
　　　d. *Alycia$_i$ forced the frogs$_j$ to like herself

The PRED/ARG structure of (3.28a), after the application of the index insertion rule and the SRA rule, is (3.29):

(3.29)   SEE $_{NP}$[+REFLEX] $_{NP}$[i]
　　　　　　　　α　　　　　　　β

The GCR as formulated in (2.27) does not apply to this structure. The target ψ is the [+REFLEX] argument, and no potential antecedent φ precedes it in the structure. Consequently, this is the derived F-structure of (3.28a).   Structure (3.29), however, is not well-formed. It contains an NP argument (the [+REFLEX] NP) which bears an SR, but no index, in violation of WFC I. This explains the ungrammaticality of example (3.28a).

　　The PRED/ARG structure of example (3.28b) after the application of the index insertion rule and the SRA rule is shown in (3.30):

(3.30) BELIEVE $_{NP}$[i] [[BE[INTELLIGENT][+T]] $_{NP}$[+REFLEX]]
　　　　　　　　　α　　　　　　　　　　　　　　　　　　　α

In this structure, the only potential antecedent for the $_{NP}$[+REFLEX] argument is the $_{NP}$[i] argument of BELIEVE. However, in contrast with the PRED/ARG structures discussed earlier, this structure contains a tensed (+T) complement. Let us assume that the reflexive/reciprocal subcase of the GCR is subject to the condition in (3.31):

(3.31)   If φ is an NP argument of PRED$_x$ and ψ is an NP argument of PRED$_y$, then PRED$_y$ must have the feature [-TENSE].

This is the second and last condition peculiar to this subcase that is required by the theory. According to Condition (3.31), the GCR can apply to φ/ψ pairs when both the antecedent and target are arguments of the same predicate, in structures like (3.2), (3.19), and (3.22); and to φ/ψ pairs when φ and ψ are arguments of different predicates and $PRED_y$ is the predicate of a [-TENSE] XP complement, as in structures (3.16), (3.18), (3.21), and so forth; or $PRED_y$ is a prepositional predicate of a [-TENSE] PP complement, as in Structures (3.5a), (3.10).[6] The condition in (3.31), however, prevents the application of the reflexive/reciprocal subcase of the GCR to the $NP[i]$ antecedent and the $NP[+REFLEX]$ target in structures like (3.30). Consequently, the $NP[+REFLEX]$ argument cannot be indexed, and the structure, which is the derived F-structure of (3.28b), violates WFC I. This accounts for the ungrammaticality of example (3.28b).

The PRED/ARG structure of Example (3.28c), after the application of the Index Insertion rule, the SRA rule, and the Raqui subcase of the GCR, is shown in (3.32):

(3.32)   BELIEVE $NP[i]$ [LIKE $NP[j]$ $NP[+REFLEX]$]]
$\qquad\qquad\quad \alpha \qquad\qquad\ \alpha \qquad \beta$

In this structure, both the 1-NP argument of BELIEVE, $NP[i]$, and the 1-NP argument of LIKE, $NP[j]$, are potential antecedents of the $NP[+REFLEX]$ argument. The FMDP chooses the closest one, $NP[j]$, and the GCR applies to produce the structure in (3.33):

(3.33)   BELIEVE $NP[i]$ [LIKE $NP[j]$ $NP[+REFLEX_j]$]]
$\qquad\qquad\quad \alpha \qquad\qquad\ \alpha \qquad \beta$

However, in example (3.28c), the reflexive form *herself* can only refer to *Alycia*, the $NP[i]$ constituent, and not to *the frogs*, the $NP[j]$ constituent, and as a result, this example is ungrammatical.

The PRED/ARG structure of example (3.28d), after the application of the index insertion rule, the SRA rule, and the co-indexing and Raqui subcases of the GCR, appears in (3.34):

(3.34)   FORCE $NP[i]$ $NP[j]$ [LIKE $NP[j]$ $NP[+REFLEX]$]]
$\qquad\qquad\ \ \alpha \qquad \beta \qquad\qquad \alpha \qquad \beta$

In this structure, both the $NP[i]$ and $NP[j]$ arguments of FORCE, and the $NP[j]$ argument of LIKE are potential antecedents of the $NP[+REFLEX]$ argument. The FMDP applies to choose the $NP[j]$ argument of LIKE as the antecedent, and the GCR applies to produce the derived F-structure of example (3.28d), which appears below:

(3.35)   FORCE $NP[i]$ $NP[j]$ [LIKE $NP[j]$ $NP[+REFLEX_j]$]]
$\quad\quad\quad\quad\quad\alpha\quad\;\;\beta\quad\quad\quad\quad\alpha\quad\;\;\beta$

As above, the reflexive form *herself* can refer only to *Alycia*, and not to *the frogs*. This explains the ungrammaticality of (3.28d).

We see, then, that the reflexive/reciprocal rule in (3.3) is a subcase of the GCR as formulated in (2.27). The GCR, and associated principles, accounts for the distribution and interpretation of bound anaphors. For this subcase, the antecedent φ is an indexed NP argument in the PRED/ARG structure and the target ψ is an unindexed NP argument with the feature [+ANAPHOR]. The theory explains the contrast between grammatical sentences like (3.1), (3.4), (3.9), and (3.14), and ungrammatical sentences like (3.28). For languages like English, Condition (3.13) is optional. The FMDP dictates that the GCR can co-index a [+ANAPHOR] target with either the closest indexed NP argument or the closest indexed 1-NP argument in the PRED/ARG structure. In Structures (3.19), (3.22), (3.32), and (3.34), the closest indexed NP argument to the target is the closest indexed 1-NP argument, and this must be the antecedent φ. Only in structures like (3.5) and (3.10) are these arguments distinct. For languages like Polish, the condition in (3.13) is obligatory. The FMDP dictates that the antecedent φ of a [+ANAPHOR] target is the closest indexed 1-NP argument in the PRED/ARG structure, in structures like (3.26). The so-called clause-mate condition on reflexive and reciprocal forms and their antecedents is a consequence of the FMDP and the condition in (3.31). Finally, if the antecedent NP argument is an NP[θ] argument of some predicate, and is deleted in accordance with the optional component of the GCR in (2.27) in structures like the ones discussed in this section, the resulting derived F-structure will lack an argument and cannot be the basis for a complete interpretation of the relevant sentence. However, just as this need not be blocked for the co-indexing subcase, as discussed in Section 2, it need not be blocked for the reflexive/reciprocal subcase.[7]

I turn now to disjoint reference data. The indices of pronominal forms have two sources: the general S-structure indexing operation discussed in Chapter II and an S-structure co-indexing operation. Either operation can apply to the following example:

(3.36)   Ladurie$_i$ said that he believed that the Great Atlantic
Optimum$_j$ prevailed throughout the third millenium BC$_k$

The general indexing operation can assign an arbitrary index, say m, to
the pronoun *he*, or alternatively, the co-indexing operation can assign
the index i of the NP *Ladurie* to this pronoun. The resulting derived F-
structures appear in (3.37), below:

(3.37)a.   SAY $_{NP[i]}$ [BELIEVE $_{NP[m]}$ [PREVAIL $_{NP[j]}$
α α α
[THROUGHOUT $_{NP[k]}$]]]
α

   b.   SAY $_{NP[i]}$ [BELIEVE $_{NP[i]}$ [PREVAIL $_{NP[j]}$
α α α

[THROUGHOUT $_{NP[k]}$]]]
α

The structure in (3.37a) is the basis for the interpretation of (3.36) in
which Ladurie says that someone else holds the belief, and the structure
in (3.37b) is the basis for the interpretation in which Ladurie says that
he, Ladurie, holds the belief. This accounts for the ambiguity of this
sentence.

Now consider the following example:

(3.38)   Hortense$_i$ disliked her

Again, either operation can apply. The general indexing operation can
assign the pronoun *her* an arbitrary index, say j, or the co-indexing
operation can assign this pronoun the index i of *Hortense*. The resulting
derived F-structures appear in (3.39a and b), respectively:

(3.39)a.   DISLIKE $_{NP[i]}$ $_{NP[j]}$
α β
   b.   DISLIKE $_{NP[i]}$ $_{NP[i]}$
α β

The structure in (3.39a) is well-formed and is the basis for the only
interpretation of (3.38), in which Hortense dislikes some other person,
the disjoint reference interpretation. In Structure (3.39b), however,
two identical NP arguments appear in the argument structure of the
predicate DISLIKE. As discussed in Chapter II, this structure is equiv-

alent to the structure in (3.40), below:

(3.40)   DISLIKE $\underset{\alpha}{NP}\underset{\beta}{[i]}$

This structure is not well-formed. The NP argument bears two SRs, in violation of WFC I. Consequently, this structure, and its equivalent in (3.39b), cannot be the basis for an interpretation of example (3.38), and this example can only have the disjoint reference interpretation.[8]

The general principles of the theory, then, define those positions in which pronouns must have a disjoint reference interpretation. As a consequence of these principles, a pronoun cannot be co-indexed with an NP antecedent in the argument structure of the same predicate. Structures like (3.37b) contrast with ones like (3.39b) in this respect. In the former case, the $NP[i]$ antecedent and the $NP[i]$ target are located in the argument structures of different predicates, SAY and BELIEVE, respectively. In the latter case, both the antecedent and target are located in the argument structure of the predicate DISLIKE.[9]

As we saw in Chapter II, both prepositions and nouns can function as the predicates of uncontrolled embedded complements, which are analogous to uncontrolled S complements in examples like (3.36). The theory predicts that the pronominal arguments of such predicates can refer to antecedents in the same sentence in examples like the following:

(3.41) a. $Rambo_i$ kept a gun_j near him at all $times_m$
       b. $Portnoy_i$ liked those books about him

In example (3.41a), the pronoun *him* can refer either to Rambo or to someone else, and in example (3.41b), *him* can refer either to Portnoy or to someone else. The reason for this is that, in both cases, either the general S-structure indexing operation can apply to assign some arbitrary index, say *k*, to these pronouns, or the S-structure co-indexing operation can apply to assign the index *i*, of *Rambo* and *Portnoy* respectively, to the pronoun. The resulting derived F-structures of (3.41) in the latter case are shown in (3.42):[10]

(3.42) a.   KEEP $\underset{\alpha}{NP}[i]$ $\underset{\beta}{NP}[j]$ [NEAR $\underset{\alpha}{NP}[i]$] [AT $\underset{\alpha}{NP}[m]$]]

b.   LIKE NP[i]_α NP[[BOOK NP[DET]_α $\text{NP[i]]}_{\beta}{}_k$]
   (α   β   α   β)

These structures are analogous to the structure in (3.37b). In (3.42a), the target is the NP[i] argument of the predicate NEAR and the antecedent is the NP[i] argument of the predicate KEEP. In (3.42b), the target is the NP[i] argument of the predicate BOOK and the antecedent is the NP[i] argument of the predicate LIKE. So in both cases, the antecedent and target are located in the argument structures of different predicates. These derived F-structures are well-formed and thus form the basis for the interpretations of the sentences in (3.41) in which the pronouns do not have a disjoint reference interpretation.[11]

   The theory also explains the partial overlap in the distribution of bound anaphors and pronouns which do not have a disjoint reference interpretation in examples like (3.41). Reflexive forms can also occur in such examples, as shown in (3.43):

(3.43) a.   ?Rambo$_i$ kept a gun$_j$ near himself at all times$_k$
       b.   Portnoy$_i$ liked books about himself

These examples have PRED/ARG structures like the following after the application of the index insertion rule and the SRA rule:

(3.44) a.   KEEP NP[i] NP[j] [NEAR NP[+REFLEX]] . . .
       (α   β   α)
       b.   LIKE NP[i] NP[[BOOK NP NP[+REFLEX]]_k]
       (α   β   α   β)

The reflexive subcase of the GCR applies to Structure (3.44a) as discussed above to co-index the [+REFLEX] NP target in the tenseless embedded complement and the NP[i] argument of KEEP, which is the closest 1-NP argument to the target. This produces the derived F-structure of (3.43a), which appears in (3.45), below:[12]

(3.45)   KEEP NP[i] NP[j] [NEAR $\text{NP[+REFLEX}_i\text{]]}$ . . .
       (α   β   α)

   To produce the derived F-structure of example (3.43b) from the structure in (3.44b), the long-range subcase of the GCR which is discussed in Section 4 applies to co-index the initial NP argument of BOOK and the $NP[i]$ argument of LIKE. This produces the structure in (3.46):

$$(3.46) \quad \text{LIKE} \underset{\alpha}{NP[i]} \underset{\beta}{NP[[BOOK} \underset{\alpha}{NP[i]} \underset{\beta}{NP[+REFLEX]]_k]}$$

Now, the reflexive subcase of the GCR applies in the normal way to co-index the [+REFLEX] NP argument and the $NP[i]$ argument of BOOK, to produce the structure in (3.47):

$$(3.47) \quad \text{LIKE} \underset{\alpha}{NP[i]} \underset{\beta}{NP[[BOOK} \underset{\alpha}{NP[i]} \underset{\beta}{NP[+REFLEX_i]]_k]}$$

This structure is well-formed, and is the basis for the relevant interpretation of the example.[13]

As I have suggested in several places throughout this chapter and Chapter II, prepositions do not always function as predicates. In the following examples, the prepositions are not independent predicates, and their S-structure NP objects are the correlates of NP arguments of the verbs in the sentences:

(3.48) a.   Petruccio$_i$ talked about Flora$_j$
     b.   Ethyl$_i$ depended on Randolf$_j$
     c.   Maureen$_i$ speaks of South Africans$_j$ quite highly

The predicates *talk about, depend on,* and *speak of* have basic F-structures that contain two $NP[\theta]$ arguments. The S-structure correlate of the 2-$NP[\beta]$ argument of *talk about* is the object of the preposition *about;* the S-structure correlate of the 2-$NP[\beta]$ argument of *depend on* is the object of the preposition *on;* and the S-structure correlate of the 2-$NP[\beta]$ argument of *speak of* is the object of the preposition *of.* The derived F-structures of the examples in (3.48) are shown in (3.49):

$$(3.49) \text{ a.} \quad [\text{TALK ABOUT}] \underset{\alpha}{NP[i]} \underset{\beta}{NP[j]}$$

$$\text{b.} \quad [\text{DEPEND ON}] \underset{\alpha}{NP[i]} \underset{\beta}{NP[j]}$$

$$\text{c.} \quad [\text{SPEAK OF}] \underset{\alpha}{NP[i]} \underset{\beta}{NP[j]}$$

It is easy to see that the proposed theory correctly predicts that either bound anaphors or pronouns with a disjoint reference interpretation, but not pronouns with a non-disjoint reference interpretation, can occupy the 2-NP[β] argument positions of such predicates. This is illustrated by the following examples:

(3.50)a. Petruccio$_i$ talked about him/himself
    b. Ethyl$_i$ depended on her/herself
    c. Maureen$_i$ speaks of her/herself quite highly

The pronouns in these examples, *him* in (3.50a) and *her* in (3.50b and c), can only refer to someone other than *Petruccio, Ethyl,* or *Maureen.* If the pronouns and the $_{NP}[i]$ constituents are co-indexed, the resulting derived F-structures are not well-formed for the reasons discussed above. Consequently, only if the pronouns bear some arbitrary index other than i in these examples can a well-formed derived F-structure be produced. This explains why the pronouns in these examples only have a disjoint reference interpretation. The reflexive subcase of the GCR can apply to the PRED/ARG structures of these examples when they contain [+ANAPHOR] NP arguments to produce well-formed derived F-structures, explaining the grammaticality of (3.50) with reflexive forms.

The situation is actually more complicated than these examples suggest. Other factors may well play a role and obscure the distributional patterns of bound anaphors and pronouns with and without a disjoint reference interpretation. However, the GCR analysis, along with various other elements of the proposed theory discussed here and in other chapters, provides the basis of an explanation of these data.[14]

4. The Long-Range Control Relation

The following examples illustrate the long-range control relation:

(4.1) a. Shaving himself in the morning was hard for Morrison$_i$
    b. Morrison$_i$ thought that shaving himself would disturb Mabel$_j$

The derivation of the F-structures of examples like these involves a rule that I call Subject Interpretation (SI). It is the analog of a cluster of rules that have been referred to as, among other names, super equi (Grinder (1970)), dative deletion, and picture noun reflexivization. In examples (4.1a and b), the NP *Morrison* is interpreted as the subject of the embedded predicate *shaving* and the antecedent of the reflexive form *himself*.

At the level of S-structure, the complement constructions, *shaving himself* in each case, are subjectless VPs embedded in NP positions, the subject position of the predicate *be hard* in (4.1a) and the subject position of *disturb* in (4.1b). The PRED/ARG structures of these sentences, after the application of the Index Insertion rule and the SRA rule, are shown in (4.2a and b), respectively:

(4.2) a.   [BE[HARD]] $_{NP}$[[SHAVING NP $_{NP}$[+REFLEX]]]
           [FOR $_{NP}$[i]]

    b.   THINK $_{NP}$[i] [DISTURB $_{NP}$[[SHAVING NP
           $_{NP}$[+REFLEX]]] $_{NP}$[j]]

All irrelevant information, including SRs and NP labels in some cases, will be omitted from the representations of F-structures throughout this discussion.

In the PRED/ARG structures in (4.2), the complements, *shaving himself* in each case, are embedded in the appropriate 1-NP argument positions of the predicates [BE[HARD]] and DISTURB, as discussed in Chapter II, Section 4. In these structures, the unindexed NP argument of SHAVING and the $_{NP}$[i] argument of FOR and THINK, respectively, must be co-indexed. This is accomplished by the SI rule, which is formulated in (4.3):

(4.3)   <u>Subject Interpretation</u>: Co-index the $_{NP}$[i] argument and the unindexed 1-NP argument in the following PRED/ARG structures:
      (a)   [... $_{NP}$[i] ...[PRED$_X$ 1-NP ...] ...]
      (b)   [... [PRED$_X$ 1-NP ...] ... $_{NP}$[i] ...]

Here, PRED$_X$ represents the predicate of the embedded complement. This rule is bidirectional. Structure (b) represents PRED/ARG structures like (4.2a), and Structure (a) represents PRED/ARG structures like (4.2b) and (3.44b) of examples like (3.43b). The latter example and PRED/ARG structure are repeated below:

(3.43) b. Portnoy$_i$ liked books about himself

(3.44) b. LIKE $_{NP}[i]$ $_{NP}[[$BOOK NP $_{NP}[$+REFLEX$]]_k]$
$\qquad\qquad\quad \alpha \qquad\quad \beta \qquad\quad \alpha \qquad \beta$

The SI rule applies as previously discussed to Structure (3.44b) to ultimately produce the derived F-structure of example (3.43b). This rule applies to the PRED/ARG structures in (4.2) to produce the PRED/ARG structures in (4.4), below:

(4.4) a. [BE[HARD]] $_{NP}[[$SHAVING $_{NP}[i]$ $_{NP}[$+REFLEX$]]]$ [FOR $_{NP}[i]]$

b. THINK $_{NP}[i]$ [DISTURB $_{NP}[[$SHAVING $_{NP}[i]$ $_{NP}[$+REFLEX$]]]$ $_{NP}[j]]$

Now the reflexive subcase of the GCR applies to co-index the [+RE-FLEX] NP argument of SHAVING in each structure and the $_{NP}[i]$ argument of SHAVING. The resulting structures, which are the derived F-structures of the examples in (4.1), appear in (4.5):

(4.5) a. [BE[HARD]] $_{NP}[[$SHAVING $_{NP}[i]$ $_{NP}[$+REFLEX$_i]]]$ [FOR $_{NP}[i]]$

b. THINK $_{NP}[i]$ [DISTURB $_{NP}[[$SHAVING $_{NP}[i]$ $_{NP}[$+REFLEX$_i]]]$ $_{NP}[j]]$

Although it differs from them in range and directionality, the SI rule is a rule of the same formal type as the three subcases of the GCR. Here, the antecedent φ is an indexed NP argument (represented as $_{NP}[i]$ in (4.3)) and the target ψ is the unindexed 1-NP argument of an embedded PRED$_x$.

It has been observed by a number of linguists that some version of the minimal distance principle plays a crucial role in choosing the antecedent of the understood subjects of embedded complements like the ones in (4.1), as well as the antecedents of bound anaphors when these occur in such complements. This was first observed, I believe, by Rosenbaum. (See, for example, Rosenbaum (1970).) Jacobson and Neubauer (1976) discuss a constraint, the so-called Intervention Constraint (IC), which was first proposed by Grinder to apply to at least some cases of the analog in their framework of the SI rule. Jacobson and Neubauer divide the IC into three subcases, as shown in (4.6):

(4.6)   <u>A</u> may not control <u>C</u> if a potential controller <u>B</u> intervenes in one of the following syntactic configurations:

    (a) $_S$[...A... $_S$[...B...C...]...]

    (b) $_S$[... $_S$[...B...C...] ...A...]

    (c) $_S$[... $_S$[...C...B...] ...A...]

They observe that judgements vary significantly from speaker to speaker, with some accepting violations of all three subcases of the IC. The majority of speakers, however, have either a so-called unconstrained "dialect" or a constrained one. Having pointed this out, I will briefly discuss the three subcases in turn and reanalyze the data of the restricted dialect in the context of the proposed theory. The difficulty of making clearcut judgements of both the relative and absolute acceptability of sentences of these types is probably due to their relative complexity, so that performance factors, which may not be properly a part of the formal theory, tend to obscure the generalization in (4.6). I return to this point below.

    Consider the following examples of Case (a):

(4.7) a.   *Flora$_i$* knew $_S$[that *Marvin$_j$* realized that *shaving himself$_j$*
        A$_i$ B$_j$ C
        twice a day was necessary]

    b.   **Flora$_i$* knew $_S$[that *Marvin$_j$* realized that *shaving herself$_i$*
        A$_i$ B$_j$ C
        twice a day was necessary]

Example (4.7a) is grammatical. In this example, *Marvin* (<u>B</u> in (4.6a)) is interpreted as the subject of the embedded predicate *shaving* and as the antecedent of the reflexive form *himself*. In example (4.7b) the reflexive form *herself* dictates that *Flora* (<u>A</u> in (4.6a)) is the antecedent, and is therefore also interpreted as the subject of *shaving*. The ungrammaticality of this example and the contrast between it and (4.7a) indicates that only *Marvin* and not *Flora*, can have this interpretation. The PRED/ARG structure relevant to both of the examples in (4.7), after the application of the Index Insertion rule and the SRA rule, is shown in (4.8):

(4.8) KNOW NP_i [REALIZE NP_j [[BE[NECESSARY]] [SHAVING NP NP_R]]]

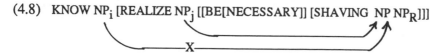

The term NP_R represents the [+REFLEX] NP argument. In this structure, the target ψ of the SI rule is the 1-NP argument of SHAVING. The only possible antecedent ϕ of this argument is the NP_j argument of REALIZE. This is indicated by the arrows in (4.8).

Before looking at subcases (b) and (c), consider the following example:

(4.9) Alfonse$_i$ knew that shaving $\left\{ \begin{array}{c} \text{himself} \\ \text{herself} \end{array} \right\}$ annoyed Gertrude$_j$

This example is analogous to (4.1b). Here, either *Alfonse* or *Gertrude* can be interpreted as the understood subject of *shaving*, and the antecedent of the reflexive argument of this predicate. The PRED/ARG structure of this sentence, after the application of the Index Insertion rule and the SRA rule, and before the application of the SI rule, is shown in (4.10):

(4.10) KNOW NP_i [ANNOY [SHAVING NP NP_R] NP_j]

In this structure, the target ψ is the NP argument of SHAVING. Either the NP_i argument of KNOW or the NP_j argument of ANNOY can be the antecedent ϕ of this target. This is indicated by the arrows in (4.10). The structure in (4.10) differs from the structure in (4.8). In (4.8), both potential antecedents are to the left of the target, while in (4.10), one of them is to the left of the target and the other is to the right of the target.

Now let us look at two examples of subcase (b):

(4.11) a. $_S$[That *Myrtle*$_i$ was angry that *dressing herself in sackcloth*
$\qquad\qquad$ B $\qquad\qquad\qquad\qquad\qquad\qquad$ C
$\quad$ frightened *the children*$_j$] astonished *Phillip*$_k$
$\qquad\qquad\qquad\qquad\qquad\qquad\qquad\qquad\qquad\qquad$ A

b. *$_S$[That *Myrtle*$_i$ was angry that *dressing himself in*
$\qquad\qquad$ B $\qquad\qquad\qquad\qquad\qquad\qquad$ C
$\quad$ *sackcloth* frightened *the children*$_j$] astonished *Phillip*$_k$
$\qquad\qquad\qquad\qquad\qquad\qquad\qquad\qquad\qquad\qquad\qquad$ A

(4.12) $\quad$ $_S$[That *Myrtle*$_i$ was angry that *dressing themselves in*
$\qquad\qquad\quad$ B $\qquad\qquad\qquad\qquad\qquad\qquad$ C
$\quad$ *sackcloth* frightened *the children*$_j$] astonished *Phillip* $_k$
$\qquad\qquad\qquad\qquad\qquad\qquad\qquad\qquad\qquad\qquad$ A

In example (4.11a), *Myrtle* (B in (4.6b)) is interpreted as the understood subject of the predicate *dressing*, and as the antecedent of the reflexive form *herself*. The ungrammaticality of (4.11b) shows that *Phillip* (A in (4.6b)) cannot be interpreted as the subject of *dressing* and the antecedent of the reflexive form *himself*, which forces this interpretation. In example (4.12), *the children* is interpreted as the understood subject of *dressing* and the antecedent of the reflexive form *themselves*. The PRED/ARG structure relevant to both of the examples in (4.11) before the application of the SI rule is shown in (4.13), and the PRED/ARG structure of example (4.12), before the application of the SI rule, is shown in (4.14):

(4.13) $\quad$ ASTONISH [[BE[ANGRY]]
$\qquad\qquad$ NP$_i$ [FRIGHTEN [DRESSING NP NP$_R$] NP$_j$]] NP$_k$

(4.14) $\quad$ ASTONISH [[BE[ANGRY]]
$\qquad\qquad$ NP$_i$ [FRIGHTEN [DRESSING NP NP$_R$] NP$_j$]] NP$_k$

In both of these structures, the target ψ is the 1-NP argument of DRESSING. As before, the arrows indicate the permissible antecedent/target (φ/ψ) pairs, and distinguish these from the impossible pairs.

Finally, consider the following examples of subcase (c):

(4.15) a. $_S$[That *dressing herself in sackcloth*   annoyed *Myrtle$_i$*]
                            C   B

           surprised *Phillip$_j$*
                      A

   b.   *$_S$[That *dressing himself in sackcloth*   annoyed *Myrtle$_i$*]
                              C   B

           surprised *Phillip$_j$*
                      A

In example (4.15a), *Myrtle* (B in (4.6c)) is interpreted as the subject of the predicate *dressing* and the antecedent of the reflexive form *herself*. The ungrammaticality of (4.15b) shows that *Phillip* (A in (4.6c)) cannot be interpreted as the subject of *dressing* and the antecedent of the reflexive form *himself*, which forces this interpretation. The PRED/ARG structure relevant to these examples is shown in (4.16):

(4.16)   SURPRISE [ANNOY [DRESSING NP NP$_R$ ...] NP$_i$] NP$_j$

The target ψ is the 1-NP argument of DRESSING.   Again, the arrows indicate the permissible antecedent/target pair and distinguish this from the impossible pair.

If we compare the PRED/ARG structures of all of these examples, we see that the SI rule must co-index the target ψ and the closest indexed NP. In Structure (4.8), both of the potential antecedents, NP$_i$ and NP$_j$ are to the left of the target, and the NP$_j$ argument is the closest one to the target. In Structure (4.10), one of the potential antecedents, NP$_i$, is to the left of the target and the other, NP$_j$, is to the right. Both are equally close to the target in the sense that there is no other indexed NP argument between either of them and the target, and both can be its antecedent.   Similarly, in Structures (4.13) and (4.14), the NP$_i$ argument (to the left of the target) and the NP$_j$ argument (to the right of the target) are equally close to the target and either can be its antecedent. The NP$_k$ argument in these structures is more distant, and cannot therefore be the antecedent of this target. In Structure (4.16), both potential antecedents, the NP$_i$ argument and the NP$_j$ argument, are to the right of the target.   Only the NP$_i$ argument, which is the closest indexed NP argument to the target can be the antecedent of this target. These data can be accounted for in the context of the proposed theory by the analog of the IC formulated in (4.17), below:

(4.17)   The unindexed 1-NP argument of an embedded predicate must
be co-indexed with the closest indexed NP argument to its left
or right in the PRED/ARG structure.

This, of course, is the FMDP, with certain additional details which
pertain to the SI rule itself. However, since the SI rule is a co-indexing
rule, the FMDP as formulated in (2.17), above, applies to it, and this
more detailed subcase is not required.

The SI rule applies to the PRED/ARG structures in (4.8), (4.10),
(4.13), (4.14), and (4.16) to co-index the 1-NP argument of the relevant
embedded predicate and the appropriate indexed NP antecedent. The
application of this rule to (4.8) produces the following PRED/ARG
structure:

(4.18)   KNOW NP_i [REALIZE NP_j [[BE[NECESSARY]]
         [SHAVING NP_j NP_R]]]

The reflexive subcase of the GCR applies to this structure to co-index
the NP_R argument of SHAVING and the NP_j argument of SHAVING.
This produces the derived F-structure of example (4.7a), which appears
in (4.19), below:

(4.19)   KNOW NP_i [REALIZE NP_j [[BE[NECESSARY]]
         [SHAVING NP_j NP_{Rj}]]]

The derived F-structures of the other examples are produced in the
same way.

The SI rule is specifically formulated in (4.3) to co-index the 1-NP
argument of an embedded $PRED_x$ and an indexed NP argument elsewhere in the PRED/ARG structure. Various general principles of the
theory, however, render this specific statement of the rule unnecessary.
To see this, first consider the following example:

(4.20)   Murphy$_i$ knew that Marvin$_j$ realized that killing Schaefer$_k$
         was necessary

The PRED/ARG structure of this example, before the application of the
SI rule is the following:

(4.21)   KNOW   NP$_i$ [REALIZE   NP$_j$ [[BE[NECESSARY]]
          [KILLING NP NP$_k$]]]

In this structure, the target ψ is the 1-NP argument of KILLING. The NP$_j$ argument and the NP$_k$ argument are equally close to the target, in the above sense, and both are therefore potential antecedents. The rule as formulated in (4.2) cannot apply to co-index the target and the NP$_k$ argument because these are in the argument structure of the same predicate, KILLING. However, if these two NP arguments were co-indexed, the following PRED/ARG structure would result:

(4.22)   KNOW   NP$_i$ [REALIZE   NP$_j$ [[BE[NECESSARY]]
          [KILLING NP$_k$ NP$_k$]]]

This structure violates WFC I for the reasons discussed earlier, and is not well-formed. However, the following well-formed derived F-structure can be produced for this example by co-indexing the NP$_j$ argument and the target:

(4.23)   KNOW   NP$_i$ [REALIZE   NP$_j$ [[BE[NECESSARY]]
          [KILLING NP$_j$ NP$_k$]]]

Consequently, the derivation of Structure (4.22) need not be prevented, and the statement of the SI rule need not mention PRED$_x$ or specify that the antecedent and target be in the argument structure of different predicates. The statement of the rule can be simplified as shown below:

(4.24)   <u>Subject Interpretation 2</u>: Co-index the $_{NP}$[i] argument and the unindexed 1-NP argument in the following PRED/ARG structures:
          (a) [... $_{NP}$[i] ... 1-NP ...]
          (b) [... 1-NP ... $_{NP}$[i] ...]

As discussed at the end of Chapter II, unindexed S-structure NPs are generally not represented in PRED/ARG structures. The 1-NP arguments of XP complements, NP* [-GR] arguments, and, as discussed in Section 3, NP arguments with the feature [+ANAPHOR], are the only unindexed NP arguments that appear in PRED/ARG structures after the application of the Index Insertion rule. Therefore, the statement of the SI rule need not specify that the target is a 1-NP argument rather than, say, a 2-NP argument or a 3-NP argument, and it can be further simplified and reformulated as shown below:

(4.25)   <u>Subject Interpretation 3</u>: Co-index φ and ψ in the following PRED/ ARG structures:
   (a)   [...φ...ψ...]
   (b)   [...ψ...φ...]

where the antecedent φ is an indexed NP argument and the target ψ is an unindexed NP argument.

We have seen that the FMDP applies to this rule. However, this principle can be, at least partially, overridden under certain circumstances. As I pointed out at the beginning of this section, judgements of these types of examples vary from speaker to speaker. Chomsky (1982) suggests a factor which we may think of as weakening the FMDP in a definable way and forming the basis of an account of at least some of the variation in judgements. He discusses examples like the following, shown with his S-structures:

(4.26) a.   They$_i$ thought I$_j$ had suggested [PRO feeding each other]
   b.   They$_i$ thought I$_j$ had suggested that [PRO feeding each other] would be difficult
   c.   They$_i$ told John$_j$ that [PRO feeding himself] was impossible
   d.   John$_i$ told them$_j$ that [PRO feeding himself] was impossible

For Chomsky, (4.26b) is better than (4.26a), and (4.26d) is better than (4.26c). He suggests that PRO may look for a controller first within its own clause, and then look outside that clause if it fails to find one.

   In the present context, we can say that the FMDP operates with varying degrees of strength as we progress outward from the PRED/ ARG structure of the predicate that contains the target NP. The PRED/ ARG structures of the examples in (4.26), before the application of the SI rule, are shown in (4.27), below. NP$_r$ represents a [+RECIPRO-CAL] argument and NP$_R$, a [+REFLEX] one:

(4.27) a.   THINK NP$_i$ [SUGGEST NP$_j$ [FEEDING NP NP$_r$]]

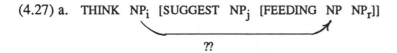

??

b.   THINK NP$_i$ [SUGGEST NP$_j$ [[BE[DIFFICULT]] [FEEDING NP
NP$_r$]]]

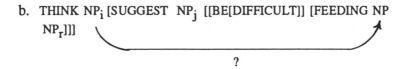

?

c.   TELL NP$_i$ NP$_j$ [[BE[IMPOSSIBLE]] [FEEDING NP NP$_R$]]

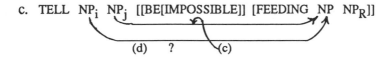

(d)   ?   (c)

Structure (4.27c) is the PRED/ARG structure relevant to both (4.26c) and (4.26d). For example (c), i = *they* and j = *John* ; for example (d), i = *John* and j = *them*. The target in each of the structures in (4.27) is the initial NP argument of FEEDING, and the antecedent/target pairs corresponding to the interpretations are indicated by the arrows. Both that of (4.26c) and (4.26d) are indicated in Structure (4.27c).

Example (4.26a) is ungrammatical because the closest and therefore most likely antecedent is the NP$_j$ argument of SUGGEST in (4.27a), but the reciprocal form *each other* cannot refer to the NP I, and therefore forces an interpretation in which the understood subject of *feeding* is *they*. This interpretation presupposes that the NP$_i$ argument of THINK is the antecedent, as diagrammed, in violation of the FMDP in its strictest sense. The following example, in contrast, is perfectly acceptable:

(4.28)   They$_i$ thought that I$_j$ had suggested feeding myself

The derived F-structure of this example appears in (4.29):

(4.29)   THINK NP$_i$ [SUGGEST NP$_j$ [FEEDING NP$_j$ NP$_{Rj}$]]

Here the antecedent of the NP argument of FEEDING is the NP$_j$ argument of SUGGEST, as diagrammed. The FMDP is not violated.

Example (4.26b) is more acceptable than (4.26a) because the FMDP applies more weakly as we progress further away from the target NP. Compare the PRED/ARG structure of this example, in (4.27b), with that of example (4.26a), in (4.27a). In Structure (4.27b), the NP_j argument of SUGGEST is closer to the target than the NP_i argument of THINK. However, in this structure, both potential antecedents are separated from the target by two predicate boundaries, that of FEEDING and that of [BE[DIFFICULT]], while in Structure (4.27a), the NP_j argument is separated from the target by a single predicate boundary, that of FEEDING. Consequently, in Structure (4.27b), the FMDP can be overridden more easily. Note, however, that the following sentence is better than (4.26b):

(4.30)   They$_i$ thought that I$_j$ had suggested that feeding myself
             would be difficult

This sentence in fact is perfectly grammatical. Its derived F-structure is the following:

(4.31)   THINK NP_i [SUGGEST NP_j [[BE[DIFFICULT]] [FEEDING NP_j
             NP_{Rj}]]]

Here, the antecedent of the 1-NP argument of FEEDING is the NP_j argument of SUGGEST, as diagrammed. This is the closest indexed NP to the target and the FMDP is not violated.

   Example (4.26c) is odd for independent reasons, possibly because of the properties of the verb *tell*. It sounds odd to tell someone about himself under certain circumstances. Note the contrast between (4.32a and b), below:

(4.32) a.   ??I told John about himself
         b.   I told John about myself

Also, observe that the following is perfectly acceptable:

(4.33)   They$_i$ told John$_j$ that feeding himself would be impossible

The PRED/ARG structure of this example is equivalent (as far as the co-indexing rule is concerned) to that of example (4.26c), shown in (4.27c)

above. In neither case is the FMDP violated.

Example (4.26d) does not have this problem, which makes it seem better than (4.26c) by comparison. In the PRED/ARG structure of this example, Structure (4.27c), the NP_i argument has been chosen as the antecedent of the 1-NP argument of FEEDING. The NP_j argument of TELL is the closest argument to the target. However, both the NP_i argument and the NP_j argument are as distantly removed from the target in this structure as they are in Structure (4.27b). Consequently, the FMDP applies more weakly, and (4.26d) is not blatantly unacceptable. It is less acceptable, however, than the following example:

(4.34) $John_i$ told $them_j$ that feeding themselves would be impossible

The derived F-structure of this example is shown in (4.35):

(4.35)   TELL NP_i NP_j [[BE[IMPOSSIBLE]] [FEEDING NP_j NP_{Rj}]]

Here, the antecedent of the 1-NP argument of FEEDING is the NP_j argument of TELL, as diagrammed. This is the closest potential antecedent, and the FMDP is not violated.

We see, then, that examples in whose PRED/ARG structures the FMDP is not violated are always better than ones in whose PRED/ARG structures this condition is violated. However, among the latter examples, there are different degrees of acceptability. Thus certain cases of disagreement from speaker to speaker over the acceptability of sentences of this type reflect the subtle effects of increasing complexity on the application of the SI rule. This complexity seems to correlate with the number of predicate boundaries that separate the target and its potential antecedents.[15]

No further conditions on the SI rule itself are required. The output of the rule is, of course, subject to WFC I, as we have seen. However, this condition applies to derived F-structures regardless of the rules involved in their derivation.[16]

As suggested in Section 3, the SI rule applies without modification to examples like (4.1) whose complements are not VPs. Consider the following examples:

(4.36) a.   Morrison$_i$ thought that pictures of himself would disturb
            Mabel$_j$
        b.   Portnoy$_i$ liked books about himself

In these examples, the embedded complement is an NP whose predicate
is a picture noun. In (4.36a), the reflexive form *himself* refers to
Morrison, and in (4.36b), the reflexive form refers to *Portnoy*. The
PRED/ARG structures of these examples before the application of the SI
rule are the following:

(4.37) a.   THINK NP$_i$ [DISTURB [PICTURES NP NP$_R$] NP$_j$]
        b.   LIKE NP$_i$ [BOOK NP NP$_R$]

In Structure (4.37a), the target is the 1-NP argument of PICTURES and
the antecedent is the NP$_i$ argument of THINK. In Structure (4.37b), the
target is the 1-NP argument of BOOK and the antecedent is the NP$_i$
argument of LIKE. The SI rule applies to (4.37) to produce the
structures in (4.38):

(4.38) a.   THINK NP$_i$ [DISTURB [PICTURES NP$_i$ NP$_R$] NP$_j$]
        b.   LIKE NP$_i$ [BOOK NP$_i$ NP$_R$]

It is clear that these applications conform to the FMDP. The reflexive
subcase of the GCR applies to the structures in (4.38) to produce the
derived F-structures of the examples in (4.36). These appear in (4.39),
below:[17]

(4.39) a.   THINK NP$_i$ [DISTURB [PICTURES NP$_i$ NP$_{Ri}$] NP$_j$]
        b.   LIKE NP$_i$ [BOOK NP$_i$ NP$_{Ri}$]

    Now consider the following examples:

(4.40) a.   Mabel$_i$ thinks that Portnoy$_j$ likes books about $\left\{ \begin{array}{l} *\text{herself} \\ \text{himself} \end{array} \right\}$

        b.   Murphy$_i$ knew that Mabel$_j$ realized that books about
            $\left\{ \begin{array}{l} *\text{himself} \\ \text{herself} \end{array} \right\}$ were boring

In example (4.40a), the reflexive form can refer to *Portnoy*, but not to

Mabel, as shown by the ungrammaticality of the sentence with the particular form that forces the latter interpretation. Similarly, in Example (4.40b), the reflexive form can refer to *Mabel*, but not to *Murphy*. The PRED/ARG structures of these examples before the application of the SI rule are shown in (4.41):

(4.41) a.   THINK NP$_i$ [LIKE NP$_j$ [BOOK NP NP$_R$]]

   b.   KNOW NP$_i$ [REALIZE NP$_j$ [[BE[BORING]] [BOOK NP NP$_R$]]]

The target in each structure is the 1-NP argument of BOOK. In Structure (4.41a), the indexed NP argument closest to the target is the NP$_j$ argument of LIKE, and in Structure (4.41b), the indexed NP argument closest to the target is the NP$_j$ argument of REALIZE. The FMDP chooses these arguments as antecedents. The SI rule and the reflexive subcase of the GCR apply to these structures to produce the derived F-structures of (4.40), which are shown below:

(4.42) a.   THINK NP$_i$ [LIKE NP$_j$ [BOOK NP$_j$ NP$_{Rj}$]]

   b.   KNOW NP$_i$ [REALIZE NP$_j$ [[BE[BORING]] [BOOK NP$_j$ NP$_{Rj}$]]]

This accounts for the interpretations of these sentences.

   Finally, consider the following examples:

(4.43) a.   Mabel$_i$ thinks that Murphy$_j$ sells pictures of $\left\{\begin{array}{l}*\text{herself}\\ \text{himself}\end{array}\right\}$

   b.   Mabel$_i$ thinks that pictures of $\left\{\begin{array}{l}\text{herself}\\ \text{himself}\end{array}\right\}$ are sold by Murphy$_j$

In (4.43a), the reflexive form can only refer to *Murphy*, as shown by the ungrammaticality of the sentence with *herself*, which forces the other interpretation. In (4.43b), however, the proper reflexive form can refer either to *Mabel* or *Murphy*. The PRED/ARG structures of these examples before the application of the SI rule are the following:

(4.44) a.   THINK NP_i [SELL NP_j [PICTURE NP NP_R]]

   b.   THINK NP_i [[BE[SOLD]] [PICTURE NP NP_R] [BY NP_j]]

The target in each structure is the 1-NP argument of PICTURE. In Structure (4.44a), the closest indexed NP argument to the target is the NP_j argument of SELL. The FMDP chooses this argument as the antecedent. In Structure (4.44b), the NP_i argument of THINK and the NP_j argument of BY are equally close to the target (as before, in the sense that no other indexed NP argument appears between either of them and the target), and either can be selected as the antecedent. The SI rule and the reflexive subcase of the GCR apply to (4.44a) to produce the derived F-structure of (4.43a). This is shown in (4.45):

(4.45)   THINK NP_i [SELL NP_j [PICTURE NP_j NP_{Rj}]]

This accounts for the interpretation of (4.43a).

   Either of the derived F-structures in (4.46) can be produced for example (4.43b) by the application of the SI rule and the reflexive subcase of the GCR rule to Structure (4.44b):

(4.46) a.   THINK NP_i [[BE[SOLD]] [PICTURE NP_i NP_{Ri}] [BY NP_j]]

   b.   THINK NP_i [[BE[SOLD]] [PICTURE NP_j NP_{Rj}] [BY NP_j]]

This accounts for the interpretations of (4.43b).

   This completes the discussion of the SI rule. The theory explains the patterns of the long-range control relation and also automatically explains why both the reference of picture noun reflexives in examples like (4.36), (4.40), and (4.43), and the interpretation of the subject of embedded VP complements in examples like (4.1), (4.7), (4.9), and so forth, pattern in the same way. The SI rule is involved in producing the derived F-structures of examples which contain both constructions. For more examples and discussion, see Horn (1979b) and (1983a).

5. Unification

The Co-indexing rule, the Raqui rule, and the Reflexive/Reciprocal rule are all unidirectional co-indexing rules, and are, in fact, subcases of a single general co-indexing rule. This rule, the GCR, which was formulated in (2.27), is repeated below:

(2.27)   <u>General Co-indexing Rule (GCR)</u>: In the structure: $[...\varphi... \psi...]$, co-index φ and ψ, and optionally delete φ, where φ is the indexed NP antecedent and ψ is the unindexed NP target.

Whenever the antecedent φ is an NP[θ] argument of some predicate and it is deleted, the derived F-structure ultimately produced is the basis for only a partial interpretation of the relevant sentence. However, this deletion process need not be blocked for any of the subcases.

The SI rule, as pointed out in Section 4, is a rule of the same formal type as the GCR. That is, it is a co-indexing rule. Moreover, the same general principle, the FMDP, applies to it. This suggests that it is not an independent rule, but is rather a fourth subcase of a single general co-indexing rule.

The SI rule, unlike the GCR, is a bidirectional rule. Its formulation in (4.25) is repeated below:

(4.25)   <u>Subject Interpretation Rule (SI)3</u>: Co-index φ and ψ in the following PRED/ARG structures:

    (a) $[...\varphi...\psi...]$

    (b) $[...\psi...\varphi...]$

where the antecedent φ is an indexed NP argument and the target ψ is an unindexed NP argument.

If we compare the GCR in (2.27) and the SI rule in (4.25), we see that, except for details, the only significant difference between the two is that the latter is a more inclusive rule than the former. Both of these rules can be combined as a general co-indexing rule, of which the SI rule is a fourth subcase, along with the three subcases of the original GCR. This more inclusive co-indexing rule is formulated in (5.1), below:

(5.1)   General Co-indexing Rule (GCR 2): Co-index φ and ψ in
the following PRED/ARG structures:
    (a) $[...\varphi...\psi...]$
    (b) $[...\psi...\varphi...]$
and optionally delete φ, where φ is the indexed NP
antecedent and ψ is the unindexed target.

The antecedent φ of the target ψ in the SI subcase is an NP[θ]
argument of some predicate. Consequently, if it is deleted in PRED/
ARG structures like the ones in Section 4, the derived F-structures that
are produced are the basis for only partial interpretations of the relevant
sentences. The situation here is therefore the same as the situation relating to the co-indexing and reflexive/reciprocal subcases of the GCR, and
the optional deletion process need not be blocked for the SI subcase of
the GCR 2.

Similarly, the co-indexing subcase and Raqui subcase can be allowed
to apply in either direction. Misapplications of the co-indexing subcase
violate WFC I. To see this more clearly, consider the following
example, shown with its PRED/ARG structure after the application of
the Index Insertion rule and the SRA rule:

(5.2) a.   Rhonda$_i$ forced her snails$_j$ to commit unnatural acts$_k$

    b.   FORCE NP$_i$ NP$_j$ [(NP*)[COMMIT NP NP$_k$]]
                   α β α β

The two targets in this structure are the NP* argument and the 1-NP
argument of COMMIT. The NP$_j$ argument of FORCE and the NP$_k$
argument of COMMIT are the closest indexed NP arguments to these
respective targets. If the NP$_k$ argument of COMMIT and the 1-NP argument of COMMIT are co-indexed, the resulting PRED/ARG structure
is the following:

(5.3)   FORCE NP$_i$ NP$_j$ [(NP*)[COMMIT NP$_k$ NP$_k$]]
                   α β α β

In this structure, COMMIT has two identical NP arguments, one bearing the SR α and the other bearing the SR β, and the structure
violates WFC I. Morcover, suppose that the NP$_j$ argument and the NP*

argument in this structure are co-indexed. This produces the structure in (5.4):

(5.4)   FORCE $\underset{\alpha}{NP_i}$ $\underset{\beta}{NP_j}$ [(NP$_j$*)[COMMIT $\underset{\alpha}{NP_k}$ $\underset{\beta}{NP_k}$]]

The Raqui subcase of the GCR cannot apply to this structure since there is no available target. This structure contains an indexed NP argument, the NP*$_j$ argument, that does not bear an SR. This is a further violation of WFC I. Since this structure is not well-formed, it cannot be the basis for an interpretation of example (5.2). However, a well-formed derived F-structure can be produced for this example by applying the co-indexing subcase of the GCR to the NP$_j$ argument and the NP* argument, and the Raqui subcase of the GCR to the NP*$_j$ argument and the 1-NP argument of COMMIT. This structure appears in (5.5):

(5.5)   FORCE $\underset{\alpha}{NP_i}$ $\underset{\beta}{NP_j}$ [COMMIT $\underset{\alpha}{NP_j}$ $\underset{\beta}{NP_k}$]

The derivation of the structure in (5.4) need not be blocked and the co-indexing subcase of the GCR can be allowed to apply in either direction.

I turn now to the Raqui subcase of the GCR. Consider the following example, shown with its PRED/ARG structure after the application of the Index Insertion rule and the SRA rule:

(5.6) a.   Melvin$_i$ believed Rhonda$_j$ to have murdered her snails$_k$

   b.   BELIEVE $\underset{\alpha}{NP_i}$ [(NP*$_j$)[MURDER $\underset{\alpha}{NP}$ $\underset{\beta}{NP_k}$]]

Indexed NP* arguments appear in PRED/ARG structures like the one in (5.6b) with verbs like *believe*, and in the PRED/ARG structures of verbs like *force* in examples like (5.2a). The PRED/ARG structure of (5.2a), after the application of the Index Insertion rule, the SRA rule, and the co-indexing subcase of the GCR is the following:

(5.7)   FORCE $\underset{\alpha}{NP_i}$ $\underset{\beta}{NP_j}$ [(NP*$_j$)[COMMIT $\underset{\alpha}{NP}$ $\underset{\beta}{NP_k}$]]

The only target in Structure (5.6b) is the 1-NP argument of MURDER, and the only target in Structure (5.7) is the 1-NP argument of COM-

MIT. Consequently, the NP* arguments can only be co-indexed with these, and the directionality of the Raqui subcase is not an issue.

Now consider the example in (5.8), below:

(5.8) Ned_i made $Melvin_j$ believe $Rhonda_k$ to have forced her $snails_m$ to commit unnatural $acts_o$

This example is odd for reasons unconnected with the present discussion, and is more acceptable if *believe* occurs with a *that* complement. I will, however, ignore this. The partial PRED/ARG structure of this example after the application of the Index Insertion rule and the SRA rule is the following:

(5.9)   MAKE NP_i NP_j $[(NP*)[BELIEVE$ NP $[(NP*_k)[FORCE$ NP
         $\quad\quad\quad\; \alpha \quad\; \beta \quad\quad\quad\quad\quad\quad\quad\quad \alpha \quad\quad\quad\quad\quad\quad\quad \alpha$
         $NP_m ...]]]]$
         β

In this structure, the Raqui subcase of the GCR can apply to co-index the $NP*_k$ argument and either the closest unindexed NP to its left, the 1-NP argument of BELIEVE, or the closest unindexed NP argument to its right, the 1-NP argument of FORCE. If the $NP*_k$ argument and the 1-NP argument of BELIEVE are co-indexed, the following structure is produced (assuming that the antecedent φ is deleted):

(5.10)   MAKE NP_i NP_j $[(NP*)[BELIEVE$ NP_k $[FORCE$ NP $NP_m ...]]]$
          $\quad\quad\quad\;\; \alpha \;\; \beta \quad\quad\quad\quad\quad\quad\quad \alpha \quad\quad\quad\quad\; \alpha \;\; \beta$

The remaining NP* argument and the NP_j argument of MAKE can be co-indexed. This produces the structure in (5.11):

(5.11)   MAKE NP_i NP_j $[(NP*_j)[BELIEVE$ NP_k $[FORCE$ NP $NP_m ..]]]$
          $\quad\quad\quad\;\; \alpha \;\; \beta \quad\quad\quad\quad\quad\quad\quad\; \alpha \quad\quad\quad\quad\; \alpha \;\; \beta$

In this structure, the only available target is the 1-NP argument of FORCE, and the FMDP dictates that the antecedent of this target be the NP_k argument of BELIEVE (or the NP_m argument of FORCE.) Consequently, the derived F-structure produced from (5.11) is one which contains an indexed NP argument, the $NP*_j$ argument, which bears no SR. The structure thus violates WFC I. As in the previous example, however, a well-formed derived F-structure for (5.8) can be produced, so the derivation of Structure (5.11), or, more accurately, the structure produced from (5.11), need not be blocked, and the Raqui subcase of the GCR can be allowed to apply in either direction.

The situation is somewhat different for the reflexive/reciprocal subcase of the GCR. Consider the following ungrammatical example:

(5.12)   *Himself disliked Merv$_i$

The PRED/ARG structure of this sentence, after the application of the Index Insertion rule and the SRA rule is shown in (5.13), below:

(5.13)   DISLIKE $_{NP[+REFLEX]}$ NP_i
                  α β

Analogous sentences do not occur in Type Y languages (Condition (3.13) above) because the antecedent of a [+ANAPHOR] target must be a 1-NP argument. Consequently, the [+REFLEX] argument in structures like (5.13) cannot be indexed and the resulting derived F-structures are not wellformed. To account for the ungrammaticality of such examples in Type X languages like English, we need only assume the following hierarchy of argument positions, HA, {1-NP, 2-NP, 3-NP, NPp}, and add the stipulation in (5.14) to (3.13):

(5.14)   The antecedent of a [+ANAPHOR] target is the highest appropriate argument which is above or on the same level as the target in the HA hierarchy.

This accounts for the ungrammaticality of (5.12) as well as the following pattern:

(5.15) a. Merv$_i$ told the Smoots$_j$ about {himself/each other}
              TELL NPi NPj [ABOUT NP$_{R/r}$]
       b. Merv$_i$ talked about {himself/*herself} to Meryl$_j$
              TALK NP$_i$ [ABOUT NP$_R$] [TO NP$_j$]

In the F-structure of (5.15a), NP$_j$ is the closest potential, and therefore appropriate, antecedent, but the FMDP can be optionally "weakened" to allow NP_i to be the antecedent as before. In (5.15b), NP_i and NP_j are equally close to the target and both are appropriate antecedents. NP_i is above NP_j in HA and is the only possible antecedent.

In Section 4, we saw that only three unindexed NP argument types appear in PRED/ARG structures after the application of the Index Insertion rule and the SRA rule. These are listed in (5.16), below:

(5.16) a.   NP* arguments of control verbs like *force* (which have the feature [-GR])
   b.   NP arguments with the feature [+ANAPHOR]
   c.   1-NP arguments of appropriate XP complements (which have no S-structure correlate)

Consequently, only these are available as targets ψ for the GCR. The configurations of the PRED/ARG structures in which the various target types can occur and the general principles of the theory determine the overall application of the GCR and render the specification of subcases unnecessary.

Unindexed NP* arguments always occur in PRED/ARG structures like the following:

(5.17) $PRED_1$ ... NP_i ... [(NP*)[$PRED_2$ 1-NP ... NP_j ...

$PRED_1$ represents the class of control predicates like *force*, and $PRED_2$ is the predicate of the embedded complement of $PRED_1$. Here, the unindexed NP* argument is the target ψ of the GCR. (The unindexed 1-NP argument of $PRED_2$ is also a target. This case is discussed below.) The FMDP dictates that the closest indexed NP argument to the NP* target, which is always an NP[θ] argument of $PRED_1$, is the antecedent ϕ. This will be NP_i in (5.17) provided no other NP argument of $PRED_1$ intervenes between it and the NP* argument. This is the co-indexing subcase of the GCR.

Unindexed NP arguments with the feature [+ANAPHOR] occur in PRED/ARG structures like (5.18):

(5.18)   ... NP_i ... $PRED_2$ ... NP[+ANAPHOR] ...

In this structure, the unindexed [+ANAPHOR] NP argument is the target ψ of the GCR. Let us first assume that PRED$_2$ has the feature [-TENSE] and that the [+ANAPHOR] NP argument occupies the 1-NP argument position of PRED$_2$. The FMDP, the stipulation in (5.14), and Condition (3.13) dictate that the antecedent ϕ is the closest indexed 1-NP argument to the left of the target. This will always be an NP argument in the adjacent argument structure; that is, an NP argument of the predicate in whose PRED/ARG structure the PRED/ARG structure of PRED$_2$ is embedded. If NP$_i$ in (5.18) satisfies this prerequisite, it is chosen as the antecedent ϕ.

Now let us suppose that PRED$_2$ in (5.18) has the feature [+TENSE]. As before, the FMDP and the stipulation in (5.14) dictate that the antecedent ϕ is the closest indexed 1-NP argument to the left of the target. However, the tense condition in (3.31) blocks the application of the GCR into the PRED/ARG structure of PRED$_2$, and the [+ANAPHOR] NP argument cannot be assigned an index. Derived F-structures containing unindexed NP arguments violate WFC I and are not well-formed.

Finally, suppose that the target [+ANAPHOR] NP argument is not the 1-NP argument of PRED$_2$, but is rather the 2-NP or 3-NP argument of this predicate. The FMDP, the stipulation in (5.14), and Condition (3.13) dictate that the antecedent ϕ is the closest indexed NP argument or 1-NP argument to the left of the target. Therefore, in this case, the antecedent is always an NP argument of PRED$_2$. This situation and the two situations discussed just before this are variants of the reflexive/reciprocal subcase of the GCR.

Unindexed 1-NP arguments occur in PRED/ARG structures like (5.19a and b).

(5.19) a. PRED$_1$ ... NP$_i$ ... [(NP*$_j$)[PRED$_2$ 1-NP ... NP$_k$ ...
     b. ... NP$_i$ ... PRED$_2$ 1-NP ... NP$_j$ ...

In Structure (5.19a), the NP* argument is indexed. PRED$_1$ here represents the class of control predicates like *force* (where j=i) and the class of predicates like *believe*. As in (5.17), PRED$_2$ is the predicate of the [(NP*)XP] complement of PRED$_1$. Structure (5.19)b represents the PRED/ARG structures of examples like the ones discussed in Section 4, which contain XP complements embedded in NP argument positions.

$PRED_2$ is the predicate of the XP complement. The F-structure representations of such complements contain no NP* argument.

In both structures, the unindexed 1-NP argument of $PRED_2$ is the target ψ. In Structure (5.19a), the FMDP dictates that either the NP*$_j$ argument, which is the closest indexed NP argument to the left of the target, or the closest indexed NP argument to the right of the target is the antecedent φ. The closest indexed NP argument to the right of the target is NP_k provided that no other NP argument intervenes between it and the 1-NP target. As we saw earlier, if the NP*$_j$ argument is not chosen as the antecedent, the resulting derived F-structure will violate WFC I. So, whenever indexed NP* arguments occur in PRED/ARG structures, they can be chosen as antecedents, and a well-formed derived F-structure is produced only if they are chosen as antecedents in the relevant structures. This is the Raqui subcase of the GCR.

In Structure (5.19b), the FMDP dictates that the antecedent φ is the closest indexed NP argument to the left or right of the target. If no other NP arguments intervene, either NP_i or NP_j is chosen as the antecedent, subject to other factors as discussed in Section 4. This, of course, is the SI subcase of the GCR.

The four subcases (the Co-indexing rule, the Raqui rule, the Reflexive/reciprocal rule, and the SI rule) follow from the GCR 2 and related general principles and need not be specified as separate operations.

6. The Generalized Co-Indexing System

The GCR as formulated in (5.1) and the associated principles are the components of the Generalized Co-Indexing System (GCS) of UG. The GCR is repeated below:

(6.1)   <u>General Co-indexing Rule (GCR)</u>: Co-index φ and ψ in the following PRED/ARG structures:

        (a)   [...φ...ψ...]

        (b)   [...ψ...φ...]

and optionally delete φ, where φ is the indexed NP antecedent and ψ is the unindexed target.

The general conditions, which apply regardless of the nature of the antecedent φ and the target ψ in the relevant PRED/ARG structure are the following:

(6.2) a. <u>FMDP</u>: The GCR must involve the antecedent/target pair relevant to the operation whose members φ and ψ are least distantly separated.

b. <u>The Default Principle</u>: If the antecedent φ is located in the PRED/ARG structure of $PRED_x$ and the target ψ is not located in the PRED/ARG structure of $PRED_x$, then φ must be the 1-NP argument of $PRED_x$.

The formulations of the FMDP and Default Principle which appear in (6.1a and b) are slightly modified versions of the earlier formulations. Some additional remarks concerning the domain and interpretation of both of these principles are in order.

Firstly, the FMDP applies to PRED/ARG structures of the general form represented in (6.3):

(6.3)   ... NP_i ... NP_j ... $\underline{NP}_1$ ... $\underline{NP}_2$ ... NP_k ... $\underline{NP}_3$ ... NP_m ...

Here, I assume that the positions represented as ... contain no NP arguments. The unindexed NPs, $\underline{NP}_1$, $\underline{NP}_2$, and $\underline{NP}_3$ are targets, and the indexed NPs are potential antecedents. Consider the target (ψ) $\underline{NP}_1$. NP_j and NP_k are the closest indexed NP arguments to $\underline{NP}_1$. However, NP_k is closer to the $\underline{NP}_2$ target than it is to the $\underline{NP}_1$ target. Hence NP_j and $\underline{NP}_1$ are the least distantly separated φ/ψ pair whose ψ member is $\underline{NP}_1$, and the FMDP chooses NP_j as the antecedent φ member of this pair. NP_k is the closest indexed NP argument to the target $\underline{NP}_2$, and the FMDP chooses it as the antecedent φ member of the pair whose ψ member is $\underline{NP}_2$. NP_k and NP_m are equally close to the target $\underline{NP}_3$, and either can be chosen by the FMDP as the antecedent φ member of the pair whose ψ member is $\underline{NP}_3$. The least distantly separated φ/ψ pairs are indicated by the arrows in (6.3).

The FMDP applies without exception (apart from the cases discussed in Section 4) whenever φ and ψ are located in the PRED/ARG structure of the same predicate, which we may arbitrarily label $PRED_x$.

This is illustrated by the following structures from previous sections, repeated below along with the relevant example sentences. In these structures, the relevant targets are labelled as ψ, and the potential antecedents are labelled as φ:

(6.4) a.   Kelly$_i$ forced Cynthia$_j$ to commit unnatural acts$_k$

 b.   FORCE NP$_i$ NP$_j$ [(NP*)[COMMIT NP NP$_k$]]
        φ φ ψ

(6.5) a.   Keyser$_i$ depended on Postal$_j$ to know the answers$_k$

 b.   [DEPEND ON] NP$_i$ NP$_j$ [(NP*)[KNOW NP NP$_k$]]
          φ φ ψ

(6.6) a.   Shaving himself was hard for Morrison$_i$

 b.   [BE[HARD]] $_{NP}$[[SHAVING NP NP$_R$]] [FOR NP$_i$]
              ψ φ

(6.7) a.   Morrison$_i$ thought that shaving himself would disturb Mabel$_j$

 b.   THINK NP$_i$ [DISTURB $_{NP}$[[SHAVING NP NP$_R$]] NP$_j$]
        φ ψ φ

(6.8) a.   Flora$_i$ knew that Marvin$_j$ realized that shaving himself was necessary

 b.   KNOW NP$_i$ [REALIZE NP$_j$ [[BE[NECESSARY]]
          φ φ

      [SHAVING NP NP$_R$]]]
              ψ

(6.9) a.   Alfonse$_i$ knew that shaving himself/herself annoyed Gertrude$_j$

 b.   KNOW NP$_i$ [ANNOY [SHAVING NP NP$_R$] NP$_j$]
          φ ψ φ

Structures (6.4b) and (6.5b) contain controlled complements of the form [(NP*)XP] and Structures (6.6b), (6.7b), (6.8b), and (6.9b) contain XP complements embedded in NP argument positions. In Structures (6.4b) and (6.5b), the potential antecedents, NP$_i$ and NP$_j$, and the target, NP*, are located in the PRED/ARG structure of the same predicate, FORCE in (6.4b) and DEPEND ON in (6.5b). The FMDP chooses the NP$_j$ argument as antecedent in each case.

In Structure (6.6b), the target ψ is located in the PRED/ARG structure of SHAVING and the antecedent φ is located in the PRED/ARG structure of FOR. However, both the PRED/ARG structure of SHAVING and that of FOR are themselves located in the PRED/ARG structure of [BE[HARD]]. Consequently, φ and ψ are ultimately located in the PRED/ARG structure of [BE[HARD]], which is PRED$_x$ in this case. It is easy to see that in (6.7b), (6.8b), and (6.9b), the situation is similar. In (6.7b), the potential antecedents, NP$_i$ and NP$_j$, and the target ψ are located in the PRED/ARG structure of THINK; in (6.8b), both the potential antecedents, NP$_i$ and NP$_j$, and the target ψ are located in the PRED/ARG structure of KNOW; and in (6.9b), both the potential antecedents, NP$_i$ and NP$_j$, and the target ψ are located in the PRED/ARG structure of KNOW. In each case, the FMDP applies as discussed above to choose the antecedent.[18]

Now consider the following examples:

(6.10) a.   Aethelbert$_i$ gave the manuscript$_j$ to Boris$_k$ naked
     b.   [GIVE NP$_i$ NP$_j$ [TO NP$_k$]][(NP*)[NAKED NP]]
               φ φ ψ

(6.11) a.   Sebastian$_i$ served the koalaburgers$_j$ naked
     b.   [SERVE NP$_i$ NP$_j$][(NP*)[NAKED NP]]
                φ φ ψ

In Structures (6.10b) and (6.11b), the potential antecedents, NP$_i$ and NP$_j$ are located in the PRED/ARG structures of GIVE and SERVE, respectively. However, the target NP* in each structure is not located in the PRED/ARG structure of GIVE or SERVE. In this situation, the FMDP does not apply, and the Default Principle chooses the 1-NP argument of PRED$_x$ as the antecedent. IN (6.10b), this is the NP$_i$ argument of GIVE, and in (6.11b), it is the NP$_i$ argument of SERVE.

The following special conditions apply to particular target types:

(6.12)   If the target ψ is the NP* argument of a controlled complement of the form [(NP*)XP] embedded in the PRED/ARG structure of a predicate, PRED$_x$, then:
      (a) the antecedent φ must be an NP argument of PRED$_x$;

(b) for predicates of class X, the antecedent φ is the NP argument of the predicate that bears the designated SR, θ_x.

(6.13) If the target ψ is an NP argument with the feature [+ANAPHOR], then:

(a) 1. the antecedent φ is the 1-NP argument of the relevant predicate - optionally in languages of type X and obligatorily in languages of type Y;

2. Alternatively, in Type X languages, the antecedent φ is the highest appropriate argument which is above, or on the same level as, the target in HA;

(b) If φ is an argument of $PRED_x$ and ψ is an argument of $PRED_y$, then $PRED_y$ must have the feature [-TENSE].

The conditions in (6.12), which apply to obligatorily controlled complements, are similar (at least in spirit) to ones suggested by Chomsky (1981) and Bresnan (1982d) for other theories. Condition (6.13) is a combined statement of (3.13), (3.31), and (5.14).

The Generalized Co-Indexing System provides a unified explanation of the short-range control relation (the analog of the standard theory raising rule and PRO interpretation rule), the anaphora relation, and the long-range control relation. The GCS satisfies the requirements for an adequate theory of control. It defines the notions "possible controller (antecedent φ)" and "possible controlled position (target ψ)", and general principles choose the controller/antecedent from several possible ones in the appropriate PRED/ARG structures. The core set of transparent positions in the sense of Chomsky (1980 & 1981) is defined by the general principles of the GCS and the general principles of the theory as a whole (such as WFC I.) The patterns of control and anaphora are a consequence of the interaction of these principles and the configurational properties of PRED/ARG structures. Moreover, the GCS theory accounts for the constraints on possible raising and control predicates (like *believe* and *force*.)

Because PRED/ARG structure types are universal, the theory applies in the same way to all languages regardless of their syntactic character. In particular, it explains the fact that both configurational languages and non-configurational languages display the same patterns (in the relevant respects) of control and anaphora. I will close the chapter with a look at some illustrative examples from various languages. Consider the following Samoan, Japanese, and Modern Irish sentences:

(6.14)   Na fosi e Ioane$_i$ Mele$_j$ ave le taavale
          TENSE FORCE (SUBJ)-Ioane Mele drive the car
          Ioane forced Mele to drive the car

(6.15)   Taroo wa$_i$ Hanako o$_j$ baka da to omotte ita
          Taro (NOM) Hanako (ACC) fool be thinking was
          Taro thought Hanako to be a fool

(6.16)   Chomhairligh me$_i$ do Chiaran$_j$ bean og$_k$ a phosadh
          advised   I   to Ciaran   woman young to marry
          I advised Ciaran to marry a young woman

The sentences in (6.14) and (6.16) contain control verbs, like English *force*, and the sentence in (6.15) contains a verb of the same class as the English verb *believe*. The different languages have different S-structure patterns and grammatical relations indicators. Therefore, they have different language-particular correlation statements. However, the PRED/ARG structures of these sentences are the universal types associated with predicates of these classes. These structures, before the application of the GCR, appear as shown in (6.17a, b, and c), respectively:

(6.17) a.   NA FOSI NP$_i$ NP$_j$ [(NP*)[[E AVE] NP NP$_k$]]
       b.   OMOTTE ITA NP$_i$ [(NP*$_j$)[DA[BAKA]] NP]]
       c.   CHOMHAIRLIGH NP$_i$ NP$_j$ [(NP*)[PHOSADH NP NP$_k$]]

In Structures (6.17a) and (6.17c), the FMDP chooses the NP$_j$ argument as the antecedent of the NP* target. After the NP* argument is assigned an index, the FMDP chooses it as the antecedent of the NP argument of the predicate of the controlled complements, AVE and PHOSADH, respectively. In Structure (6.17b), the FMDP chooses the indexed NP* argument as the antecedent of the NP argument of [DA[BAKA]]. The application of the GCR to these structures produces the derived F-structures of the examples in (6.14), (6.15), and (6.16). These are shown in (6.18):

(6.18) a.   NA FOSI NP_i NP_j [[E AVE] NP_j NP_k]
    b.   OMOTTE ITA NP_i [[DA[BAKA]] NP_j]
    c.   CHOMHAIRLIGH NP_i NP_j [PHOSADH NP_j NP_k]

The theory accounts for the fact that sentences which contain predicates of these types are interpreted in the same way in all languages.

Finally consider the following Malagasy examples:

(6.19) a.   Tia tena $Rabe_i$
        PRES-like self Rabe
        Rabe likes himself
    b.   Namono tena $Rasoa_i$
        PAST-kill self Rasoa
        Rasoa killed herself

In the S-structures of these sentences the reflexive forms precede their antecedents. However, the PRED/ARG structures of these sentences, after the application of the Index Insertion rule and the SRA rule, appear as shown in (6.20):

(6.20) a.   TIA $\underset{\alpha}{NP_i}$ $\underset{\beta}{NP[+REFLEX]}$

    b.   NAMONO $\underset{\alpha}{NP_i}$ $\underset{\beta}{NP[+REFLEX]}$

The GCR applies to these structures to produce the derived F-structures of (6.19), which are shown in (6.21):

(6.21) a.   TIA $\underset{\alpha}{NP_i}$ $\underset{\beta}{NP[+REFLEX_i]}$

    b.   NAMONO $\underset{\alpha}{NP_i}$ $\underset{\beta}{NP[+REFLEX_i]}$

The theory accounts for the fact that bound anaphors refer to the subjects of sentences which contain two-argument predicates like the ones in (6.19) in all languages, regardless of their syntactic characteristics.

NOTES

1. Non-initial NP arguments in embedded complements are externally controlled in examples like the following:

(i) a.   Herbert$_i$ was easy for the zoo keepers$_j$ to feed
   b.   The nose flute$_i$ is difficult to play sonatas$_j$ on

The PRED/ARG structures of these examples do not contain obligatorily controlled complements of the form [(NP*)XP]. These examples are discussed in Horn (1983a) and Chapter V.

2. These optional adjuncts are independent lexical items, with their own lexical entries and F-structure representations. Two examples appear below:

(i)
$$
\begin{bmatrix}
\text{UNOPENED} \\
\text{+A/COMP} \\
\\
\cdots \\
\\
[(\text{NP*})[\text{UNOPENED NP}]] \\
\qquad\qquad\qquad\quad \alpha
\end{bmatrix}
$$

(ii)
$$
\begin{bmatrix}
\text{RAW} \\
\text{+A/COMP} \\
\\
\cdots \\
\\
[(\text{NP*})[\text{RAW NP}]] \\
\qquad\qquad\quad \alpha
\end{bmatrix}
$$

3. *Make* in a second sense occurs in examples like (2.5a), repeated below:

(2.5) a.   Roth$_i$ made Gertrude$_j$ a virtuous woman

The basic F-structure of *make* in this sense is functionally identical to (2.41b).

However, this verb has a different thematic structure than *make* in examples like (2.40b). *Make* in the sense of (2.5a) is not exceptional. It conforms to the FMDP, which dictates that the 2-NP[β] argument is the antecedent of the NP* argument.

Actually, neither *promise* nor *make* in the sense of (2.40b) requires a second NP[θ] argument. These predicates also occur in sentences like the following:

(i) a. Thor$_i$ promised to leave
    b. Davis$_i$ will make a good husband

Their basic F-structures relevant to these examples are shown in (ii):

(ii) a.   PROMISE 1-NP[α]   [(NP*)VP]
    b.   MAKE 1-NP[α]   [(NP*)NP]

The PRED/ARG structures of the sentences in (i), after the application of the Index Insertion rule and the SRA rule, are shown in (iii):

(iii) a.   PROMISE $_{NP}[i]$ [(NP*)[LEAVE NP]]
           α α
    b.   MAKE $_{NP}[i]$ [(NP*)[[GOOD HUSBAND] NP]
         α α

Here, the $_{NP}[i]$ arguments of PROMISE and MAKE are the closest possible antecedents of the NP* argument. The subcases of the GCR apply to produce the derived F-structures of (i), which are shown below:

(iv) a.   PROMISE $_{NP}[i]$ [LEAVE $_{NP}[i]$]
           α α
    b.   MAKE $_{NP}[i]$ [[GOOD HUSBAND] $_{NP}[i]$]
         α α

This analysis also accounts for the ungrammaticality of (v a) and the fact that (v b) is not the passive counterpart of (i b):

(v) a.   *Thor$_i$ was promised to leave
    b.   Davis$_i$ was made a good husband

The PRED/ARG structures of these examples, after the application of the Index Insertion rule and the SRA rule, are shown in (vi):

(vi) a. $_{Sp}VP[BE][PROMISED]$ $_{NP}[i]$ $[(NP^*)[LEAVE\ NP]]$
$\beta\alpha$

b. $_{Sp}VP[BE][MADE]$ $_{NP}[i]$ $[(NP^*)[[GOOD\ HUSBAND]\ NP]]$
$\beta\alpha$

These PRED/ARG structures are produced from the two-argument basic F-structures of PROMISE and MAKE in (2.42) by rules and procedures that are discussed in Chapter IV. The $_{NP}[i]$ argument in each structure bears the SR β, which is the SR borne by the 2-NP argument of each predicate in its basic F-structure. Therefore, in neither case does the only argument of the matrix predicate bear the specified SR, θ_p or θ_m. Consequently, the co-indexing subcase of the GCR cannot apply, and the resulting F-structures, in (vi), above, violate WFC I. Each one contains an NP argument (of the embedded predicate) which bears an SR, but no index. Thus (v a) is ungrammatical and (v)b does not have an interpretation based on the F-structure in (vi b).

The following sentences contain *by*-phrases:

(vii) a. *Thor$_i$ was promised to leave by Agnes$_j$
   b. *Davis$_i$ was made a good husband by Mavis$_j$

The PRED/ARG structures of these sentences after the application of the Index Insertion rule and the SRA rule, are shown in (viii):

(viii) a. $_{Sp}VP[BE][PROMISED]$ $_{NP}[i]$ $[(NP^*)[LEAVE\ NP]]$ $[BY$
$\beta\alpha$
$NP[j]]$
α

b. $_{Sp}VP[BE][MADE]$ $_{NP}[i]$ $[(NP^*)[[GOOD\ HUSBAND]\ NP]]$
β
$[BY\ NP[j]]$
α

In these structures, the $_{NP}[i]$ constituent is an argument of BY, and not of the predicates PROMISED or MADE. Consequently, these arguments are not possible antecedents, and as before, the GCR cannot apply to these structures. The derived F-structures of the examples in (vii) are not well-formed, and this accounts for their ungrammaticality.

The example in (v b) can only be interpreted as the passive counterpart of the following:

(ix)   Mavis$_i$ made Davis$_j$ a good husband

This sentence contains *make* in its other sense, which was briefly discussed earlier. In this sense, *make* behaves like *force*. The PRED/ ARG structure of (ix), after the application of the Index Insertion rule and the SRA rule, is shown in (x):

(x)   MAKE $\underset{\alpha}{\text{NP}[i]}$ $\underset{\beta}{\text{NP}[j]}$ $[(\text{NP*})[[\text{GOOD HUSBAND}] \underset{\alpha}{\text{NP}}]]$

The subcases of the GCR apply to (x) in the normal way to produce (xi):

(xi)   MAKE $\underset{\alpha}{\text{NP}[i]}$ $\underset{\beta}{\text{NP}[j]}$ $[[\text{GOOD HUSBAND}] \underset{\alpha}{\text{NP}[i]}]$

This is the derived F-structure of (ix). The PRED/ARG structure of (v b), with *make* in this sense, after the application of the Index Insertion rule and the SRA rule, is shown in (xii):

(xii)   S$_P$VP[BE][MADE] $\underset{\beta}{\text{NP}[i]}$ $[(\text{NP*})[[\text{GOOD HUSBAND}] \underset{\alpha}{\text{NP}}]]$

The GCR applies to this structure to produce (xiii), which is the derived F-structure of example (v b):

(xiii)   S$_P$VP[BE][MADE] $\underset{\beta}{\text{NP}[i]}$ $[[\text{GOOD HUSBAND}] \underset{\alpha}{\text{NP}[i]}]$

4. See the alternative structures in Chapter II. The choice of which of these structures are assigned to these examples does not affect the analysis proposed here.

5. I assume that co-indexing rules transfer certain features, such as [+ANAPHOR], as well as indices.

6. The reflexive/reciprocal subcase of the GCR also applies into tense-less embedded sentential complements in examples like the following:

(i) a.   Bertram and Edwin$_i$ would prefer for themselves to be victorious

b.   The bullfrogs$_i$ would prefer for each other to drown

The S-structures of these examples are shown in (ii), and the basic F-structure of PREFER appears in (iii):

(ii)

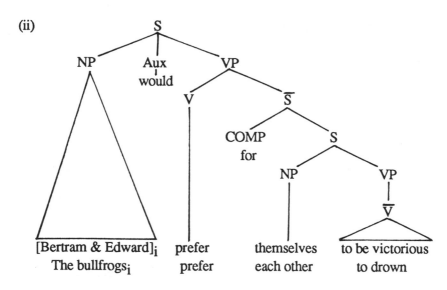

(iii)   PREFER   1-NP[α]   S

This predicate occurs with an S argument, which is the F-structure correlate of an S-structure $\overline{S}$ complement. The PRED/ARG structures of (i) are shown in (iv), after the application of the Index Insertion rule and the SRA rule:

(iv) a.   PREFER   NP[i]   [[BE[VICTORIOUS]]   NP[+REFLEX]]
              α   α

b.   PREFER   NP[i]   [DROWN   NP[+RECIPROCAL]]
              α   α

These structures contain uncontrolled [-tense] complements, analogous to ones of category PP. The reflexive/reciprocal subcase of the GCR applies to these structures in the normal way to produce the derived F-structures of these examples, which are shown in (v):

(v) a.   PREFER   NP[i]   [[BE[VICTORIOUS]]   NP[+REFLEX$_i$]]
              α   α

b.   PREFER $_{NP[i]}$ [DROWN $_{NP[+RECIPROCAL_i]}$]]
  α α

7. To see this more clearly, consider the following example:

(i)   Jocelyn$_i$ hated herself

The PRED/ARG structure of this example, after the application of theIindex Insertion rule and the SRA rule is the following:

(ii)   HATE $_{NP[i]}$ $_{NP[+REFLEX]}$
         α β

The reflexive subcase of the GCR applies to produce the structure in (iii):

(iii)   HATE $_{NP[i]}$ $_{NP[+REFLEX_i]}$
          α β

If the antecedent φ, the $_{NP[i]}$ argument of HATE, is deleted, the following derived F-structure is produced:

(iv)   HATE $_{NP[+REFLEX_i]}$
             β

In this structure, there is no correlate of the $_{NP[i]}$ constituent in example (i), so this structure cannot be the basis of a complete interpretation of example (i). However, since an adequate derived F-structure, Structure (iii), can be produced for this example, there is no need to block the derivation of (iv). It is easy to see that this applies to any F-structure in which an NP[θ] argument is deleted.

8. At the level of F-structure, pronominal NPs are represented in the same way as all lexical NPs. In contrast, bound anaphors, as we have seen, are represented at the level of F-structure as NP arguments with the feature [+ANAPHOR], and are not identical to other indexed NP arguments. Consequently, bound anaphors can be co-indexed with antecedents in the argument structure of the same predicate, and the resulting derived F-structures do not violate WFC I.

9. It is perhaps more accurate to say that the principles which govern the S-structure co-indexing rule define the set of configurations in which pronominal anaphora is possible. For example, they preclude pronominal anaphora in examples like (i), below, where the pronoun, *he*, precedes and commands the NP *Elroy*, while allowing it in examples like (3.36):

(i)   *He$_i$ liked Elroy$_i$ most of all

The F-level principles discussed here further eliminate the possibility of pronominal anaphora in certain environments in which the S-level principles allow it.

10. The predicate BOOK has the basic two-argument F-structure in (i), below:

(i)   BOOK 1-NP[α]   2-NP[β]

The noun *book* is typical of the class of picture nouns when they function as predicates, and this noun class is analogous to nominals like *destruction*, which also have two-argument basic F-structures as shown in example (2.1d), Chapter II.The S-structure correlate of the 1-NP[α] argument of such [+N] predicates is the DET/NP$_{poss}$ constituent, and the S-structure correlate of the 2-NP[β] argument is the NP object of a designated preposition. This is generally the prepositon *of* for nominals like *destruction*, and is the preposition *about* for *book*. In this respect, [+N] predicates are analogous to verbs like *depend on*.

In Structure (3.42b), the PRED/ARG structure of BOOK is embedded in the NP[β] argument position in the PRED/ARG structure of LIKE. This type of embedding is discussed in Chapter II, Section 4. The index $\underline{k}$ is assigned to the entire NP[β] argument.

In example (3.41b), the S-structure correlate of the 1-NP argument of BOOK is the determiner *those,* whose F-structure representation has the same formal status as [+INDEF] 1-NP arguments in XP complements of the type discussed in Chapter II.

11. The parallelism between sentences with uncontrolled S complements, like (3.36), and sentences with NP complements like (3.41b)

becomes more apparent when we consider sentences like the following:

(i) a.   Portnoy$_i$ liked Alfred's$_j$ books about $\left\{ \begin{array}{c} \text{him} \\ \text{himself} \end{array} \right\}$

   b.   Portnoy$_i$ believed that Alfred$_j$ liked $\left\{ \begin{array}{c} \text{him} \\ \text{himself} \end{array} \right\}$

The PRED/ARG structure of (i a), after the application of the Index Insertion rule and the SRA rule, is shown in (ii a), below, and the PRED/ARG structure of (i b), after the application of the Index Insertion rule and the SRA rule, is shown in (ii b) below:

(ii) a.   LIKE $_{\text{NP}}[i]$ $_{\text{NP}}[[\text{BOOK}$ $_{\text{NP}}[j]$ $_{\text{NP}}[\text{XXX}]]_k]$
$\qquad\qquad\quad \alpha \qquad \beta \qquad\quad \alpha \qquad \beta$

   b.   BELIEVE $_{\text{NP}}[i]$ [LIKE $_{\text{NP}}[j]$ $_{\text{NP}}[\text{XXX}]]$
$\qquad\qquad\qquad\quad \alpha \qquad\qquad \alpha \qquad \beta$

In these structures, $_{\text{NP}}[\text{XXX}]$ represents an arbitrarily indexed argument, or a [+REFLEX] argument.

If the pronoun *him* in each case is assigned an arbitrary index, say *m*, the following derived F-structures are produced:

(iii) a.   LIKE $_{\text{NP}}[i]$ $_{\text{NP}}[[\text{BOOK}$ $_{\text{NP}}[j]$ $_{\text{NP}}[m]]_k]$
$\qquad\qquad\qquad \alpha \qquad \beta \qquad\quad \alpha \qquad \beta$

   b.   BELIEVE $_{\text{NP}}[i]$ [LIKE $_{\text{NP}}[j]$ $_{\text{NP}}[m]]$
$\qquad\qquad\qquad\qquad \alpha \qquad\qquad \alpha \qquad \beta$

If the pronoun *him* in each case is co-indexed with the $_{\text{NP}}[j]$ argument, the following derived F-structures are produced:

(iv) a.   LIKE $_{\text{NP}}[i]$ $_{\text{NP}}[[\text{BOOK}$ $_{\text{NP}}[j]$ $_{\text{NP}}[j]]_k]$
$\qquad\qquad\qquad \alpha \qquad \beta \qquad\quad \alpha \qquad \beta$

   b.   BELIEVE $_{\text{NP}}[i]$ [LIKE $_{\text{NP}}[j]$ $_{\text{NP}}[j]]$
$\qquad\qquad\qquad\qquad \alpha \qquad\qquad \alpha \qquad \beta$

These structures are not well-formed, for the reason discussed in the text. Finally, if the pronoun *him* is co-indexed with the $_{\text{NP}}[i]$ argument in each case, the following derived F-structures are produced:

(v) a.   LIKE $_{\text{NP}}[i]$ $_{\text{NP}}[[\text{BOOK}$ $_{\text{NP}}[j]$ $_{\text{NP}}[i]]_k]$
$\qquad\qquad\qquad \alpha \qquad \beta \qquad\quad \alpha \qquad \beta$

b. BELIEVE $_{NP[i]}$ [LIKE $_{NP[j]}$ $_{NP[i]}$]
$\quad\quad\quad\quad\,\,\alpha\quad\quad\quad\quad\,\,\alpha\quad\,\beta$

The structures in (iii) are the basis for interpretations in which the pronoun refers to someone other than Portnoy or Alfred.The structures in (v) are the basis for interpretations in which the pronoun refers to Portnoy. The structures in (iv) are the basis for interpretations in which the pronoun refers to Alfred, but these structures are not well-formed. This explains why the examples in (i), with pronouns, only have the first two interpretations, and not the third.

The PRED/ARG structures of these examples with reflexive forms are shown in (vi), below:

(vi) a. LIKE $_{NP[i]}$ $_{NP[[BOOK}$ $_{NP[j]}$ $_{NP[+REFLEX]]_k]}$
$\quad\quad\quad\quad\,\,\alpha\quad\quad\,\,\beta\quad\quad\quad\alpha\quad\quad\,\beta$
    b. BELIEVE $_{NP[i]}$ [LIKE $_{NP[j]}$ $_{NP[+REFLEX]]}$
$\quad\quad\quad\quad\quad\quad\,\,\alpha\quad\quad\quad\quad\,\,\alpha\quad\quad\,\beta$

In both cases, the reflexive subcase of the GCR can only co-index the [+REFLEX] NP target and the $_{NP[j]}$ argument of BOOK and LIKE, respectively. This produces the derived F-structures shown in (vii):

(vii) a. LIKE $_{NP[i]}$ $_{NP[[BOOK}$ $_{NP[j]}$ $_{NP[+REFLEX_j]]_k]}$
$\quad\quad\quad\quad\,\,\alpha\quad\quad\,\,\beta\quad\quad\quad\alpha\quad\quad\,\,\,\beta$
    b. BELIEVE $_{NP[i]}$ [LIKE $_{NP[j]}$ $_{NP[+REFLEX_j]]}$
$\quad\quad\quad\quad\quad\quad\,\,\alpha\quad\quad\quad\quad\,\,\alpha\quad\quad\,\,\,\beta$

This explains why the bound anaphor in each example can only refer to *Alfred* and not to *Portnoy*.

12. The closest indexed NP in the PRED/ARG structure can also be the antecedent of the anaphor in examples like this under the right circumstances. The following sentence is structurally identical to (3.43a):

(i)   Axelrod$_i$ kept the twins$_j$ near each other

The PRED/ARG structure of this example, immediately before the application of the reflexive/reciprocal subcase of the GCR is the following:

(ii)   KEEP $_{NP}$[i] $_{NP}$[j] [NEAR $_{NP}$[+RECIPROCAL]]
         α   β   α

The reciprocal subcase of the GCR applies to this structure to co-index the [+RECIPROCAL] NP target and the $_{NP}$[j] argument of KEEP to produce the derived F-structure of (i), which appears in (iii):

(iii)   KEEP $_{NP}$[i] $_{NP}$[j] [NEAR $_{NP}$[+RECIPROCAL$_j$]]
          α   β   α

13. Additional examples like (3.41) and (3.43) are shown in (i):

(i) a. Dracula$_i$ constantly looked around him$_i$/himself when he
        walked through graveyards
    b. Insecure people$_i$ build walls around them$_i$/themselves as
        psychological protection

14. At this point, it might be useful to collate the evidence that prepositions can function either as independent predicates, in examples like (i), or as non-predicates, in examples like (ii):

(i) a. Rambo$_i$ kept a gun near the bed$_j$ at all times$_k$
    b. Ferdinand$_i$ drove near the obelisk$_j$
    c. Archibald$_i$ walked to the crematorium$_j$
    d. Dracula$_i$ constantly looked around him when he walked
        through graveyards
    e. Insecure people$_i$ build walls around them as psychological
        protection

(ii) a. Petruccio$_i$ talked about Flora$_j$
     b. Ethyl$_i$ depended on Randolf$_j$
     c. Maureen$_i$ speaks of South Africans$_j$ quite highly

In the PRED/ARG structures of the examples in (i), the prepositions are the predicates of PP complements, and are represented as shown in (iii):

(iii)   .....[PREP $_{NP}$[i]] ...
                     α

In the PRED/ARG structures of the examples in (ii), the NP objects of the prepositions are arguments of the verbs, and these structures do not contain embedded PP complements.

When prepositions function as predicates, their NP objects have the following cluster of properties:

(iv) a. they may be bound anaphors;
b. they can be pronouns which do not have a disjoint reference interpretation;
c. they cannot be antecedents of the NP* arguments of controlled XP complements;
d. they cannot occur as the subject (i.e. the S-structure correlate of the 1-NP argument) of the passive participle of the relevant verb.

This is illustrated by the pattern of grammaticality of the examples in (v), in which the preposition NEAR functions as a predicate:

(v) a. Rambo$_i$ kept a pistol near himself at all times
b. Rambo$_i$ kept a pistol near him$_i$ at all times
c. Rambo$_i$ kept his fighter plane$_j$ near the hangar$_k$ unlocked
d. *Rambo's hangar$_i$ was kept a fighter plane$_j$ near at all times

In (v c), the controller of the complement *unlocked* can be *his fighter plane*, which is the 2-NP[β] argument of the predicate KEEP, but not *the hangar*, which is the NP[α] argument of the prepositional predicate NEAR. In examples like (v d), only the 2-NP[β] argument of KEEP has a 1-NP argument analog in sentences which contain the passive participle of this verb, KEPT. *Rambo's hangar* is not an argument of KEEP, and therefore has no such analog. The other examples in (i) pattern in the same way (except for unrelated restrictions on the occurrence of anaphors in (b and c).

In contrast, when prepositions do not function as independent predicates, their S-structure NP objects have the following cluster of properties:

(vi) a. they may be bound anaphors;

  b. they can be pronouns, but must have a disjoint reference
   interpretation;
  c. they can be the antecedents of the NP* arguments of controlled
   XP complements;
  d. they can occur as the subject of the passive participle of the
   relevant verb

This cluster of properties is illustrated by the pattern of grammaticality of the examples in (vii), in which the preposition *on* does not
function as a predicate:

(vii) a. Ethyl$_i$ depends on herself
  b. *Ethyl$_i$ depends on her$_i$
  c. Ethyl$_i$ depends on Randolf$_j$ to do the housework
  d. Randolf$_i$ is depended on by everyone

The other examples in (ii) pattern in the same way.

15. This analysis also explains why judgements concerning sentences
which contain obligatorily controlled complements like the following
are more clearcut:

(i) a. Jackson$_i$ forced Scott$_j$ to kiss a toad$_k$
 b. Everyone$_i$ considered Jumbo$_j$ large

The PRED/ARG structures of these examples, after the application of
the Index Insertion rule and the SRA rule, are the following:

(ii) a. FORCE NP$_i$ NP$_j$ [(NP*)[KISS NP NP$_k$]]
      α β α β
  b. CONSIDER NP$_i$ [($_{NP*}$[j])[LARGE NP]]
        α α

In structure (ii a), the target, NP*, and the potential controllers, NP$_i$ and
NP$_j$ are located in the argument structure of the same predicate,
FORCE. The FMDP applies without exception to such structures. In
both structures, the antecedent for the Raqui subcase of the GCR, NP*,
and the target, the 1-NP argument of KISS and LARGE, respectively,
are located in adjacent argument structures, and the FMDP applies

without exception in this case also.

16. The SI rule is optional and need not apply to the PRED/ARG structures of examples like the ones discussed in this section. If it does not apply, the subject of the embedded complement is interpreted as having indefinite reference by the convention suggested in Chapter II. This is illustrated by the following examples:

(i) a. Morrison$_i$ thought that shaving oneself in public was impolite
   b. Flora$_i$ knew that Marvin$_j$ realized that dressing oneself in sackcloth was frowned upon

The derived F-structures of these examples are shown in (ii):

(ii) a. THINK NP$_i$ [[BE[IMPOLITE]] [SHAVING [+INDEF] NP$_R$[+INDEF]]]

   b. KNOW NP$_i$ [REALIZE NP$_j$ [[BE[FROWNED UPON]] [DRESSING [+INDEF] NP$_R$[+INDEF]]]]

In some cases, the interpretation in which one of the NPs is the understood subject of the complement is the preferred one, for reasons that probably have nothing to do with the SI rule. An example in which this is the case is the following:

(iii) Marvin$_i$ knew that shaving in the living room would disturb his pet alligator$_j$

However, the interpretation in which anyone's shaving in the living room would have this result is also possible for this example.

17. As was the case for examples like (4.1b), the NP$_j$ argument in structures like (4.39a) can also be the antecedent, under the right circumstances. This is illustrated by example (i), below, shown with its derived F-structure:

(i) a. Morrison$_i$ thought that pictures of herself would disturb Mabel$_j$

b. THINK NP_i [DISTURB [PICTURES NP_j NP_{Rj}] NP_j]

18. The NP_i argument in (6.6b) and the NP_j arguments in (6.7b) and (6.9b) are closer to the unindexed NP_R arguments in these structures than they are to the designated target ψ. However, in each of these structures, a 1-NP argument is equally close to the NP_R argument, and according to Stipulation (5.14) must be its antecedent. Therefore, the NP_R arguments are not possible targets for NP_i in (6.6b) and NP_j in (6.7b) and (6.9b). Consequently, these latter arguments are potential antecedents of the ψ targets. In (6.6b), the NP_i/NP pair is the only possible φ/ψ pair relevant to the co-indexing operation, and is therefore the one whose members are least distantly separated. In (6.7b) and (6.9b), the NP_j/NP pairs as well as the NP_i/NP pairs are the φ/ψ pairs relevant to the co-indexing operation whose members are least distantly separated.

Chapter IV

The Argument Reduction System: A Reanalysis of Bounded Movement and Deletion

1. Introduction

A minimal requirement for an adequate theory of UG is that it provide an explanation for the general patterns of movement and deletion that are observed in language. Here, I will look at two categories of movement: (a) movement relevant to Chomsky's "Move NP" rule, and (b) movement attributed to the operation of various lexical transformations. Additionally, I will consider a case of uncontrolled deletion: so-called "object deletion". I will formulate the second of the three rule systems of UG, the Argument Reduction System. This provides a unified account of these three syntactic and lexical phenomena, operating in conjunction with general principles of the theory to properly constrain them. At the same time, the theory explains the cross-language variation in these general patterns.

The principal subcases of the general "Move NP" rule in the standard theory are passivization and raising to subject position. Raising to object position has been eliminated from that theory. In the first case, an NP is moved from some non-subject position to subject position, as diagrammed in (1.1a), and in the second case, an NP is moved from the subject position of a complement sentence to the subject position of a higher sentence, as diagrammed in (1.1b):

(1.1) a.

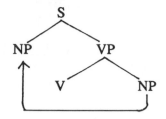

b.

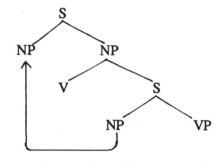

Chomsky's insight was that NP movement, broadly speaking, patterns as follows: In effect, NPs can be moved to subject position from some non-subject position (or from complement subject position), but not from subject position to some non-subject position. In hierarchical languages like English, this entails moving NPs from lower to higher positions in phrase markers, but not vice versa. The principles and conditions associated with trace theory, in effect, constrain NP movement and account for these patterns as well as the partial similarity of the patterns of NP movement and those of control and anaphora, which were discussed in the preceding chapter.[1] These are discussed in a myriad of references. Two of the most important recent ones are Chomsky (1981) and Chomsky (1985).

As examples of the second type of movement, consider the following sentence pairs:

(1.2) a.   Someone broke the window
    b.   The window broke

(1.3) a.   The army's destruction of the village
    b.   The village's destruction (by the army)

(1.4) a.   Everyone loved Mickey
     b.   Mickey was lovable

The sentence pairs in these examples are related by lexical processes, all of which mirror in a sense the patterns of syntactic NP movement. That is, some NP in a non- subject position of the (a) member of each pair corresponds to an NP in subject position of the (b) member of each pair. Since the output of lexical operations must be compatible with the syntactic structures and patterns of the relevant language, this is not surprising.

Sentence pairs like the following are examples of the process of object deletion:

(1.5) a.   Priam drinks beer
     b.   Priam drinks

(1.6) a.   Merv drove his car to work
     b.   Merv drove to work

The Object Deletion relation is observed for certain verbs or verb classes, and is probably attributable to a lexical transformation rather than a non-lexical rule.

As discussed in Chapter I, "movement" may be defined as a particular type of relation between sentence pairs. In the context of the proposed theory, we can redefine (lexical and non-lexical) "movement" of a particular type, say NP movement, in terms of pairs of related F-structures, as the set of FS_1/FS_2 pairs that some specific rule system of the theory relates. In this way, the notion of movement can be generalized to the notion "grammatical process", which encompasses the analogs of syntactic movement, certain lexical processes, and deletion in earlier theories.

In this framework, the rules of the proposed Argument Reduction System (which is a generalized version of the one proposed in Horn (1983a) and (1983b)) relate the sets of FS_1/FS_2 pairs that correspond to sentence pairs related by cases of the NP movement rule (other than raising to subject and object positions, which have been discussed), as well as the lexical processes illustrated by examples (1.2) - (1.4), and the Object Deletion rule illustrated in example (1.5). These FS pairs fall into two categories: argument reduction pairs and object deletion pairs.

The Argument Reduction System, in effect, defines the set of possible Argument Reduction (AR) FS pairs and Object Deletion (OD) FS pairs. The set of possible AR and OD FS pairs is the analog of the set of possible sentence-pairs related by the NP movement rule and other processes discussed here. So the proposed theory explains the patterns, illustrated in (1.1a), that Chomsky attributes to the NP movement rule, in particular, the residue of cases not discussed in Chapter III.

In the next section, I will define the Argument Reduction relation as an FS pair type, and look at some examples of non-lexical and lexical argument reduction in English and other languages. I will conclude the section with a first pass at the formulation of the Argument Reduction System.

In Section 3, I will look at additional examples of the Argument Reduction relation, as well as the Object Deletion relation, and demonstrate that the same sorts of non-lexical and lexical rules relate both types of FS pairs. These rules can be formulated as components of a generalized Argument Reduction System. This explains why the output of a large class of lexical transformations mirrors the NP movement pattern.

In Section 4, I will demonstrate that no additional conditions peculiar to the generalized Argument Reduction System are required. The nature of the rules and independently motivated general principles of the theory sufficiently constrain the Argument Reduction and Object Deletion processes. Moreover, the generalized Argument Reduction System analysis is equally applicable to configurational and non-configurational languages.

Section 5 is a summary of the main points, and a discussion of a constraint on lexical rules that accounts for the non-occurrence of the analog of raising to object position in NPs.

2. The Argument Reduction Relation

This is the relation between the members of the set of FS_1/FS_2 pairs such that:

(a)   the 2-NP[β] argument of FS_1 corresponds to the 1-NP[β] argument of FS_2;

(b) FS_2 contains one x-NP[θ] argument less than FS_1;

(c) no obligatory x-NP[θ] argument of FS_2 bears the SR α, which is borne by the 1-NP argument of FS_1.

The Argument Reduction relation may be schematized as shown in (2.0):

(2.0) $PRED_1$ 1-NP[α]   2-NP[β]   ...   / $PRED_2$ 1-NP[β]   ...

where the lefthand F-structure is FS_1 and the righthand F-structure is FS_2.

The principal, and perhaps only, manifestation of non-lexical argument reduction in English is the active verb/verbal participle relation. The following sentence pairs illustrate this relation:

(2.1) a.   Annette$_i$ gave Archibald$_j$ a book$_k$

   b.   Archibald$_i$ was given a book$_j$ (by Annette)

(2.2) a.   Lex$_i$ helped Alfred$_j$

   b.   Alfred$_i$ was helped (by Lex)

(2.3) a.   Mac$_i$ saw Jack$_j$

   b.   Jack$_i$ was seen (by Mac)

The properties of this relationship are well-known and need not be discussed here. I assume, following Wasow (1978), that there are both lexical and non-lexical passives in English, and that the latter contain verbal participles.

The derived F-structures of examples (2.1a), (2.2a), and (2.3a) are produced as discussed in Chapter II. They are shown below:

(2.4) a.   GIVE $NP^{[i]}_\alpha$ $NP^{[j]}_\beta$ $NP^{[k]}_\gamma$

   b.   HELP $NP^{[i]}_\alpha$ $NP^{[j]}_\beta$

   c.   SEE $NP^{[i]}_\alpha$ $NP^{[j]}_\beta$

Verbal participles are inflectional variants of the verbs that they are related to, and are derived from these verbs by the following Word Formation Rule (WFR):

(2.5)   VERB –> [VERB + EN]$_V$

As the inflectional *-en* variants of verbs, verbal participles do not have their own lexical entries and their basic F-structures are (necessarily) identical to those of the verbs that they are derived from. The derived F-structures of sentences containing verbal participles are produced as shown below for examples (2.1b) and (2.2b).

Since the verbal participles *given* and *helped* are inflectional variants of the verbs *give* and *help*, they occur in the same type of syntactic structures. The S-structures of these examples are shown below:

(2.6) a.

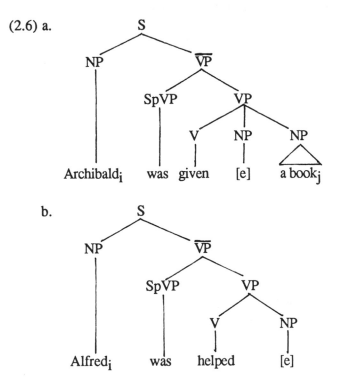

b.

The basic F-structures of *helped* and *given* (which are also the basic F-structures of *help* and *give*) are shown in (2.7):

(2.7) a.   HELPED   1-NP[α]   2-NP[β]

b.   GIVEN   1-NP[α]   2-NP[β]   3-NP[ɣ]

In (2.6a), *Archibald*$_i$ is the S-structure correlate of the 1-NP argument of GIVEN, and *a book*$_j$ is the S-structure correlate of the 3-NP argument. In (2.6b), *Alfred*$_i$ is the S-structure correlate of the 1-NP argument of HELPED.

The derived F-structures of these examples are produced from the following bare PRED/ARG structures:

(2.8) a. $_{Sp}$VP[BE][GIVEN   1-NP   2-NP   3-NP]
      b. $_{Sp}$VP[BE][HELPED   1-NP   2-NP]

These structures are produced by combining $_{Sp}$VP[BE] and the basic PRED/ARG structures of the relevant predicates.

First, the indices of the S-structure NPs are inserted into the appropriate NP argument positions in the structures in (2.8) to produce the following:

(2.9) a. $_{Sp}$VP[BE][GIVEN $_{NP}$[i] $_{NP}$[j]]
      b. $_{Sp}$VP[BE][HELPED $_{NP}$[i]]

The empty nodes [e] are unindexed and do not appear at the F-structure level.

At this point, the Semantic Relations Assignment rule (SRA) must apply. However, in (2.9a), the SR β must be assigned to $_{NP}$[i] and the SR ɣ must be assigned to $_{NP}$[j]. In Structure (2.9b), the SR β must be assigned to $_{NP}$[i]. The SRA rule, as formulated in Chapter II, is repeated below:

(2.10)   <u>SRA</u>:   Assign the semantic relations, α, β, ɣ to x-NP arguments in the PRED/ARG structure in the order in which these appear in the basic F-structure of the relevant PRED.

To produce the F-structures of (2.1b) and (2.2b), SRA must be reformulated as shown in (2.11):

(2.11)   <u>SRA(b)</u>:
        (1) To produce derived F-structures from PRED/ARG struc-

tures of the form:

$$[\phi][PRED\ NP_i\ NP_j\ ...,$$

delete the SR α in the basic F-structure of the relevant PRED;

(2) Assign the (remaining) SRs, (α), β, γ, ... to x-NP arguments in the PRED/ARG structure in the order in which these appear in the basic F-structure of the relevant PRED.

In this rule, $\{\phi\}$ is the set of syntactic markers in S-structures that trigger α-deletion. For English, this set includes $_{Sp}VP[BE]$, as well as $_{Sp}VP[GET]$. The set $\{\phi\}$ differs from language to language. I will return to this point below.

SRA(b) applies to the structures in (2.9) to produce the following:

(2.12) a. $_{Sp}VP[BE][GIVEN\ \underset{\beta}{NP^{[i]}}\ \underset{\gamma}{NP^{[j]}}]$

b. $_{Sp}VP[BE][HELPED\ \underset{\beta}{NP^{[i]}}]$

These are the derived F-structures of examples (2.1b) and (2.2b). This explains the relationship between the F-structures of active and passive sentences. The FS_1/FS_2 pairs for sentences like (2.1) to (2.3) are examples of the general pattern shown in (2.13), the English Passive subcase of the Argument Reduction pattern:[2]

(2.13) $PRED_x\ NP[\alpha]\ NP[\beta]\ ...\ /PRED_y\ NP[\beta]\ ...$
where $PRED_x = VERB$ and $PRED_y = [VERB+EN]_V$

The non-lexical argument reduction process manifests itself in different ways in different languages. A widespread pattern involves the occurrence of reflexive forms in sentences that are not, semantically or functionally, transitive reflexive sentences. Examples of this pattern in Polish and Italian are shown in (2.14), below. These examples correspond to intransitive sentences in English:

(2.14) a.   Okno zbiło się
window (NOM) broke REFLEX
The window broke

b.   Lód stopił się
     ice (NOM) melted REFLEX
     The ice melted

c.   Drzwi otworzyły się
     door (NOM) opened REFLEX
     The door opened

(2.15) a.   La finestra si ruppe
            the window REFLEX broke
            The window broke

b.   Il ghiaccio si scioglie
     the ice REFLEX is melting
     The ice is melting

c.   Il cielo si arrossa
     the sky REFLEX is turning red
     The sky is turning red

This pattern is quite widespread in Polish, extending beyond the so-called inchoative verb class. The following examples illustrate this:

(2.16) a.   Jan urodził się w 1948 roku
            Jan (NOM) born REFLEX in 1948 year(LOC)
            Jan was born in 1948

b.   Szkoła utworzyła się w Poznaniu
     school (NOM) founded REFLEX in Poznań (LOC)
     The school was founded in Poznań

c.   Jan wychował się u dziadka
     Jan (NOM) brought up REFLEX at grandfather (GEN)
     Jan was brought up at his grandfather's home

In these examples, the reflexive particle (Polish *się*/Italian *si*) in its non-reflexive usage occurs with verbs that are functionally transitive just in case these verbs occur with only a single lexical NP. All of the above verbs occur in transitive sentences as shown below:

(2.17) a.   Jan$_i$ zbił okno$_j$
Jan (NOM) broke window (ACC)
Jan broke the window

b.   Marek$_i$ stopił lód$_j$
Marek (NOM) melted ice (ACC)
Marek melted the ice

c.   Jan$_i$ otworzył drzwi$_j$
Jan (NOM) opened door (ACC)
Jan opened the door

d.   Maria$_i$ urodziła Jana$_j$
Maria (NOM) bore Jan (ACC)
Maria gave birth to Jan

e.   Profesorowie$_i$ utworzyli szkołę$_j$ w Poznaniu$_k$
Professors (NOM) founded school (ACC) in Poznań (LOC)
The professors founded the school in Poznań

f.   Marek$_i$ wychował Jana$_j$
Marek (NOM) raised Jan (ACC)
Marek raised/brought up Jan

(2.18) a.   Giovanni$_i$ ruppe la finestra$_j$
Giovanni broke the window

b.   Luigi$_i$ scioglie il ghiaccio$_j$
Luigi is melting the ice

To generalize, reflexive particles in their non-reflexive usage occur with n-place verbs, just in case these verbs are inserted into S-structures containing n-1 lexical NP constituents. Moreover, the subjects of examples like (2.14) - (2.16) bear the SR β, which is assigned to the objects of the verbs in (2.17) and (2.18), and no NP constituent in (2.14) - (2.16) is assigned the SR α, which is assigned to the subjects of

examples like (2.17) and (2.18). In functional terms, the relationship
between examples like (2.14) - (2.16) on the one hand and examples like
(2.17) and (2.18) on the other is identical to the relation between
English passive and active sentences.

The derived F-structures of examples (2.17) - (2.18) are produced as
discussed in Chapter II. Three of these are shown below (for (2.17a),
(2.17f), and (2.18a), respectively):

(2.19) a.   ZBIĆ   NP[i] NP[j]
                    α   β

       b.   WYCHOWAĆ   NP[i] NP[j]
                       α   β

       c.   ROMPERE   NP[i] NP[j]
                      α   β

Since the reflexive/intransitive sentences in (2.14) - (2.16) contain
the same verbs as their transitive counterparts, the S-structures of
both sentence types are identical (down to category level). The S-
structures of (2.14a) and (2.16a) are shown below:

(2.20) a.

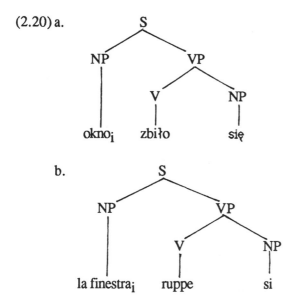

       b.

The reflexive particles in these sentences are functionally analogous to
the English SpVP[BE] and SpVP[GET]. That is, they are elements of
the set {φ}, and trigger the rule in SRA(b)(1), α–> ø.

The derived F-structures of these examples are produced from the following bare PRED/ARG structures, which are formed by combining the elements of the set $\{\phi\}$ with the F-structures of the relevant predicates:

(2.21) a.   [SIĘ][ZBIĆ 1-NP 2-NP]
     b.   [SI][ROMPERE 1-NP 2-NP]

As elements of $\{\phi\}$, the particles are marked [-Grammatical Relation]. As a consequence, no correlation statement applies to them since correlation statements are sensitive to grammatical relation indicators.[3] So the object NP constituents in (2.20) are equivalent to the $_{NP}[e]$ constituents in the structures of the English passives discussed earlier. As a result, the insertion of the appropriate indices into the structures in (2.21) and the application of SRA(b) produces the derived F-structures of (2.14a) and (2.15a).

(2.22) a.   [SIĘ][ZBIĆ $_{NP}^{[i]}_{\beta}$]

     b.   [SI][ROMPERE $_{NP}^{[i]}_{\beta}$]

We see, then, that the non-lexical argument reduction process explains the relationship between transitive sentences like (2.17) and (2.18) and their intransitive-reflexive counterparts like (2.14) - (2.16). A comparison of the derived F-structures in (2.19) and (2.22) reveals that the FS_1/FS_2 pairs for these sentence types are examples of the general argument reduction pattern. This is illustrated below:

(2.23) $PRED_x$ NP[α] NP[β] ... / $PRED_y$ NP[β]
      where $PRED_x$ = VERB and $PRED_y$ = [[REFLEX][VERB]]

The same non-lexical rules of Index Insertion (in accordance with the appropriate correlation statements of the particular languages) and SRA, with and without α-deletion, apply to produce the F-structures of the English active/passive pairs and the Polish and Italian transitive/intransitive-reflexive pairs.[4]   The set of related predicates, $PRED_x$ and $PRED_y$, and the membership of the set $\{\phi\}$ differ from language to language.

I turn now to movement which is attributed to the operation of various lexical transformations. One example of this is adjectival passivization in English, illustrated by the following examples:

(2.24) a.   Someone broke the window
    b.   The window was broken   (the broken window)

(2.25) a.   White farmers inhabited South Africa in the 19th
      century
    b.   South Africa is inhabited

(2.26)   That food is untouched (by human hands)

The passive sentences in these examples are clearly related to their active counterparts (if such active counterparts exist) in the same way that English verbal passives are related to their active counterparts. This is another manifestation of the Argument Reduction relation.

However, unlike verbal participles, adjectival participles like *broken*, *inhabited*, and *untouched*, are independent lexical items, with their own lexical entries, and their own basic F-structures. The basic F-structures of the verbs *break* and *inhabit* are shown in (2.27) and those of the adjectival participles *broken*, *inhabited*, and *untouched* are shown in (2.28):

(2.27) a.   BREAK 1-NP[α] 2-NP[β]
    b.   INHABIT 1-NP[α] 2-NP[β]

(2.28) a.   BROKEN 1-NP[α]
    b.   INHABITED 1-NP[α]
    c.   UNTOUCHED 1-NP[α]

The SR α in the F-structures of (2.28) is the same as the SR β in the F-structures of (2.27).

The derivations of the F-structures of all the examples in (2.24), (2.25), and (2.26) are straightforward. The S-structures of (2.24a), (2.24b), and (2.26) are shown below:

(2.29) a.

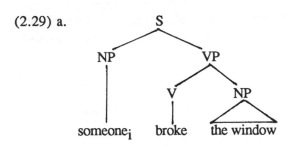

someone$_i$ broke   the window

b.

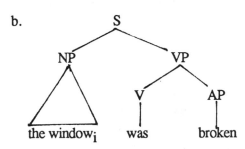

the window$_i$ was   broken

c.

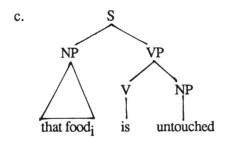

that food$_i$ is   untouched

(In structures (b) and (c), the form of BE is a main verb rather than SpVP.)

The derived F-structures of these examples are produced from the following PRED/ARG structures. Structures (b) and (c), are formed by combining the PRED/ARG structures of the main verb BE and the relevant predicates:

(2.30) a.   BREAK 1-NP 2-NP
       b.   BE[BROKEN] 1-NP
       c.   BE[UNTOUCHED] 1-NP

The application of the Index Insertion rule and the SRA rule (without α-deletion) produces the following derived F-structures:

(2.31) a.   BREAK NP[i]_{α} NP[j]_{β}

    b.   BE[BROKEN] NP[i]_{α}

    c.   BE[UNTOUCHED] NP[i]_{α}

As in the non-lexical cases, a comparison of the derived F-structures of examples like (2.24a) and (2.25a), on the one hand, and those of examples like (2.24b), (2.25b), and (2.26), on the other, reveals that the FS_1/FS_2 pairs for these sentences are examples of the general argument reduction pattern. This is shown below:

(2.32) $PRED_x$ NP[α] NP[β] / $PRED_y$ NP[β]
        where $PRED_x$ = VERB and $PRED_y$ = $[VERB+EN]_A$

The relationship between active sentences and their counterparts containing adjectival particles is explained by deriving the adjectival participle from the active verb, or, perhaps more accurately, relating the active verb and the corresponding adjectival participle. Two lexical rules, a lexical transformation and a WFR, do this. These rules are shown in (2.33):

(2.33) a.   VERB -> $[VERB+EN]_A$
     b.   VERB 1-NP[α] 2-NP[β] <-> $[VERB+EN]_A$ 1-NP[β]
        Condition: β = theme

The active/passive relation in Polish is the analog in that language of the English lexical passivization process. The following Polish sentences illustrate this relation:

(2.34) a. Jan_i widział Marię_j
        Jan (NOM) saw Maria (ACC)
        Jan saw Maria

     b. Maria_i była wydziana   (przez Jana)
        Maria (NOM) was seen (by Jan (GEN))
        Maria was seen (by Jan)

As in English, the active sentence, example (2.34a), contains two NP constituents and the passive sentence contains a single obligatory constituent, which bears the same SR as that assigned to the object NP constituent of the active sentence. It is easy to see that such sentence pairs are related by the Argument Reduction relation.

Additional passive sentences are shown below:

(2.35)a.   Okno$_i$ było wybite (przez Jana)
window (NOM) was broken (by Jan (GEN))
The window was broken (by Jan)

b.   Książka$_i$ była przeczytana
book (NOM) was read
The book was read

c.   Człowiek$_i$ był pobity
man (NOM) was beaten up
The man was beaten up

In contrast to English, however, all passive participles in Polish are truly adjectival. That is, they behave morphologically like adjectives in that they agree in gender, number, and case with the nouns that they are related to, and they can occupy all of the syntactic positions that adjectives occur in (prenominal as well as predicate positions). There is thus no syntactic evidence for a separate class of verbal participles as there is in English.

In the context of the proposed thoery, then, both active verbs and participles are independent lexical items, with their own lexical entries and basic F-structures. The basic F-structure of the active verb, *widzieć* is shown in (2.36), and the basic F-structures of *widziany*, *wybity*, and *przeczytany*, the passive participles, are shown in (2.37):

(2.36)   WIDZIEĆ 1-NP[α] 2-NP[β]

(2.37)a.   WIDZIANY 1-NP[α]
b.   WYBITY 1-NP[α]
c.   PRZECZYTANY 1-NP[α]

The SR α assigned to the 1-NP argument of WIDZIANY is the same as the SR β assigned to the 2-NP term of WIDZIEĆ, and the SRs α of the 1-NP arguments of the participles WYBITY and PRZECZYTANY are the same as the SRs assigned to the 2-NP arguments of the corresponding active verbs (by convention, represented as β in the F-structures of the latter).

The derived F-structures of these examples are produced as discussed in Chapter II. The S-structures of (2.34a and b) are shown below:

(2.38) a.

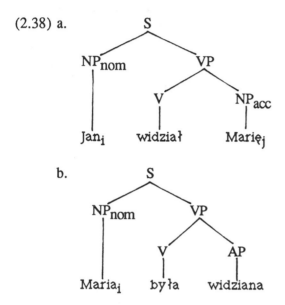

b.

The S-structures of (2.35) are identical to (2.38b) down to and including the level of syntactic categories.

The derived F-structure of (2.34a) is produced from the bare PRED/ARG structure of (2.36) and the derived F-structures of (2.34b) and (2.35) are produced from PRED/ARG structures formed by combining the PRED/ARG structure of the main verb BYC and those of the relevant predicates. The Index Insertion rule and the SRA rule (without α-deletion) apply to produce the following:

(2.39)   WIDZIEĆ $NP[i]_{\alpha}$ $NP[j]_{\beta}$

(2.40) a. BYĆ[WIDZIANA] $NP[i]_{\alpha}$

b.   BYĆ[WYBITE] $_{NP[i]}$
α

c.   BYĆ[PRZECZYTANA] $_{NP[i]}$
α

The structure in (2.39) is the derived F-structure of example (2.34a), and the structures in (2.40) are the derived F-structures of (2.34b), (2.35a), and (2.35b), respectively.

As in the previously discussed cases, a comparison of the derived F-structures of examples like (2.34a), on the one hand, and (2.34b) and (2.35) on the other, reveals that the FS_1/FS_2 pairs for this sentence-type are examples of the argument reduction pattern. This is illustrated in (2.41):

(2.41) $PRED_x$ 1-NP[α] 2-NP[β] / $PRED_y$ 1-NP[β]
where $PRED_x$ = VERB and $PRED_y$ = [VERB + ANY]$_A$

As in English, the relationship between Polish active and passive sentences is explained by relating active verbs and their corresponding passive participles by means of a lexical transformation and a WFR. These are shown below:

(2.42) a.   VERB -> [VERB + ANY]$_A$

b.   VERB 1-NP[α] 2-NP[β] W <-> [VERB + ANY]$_A$
1-NP[β] W
Condition: β = theme; W = variable

(See (1983b) for a more extensive discussion of passivization in Polish.)

Now consider the following Polish sentence pairs:

(2.43) a.   Jan$_i$ topi lód$_j$
Jan (NOM) melts ice (ACC)
Jan is melting the ice

   b. Lód$_i$ topnieje
       ice (NOM) melts
       The ice is melting

(2.44) a. Krew$_i$ czerwieni wodę$_j$
           blood (NOM) reddens water (ACC)
           Blood is turning the water red

   b. Niebo$_i$ czerwienieje
       sky (NOM) reddens
       The sky is turning red

The (a) members of each pair contain transitive verbs, *topić* and
czerwienić which occur with two NP constituents. (These verbs also
occur in intransitive-reflexive sentences like those discussed earlier:
Lód topi się (The ice is melting) and *Niebo czerwieni się* (The sky is
turning red).) The (b) members of each pair contain the intransitive
verbs *topnieć* and *czerwienieć*, which are morphologically related to
the transitive verbs, and occur with a single NP constituent. The SR
borne by the single NP constituent is the same as that borne by the object
NP in the (a) examples, and no NP constituent bearing the SR α (of
the subjects of the (a) examples) appears. So the relation between these
sentence pairs is another example of the Argument Reduction relation.

Both the transitive verbs and the intransitive verbs are independent
lexical items with their own basic F-structures. The basic F-structures
of *topić* and *topnieć* are shown below:

(2.45) a. TOPIĆ   1-NP[α]   2-NP[β]
       b. TOPNIEĆ 1-NP[α]

The SR α of the 1-NP argument of TOPNIEĆ is the same as the SR
β of the 2-NP argument of TOPIĆ.

The S-structures of (2.45) are shown below:

(2.46) a.

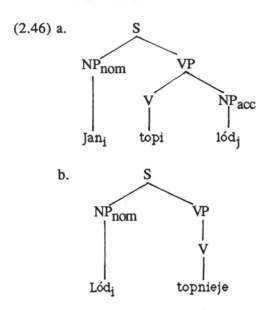

The derivations of the F-structures of these examples is straight-forward. The Index Insertion rule and the SRA rule apply to produce the structures shown in (2.47):

(2.47) a.   TOPIĆ   NP[i]   NP[j]
                      α β

 b.   TOPNIEĆ   NP[i]
                        α

Comparing these structures, we see that the FS_1/FS_2 pairs for sentences of this type are examples of the argument reduction pattern:

(2.48) $PRED_x$ NP[α] NP[β] / $PRED_y$ NP[β]
         where $PRED_x$ = VERB and $PRED_y$ = [VERB + Iaf]$_{Vi}$
         Iaf = intransitive affix

The relationship between transitive verbs (of this class) and their intransitive counterparts is explained by the following WFR and lexical transformation:

(2.49) a.   VERB -> [VERB + NIEĆ]$_{V_i}$

b.   VERB 1-NP[α]   2-NP[β]   <-> [VERB+NIEĆ] 1-NP[β]

Finally, consider the English sentence-pairs in the following examples:

(2.50) a.   Alex$_i$ broke the window$_j$
        The window$_i$ broke

(2.51) a.   Ralph$_i$ opened the door$_j$
        The door$_i$ opened

(2.52) a.   Everyone$_i$ loved Gwen$_j$
     b.   Gwen$_i$ is quite lovable

A number of verbs in English (of different classes) occur in both transitive and intransitive sentences. Two examples are *break* and *open*, and others include verbs that appear in pairs like: *Alex peeled the oranges/Those oranges peel easily, Everyone read that book/That book reads easily*, and so forth. There are, perhaps, many interesting questions to ask about the semantics (and syntax) of these examples, but, from a functional viewpoint, these sentence pairs are related in the same way as the other sentence pairs discussed in this section. In each case, the second member of the pair contains one less NP constituent than the first member, and the SR of that one NP is the same as the SR of the object NP of the first member. This is another example of the Argument Reduction relation.

Each of the predicates in these examples is an independent lexical item. The derived F-structures of (2.50) and (2.52) are shown below:

(2.53) a.   BREAK NP[i]_α NP[j]_β

     b.   BREAK NP[i]_α

(2.54) a.   LOVE NP[i]_α NP[j]_β

     b.   LOVABLE NP[i]_α

As before, the SR α of the 1-NP argument of the (b) examples is the same as the SR β of the 2-NP argument of its counterpart in (a).

It is easy to see that the FS_1/FS_2 pairs of these sentence types are cases of the argument reduction pattern:

(2.55) $PRED_x$ NP[α] NP[β] / $PRED_y$ NP[β]
where $PRED_x$ = $VERB_{Trans}$ and $PRED_y$ = $VERB_{Intrans}$
or $PRED_x$ = VERB and $PRED_y$ = $[VERB + ABLE]_A$

These relationships are explained by the following lexical transformations:

(2.56) a.   VERB   1-NP[α]   2-NP[β]   <-->   VERB   1-NP[β]
      b.   VERB   1-NP[α]   2-NP[β]   <--> $[VERB + ABLE]_A$
              1-NP[β]

The second transformation is accompanied by the WFR shown in (2.57):

(2.57)   VERB --> $[VERB + ABLE]_A$

The data discussed in this section include several syntactic and lexical processes in three different languages, which are representative of the sorts of processes that occur in most, if not all, languages in some form. All of these diverse processes can be analyzed as specific cases of a single general argument reduction process. Both the lexical and non-lexical rules involved in the derivations effectively relate the same general type of FS_1/FS_2 pairs, schematised below:

(2.58) $PRED_x$ NP[α] NP[β] W / $PRED_y$ NP[β] W
W = variable

Two general non-lexical operations on F-structures, Index Insertion and SRA, apply in the derivations of the F-structures of the examples discussed in this section in the same way that they apply to all derivations of F-structures in the theory, as discussed in Chapter II. The formulations of these rules appear below:

(2.59) a.   Index Insertion: Insert the indices of the S-structure NP constituents into the proper argument positions of the PRED/ARG structure in accordance with the correlation statements of the language.

b. <u>SRA</u>: Assign the (relevant) semantic relations, $\theta_1, \theta_2, \theta_3$, ..., to x-NP arguments in the PRED/ARG structure in the order in which the SRs appear in the basic F-structure of the relevant PRED.

The SRA rule, as reformulated here, is a generalized version of (2.10) and (2.11), and is applicable to all derivations, whether or not α-deletion applies to them.

The non-lexical rule which relates specifically to the Argument Reduction process is shown in (2.60):

(2.60) $\alpha \rightarrow \varnothing$ in the production of derived F-structures from PRED/ARG structures of the form: $[\phi]$PRED...x-NP..., where ϕ is a member of the set $\{\phi\}$ of designated syntactic (S-structure-level) markers or triggers in the relevant language, L_x.

The lexical transformations which pertain to the argument reduction process may be generalized as follows:

(2.61) $[..PRED_x..]$ 1-NP$[\alpha]$ 2-NP$[\beta]$ W $\longleftrightarrow$ $[..PRED_y..]$ 1-NP$[\beta]$ W

Since all basic F-structures have the same form, the structural description of the generalized lexical transformation need not be explicitly stated. Consequently, the rules of UG which comprise what we may think of as the Argument Reduction System can be formulated as follows:

(2.62)   <u>The Argument Reduction System</u>
(a)   To produce derived F-structures from PRED/ARG structures of the form:
$[\phi]$PRED$_x$ ...x-NP$[\theta]$ ..., $\phi \in \{\phi\}$;
SR α of PRED$_x$ $\rightarrow \varnothing$

(b)   To relate the pair FS_x/FS_y of $PRED_x$ and $PRED_Y$,

$$1\text{-NP}[\alpha]_{PREDx} \rightarrow \emptyset$$

where $PRED_x$ and $PRED_y$ $\in$ $\{PRED_x <\text{-}> PRED_y\}$

The non-lexical rule of α-deletion, (a) above, is triggered by some element ϕ of the set $\{\phi\}$, and SRA applies to assign the remaining SRs in the basic F-structure of the relevant PRED to NP arguments in the PRED/ARG structure. Those elements which are members of the set $\{\phi\}$ are independent lexical items in the sense that they are free morphemes inserted into Phrase-markers independently of other lexical items, and are not attached to other forms by WFRs. Ideally, the theory should limit the types of syntactic elements that can function as ϕ triggers, but I will not pursue this problem here. A first pass at a solution might be to limit such elements to semantically empty N and AUX categories, although this is admittedly not a particularly natural set.

The lexical rule in (b) deletes the 1-NP argument in the basic F-structures of designated predicates to produce the basic F-structures of those predicates that are related to them. As a result of the application of this rule, the original 2-NP[β] argument of the predicate, shown in the F-structure on the left-hand side of the rule in (2.61), becomes the 1-NP argument of the derived predicate, or perhaps more accurately, the related predicate shown in the right-hand F-structure in (2.61), since F-structure arguments are ordered.

The set of related predicates $\{PRED_x <\text{-}> PRED_y\}$ is specified as a list of the appropriate WFRs of the language. WFRs specify the lexical categories and sub-categories of the forms that they relate and the morphological relationship between those forms (as well as the phonological specifications of the forms.) The symbol "$<\text{-}>$" signifies that the relationships expressed by WFRs may be considered to be bidirectional since both of the related predicates in each case are independent members of the lexicon.

Although the domain of the Argument Reduction process is functionally coherent and defines a single class of FS_1/FS_2 pairs, it is not semantically, syntactically, or morphologically coherent. That is, the argument reduction relation manifests itself in diverse ways, relating different classes of predicates (and sentence types) both within particular languages and across languages. This is especially clear when we compare Polish intransitive-reflexive/transitive pairs and English transitive/ intransitive pairs, or Polish lexical passive/transitive pairs, and English transitive verb/-*able*-adjective pairs, as well as the sentence pairs discussed in Section 3, below.

In the proposed theory, the diversity of the Argument Reduction pattern can be explained as a consequence of varying the values of two principal parameters of the Argument Reduction System in (2.62): (a) membership of the set $\{\phi\}$; and (b) membership in the set $\{PRED_x <\rightarrow PRED_y\}$. For each language, the set $\{\phi\}$ must be specified. In English, as we have seen, this set includes the auxiliary verbs $_{Sp}VP[BE]$ and $_{Sp}VP[GET]$, but not the main verb BE, whereas in Polish, it includes the particle SIE with the feature [-Grammatical Relation], but not the verb BYĆ (*be*), which functions only as a main verb in that language. Secondly, the set of WFRs which identify the argument reduction predicates of the language must be listed. This information is shown below for English and Polish:

(2.63) a. <u>English</u>: $\{PRED_x <\rightarrow PRED_y\}$
   1. Transitive Verbs/Passive Participles (AR subcase 1):
   $$VERB \rightarrow [VERB + EN]_A$$

   2. Transitive Verbs/Adjectives (AR subcase 2):
   $$VERB_X \rightarrow [VERB_X + ABLE]_A$$

   3. Transitive Verbs/Intransitive Verbs (AR subcase 3):
   $$VERB_Y \rightarrow [VERB_Y + \emptyset]_{Vi}$$

b. <u>Polish</u>: $\{PRED_x <\rightarrow PRED_y\}$
   1. Transitive Verbs/Passive Participles (AR subcase 1):
   $$[VERB\ STEM] \rightarrow [[VERB\ STEM]] + NY]_A$$

   2. Transitive Verbs/Intransitive Verbs (AR Subcase 2):
   $$[VERB\ STEM] \rightarrow [[VERB\ STEM] + NIEĆ]_{Vi}$$

The term $VERB_X$ in (2.63a) represents the class of verbs (defined morphologically or semantically) which have -*able* adjective counter-parts, and $VERB_Y$ represents the class of verbs (probably defined semantically) which have intransitive counterparts with the same morphological shape.

Both English and Polish passive sentences may contain a prepositional phrase (with *by* in English and *przez* in Polish), as shown in
(2.3b) and (2.34b), repeated below:

(2.3)   b.   Jack$_i$ was seen by Mac$_j$

(2.34) b.   Maria$_i$ była widziana przez Jana$_j$

The derived F-structures of passive sentences containing *by*-phrases (or
their analogs) are produced by first combining the PRED/ARG structures of the participles and the PRED/ARG structures of the prepositions, BY and PRZEZ. The Index Insertion rule and the SRA rule
(with or without α-deletion) apply to the NP[θ] arguments of the
participles and the prepositions in the normal way to produce the
following, which are the derived F-structures of (2.3b) and 2.34b):

(2.64) a. $_{S}[_{VP}$[BE][SEEN $\underset{\beta}{NP[i]}$ [BY $\underset{\alpha}{NP[j]}$]]]

b.   [BYĆ][WIDZIANA $\underset{\beta}{NP[i]}$ [PRZEZ $\underset{\alpha}{NP[j]}$]]]

By convention, the NP argument of the English preposition *by*, or its
analog in the relevant language (such as *przez* in Polish), bears the SR
α borne by the 1-NP argument of the transitive verb corresponding
to the participle.

The members of the sentence pairs whose predicates are related by
the lexical and non-lexical rules of the Argument Reduction System
automatically conform to the general syntactic patterns of the relevant
language. The reason for this is that the D- and S-structures of both
members of each pair are produced by the base rules (PS rules and
lexical insertion rules) alone. Consequently, the theory predicts that
sentences containing argument reduction predicates, [+A] passive participles, intransitive verbs with transitive counterparts, *-able* adjectives,
and so forth, are no different in any relevant respect from sentences
containing other predicates of the same syntactic categories. That is,
there are no differences in word order, types of constituents that occur
in them, agreement patterns, case frames and so forth, that distinguish

these sentences from others in the language.

This prediction is correct.   For example, all adjectives in English, and not just [+A] passive participles, occur in sentences with some form of the main verb *be* (or *get*) when they function as ·S-structure predicates.   Other non-finite verb forms, such as present and past participles, and not just verbal [+V] passive participles, occur in sentences with auxiliary verbs (*be* and/or *have*).   Similarly, Polish [+A] passive participles behave like all adjectives in that language. These occur with the main verb *być* when they are S-structure predicates, and occur in pre- or post-nominal position in S-structure NP constituents. In both languages, intransitive verbs with transitive counterparts occur in the same sentence types as any intransitive verb in the relevant language. Finally, the ϕ triggers, $_{Sp}VP$[BE] and $_{NP}$[+REFLEX], occur in the same sentence positions and display the same morphological and syntactic characteristics as other lexical items of the same categories. (For example, the trigger BE is marked for tense and subject agreement like any verb.) Thus no syntactic constraints or conditions peculiar to sentences which are members of argument reduction pairs are required in UG.

Furthermore, many of the restrictions on the sub-classes of predicates that participate in the argument reduction process are actually general restrictions on the definition of "possible lexical item/predicate" in the relevant language, L_x. For example, only some transitive verbs in English and Polish have corresponding adjectival passive participles. These are verbs whose 2-NP arguments bear the SR *theme*. This was accounted for earlier by specifying this as a condition on the application of the lexical passive subcase of the argument reduction process. However, this condition follows from the greater generalization that all adjectives and intransitive verbs in these languages have 1-NP arguments that bear the SR *theme*.[5] This is not a property peculiar to adjectival passive participles.

The lexical passive subcase of the argument reduction process in English only applies to verbs whose basic F-structures contain two NP[θ] arguments, and not to verbs whose basic F-structures contain three such arguments. The process does not apply to produce adjectival participles whose basic F-structures contain two NP[θ] arguments. This might be accounted for by stipulating that the variable W in (2.61) not contain an x-NP[θ] argument. However, it is a general property of

English phrase structure that APs do not have NP complements, and there are no two-argument, or transitive, adjectives of any sort in English. This is not a property peculiar to adjectival passive participles. Similarly, the Polish *-nieć* attachment WFR specifies that the element with this affix is an intransitive verb (V_i). Since intransitive verbs have basic F-structures which contain only a single NP[θ] argument, it need not be specified that in this subcase of the lexical Argument Reduction rule the rule can only apply to relate two-, and not three-argument predicates to *-nieć* predicates.

So, the application of the relevant Argument Reduction rule in each of these forbidden cases produces a lexical item that violates general principles, some of which are possibly peculiar to the particular language, and others of which are universal. These general principles, in effect, define the notion "possible predicate in L_x" and need not be stipulated in the rules of the Argument Reduction System itself at the level of UG. Therefore, the Argument Reduction System as formulated in (2.62), with the mechanism of parametric variation in the form of the two-parameter system discussed here, is sufficient to account for the range of cross-language argument reduction phenomena. Before generalizing the rules in (2.62) further, I will look at some additional data.

3. Extensions: The Generalized Argument Reduction System

The active/passive relation (following the English/Polish pattern) is quite widespread, and occurs in most, if not all, languages. The argument reduction relation, of which it is a subcase, is most probably universal. In this section, I will look at some additional types of related sentence pairs in various languages, and show that their FS_1/FS_2 pairs, in each case, fall into one of two general categories: those which define the Argument Reduction relation, and are thus related by special cases of the rules in (2.62); and those which define the Object Deletion relation. I will show that the Argument Reduction rules and the Object Deletion rules are part of a generalized rule system that relates both types of FS_1/FS_2 pairs.

First, consider the following sentence pairs from Japanese and Malagasy:

(3.1) a.   Naomi-ga Seiji-o ut-ta
Naomi-SUBJ Seiji-OBJ hit-PAST
Naomi hit Seiji

     b.   Seiji-ga (Naomi-ni) ut-are-ta
Seiji-SUBJ (Naomi-BY) hit-PASSIVE-PAST
Seiji was hit (by Naomi)

(3.2) a.   Manasa ny lamba ity Rasoa
TRANS-wash the clothes this Rasoa
Rasoa is washing the clothes

     b.   Sasan-dRasoa ny lamba
washed-PASSIVE-Rasoa the clothes
The clothes are being washed by Rasoa

     c.   Sasana ny lamba
washed-PASSIVE the clothes
The clothes are being washed

Although Japanese and Malagasy differ from each other and from English syntactically in a number of ways, it is easy to see that the sentence pairs in (3.1) and (3.2) (that is, the pair (3.2a/b) and the pair (3.2a/c)), are the analogs in these languages of active/passive sentence pairs in English. They are examples in these languages of the Argument Reduction relation, as defined in Section 2.[6]

Both the active and passive verbs in these examples are independent lexical items with their own basic F-structures. The basic F-structures of the predicates (3.1) and (3.2a and c) are shown in (3.3) and (3.4), below:

(3.3) a.   UT-   1-NP[α]   2-NP[β]
     b.   UT-ARE-   1-NP[α]

(3.4) a.   MANASA   1-NP[α]   2-NP[β]
     b.   SASANA   1-NP[α]

In these examples, the SR α of the 1-NP argument of the (b) F-structures is identical to the SR β of the 2-NP argument of the (a) F-structures.

Let us assume that the S-structures of (3.1) and (3.2a and c) are the following:

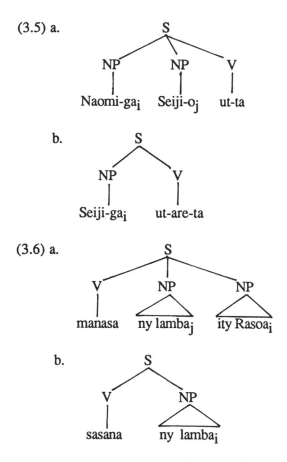

(3.5) a.

S

NP   NP   V

Naomi-ga$_i$ Seiji-o$_j$ ut-ta

b.

S

NP   V

Seiji-ga$_i$ ut-are-ta

(3.6) a.

S

V   NP   NP

manasa   ny lamba$_j$ ity Rasoa$_i$

b.

S

V   NP

sasana   ny lamba$_i$

(Here, I have represented Malagasy as a non-configurational language. It makes no difference to the present discussion whether sentences like the above are assigned the structure shown or a structure which contains a VP.)

The derivations of the F-structures of these examples proceed as discussed in Chapter II and Section 2 of this chapter. The index insert-ion rule, in accordance with the correlation statements relevant to each language, applies to insert the S-structure indices into the proper PRED/ARG structure positions. SRA (without α-deletion) then applies to produce the following:

(3.7) a.   UT-TA NP[i]_α NP[j]_β

    b.   UT-ARE-TA NP[i]_α

(3.8) a.   MANASA NP[i]_α NP[j]_β

    b.   SASANA NP[i]_α

A comparison of these structures reveals that the FS_1/FS_2 pairs for examples like (3.1) and (3.2) are cases of the argument reduction pattern:

(3.9) PRED_x $\text{NP}[\alpha]$ $\text{NP}[\beta]$ / PRED_y $\text{NP}[\beta]$

For both languages, PRED_x is the active verb form and PRED_y is the passive verb form. These forms are related by a WFR and a lexical transformation. These are shown below for Japanese:

(3.10) a.   [VERB STEM] $\to$ [VERB STEM + (R)ARE]
      b.   VERB 1-NP$[\alpha]$ 2-NP$[\beta]$ $\longleftrightarrow$ [VS + (R)ARE] 1-NP$[\beta]$

The lexical transformation for the Malagasy forms is identical to the one in (3.10b). Only the WFR differs. These are special cases of the lexical rule in (2.62).

We see, then, that the lexical rule of the Argument Reduction System, as formulated in (2.62), accounts for the analog of the active/passive relation in Japanese and Malagasy. The set $\{\text{PRED}_x <\!\!-\!\!> \text{PRED}_y\}$, as expected, differs for each of these languages. The appropriate WFRs must be specified for each.

The following examples represent a rather widespread pattern which is syntactically and semantically distinct from, but functionally identical to, the English active/ passive pattern. This is illustrated by the following Turkish sentence pairs:

(3.11) a.   Mehmet$_i$ Hasani$_j$ öldürdü
            Mehmet (SUBJ) Hasan (OBJ) caused-die
            Mehmet killed Hasan

       b.   Hasan$_i$ öldü
            Hasan (SUBJ) died
            Hasan died

(3.12) a.   Hasan$_i$ işi$_j$ bitirdi
            Hasan (SUBJ) job (OBJ) finished
            Hasan finished the job

       b.   Iş$_i$ bitti
            job (SUBJ) ended
            The job ended

(3.13) a.   Ahmet Bey$_i$ herkesi$_j$ masaya$_k$ oturttu
            Ahmet Bey (SUBJ) everyone (OBJ) (at)table caused-sit
            Ahmet Bey made everyone sit at the table

       b.   Herkes$_i$ masaya$_j$ oturdu
            everyone (SUBJ) (at)table sat down
            Everyone sat down at the table

Comparing the sentence pairs in these three examples, we see that the (a) examples contain one more NP than the (b) examples and that no NP in the (b) examples bears the SR α of the (a) examples. This, of course, is the Argument Reduction relation.

As was the case for Japanese and Malagasy, all of the predicates in the Turkish examples are independent lexical items. The basic F-structures of the predicates in (3.11) are shown below:

(3.14) a.   OLDURMEK   1-NP[α]   2-NP[β]
       b.   OLMEK   1-NP[α]

The SR α in Structure (b) is the same as the SR β in Structure (a).
    The Index Insertion rule (in accordance with the correlation statements of the language) and the SRA rule (without α-deletion) apply

to produce the derived F-structures of these examples. (Their S-structures are not shown.) These appear below:

(3.15) a. ÖLDÜRDÜ $NP[i]_\alpha$ $NP[j]_\beta$

    b. ÖLDÜ $NP[i]_\alpha$

(3.16) a. BITIRDI $NP[i]_\alpha$ $NP[j]_\beta$

    b. BITTI $NP[i]_\alpha$

(3.17) a. OTURTTU $NP[i]_\alpha$ $NP[j]_\beta$

    b. OTURDU $NP[i]_\alpha$ ...

We see that the FS_1/FS_2 pairs for sentences like those in (3.11) to (3.13) are cases of the argument reduction pattern as schematized below:

(3.18) $PRED_x$ NP[α] NP[β] W / $PRED_y$ NP[β] W

Here, $PRED_x$ is the causative verb form, produced by adding a phono-logically conditioned variant of a general causative affix to the verb stem, and $PRED_y$ is the basic verb form. These predicate types are related by a WFR and lexical transformation formulated more or less as shown in (3.19):

(3.19) a. [VERB STEM] $\rightarrow$ [[VERB STEM]+CAUSATIVE AFFIX]$_V$

    b. [VERB STEM+X] 1-NP[β] W <-> [VB STEM+CAUS AF]
        1-NP[α] 2-NP[β] W

In (3.19b), the order of the F-structures has been reversed. That is, the F-structure with fewer arguments appears on the left-hand side of the lexical transformation. In the proposed framework, however, lexical transformations are thought of as relating the F-structures of independent lexical items, as discussed previously, and the relationship itself is, of course, non-directional. Consequently, Rule (3.19b) can be formulated as above, or with the right-hand and left-hand terms in the opposite order, which is the format used in the preceding discussions.

This rule is another special case of the general lexical rule of the Argument Reduction System. Only the set $\{\text{PRED}_x <-> \text{PRED}_y\}$, which lists the relevant WFRs, must be specified.

This argument reduction pattern is quite widespread in Turkish. The analysis without modification extends to sentence pairs like the following:

(3.20) a. Kasap$_i$ eti$_j$ kesti
           butcher (SUBJ) meat (OBJ) cut
           the butcher cut the meat

     b. Yusuf$_i$ kasaba$_j$ eti$_k$ kestirdi
           Yusuf (SUBJ) butcher (DAT) meat (OBJ) cause-cut
           Yusuf had the butcher cut the meat

(3.21) a. Mehmet$_i$ Hasani$_j$ öldürdü
           Mehmet (SUBJ) Hasani (OBJ) cause-die
           Mehmet killed Hasan

     b. Polis$_i$ Mehmede$_j$ Hasani$_k$ öldürttü
           police (SUBJ) Mehmet (DAT) Hasan (OBJ) cause- [cause-
               die]
           The police had Mehmet kill Hasan

Unlike their English counterparts, these sentences consist of single clauses at S-structure level (and at D-structure level in the proposed analysis). The predicates in these pairs are related by the rule in (3.19a), which can apply to its own output in the case of (3.21), and by the lexical transformation in (3.19b). The FS_1/FS_2 pairs of these examples are shown below:

(3.22) a. KESTI $\underset{\beta}{\text{NP}^{[i]}}$ $\underset{\gamma}{\text{NP}^{[j]}}$

     b. KESTIRDI $\underset{\alpha}{\text{NP}^{[i]}}$ $\underset{\beta}{\text{NP}^{[j]}}$ $\underset{\gamma}{\text{NP}^{[k]}}$

(3.23) a. ÖLDÜRDÜ $\text{NP}^{[i]}_{\beta}$ $\text{NP}^{[j]}_{\gamma}$

b. ÖLDÜRTTÜ $\text{NP}^{[i]}_{\alpha}$ $\text{NP}^{[j]}_{\beta}$ $\text{NP}^{[k]}_{\gamma}$

Here I have departed from the usual convention on labelling SRs to make clear the relation between the members of these two-argument and three-argument FS pairs.

Finally, consider the following examples:

(3.24) a. Ben$_i$ çalişdim
I (SUBJ) worked
I worked

b. Bu saatte çalişilir mi
at this hour works QUESTION
Does (one) work at this hour?

This pair represents the minimal case of the argument reduction relation in Turkish. In example (a), the verb, *çalişdim* occurs with a single NP constituent, and in example (b), the related verb *çalişilir* occurs with no NP constituent at all. This can be accounted for by allowing the lexical rule of the Argument Reduction System to delete the lone 1-NP[θ] argument of certain predicates. The WFRs that relate the appropriate predicates for this subcase must be listed. The FS_1/FS_2 pairs of examples like these are shown in (3.25):

(3.25) a. ÇALIŞDIM $\text{NP}^{[i]}_{\alpha}$

b. ÇALIŞILIR [ADVERBIAL]; ADVERBIAL = *bu saatte*

Analogs, at least partial ones, of this case of the Argument Reduction relation occur in a number of other languages. This pattern is represented by sentence pairs like (3.26) in Japanese and (3.27) and (3.28) in Guugu Yimidhirr (an Australian Aboriginal language):

(3.26) a.   Taroo wa$_i$ Hanako ni$_j$ piano o$_k$ hik-ase-ta
Taro (NOM) Hanako (DAT) piano (ACC) play-CAUSE-
PAST
Taro forced Hanako to play the piano

   b.   Hanako ga$_i$ piano o$_j$ hii-ta
Hanako (NOM) piano (ACC) play-PAST
Hanako played the piano

(3.27) a.   Yugu$_i$ buli
tree (ABS) fell
The tree fell

   b.   Ngayu$_i$ yugu$_j$ bulii-mani
I (NOM) tree (ABS) fall-CAUSE-PAST
I made the tree fall

(3.28) a.   Nambal$_i$ duday
rock (ABS) roll away-PAST
The rock rolled away

   b.   Yarrga-ngun$_i$ nambal$_j$ dudaay-mani
boy (ERG) rock (ABS) roll away-CAUSE-PAST
The boy rolled the rock away

(In (3.27) and (3.28), ABS = absolutive case, which marks NP subjects of intransitive verbs and NP objects of transitive verbs; ERG = ergative case, which marks NP subjects of transitive verbs. Pronouns display NOM/ACC case-marking.)

Like their Turkish counterparts, all of these examples are non-complex sentences. Each pair is quite clearly a subcase of the Argument Reduction relation, and each of the predicates is an independent lexical item with its own basic F-structure. These are shown below for the predicates in (3.26) and (3.27):

(3.29) a.   [HIK-ASE-]   1-NP[α]   2-NP[β]   3-NP[γ]

   b.   [HIK-]   1-NP[β]   2-NP[γ]

(3.30) a.   [BULLII-MANI]   1-NP[α]   2-NP[β]
        b.   [BULI]   1-NP[β]

(Again, I have departed from the usual convention on labelling SRs in order to show the relationship between these pairs more clearly.)

These pairs of predicates are related in each language by a special case of the lexical Argument Reduction rule. The generalized lexical transformation that applies to both languages is shown in (3.31), and the WFRs for each language are shown in (3.32):

(3.31)   [..PRED$_x$..]   1-NP[α]   2-NP[β]   W <--> [..PRED$_y$..]
        1-NP[β]   W

(3.32) a.   <u>Japanese</u>:
        [VERB STEM] -> [[VERB STEM]+(S)ASE]$_{VERB STEM}$

    b.   <u>Guugu Yimidhirr</u>:
        [VERB STEM] -> [[VERB STEM]+MANI]$_V$

In these WFRs, the left hand predicates are PRED$_y$ and the right-hand predicates are PRED$_x$.

The derivations of the F-structures of these examples are straight-forward. The Index Insertion rule and the SRA rule (without α-deletion) apply to produce the following derived F-structures for examples (3.26) and (3.27):

(3.33) a.   [HIK-ASE-TA]   NP[i]   NP[j]   NP[k]
                            α   β   γ
        b.   [HII-TA]   NP[i]   NP[j]
                         α   β

(3.34) a.   BULI   NP[i]
                    α
        b.   BULII-MANI   NP[i] NP[j]
                           α   β

(In these examples, I have returned to the convention on labelling SRs used throughout the book.)

Now, consider the following Maninka examples:

(3.35) a. U_i bara daba$_j$ ti
            they PERFECT hoe break
            They have broken the hoe

    b.   Daba$_i$ bara ti
            hoe PERFECT break
            The hoe has broken

(3.36) a. U_i be ji$_j$ min
            they CONTINUOUS water drink
            They are drinking water

    b.   Ji$_i$ be min
            water CONTINUOUS drink
            The water is being drunk

(3.37) a.   Fanta$_i$ bena Baba$_j$ fo
            Fanta FUTURE Baba greet
            Fanta will greet Baba

    b.   Baba$_i$ bena fo
            Baba FUTURE greet
            Baba will be greeted

This pattern is quite regular in Maninka, and virtually any transitive verb can be used intransitively also, as shown in these examples. This pattern, syntactically, is analogous to the English transitive/intransitive pattern discussed in Section 2, but the latter is much more restricted as we saw.

It is easy to see that these examples are cases of the general Argument Reduction relation. Transitive verbs in this language have intransitive counterparts which are related to them by the lexical Argument Reduction rule as shown below:

(3.38) $VERB_T$ 1-NP[α] 2-NP[β] <--> $VERB_I$ 1-NP[β]

The WFR associated with this rule may be formulated as shown in (3.39):

(3.39) $VERB_T \rightarrow [VERB + \emptyset]_I$

The Index Insertion rule and the SRA rule apply as in the previous examples to produce the derived F-structures of these sentences. The derived F-structures for (3.37) are shown below:

(3.40) a.   [BENA][FO] $\underset{\alpha}{NP[i]}$ $\underset{\beta}{NP[j]}$

      b.   [BENA][FO] $\underset{\alpha}{NP[i]}$

(In these structures, the SR α of the NP argument in (b) is identical to the SR β of the right-most NP argument in (a).)

A pattern which is syntactically analogous to this occurs in Samoan. This pattern is illustrated by the following examples:

(3.41) a.   Na kuka e Mele$_i$ le meaai$_j$
          TENSE cook (SUBJ) Mele the meal
          Mele cooked the meal

      b.   Na kuka le meaai$_i$
          TENSE cook the meal
          The meal was cooked

(3.42) a.   Na faatau e Ioane$_i$ le fale$_j$
          TENSE sell (SUBJ) Ioane the house
          Ioane sold the house

      b.   Na faatau le fale$_i$
          TENSE sell the house
          The house was sold

(3.43) a.   Na ave e Mele$_i$ le taavale$_j$
          TENSE drive (SUBJ) Mele the car
          Mele drove the car

b.   Na ave le taavale$_j$
     TENSE drive the car
     The car was driven

(3.44) a.   Na tatala e Ioane$_i$ le faitotoa$_j$
            TENSE open (SUBJ) Ioane   the window
            Ioane opened the window

b.   Na tatala le faitotoa$_i$
     TENSE open the window
     The window was opened/opened

Comparing these sentence pairs, we see that they are yet another case of
the Argument Reduction relation. In the (a) examples, the verb occurs
with a subject, marked by the particle *e*, and an unmarked object. In
the (b) examples, the verb occurs with a single unmarked NP subject.
(Samoan, like Guugu Yimidhirr, is an ergative language, at least as
regards S-structure case-marking.) Not all transitive verbs in Samoan
can be used intransitively in this way, but I will not discuss the constraints on this relation.[7] The important point here is that transitive
verbs of a particular class or classes have intransitive counterparts and
that these verb pairs are related by a subcase of the lexical Argument
Reduction rule, as shown below:

(3.45)   VERB$_{Tx}$ 1-NP[α]   2-NP[β]   <-->   VERB$_{Ix}$ 1-NP[β]

Here, $\underline{x}$ represents the class of predicates that the relationship applies to.
The WFR that accompanies this rule may be formulated as in (3.46):

(3.46)   [VERB$_x$]$_{VT}$ ->   [[VERB$_x$] + Ø]$_{VI}$

The derived F-structures of examples (3.41a and b), produced by the
application of the Index Insertion rule and SRA rule to basic one- and
two-argument PRED/ARG structures, are the following:

(3.47) a.   [NA][KUKA]   NP[i]   NP[j]
                          α β

b. [NA][KUKA] NP[i]
            α

(As above, the SR α in (3.47b) is the same as the SR β in (3.47a).)

Two final examples of the argument reduction pattern are Polish impersonal/transitive sentence pairs, and English active/passive nominal pairs. I will close the discussion of the Argument Reduction relation with a brief look at both of these cases.

The Polish transitive/impersonal relation is illustrated by the following examples:

(3.48) a. Adam dał Janowi książkę
           Adam (NOM) gave Jan (DAT) book (ACC)
           Adam gave Jan a book

       b. Dano Janowi książkę
           give (impersonal form) Jan (DAT) book (ACC)
           Someone gave Jan a book

(3.49) a. Jan wybił okno
           Jan (NOM) broke window (ACC)
           Jan broke the window

       b. Wybito okno
           break (impersonal form) window (ACC)
           Someone broke the window

(3.50) a. Adam zazdrościł Janowi jego dziewczyny
           Adam (NOM) envied Jan (DAT) his girlfriend (GEN)
           Adam envied Jan his girlfriend

       b. Zazdroszczono Janowi dziewczyny
           envy (impersonal form) Jan (DAT) girlfriend (GEN)
           They envied Jan his girlfriend

In such examples, at the S-structure level, the so-called impersonal form of the verb occurs with its NP objects, but no NP subject, marked for nominative case, ever appears. Impersonal verb forms are invariant (not marked for tense or subject agreement) and differ morphologically from all other verb forms. The process is relatively productive, and a wide range of verbs have impersonal forms. The NPs that appear with impersonal verbs are case-marked in the same way as the NP objects in sentences containing the corresponding transitive verbs.

In functional terms, these sentence pairs are cases of the Argument Reduction relation. The impersonal sentences in (b) occur with one NP constituent less than their non-impersonal counterparts in (a), and no NP constituent in the (b) examples bears the SR α, borne by the subjects of the (a) examples.

The verbs *dać* (give), *(wy)bić* (break), and *zazdrościć* (envy) have the basic F-structures shown in (3.51):

(3.51) a. DAĆ   1-NP[α]   2-NP[β]   3-NP[γ]
     b. WYBIĆ   1-NP[α]   2-NP[β]
     c. ZAZDROŚCIĆ   1-NP[α]   2-NP[β]   3-NP[γ]

The impersonal verbs, *dano, wybito,* and *zazdroszczono,* have basic F-structures like the following:

(3.52) a. DANO   1-NP[β]   2-NP[γ]
     b. WYBITO   1-NP[β]
     c. ZAZDROSZCZONO   1-NP[β]   2-NP[γ]

(As in previous discussions, I have departed here from the SR labelling convention in order to more clearly show the relationship between the predicates in (3.51) and (3.52).)

These predicates are related by the subcase of the lexical Argument Reduction rule shown in (3.53) with the relevant WFR:

(3.53) a. [VERB STEM]$_V$ -> [[VERB STEM] + NO]$_{V\text{impersonal}}$
     b. [VERB]$_X$ 1-NP[α]   2-NP[β]   W   <-> [V_X+NO]
        1-NP[β]   W

The derived F-structures of the sentences in (3.48a), (3.49a), and (3.50a) are produced in the normal way by the application of the Index Insertion rule and the SRA rule. The S-structure and derived F-structure of (3.48a) are shown below:

(3.54) a.

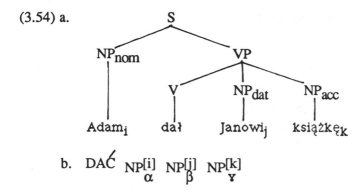

b. DAĆ NP[i] NP[j] NP[k]
         α   β   γ

Impersonal verbs, however, occur in structures that consist of a bare VP, something like the following (for (3.48b) and (3.49b)):

(3.55) a.

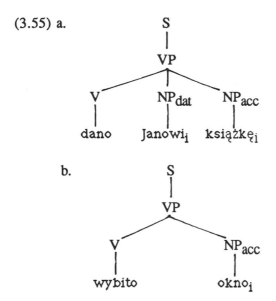

The Index Insertion rule and the SRA rule apply to produce the derived F-structures of these examples, which are shown in (3.56):[8]

(3.56) a. DANO NP[i] NP[j]
                  β   γ

b. WYBITO NP[i]
               β

The derived F-structures of the other examples are produced in the same way.

Now consider the following pairs of nominal constructions in English:

(3.57) a.   the army's destruction of the village
       b.   the village's destruction (by the army)

(3.58) a.   the witness's description of the murderer
       b.   the murderer's description (by the witness)

(3.59) a.   Maynard's murder of his stepfather
       b.   Maynard's stepfather's murder (by Fred)

(3.60) a.   Ian's killing of his sister
       b.   Ian's sister's killing

The examples in (a) contain nominals which, like their verbal counterparts, occur with two NP arguments. The examples in (b) contain the same nominals, but in these cases they only occur with a single NP argument. The SR borne by the single NP argument in the (b) examples is the same as the SR borne by the object (NP_{of}) in the (a) examples, and no NP argument in the (b) examples bears the SR of the subject (NP_{poss}) in the (a) examples. These pairs, then, represent another subcase of the Argument Reduction relation.

The basic F-structures of the nominals in the (a) examples are shown below:

(3.61) a.   DESTRUCTION   1-NP[α]   2-NP[β]
       b.   DESCRIPTION   1-NP[α]   2-NP[β]
       c.   MURDER   1-NP[α]   2-NP[β]
       d.   KILLING   1-NP[α]   2-NP[β]

The single-argument basic F-structures of the nominals in the (b) examples are shown in (3.62):

(3.62) a.   DESTRUCTION   1-NP[α]
       b.   DESCRIPTION   1-NP[α]

   c.   MURDER   1-NP[α]

   d.   KILLING   1-NP[α]

In each case, the SR α in the structures of (3.62) is identical to the SR β in the corresponding structure in (3.61).

These predicates are related by a subcase of the lexical Argument Reduction rule. This rule, with the accompanying WFR is shown in (3.63):

(3.63) a. NOM_x -> $[NOM_x + \emptyset]_N$

      b. NOM_x 1-NP[α] 2-NP[β] <-> $[NOM]_x$ 1-NP[β]

NOM_x represents the class of nominals that are related in this way. The Argument Reduction relation does not apply to all two-argument nominals. This is illustrated below:

(3.64) a. Ian's belief of the story

      b. *The story's belief (by Ian)

(3.65) a. Mabel's growing of tomatoes

      b. *The tomatoes' growing (by Mabel)

Consequently, the class NOM_x must be specified for the Argument Reduction rule.

The derivation of the F-structures of examples like (3.57) to (3.60) is straightforward. The S-structures of (3.57a and b) are shown below:

(3.66) a.

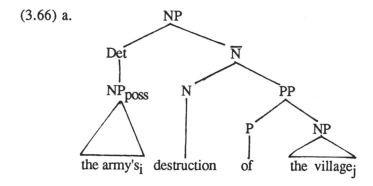

b.

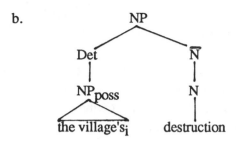

the village's₍ᵢ₎   destruction

The Index Insertion rule and the SRA rule apply in the normal way to the PRED/ARG structures of the predicates to produce the derived F-structures of these NPs. For nominal predicates, the S-structure correlate of the 1-NP argument is NP$_{poss}$ and the S-structure correlate of the 2-NP argument is NP$_{of}$. The application of these rules produces the following:

(3.67) a.   DESTRUCTION $\underset{\alpha}{\text{NP[i]}}$ $\underset{\beta}{\text{NP[j]}}$

     b.   DESTRUCTION $\underset{\alpha}{\text{NP[i]}}$

The argument reduction pattern for nominals (and other noun predicates) is obscured by certain syntactic differences between NPs and sentences. For example, NPs do not have obligatory S-level subjects. Consequently, examples like the following appear:

(3.68) a.   the destruction of the village$_i$

     b.   the murder of Maynard's stepfather$_i$

These are not examples of the argument reduction process, and, in fact, no lexical transformation applies to these cases. The derived F-structures of these examples are produced from the basic two-argument bare PRED/ARG structures of (3.61a and c). At the S-structure level, there is no NP correlate of the 1-NP argument (that is, no NP$_{poss}$). By convention, the 1-NP argument is interpreted as [+INDEF].[9] The application of the Index Insertion rule, in accordance with this convention, and the SRA rule produces the following derived F-structures:

(3.69) a.   DESTRUCTION $\underset{\alpha}{\text{NP[+INDEF]}}$ $\underset{\beta}{\text{NP[i]}}$

b. MURDER $_{NP[+INDEF]}$ $_{NP[i]}$
$\qquad\qquad\qquad\quad \alpha \qquad\qquad \beta$

Other complicating factors which tend to obscure the similarities between nominal and verbal predicates in this regard are: (a) NPs do not require objects in certain cases; (b) objects of the preposition OF have various interpretations (as in *the leg of the table, the treasure of the king('s)*); and (c) NP_{poss} constituents can also have different interpretations.

Finally, the convention on BY phrases discussed in Section 2 extends without modification to NPs. Example (3.57b) is repeated below:

(3.57) b. the village's$_i$ destruction by the army$_j$

The F-structure of this example is derived by combining the single argument PRED/ARG structure of (3.62b) and the PRED/ARG structure of BY, and then applying the Index Insertion rule and the SRA rule. The result is shown in (3.70):

(3.70) DESTRUCTION $_{NP[i]}$ [BY $_{NP[j]}$]
$\qquad\qquad\qquad\qquad \alpha \qquad\qquad \alpha$

This completes the discussion of the Argument Reduction relation. Examples like the following illustrate a different relationship between FS_1/FS_2 pairs:

(3.71) a. Malcolm drives sportscars
        b. Malcolm drives everyday

(3.72) a. Simon drinks beer after work
        b. Simon drinks after work

(3.73) a. Vanessa is cooking dinner
        b. Vanessa is cooking

The (a) examples of these pairs contain verbs that occur with two NP constituents, and in the (b) examples, the verbs occur with a single NP constituent (plus adverbials in (3.71b) and (3.72b)). However, in contrast to the examples discussed so far, the SR of the single NP constituent in the (b) sentences is identical to the SR of the subject of the corresponding (a) sentence.   These are cases of what we may refer to as the Object Deletion relation.

The Object Deletion relation applies to a rather large class of transitive verbs in English. The basic F-structures of these verbs and their intransitive, or one-argument, counterparts are shown in (3.74) and (3.75):

(3.74) a.   DRIVE   1-NP[α]   2-NP[β]
       b.   DRINK   1-NP[α]   2-NP[β]
       c.   COOK   1-NP[α]   2-NP[β]

(3.75) a.   DRIVE   1-NP[α]
       b.   DRINK   1-NP[α]
       c.   COOK   1-NP[α]

These basic F-structures can be related by a lexical rule like the following:

(3.76)   VERB$_X$ 1-NP[α]   2-NP[β]   <–>   VERB$_X$ 1-NP[α]

I will refer to this rule as the Object Deletion rule. The verb class that this rule applies to must be specified. It does not apply to all two-argument verbs as shown by the ungrammaticality of the (b) example, below:

(3.77) a.   Smyth sees Jones every morning
       b.   *Smyth sees every morning

Consequently, the membership of the relevant set {PRED$_X$ <–> PRED$_y$} must be listed. These PREDs are related by a WFR something like the following:

(3.78)   VERB$_X$ –>   [VERB$_X$ + $\emptyset$]$_{VI}$

The term VI stands for intransitive, or one-argument, verb.

Sentence pairs like (3.79) and (3.80) illustrate another subcase of the Object Deletion relation:

(3.79) a.   Elyse loves everyone
      b.   Elyse is quite loving

(3.80) a.   Barnaby cares about the poor
      b.   Barnaby is quite caring

    The (a) member of each example contains a transitive verb, and the (b) member contains an adjective, that only occurs with a single NP constituent. However, the SR borne by this single constituent, in each case, is the same as the SR borne by the subject of the transitive verb.

    The basic F-structures of the transitive verbs are shown in (3.81), and the basic F-structures of the corresponding adjectives are shown in (3.82):[10]

(3.81) a.   LOVE   1-NP[α]   2-NP[β]
      b.   CARE   1-NP[α]   2-NP[β]

(3.82) a.   LOVING   1-NP[α]
      b.   CARING   1-NP[α]

    These F-structures are related by the subcase of the Object Deletion rule shown below, along with the relevant WFR:

(3.83) a. $VERB_x$ -> [$VERB_x$ + ING]$_A$
      b. $VERB_x$ 1-NP[α] 2-NP[β]<->[$VERB_x$+ING]$_A$ 1-NP[α]

The verb class that this rule applies to is identified as $VERB_x$ in the WFR, which, as we have seen, defines the set {$PRED_x$ <-> $PRED_y$} for rule (3.83b).

    Examples of the Object Deletion relation can be found in other languages. Consider the following sentence pairs:

(3.84) a.   Sa ai e Pili le sapasui
          TENSE eat (SUBJ) Pili the chopsuey
          Pili ate the chopsuey

b.   Sa ai Pili
TENSE eat Pili
Pili ate

(3.85) a.   Sa inu e Pili le pia
TENSE drink (SUBJ) Pili   the beer
Pili drank the beer

b.   Sa inu Pili
TENSE drink Pili
Pili drank

(3.86) a.   Na faafiafia e Mele Ioane
TENSE entertain (make happy) (SUBJ) Mele Ioane
Mele entertained Ioane

b.   Na faafiafia Mele
TENSE entertain Mele
Mele entertained

It is clear that these sentence pairs are analogous to their English translational equivalents. The basic F-structures of the transitive verbs in the (a) examples and those of their intransitive counterparts are shown in (3.87) and (3.88), respectively:

(3.87) a.   AI   1-NP[α]   2-NP[β]
    b.   INU   1-NP[α]   2-NP[β]
    c.   FAAFIAFIA   1-NP[α]   2-NP[β]

(3.88) a.   AI   1-NP[α]
    b.   INU   1-NP[α]
    c.   FAAFIAFIA   1-NP[α]

As was the case with English, not all two-argument verbs have one-argument object deletion counterparts. Thus the (b) member of the followiing pair only has the argument reduction reading. It is consequently odd for semantic reasons:

(3.89) a. Na kuka e Mele le meaai
TENSE cook (SUBJ) Mele the meal
Mele cooked the meal

b. ?Na kuka Mele
TENSE cook Mele
Mele was cooked

Therefore the classes of verb pairs that are related by the Object Deletion relation, the set $\{PRED_x <-> PRED_y\}$, must be specified. The subcase of the Object Deletion rule, and the accompanying WFR, that relates the basic F-structures of the predicates in sentences like (3.84), (3.85), and (3.86) are shown below:

(3.90) a. $VERB_x \rightarrow [VERB_x + \emptyset]_{VIy}$
b. $VERB_x$ 1-NP[α] 2-NP[β] $<->$ $[VERB_x + \emptyset]_y$
1-NP[α]

Finally, consider the following pairs of English NPs:

(3.91) a. Ralph's$_i$ photograph of Randolf$_j$
b. Ralph's$_i$ photograph

(3.92) a. Nigel's$_i$ book about Nixon$_j$
b. Nigel's$_i$ book

In the (b) examples, *Ralph's* and *Nigel's* can be interpreted as the object of the noun predicate (*photograph of Ralph, book about Nigel*), or as the subject (with the same SR as in the (a) examples.) The first interpretation is due to the fact that the lexical Argument Reduction rule can apply to relate two- and one-argument F-structures for the [+N] predicates *photograph* and *book*, as discussed above. The second interpretation is the relevant one here. The basic F-structures of the predicates in the (a) examples are shown in (3.93), and the basic F-structures of the predicates in the (b) examples with the second interpretation are shown in (3.94):

(3.93) a.   PHOTOGRAPH   1-NP[α]   2-NP[β]
     b.   BOOK   1-NP[α]   2-NP[β]

(3.94) a.   PHOTOGRAPH   1-NP[α]
     b.   BOOK   1-NP[α]

These basic F-structures are related by a subcase of the Object Deletion rule. This is shown in (3.95), with the WFR that specifies the set of noun predicates it applies to:

(3.95) a. $NOUN_x$ -> $[NOUN_x + \emptyset]_N$
     b. $NOUN_x$ 1-NP[α]   2-NP[β] <-> $[NOUN + \emptyset]_N$
        1-NP[α]

The Object Deletion relation does not hold of all [+N] predicates. The nominal *destruction,* for example, in (b), below, appears to have only the argument reduction reading, in which *the army's* bears the SR normally assigned to the 2-NP argument in the two-argument F-structure:

(3.96) a.   the army's destruction of the village
     b.   the army's destruction

So *destruction*, or the class of which it is a member, is not in the set $\{PRED_x$ <-> $PRED_y\}_{OD}$.

The derived F-structures of examples (3.91) and (3.92) are produced from the PRED/ARG structures of (3.93) and (3.94) by the application of the Index Insertion rule and the SRA rule. (The S-structure correlate of the 2-NP argument of *photograph* is NP_{of}, and the S-structure correlate of the 2-NP argument of *book* is NP_{about}.) These derived F-structures are shown below.[11]

(3.97) a.   PHOTOGRAPH $NP^{[i]}_{\alpha}$ $NP^{[j]}_{\beta}$
     b.   PHOTOGRAPH $NP^{[i]}_{\alpha}$
     c.   BOOK $NP^{[i]}_{\alpha}$ $NP^{[j]}_{\beta}$

d.   BOOK $NP[i]$
α

As was the case with the Argument Reduction rules, the various lexical object deletion transformations can be generalized as the single rule shown in (3.98):

(3.98) $[..PRED_x..]$ 1-NP[α] 2-NP[β] <-> $[..PRED_y..]$ 1-NP[α]

Again, because all basic F-structures in the theory have the same form, the structural description of this rule need not be stated, and, as a consequence, the lexical Object Deletion rule reduces to the form shown in (3.99):

(3.99)   To relate the pair FS_x/FS_y of $PRED_x$ and $PRED_y$,
              2-NP[β]$_{PREDx}$ -> Ø
              where $PRED_x$ and $PRED_y$ ∊ {$PRED_x$ <-> $PRED_y$}

The rules of the Argument Reduction subsystem in (2.62) and the Object Deletion rule in (3.99) can be combined and reformulated as a more general rule system. We may refer to this as the Generalized Argument Reduction (GAR) System. It is formulated in (3.100):

(3.100)   The Generalized Argument Reduction System
              (a)   To produce derived F-structures from PRED/ARG
                    structures of the form:
                         [ϕ]$PRED_x$ ...x-NP[θ]..., ϕ ∊ {ϕ},
                    SR θ of $PRED_x$ -> Ø

              (b)   To relate the pair FS_x/FS_y, of $PRED_x$ and $PRED_y$,
                         x-NP[θ]$_{PREDx}$ -> Ø
                    where $PRED_x$ and $PRED_y$ ∊ {$PRED_x$ <-> $PRED_y$}

To account for both the Argument Reduction relation and the Object Deletion relation, the GAR System, which is part of UG, requires the following statements:

(3.101) a.   SR θ = α if φ ∈ {φ$_{AR}$}
SR θ = β if φ ∈ {φ$_{OD}$}

b.   x-NP = 1-NP if PRED$_x$ & PRED$_y$ ∈ {PRED$_x$ <->
PRED$_y$}$_{AR}$
x-NP = 2-NP if PRED$_x$ & PRED$_y$ ∈ {PRED$_x$ <->
PRED$_y$}$_{OD}$

Here, the set {φ$_{AR}$} is the set of triggers of the argument reduction variant of the non-lexical rule and {φ$_{OD}$} is the set of triggers of a hypothethical object deletion variant of this rule.[12] Similarly, the set {PRED$_x$ <-> PRED$_y$}$_{AR}$ is the set of PRED pairs that are related by the argument reduction variant of the lexical rule, and the set {PRED$_x$ <-> PRED$_y$}$_{OD}$ is the set of PRED pairs that are related by the object deletion variant of the lexical rule.

To summarize, the examples that I have looked at in this section and in Section 2, are examples of two types of relationship between FS$_1$/FS$_2$ pairs: the Argument Reduction relation and the Object Deletion relation. Both the argument reduction process and the object deletion process relate F-structure pairs whose members have different argument structures. More specifically, one member of these pairs has one more x-NP[θ] argument than the other member. I will refer to the FS pairs related by the GAR System, FS$_{AR}$ and FS$_{OD}$ pairs collectively, as asymmetric FS pairs.

The argument reduction process is the analog in the proposed theory of the syntactic rule of NP movement in the standard theory (excluding the raising cases discussed in Chapter III and the wh-movement case discussed in Chapter V) as well as certain lexical processes that may collectively be considered to be a sort of lexical analog of NP movement in the standard theory.[13] The object deletion process is the analog of object deletion, regardless of its specific formulation, in earlier theories. Both of these processes can be generalized and combined as elements of the Generalized Argument Reduction System, as shown in this section.

In this generalized rule system, both the non-lexical and lexical argument reduction and object deletion variants are processes of the same formal type, deletion. The non-lexical variants delete some SR θ under certain circumstances, and the lexical variants delete some x-NP[θ] argument under certain circumstances. Some of the consequences of this analysis have been discussed. Others are discussed below.

4. Constraints: Defining the notion "possible asymmetric FS pair"

In this section, I will demonstrate that the Generalized Argument Reduction System and various basic principles of the theory interact to define the set of possible asymmetric FS pairs. More specifically, the rules of the GAR System, in conjunction with other principles of the theory, relate all of the occurring subcases of the two asymmetric pair types, FS_{AR} and FS_{OD}, but no asymmetric FS pair types of other categories that do not occur. Moreover, SR θ in the non-lexical rule need not be arbitrarily limited to α or β, and the x-NP[θ] argument in the lexical rule need not be arbitrarily limited to 1-NP[α] or 2-NP[β]. Let us consider this latter point first.

The following basic assumptions of the theory pertain to this discussion:

(4.1) a. The argument structures of predicates are ordered, and contain one, two, or three x-NP[θ] arguments.

   b. The SRA rule assigns SRs to indexed x-NP[θ] arguments in the order in which these appear in the basic F-structure of the relevant predicate.

The first of these assumptions is discussed in detail in Chapter II. The second is embodied in the formulation of the SRA rule, which is also discussed in that chapter.

As a consequence of the first assumption, if the n-NP[θ_n] argument in an F-structure like the following is deleted by the lexical rules, the (n+1)-NP[θ_{n+1}] argument becomes the new n-NP[θ_{n+1}] argument:

(4.2)   PRED ...n-NP[θ_n] (n+1)-NP[θ_{n+1}] ...

X-NP[θ] arguments always retain their SRs in this situation.

In contrast, as a consequence of the second assumption, if an SR, θ_n, is deleted by the non-lexical rule, then the SR θ_{n+1} in the basic

F-structure of the relevant predicate is assigned to the n-NP[θ] argument of the PRED/ARG structure, as we have seen in numerous examples in the preceding sections.

In the absence of conditions stating otherwise, the following variants of the rules of the GAR System (and not only the ones in (3.101)) are possible:

(4.3) a.   Application of the non-lexical rule: $\theta \rightarrow \emptyset$:

       (1) $\theta = \alpha$

       (2) $\theta = \beta$

       (3) $\theta = \gamma$

    b.   Application of the lexical rule: n-NP[θ] $\rightarrow \emptyset$

       (1) n-NP[θ] = 1-NP[α]

       (2) n-NP[θ] = 2-NP[β]

       (3) n-NP[θ] = 3-NP[γ]

I will discuss these possibilities in turn as they relate to one-, two- and three-argument predicates.

Unless additional constraints are placed on them, members of the set of triggers of α-deletion, variant (4.3a) (1) above, can occur in sentences with one-, two-, and three-argument predicates. The derived F-structures of such sentences must be produced from PRED/ARG structures like the following:

(4.4) a.   [φ]PRED$_a$ 1-NP

    b.   [φ]PRED$_b$ 1-NP 2-NP

    c.   [φ]PRED$_c$ 1-NP 2-NP 3-NP

In these structures, φ is a member of the set $\{φ\}_{AR}$.

Consider the structure in (4.4a). Assuming that the appropriate S-structure contains an indexed NP constituent, say NP[i], the index insertion rule and the SRA rule, with α-deletion, apply to produce a structure like the following:

(4.5)   [φ]PRED$_a$ NP[i]

Because the basic F-structure of the predicate, PRED$_a$, contains a single

1-NP[α] argument, whose SR, α, is deleted, no SR can be assigned to the indexed NP in (4.5). Consequently, this F-structure violates WFC I. Therefore, sentences for which this is the only derivable F-structure are ungrammatical. This prediction is, in fact, correct. An example of such a sentence is the following:

(4.6) *Malcolm$_i$ was walked

Here, *walk* is a single-argument predicate, of type $PRED_a$, and $SpVP[BE]$ is a member of the set $\{\phi\}_{AR}$.[14]

When triggers of α-deletion occur with two- and three-argument verbs in an S-structure, the consequences are somewhat different. Let us first assume that a two-argument predicate occurs in an S-structure with an indexed NP argument, $NP[i]$, and the appropriate trigger. The application of the Index Insertion rule and the SRA rule with α-deletion to the PRED/ARG structure in (4.4b) produces the derived F-structure shown below:

(4.7) $[\phi]PRED_b \quad NP[i] \atop \beta$

This structure is well-formed. It does not violate WFC I or any other condition on F-structures. We would predict, then, that sentences with such derived F-structures are grammatical. This prediction is correct. Some examples are English passive sentences with verbal participles, and Polish intransitive reflexive sentences. An example of each of these is shown in (4.8) along with its derived F-structure:

(4.8) a. Xavier$_i$ was seen
$\quad\quad\quad$ SpVP[BE]SEEN $NP[i] \atop \beta$

$\quad$ b. Okno$_i$ zbiło się
$\quad\quad\quad$ SpVP[SIĘ]ZBIĆ $NP[i] \atop \beta$

In contrast, if sentences contain a two-argument verb, a trigger of α-deletion, and two indexed NP constituents, the application of the Index Insertion rule and the SRA rule will produce a derived F-structure like the following:

(4.9) $[\phi]\text{PRED}_b$ $\text{NP}^{[i]}_{\beta}$ $\text{NP}^{[j]}$

In this case, no SR is available to be assigned to the second, $\text{NP}^{[j]}$, argument, and this F-structure violates WFC I. This predicts the ungrammaticality of examples like the following: (shown with its derived F-structure):

(4.10) a. *Ian$_i$ was seen Nigel$_j$
       b. $_{Sp}\text{VP}^{[BE]}\text{SEEN}$ $\text{NP}^{[i]}_{\beta}$ $\text{NP}^{[j]}$

The situation is similar for sentences containing three-argument verbs, a trigger of α-deletion, and two or three indexed NP arguments. In the first case, a well-formed derived F-structure like the one in (4.11a) can be produced. In the second case, only a derived F-structure like the one in (4.11b), which violates WFC I, can be produced:

(4.11) a. $[\phi]\text{PRED}_c$ $\text{NP}^{[i]}_{\beta}$ $\text{NP}^{[j]}_{\gamma}$
       b. $[\phi]\text{PRED}_c$ $\text{NP}^{[i]}_{\beta}$ $\text{NP}^{[j]}_{\gamma}$ $\text{NP}^{[k]}$

In structure (4.11b), the rightmost indexed NP argument bears no SR.

Sentences with derived F-structures like (4.11a) are grammatical as predicted, while sentences with derived F-structures like (4.11b) are not. This is illustrated below by (4.12a) and (4.12b), respectively:

(4.12) a.   Andrew$_i$ was given a book$_j$

           $_{Sp}\text{VP}^{[BE]}\text{GIVEN}$ $\text{NP}^{[i]}_{\beta}$ $[\text{NP}^{[j]}_{\gamma}$

       b. *Andrew$_i$ was given Phillip$_j$ a book$_k$

           $_{Sp}\text{VP}^{[BE]}\text{GIVEN}$ $\text{NP}^{[i]}_{\beta}$ $\text{NP}^{[j]}_{\gamma}$ $\text{NP}^{[k]}$

Let us turn now to variant (4.3a)(2) of the non-lexical rule, β-deletion. This variant is allowed by the theory, again, unless specifically prohibited. It would apply in the production of the derived F-structures of sentences containing two- and three-argument predicates, the appropriate number of indexed NP arguments, and an appropriate trigger at S-structure level. The appropriate trigger, as discussed in Section 2, must be an independent lexical item which is a member of the set that we may label $\{\phi\}_{OD}$ as shown in (3.101), above.

The derived F-structures of such sentences must be produced from PRED/ARG structures of either of the following types:

(4.13) a. $[\phi_{OD}]PRED_b$ 1-NP 2-NP

      b. $[\phi_{OD}]PRED_c$ 1-NP 2-NP 3-NP

If the relevant S-structures have the "correct" number of indexed NPs, a single $NP[i]$ constituent in the first case, and two NP constituents, $NP[i]$ and $NP[j]$, in the second case, well-formed derived F-structures of the following types can be produced by the application of the Index Insertion rule and the SRA rule with β-deletion:

(4.14) a. $[\phi_{OD}]PRED_b \underset{\alpha}{NP[i]}$

      b. $[\phi_{OD}]PRED_c \underset{\alpha}{NP[i]} \underset{\gamma}{NP[j]}$

To produce structure (b), the SR γ in the basic F-structure of the $PRED_c$ is assigned to the second indexed NP argument since the SR β in the basic F-structure of this predicate has been deleted. This is a consequence of the second assumption, discussed at the beginning of this section.

There are no examples of non-lexical object deletion with two-argument predicates in English or any of the languages discussed in Section 3. However, if they occurred, they would be analogs of the cases of lexical object deletion which occur in a number of languages. We see, then, that this variant relates the members of an existing type of asymmetric FS pair, and not those of an entirely different pair type. Therefore, there is no reason to exclude this variant at the level of UG. A hypothetical example of a non-lexical object deletion sentence in English is the following, in which OD represents the lexical item that triggers the process:

(4.15)   David$_i$ OD drinks

This example has a derived F-structure like that shown in (4.14a), above.

A hypothetical example of a non-lexical object deletion sentence containing a three-argument predicate in English is the following:

(4.16)   *?Daniel$_i$ OD gave a book$_j$

This example has a derived F-structure like that shown in (4.14b). Its ungrammaticality, or at least its oddness, is due to the fact that it cannot be completely interpreted. As we saw with the lexical object deletion process, not all two-argument verbs are related in this way to one-argument verbs. We can allow the non-lexical object deletion process to apply to such cases (in theory) and account for their oddness or ungrammaticality by independently motivated principles. There is no need to constrain the object deletion process itself.[15]

If all of the NP constituents in the S-structures of object deletion sentences are indexed, derived F-structures of the following type will be produced by the application of the Index Insertion rule and the SRA rule, with β-deletion to (4.13a and b), respectively:

(4.17) a. $[\phi_{OD}]PRED_b$ $\underset{\alpha}{NP^{[i]}}$ $NP^{[j]}$

b. $[\phi_{OD}]PRED_c$ $\underset{\alpha}{NP^{[i]}}$ $\underset{\gamma}{NP^{[j]}}$ $NP^{[k]}$

Both of these structures violate WFC I. Consequently, we can account for the ungrammaticality of hypothetical sentences which have such derived F-structures without constraining the β-deletion process itself.

Finally, consider the variant of the non-lexical rule in (4.3a) (3), γ-deletion. This is also a hypothetical case, which would apply in the production of the derived F-structures of sentences containing three-argument predicates, the requisite number of indexed NP constituents, and the appropriate trigger, an element of a set which may be labelled $\{\phi\}_{\underset{\gamma}{OD}}$.

The derived F-structures of such sentences must be produced from the following PRED/ARG structure type:

(4.18)　$[\phi OD_\gamma]PRED_c$　1-NP　2-NP　3-NP

Assuming that the relevant sentences have two indexed NP constituents at S-structure level, derived F-structures like the following can be produced by the application of the Index Insertion rule and the SRA rule with ɣ-deletion:

(4.19)　$[\phi OD_\gamma]PRED_c$　$NP_\alpha^{[i]}$　$NP_\beta^{[j]}$

An example of this sentence type is shown in (4.20):

(4.20)　*?Peter$_i$ OD gave Paul$_j$

Like example (4.16), this sentence cannot be fully interpreted. This accounts for its unacceptability. We need not, therefore, eliminate the ɣ-deletion variant at the level of UG. We can account for the ungrammaticality of the output of the rule with independently motivated principles.

As was the case with the β-deletion process, if the relevant sentences contain three indexed NP constituents at the S-structure level, no well-formed derived F- structure can be produced for them.

It is easy to see that the same sorts of arguments apply to the three variants of the lexical x-NP[θ]-deletion rule. The application of the 1-NP[α] variant to one-, two- and three-argument predicates produces basic F-structures like (4.21a), (4.21b), and (4.21c), respectively:

(4.21) a.　$PRED_y$　∅
　　　 b.　$PRED_y$　1-NP[β]
　　　 c.　$PRED_y$　1-NP[β]　2-NP[ɣ]

Examples containing related predicates with all of these structure types occur. Such predicates are members of the set $\{PRED_x$ <-> $PRED_y\}_{AR}$ in the relevant language. A Turkish example of the application of this variant to a one-argument verb is shown in (4.22a), a

Polish example of the application of this variant to a two-argument predicate is shown in (4.22b), and a Polish example of the application of this variant to a three-argument predicate is shown in (4.22c):

(4.22) a. Bu saatte çalişilir mi   (Example (3.24b))

      b. Lód topnieje   (Example (2.43b))

      c. Książka była dana Janowi
           book (NOM) was given [+ADJ] Jan (DAT)
           The book was given to Jan

The application of the 2-NP[β]-deletion variant to two- and three-argument predicates produces basic F-structures like (4.23a and b), respectively:

(4.23) a. PRED_y 1-NP[α]
      b. PRED_y 1-NP[α] 2-NP[γ]

Sentences with derived F-structures of type (a) are ones which contain one-argument predicates, PRED_y, that are members of the set {PRED_x <-> PRED_y}$_{OD}$ in the relevant language. An example from English is shown below:

(4.24)   Randy$_i$ drank

Again, in the absence of constraints stating otherwise, the 2-NP[β]-deletion variant can, in theory, apply to three-argument predicates to produce predicates with basic F-structures like (4.23b). The following example contains a hypothetical predicate of this type, a two-argument variant of *give* :

(4.25)   *?Jarrold$_i$ gave a book$_j$

This example, like its non-lexical counterpart in (4.16), is ungrammatical because it cannot be fully interpreted (except in the sense of *donate*).

     Similarly, the 3-NP[γ]-deletion variant is possible in theory. This variant applies to three-argument predicates which are members of a set $\{PRED_x \leftrightarrow PRED_y\}_{OD\gamma}$ to produce predicates with basic F-structures like the following:

(4.26) $PRED_y$ 1-NP[α]   2-NP[β]

Example (4.27), below, contains a hypothetical predicate of this type, a second two-argument variant of the verb *give* :

(4.27)   *?Jarrold$_i$ gave Nigel$_j$

This example, also, like its non-lexical counterpart in (4.20), cannot be fully interpreted.

Consequently, it is not necessary to prevent the 2-NP[β]-deletion variant from applying to three-argument verbs, nor to prevent the 3-NP[γ]-deletion variant altogether, at the level of UG. Independently motivated principles account for the ungrammaticality of the output of these variants.

We see, then, that there is no need to limit the domain of the non-lexical and lexical rules of the GAR System in (3.99) to the SRs α and β, and to 1-NP[α] and 2-NP[β] arguments, respectively. Moreover, there is no need to restrict either of these two general processes to predicates of a particular type; that is, to one- and/or two- and/or three-argument predicates. Each of the lexical and non-lexical variants can be allowed to apply to any predicate type.

In more formal terms, this means that there is no need to restrict the occurrence of members of the sets $\{\phi\}_{AR}$ and $\{\phi\}_{OD}$ to S-structures which contain certain predicate types, and there is no need to arbitrarily exclude sets like $\{\phi\}_{OD}$ and $\{\phi\}_{OD\gamma}$ from the theory. In the latter case, independent principles relating to interpretability explain the non-occurrence of OD_γ triggers.

Regarding the lexical process, it is not necessary to restrict the sets $\{PRED_x \leftrightarrow PRED_y\}_{AR}$ and $\{PRED_x \leftrightarrow PRED_y\}_{OD}$ to predicates of particular types, although certain subclasses of predicates (of all types) must be specified for each set as we saw in Section 3. Nor is it necessary to arbitrarily exclude the set $\{PRED_x \leftrightarrow PRED_Y\}_{OD\gamma}$ from the theory. As in the non-lexical case, independent principles explain the fact that this set is empty. Therefore, no further constraints on the GAR System itself are required in UG.

In fact, the rules of the GAR System, no matter how they apply, can relate only two types of asymmetric FS-pairs: argument reduction (AR) pairs and object deletion (OD) pairs. (β-deletion pairs (OD) and ɤ-deletion pairs (ODɤ) are both variants of the general OD relation.) As a consequence, there are no analogs in the proposed theory, of movement from subject position to some non-subject position, or of movement from some non-subject position to some other non-subject position.

The following diagrams illustrate syntactic movement of these types:

(4.28) a.

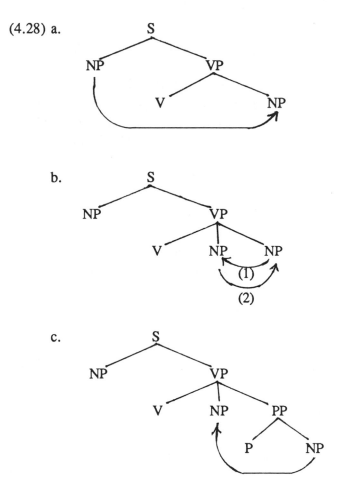

(I exclude the rule of raising to object position from this discussion. See Chapter III.)

In the proposed theory, the analogs of these rules must be non-lexical or lexical processes that relate asymmetric FS pairs like the following; which correspond to the cases of movement diagrammed in structures like (4.28a), (4.28b), and (4.28c), respectively:

(4.29) a.　　$PRED_x$　1-NP[α]　2-NP[β]　...　/　$PRED_y$　2-NP[α]

　　　b.(1)　$PRED_x$　1-NP[α]　2-NP[β]　3-NP[ɣ] / $PRED_y$
　　　　　　1-NP[α]　2-NP[ɣ]
　　　　(2)　$PRED_x$　1-NP[α]　2-NP[β]　3-NP[ɣ] / $PRED_y$
　　　　　　1-NP[α]　3-NP[β]

　　　c.　　$PRED_x$ 1-NP[α] 2-NP[β] [P NP[ɣ] / $PRED_y$
　　　　　　1-NP[α]　2-NP[ɣ]

None of the F-structure pairs in (4.29) can be related by the rules of the GAR System. To demonstrate this, I will consider each pair in turn.

To relate FS pairs like (4.29a), the rules of the theory must effect the F-structure, or F-level, modification diagrammed below:

(4.30)　PRED　1-NP[α]　2-NP[ ]

The non-lexical rule cannot do this. Here, the SR β must be deleted, but even if it is deleted, the SR α will still be assigned to the indexed 1-NP argument and not to the 2-NP argument.

Similarly, the lexical variant, 2-NP[β] -> Ø, does not produce an F-structure like the right-hand one in (4.29a), as we have seen in many examples. The remaining NP argument, by definition, is a 1-NP[α] argument. The variant, 1-NP[α] -> Ø, not only results in the old 2-NP argument becoming the new 1-NP argument, but also deletes the SR α. So this operation cannot produce an F-structure like the right-hand one in (4.29a) either.

The situation with the FS-pair in (4.29b)(1) is somewhat different. Both the non-lexical β-deletion variant and the lexical 2-NP[β]-deletion variant can relate such F-structures. However, as we saw previously, the sentences associated with the F-structures produced by these operations cannot be fully interpreted. In any case, they are not interpreted as involving movement from some non-subject position to another non-subject position.

Neither the non-lexical nor the lexical rule of the GAR System can relate FS-pairs like (4.29b)(2). This would require the F-level modification diagrammed in (4.31):

(4.31)   PRED   1-NP[α]   2-NP[β]   3-NP[ ]

The application of the non-lexical ɤ-deletion variant does not result in the reassignment of the SR β to the 3-NP argument. Instead, this variant only produces F-structures whose associated sentences cannot be fully interpreted. The lexical variant, 3-NP[ɤ] –> Ø, produces two-argument F-structures, which contain 1-NP[α] and 2-NP[β] arguments, not F-structures like the right-hand one in (4.29b)(2), whose associated sentences in any case could not be fully interpreted.

In order to relate the F-structure pair in (4.29c), the following F-level modification is required:

(4.32)   PRED   1-NP[α]   2-NP[ ]   [P NP[ɤ]]

Even if the non-lexical β-deletion variant applies, the SRA rule cannot reassign the SR ɤ of the object of the preposition P to the 2-NP argument. The reason for this is that the SRA rule cannot assign the SR of an argument of a predicate to the argument of another predicate. In this case, the preposition functions as a predicate, as discussed in Chapter II.

The lexical 2-NP[β]-deletion variant will produce only a predicate with an F-structure containing a 1-NP[α] argument and the [P NP[ɤ]] argument, and not one like the right-hand F-structure in (4.29c).

The rules of the GAR System and the principles of the theory, in effect, define the set of possible asymmetric FS pairs. This set consists of FS_{AR} and FS_{OD} pairs, but not FS pairs like the ones in (4.29). The principles of the theory also explain the occurrence of $FS_{OD\beta}$ pairs with two-argument predicates and corresponding single-argument predicates, and the non-occurrence of $FS_{OD\beta}$ pairs with three-argument predicates and corresponding two-argument predicates, and

FS$_{ODY}$ pairs.[16] I will discuss the implications of this in the next section.

5. Concluding Remarks - The GAR System

The GAR System, as formulated in (3.100) and (3.101), is repeated below:

(3.100) <u>The Generalized Argument Reduction System</u>
        (a)   To produce derived F-structures from PRED/ARG structures of the form:

$$[\phi]PRED_x \ ...x\text{-}NP[\theta]..., \quad \phi \ \subset \ \{\phi\},$$
$$SR \ \theta \ of \ PRED_x \ \rightarrow \ \varnothing$$

        (b)   To relate the pair FS$_x$/FS$_y$, of PRED$_x$ and PREDy,

$$x\text{-}NP[\theta]_{PREDx} \ \rightarrow \ \varnothing$$

        where PRED$_x$ and PRED$_y$ $\subset$ {PRED$_x$ <-> PRED$_y$}

(3.101) a.   SR θ = α if ϕ $\subset$ {ϕ_{AR}}
            SR θ = β if ϕ $\subset$ {ϕ_{OD}}
     b.   x-NP = 1-NP if PRED$_x$ & PRED$_y$ $\subset$ {PRED$_x$ <->
           PRED$_y$}$_{AR}$
           x-NP = 2-NP if PRED$_x$ & PRED$_y$ $\subset$ {PRED$_x$ <->
           PRED$_y$}$_{OD}$

This system is the second of the three rule systems of UG. Under the circumstances discussed in Sections 2, 3 and 4, the non-lexical rule deletes an SR θ, and the SRA rule assigns the remaining SRs to indexed NP arguments. The lexical rule deletes an x-NP[θ] argument. The GAR rules, in conjunction with other basic principles of the theory, define the set of possible asymmetric FS pairs (FS$_{AR}$ and FS$_{OD}$ pairs), as we have seen. The set of possible asymmetric FS pairs in this theory is analogous to the set of possible sentence pairs related by a movement (or deletion) rule in the standard theory and other earlier theories. Therefore, the GAR system and associated principles, in effect, define the analog of the standard theory notion of "possible NP movement". However, "possible asymmetric FS pair" is a more general concept than "possible sentence pair related by the NP movement rule". The proposed analysis provides a unified explanation for the patterns produced by the analogs of the NP movement rule, the Object Deletion rule, and certain other lexical rules that do not involve NP movement in any current theory, all of which are subcases of the GAR system. These patterns include such diverse phenomena as Turkish causative/non-causative sentence pairs, English active/passive sentence pairs, and Polish transitive/intransitive-reflexive sentence pairs.[17]

Because of the formal properties of the rules of the GAR system and the absence of an NP movement rule in UG, AR and OD sentence pairs necessarily conform to the general syntactic patterns of the relevant language. Variation from language to language of the types of sentence pairs which instantiate these relations is due to general structural differences of the sort discussed in Chapter II, and to differences in the membership of the sets $\{\phi\}$, $\{PRED_x <-> PRED_y\}_{AR}$, and $\{PRED_x <-> PRED_y\}_{OD}$, which must be specified for each language. Differences in the nature of ϕ triggers in Polish and English lead to the occurrence of transitive/intransitive-reflexive sentence pairs in the former language but not in the latter, and to the occurrence of active/[+V] passive sentence pairs in the latter language, but not in the former. The analysis explains the absence of intransitive-reflexive sentences (as a productive pattern) in English and the absence of [+V] passive participles in Polish.

The sets $\{PRED_x <-> PRED_y\}_{AR}$ and $\{PRED_x <-> PRED_y\}_{OD}$ are specified by the appropriate WFRs of the language, which define the morpheme inventory and permissible combinatory patterns of the morphemes of that language.[18] Differences from language to language in the set of WFRs can lead to striking contrasts. For example, Turkish and Japanese, but not English, have a CAUSATIVE (argument reduction) affix, which is attached to predicates (verbs) of certain classes in those languages. Moreover, in Turkish, the word formation process associated with this affix can, in certain cases, apply to its own output. This explains the occurrence of single-clause sentences like (3.20b) and (3.26a), repeated below, and the consequent occurrence of argument reduction sentence pairs with these as members, in Turkish and Japanese, but not in English:

(3.20) b.   Yusuf kasaba eti kestirdi
           Yusuf (SUBJ) butcher (DAT) meat (OBJ) CAUSE-cut
           Yusuf had the butcher cut the meat

(3.26) a.   Taroo wa Hanako ni piano o hik-ase-ta
           Taro (NOM) Hanako (DAT) piano (ACC) play-CAUSE-
               PAST
           Taro forced Hanako to play the piano

Most importantly, however, the Generalized Argument Reduction System analysis is essentially a structure-neutral analysis of NP movement (and the other processes). Neither of the two general rules are formulated in terms of syntactic structure, and none of the relevant assumptions or principles (such as WFC I) make reference to structural configurations or structurally defined relations. The same is true of the SRA rule. The only connection between the Generalized Argument Reduction System and the structural and/or morphological properties of individual languages is through the index insertion process, which, as discussed in Chapter II, applies in accordance with the correlation statements of the language in question; and through the relevant WFRs, which vary from language to language. Neither the Index Insertion rule nor word formation rules constrain in any way the rules of the Generalized Argument Reduction System in UG, so these latter rules apply in the same way to both configurational and non-configurational languages. The theory therefore predicts that both language types manifest the same syntactic patterns of related (or relatable) sentence pairs. This prediction is essentially correct.

There are, of course, other types of lexical rules, which are not subcases of the Generalized Argument Reduction System, and are not analogs of the NP movement rule in the GB theory. These obey different constraints and conditions, and relate other sets of FS pairs, of different types. I do not intend to discuss these in detail here, since any theory must incorporate them in some form. My goal here is more modest. I will look at the lexical transformation that relates verbs and nominals, and suggest a constraint on lexical rules that accounts for the non-occurrence of raising-analog controlled complements of the form: [(NP*[+GF])XP] in the F-structures of nominals (NPs). This discussion relates to another partial analog of NP movement, the Co-indexing rule discussed in Chapter III.

A relatively large number of lexical processes relate predicates with F-structures of the same type; that is, ones with the same number of x-NP[θ] arguments (and arguments of other categories). One example of such a rule is the Nominalization rule, shown below, which is accompanied by various WFRs in English:

(5.2)   VERB$_X$ 1-NP[α] X <--> [VERB+AF]$_N$ 1-NP[α] X

The variable X can contain one or more x-NP[θ] arguments as well as various other categories of F-level constituents.

This rule relates verbs of specified classes to their corresponding nominal forms. Both the verbs and the nominals have F-structures of the same type. That is, they contain the same number of x-NP[θ] arguments and the same arguments of other categories. However, the S-structure correlates of the NP[θ] arguments of verbs and nominals have different GR indicators (and the correlation statements for the x-NP[θ] arguments of each predicate type differ from one another, as discussed in Chapter II). Pairs like the following exemplify the verb/ nominal relation:

(5.3) a. The army$_i$ destroyed the village$_j$
       b. The army's$_i$ destruction of the village$_j$

(5.4) a. Joh$_i$ arrived (in Sydney$_j$)
       b. Joh's$_i$ arrival (in Sydney$_j$)

(5.5) a. Joh$_i$ believed that Hawke was a fool
       b. Joh's$_i$ belief that Hawke was a fool

(5.6) a. Murphy$_i$ decided to leave
       b. Murphy's$_i$ decision to leave

The basic F-structures of the predicates in (5.3) and (5.6) are shown below:

(5.7) a. DESTROY   1-NP[α] 2-NP[β]
       b. DESTRUCTION   1-NP[α] 2-NP[β]

(5.8) a.   DECIDE   1-NP[α]   [(NP*[-GR])VP]
  b.   DECISION   1-NP[α]   [(NP*[-GR])VP]

The Index Insertion rule and the SRA rule apply in the normal way to the bare PRED/ARG structures of (5.7) and (5.8) to produce the derived F-structures of examples (5.3) and (5.6), shown below:

(5.9) a.   DESTROY $\text{NP}[i]$ $\text{NP}[j]$
                 α β

  b.   DESTRUCTION $\text{NP}[i]$ $\text{NP}[j]$
                       α β

(5.10) a.   DECIDE $\text{NP}[i]$ [LEAVE $\text{NP}[i]$]
                   α α

  b.   DECISION $\text{NP}[i]$ [LEAVE $\text{NP}[i]$]
                     α α

(The Co-indexing rule, as discussed in Chapter III, has applied to produce the F-structures in (5.10).)

The following pair contrasts with the pair in (5.6):

(5.11) a.   Murphy$_i$ appeared to leave
  b.   *Murphy's$_i$ appearance to leave

Here, the nominal construction in (b) is ungrammatical. Since both (5.6b) and (5.11b) have identical S-structures (down to category level), there is no ready structural explanation for the ungrammaticality of the latter.

The difference lies in the applicability of the lexical nominal transformation, in (5.2). To understand this, some background discussion is necessary.

Lexical transformations, as we have seen, can change argument structure. For example, the lexical Argument Reduction rule deletes the 1-NP[α] argument of some predicate, PRED$_x$, and as a consequence, the 2-NP[β] argument becomes the new 1-NP[β] argument of the related predicate, PRED$_y$. As a result, the grammatical relation indicator (GRI) of the S-structure correlate of the NP[β] argument effectively changes. As an argument of PRED$_x$, its S-structure correlate bears the GRI, NP_2; and as an argument of $PRED_y$, its S-structure correlate bears the GRI, NP_1. In this situation, we may say that the lexical argument reduction transformation "involves" both the 1-NP[α] argument and the 2-NP[β] argument of $PRED_x$. It deletes the former and changes the GRI of the S-structure correlate of the latter.[19]

The Nominalization rule in (5.2) relates predicates of different categories. Here, $PRED_x$ is a verb [+V] and $PRED_y$ is a nominal [+N]. The S-structure correlates of the x-NP[θ] arguments of verbs bear different GRIs than the S-structure correlates of the x-NP[θ] arguments of nominals. As shown above, the S-structure correlate of the 1-NP[α] argument of a nominal bears the GRI, NP_{poss}, while that of the 2-NP[β] argument of a nominal bears the GRI, NP_{of}. These differ from the GRIs borne by the S-structure correlates of the 1-NP[α] and 2-NP[β] arguments of verbs: NP_1 and NP_2, respectively.

Therefore, the Nominalization rule, like the Argument Reduction rule, effectively changes the GRIs of the S-structure correlates of the NP[θ] arguments of some $PRED_x$ [+V] when relating that predicate to a corresponding $PRED_y$ [+N]. The GRI of the S-structure correlate of the NP[α] argument of the $PRED_x$ is changed from NP_1 to NP_{poss}, and that of the S-structure correlate of the NP[β] argument of the $PRED_x$ is changed from NP_2 to NP_{of}. In the above sense, then, we may say that the lexical nominalization transformation "involves" both the NP[θ] arguments of the VERB ($PRED_x$).

To produce the F-structure of DESTRUCTION in (5.7b) from that of DESTROY in (5.7a), the nominalization transformation must apply as shown:

(5.12)   DESTROY 1-NP[α] 2-NP[β] <--> [DESTRUCTION]$_N$
          1-NP[α]   2-NP[β]

It is easy to see that the rule involves both the 1-NP[α] argument and the 2-NP[β] argument of DESTROY, for the reasons cited above.

I will now propose the following constraint on the application of lexical rules:

(5.13)   Lexical transformations can involve only x-NP[θ] arguments
          of the relevant predicate

This condition, which also accounts for the boundedness of lexical operations, is not new, and, in fact, is quite similar in spirit to the earliest assumptions of the so-called lexicalist hypothesis.[20] The only innovation is the slightly broadened sense of involvement, formulated in the context of the proposed theory.

Now, let us consider the pair, DECIDE/DECISION. To derive the basic F-structure of DECISION, in (5.8b), from that of DECIDE, in (5.8a), the Nominalization rule in (5.2) must apply as shown:

(5.14)   DECIDE   1-NP[α]   [(NP*[-GR])VP]   <-> DECISION
          1-NP[α]   [(NP*[-GR])VP]

The basic F-structure of DECIDE contains only a single x-NP[θ] argument, 1-NP[α]. The NP*[-GR] argument is not an NP[θ] argument because it is not assigned an SR by the predicate DECIDE.

The application of the rule in (5.14) involves the 1-NP[α] argument. When it relates the $PRED_x$, DECIDE [+V] to the $PRED_y$, DECISION [+N], it changes the GRI of the S-structure correlate of the 1-NP[α] argument from NP_1 to NP_{poss}.

However, the rule does not involve the NP*[-GR] argument. Arguments of this category have no S-structure correlates, and consequently have no associated GRIs. Therefore, the only way that a lexical transformation can involve such arguments is by deleting them. This, of course, is not the case in (5.14).

Thus the application of the Nominalization rule in (5.14) involves only an x-NP[θ] argument, and does not violate the condition in (5.13).

This is not the case for the pair APPEAR/APPEARANCE in examples like (5.11). To relate the predicate APPEAR in this sense to the nominal APPEARANCE, the lexical transformation must apply as shown below:

(5.15)   APPEAR [(NP*[+GR])VP] <-> [APPEARANCE]$_N$
          [(NP*[+GR])VP]

APPEAR is a "raising" predicate, and contains the argument NP*[+GR]. Arguments of this category have S-structure correlates which bear a GRI. With APPEAR [+V], the F-structure correlate of this argument bears the GRI, NP_1. However, the NP*[+GR] argument is not an NP[θ]

argument because the predicate APPEAR assigns no SR to it.

It is easy to see that this application of the Nominalization rule involves this argument, since it changes the GRI of its S-structure correlate from NP_1 to NP_{poss}. It therefore violates the condition in (5.13). As a consequence, the right-hand F-structure is not a permissible one for APPEAR, and this accounts for the ungrammaticality of the example in (5.11b).

This analysis predicts that pairs like the ones in (5.16) occur:

(5.16) a. Isabella appeared
      b. Isabella's appearance

The relevant F-structure of APPEAR is shown in (5.17):

(5.17)   APPEAR   1-NP[α]

To derive the F-structure of APPEARANCE in this sense from that of APPEAR, the nominalization transformation must apply as shown in (5.18):

(5.18)   APPEAR   1-NP[α]   <-->   [APPEARANCE]$_N$ 1-NP[α]

This application does not violate the condition in (5.13).

The analysis also accounts for the ungrammaticality of the (b) members of pairs like (5.19), and the grammaticality of the (b) members of pairs like (5.20):

(5.19) a. Malcolm believed Nigel to have done that
      b. *Malcolm's belief of Nigel to have done that

(5.20) a. Joh forced Hawke to kiss Flo
      b. Joh's forcing of Hawke to kiss Flo

The analysis explains why nominals cannot have F-structures to which the analog of the raising subcase of NP movement in the GB theory can apply. This explains the non-occurrence of what is analyzed as raising to subject position in NPs in the GB theory.

NOTES

1. For non-configurational languages, with sentence structures like (i), below, neither movement from non-subject to subject position, nor movement from subject to non-subject position involves movement of NPs from lower to higher positions in P-structures (or vice versa):

(i)

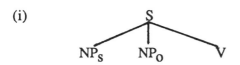

$$NP_S = subject \;\&\; NP_O = object$$

Moreover, NP movement from one non-subject position to another non-subject position in the standard theory is prevented by certain general principles of that theory, primarily by the Theta Criterion. The analog of this sort of movement in the proposed theory is discussed in Section 4.

2. See Horn (1978) and (1983b) for more extensive discussion of passivization, including the overgeneration question.

3. By assigning the feature [-Grammatical Relation] to the reflexive particles in intransitive-reflexive examples, we can also account for the fact that such particles are not marked for case, but are invariant in form (only *się* occurs). In true reflexive sentences, case-marked variants of the reflexive particle can occur. Since morphological case markers are indicators of grammatical relations in Polish, they do not occur on constituents that bear no grammatical relation.

4. A second pattern of intransitive-reflexive sentences occurs in Polish. Examples are shown in (i) and (ii):

(i)   Te pomarańcze łatwo się obiera
        those oranges (ACC/pl) easily REFLEX peel (3rd person/sg)
        Those oranges can be peeled easily

(ii)   Te bluzki dobrze się pierze
        those blouses (ACC/pl) well REFLEX wash (3rd person/sg)
        Those blouses wash easily

In these examples, the lone plural NP is marked for the accusative case, the GR indicator of direct objects, and the verb is marked for third person singlular subject agreement. Such examples are best analyzed as having S-structures like the following:

(iii)

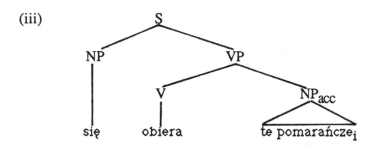

This is the S-structure of (i). The particle *się* occupies the subject position. The third person singular verb form occurs in sentences which contain dummy subjects, so this analysis accounts both for the verb form and the case-marking of the NP constituent. The argument reduction analysis applies to these examples without modification. The F-structure of (i) is derived from the following:

(iv)   [SIĘ]OBIERAĆ 1-NP 2-NP

The Index Insertion rule and the SRA rule, with α-deletion, apply to produce the following:

(iv)   [SIĘ]OBIERAĆ $NP_\beta^{[i]}$

Examples of this sort, and their analogs in Italian, are discussed in Horn (1983b).

5. This statement of the distribution of NPs which bear the SR *theme* is based in part on observations made in Anderson (1977).

6. In example (3.2a), TRANS represents a transitive verbal prefix. The verb form, *manasa* in (3.2a) is formed by combining the morphemes shown in (i):

(i) MAN + SASA

The prefix MAN- is the present tense, transitive prefix. The stem is SASA, "wash". Due to morphophonemic properties of the language, the initial consonant of the stem is deleted.

The verb form *sasana* in (3.2c) is analyzed as follows:

(ii) SASA + NA

NA is the passive suffix. When the agent NP is attached to the passive verb form, the final vowel of the passive affix is deleted. As a consequence of other phonological properties of the language, the sequence shown in (iii) becomes the form that appears in example (3.2b). This latter form is shown in (iv):

(iii) SASA + N +RASOA
(iv) SASA + N +dRASOA

7. This process, for example, does not apply to the transitive verb, *po* (hit), as illustrated by the ungrammaticality of the (b) example in the following pair:

(i) a. Na po e Ioane Mele
        TENSE hit (SUBJ) Ioane Mele
        Ioane hit Mele

  b. *Na po Mele
        TENSE hit Mele
        Mele was hit

This verb has no object deletion counterpart either. (See discussion of the OD relation below.)

8. In these examples, the index of the NP_{acc} has been inserted into the 1-NP position in the F-structures.

   In the normal situation, as discussed in Chapter II, the NP_{nom} in the S-structure is the correlate of the F-level 1-NP argument. NP_{nom} is the sister of $V^{(n)}$, the maximal projection of V^0, which is VP for Polish.

   This is consistent with the universal structure-based correlation statement for 1-NP arguments. The S-structure correlates of 2-NP and 3-NP arguments, which are sisters of V^0, are NPs marked for other cases.

   In structures like (3.55), however, the VP has no sister NP. Therefore, the NP_{acc} is the sister of the maximal projection of V^0 that has an NP sister, namely V^0 itself. So NP_{acc} satisfies the conditions of the structure-based correlation statement.

   Therefore, impersonal sentences are exceptional only with regard to the case-based correlation statement for F-level 1-NP arguments. The correlation of the NP_{dat} constituent and the 2-NP argument in the F-structure of DANO, in (3.56a), is not exceptional. NP_{dat} constituents are the S-structure correlates of the 2-NP arguments of a number of predicates. One example is the two-argument predicate *ufać* (trust), which occurs in sentences like (i), below, shown with its F-structure:

(i) a. $Adam_i$ ufał swoim $przyjacielom_j$
         Adam (NOM) trusted his friends (DAT)
         Adam trusted his friends

   b.   UFAĆ $NP^{[i]}_{\alpha}$ $NP^{[j]}_{\beta}$

   Impersonal verbs, then, occur in marked S-structures. As a consequence of this, the derivations of the F-structures of sentences containing impersonal verbs require an exception to the application of the case-based correlation statements of the language.

9. This is the same convention that applies to the 1-NP[α] arguments of [+V] predicates. As discussed in previous chapters, these have no S-structure correlates when the verbs occur in embedded VPs. An

example is the following:

(i) a. To win is desirable

   b. BE[DESIRABLE] $\underset{\alpha}{\text{NP}[[\text{WIN}]}$ $\underset{\alpha}{\text{NP}[\text{INDEF}]]}$

10. The basic F-structure of the predicate CARE, in this sense, contains two x-NP[θ] arguments, as shown in (3.81b). The S-structure correlate of the 2-NP[β] argument is the object of the preposition *about*.

11. In the argument reduction discussion, certain factors which tend to obscure the similarities between nominal and verbal predicates in that regard were mentioned. The same factors are relevant here.

As we saw in the earlier discussion, nominals like *destruction* and *murder*, when they occur with NP arguments, have the same sorts of argument structures as their corresponding verb forms, and they participate in the same sorts of Argument Reduction (AR) and Object Deletion (OD) relations. For example, the verbs *destroy* and *murder* occur in AR pairs, but not OD pairs, as illustrated in (i) and (ii):

(i) a. The army destroyed the village
      The village was destroyed
    *The army destroyed

(ii) a. John murdered his stepfather
    b. John's stepfather was murdered
    c. *John murdered

These patterns apply to the nominal forms of these verbs as well, as illustrated in the following examples:

(iii) a. The army's destruction of the village
     b. The village's destruction
     c. The army's destruction

(iv) a. John's murder of his stepfather
     b. John's stepfather's murder
     c. John's murder

Example (iii c) has only the AR interpretation, not an OD interpretation, and the same is true of (iv c). The verb/nominal pair *kill/killing* behaves the same way as shown below:

(v) a. John killed his sister
   b. John's sister was killed
   c. *John killed

(vi) a. John's killing of his sister
   b. John's sister's killing
   c. John's killing

As above, example (vi c) has only the AR interpretation.

However, nouns which are not deverbal nominals, and which can function as two-argument predicates in certain cases, also occur in what seems to be a rather wide array of structures of various types, each of which has multiple interpretations. Two examples are *photograph* and *book*, which occur in NPs like the following:

(vii) a. John's$_i$ photograph of Bill$_j$
    b. John's$_i$ photograph

(viii) a. Kissinger's$_i$ book about Nixon$_j$
     b. Kissinger's$_i$ book

(ix) a. The photograph of Bill$_i$
    b. The book about Nixon$_i$

Examples (vii a) and (viii a) are ambiguous. They can have either the interpretations in which John is the photographer and Kissinger is the author, or the interpretations in which John and Kissinger possess the photograph and book, respectively, in some sense. Examples (vii b) and (viii b) are also ambiguous, and these have three interpretations: the OD interpretation, which is associated with the F-structures shown in (3.97b and d); the AR interpretation; or an interpretation in which John and Kissinger possess the photograph and book in some sense.

This latter interpretation in all cases is associated with F-structures that are produced by substituting the SR *poss* for the SR α of the

1-NP argument in the basic one- or two-argument F-structure of the relevant predicate. (Remember that NP_{poss} constituents are the S-structure correlates of the 1-NP arguments of [+N] predicates.) Consequently, two F-structures can be produced for (vii a) and (viii a), and three each for (vii b) and (viii b). These are shown for examples (vii a) and (vii b), respectively:

(x)   a.   PHOTOGRAPH   NP[i]   NP[j]
                         α β

    b.   PHOTOGRAPH   NP[i]   NP[j]
                         poss β

(xi) a.   PHOTOGRAPH   NP[i]
                         α

    b.   PHOTOGRAPH   NP[i]
                         β

    c.   PHOTOGRAPH   NP[i]
                         poss

    The F-structures of the examples in (ix) are derived from the basic two-argument F-structures of PHOTOGRAPH and BOOK as discussed for example (3.68) in the text. The F-structure for (ix a) is shown below:

(xii)   PHOTOGRAPH   NP[INDEF]   NP[i]
                         α β

    So we can account for these patterns by assuming that these [+N] predicates can have any of the three F-structure types shown in (xiii), and that an NP_{poss} constituent in the S-structure can trigger an operation: α -> poss.

(xiii) a.   PRED   1-NP[α]   2-NP[β]
     b.   PRED   1-NP[α]
     c.   PRED   1-NP[β]

Structure (xiii a) is the basic F-structure, Structure (xiii b) is the OD F-structure, and structure (xiii c) is the AR F-structure.

    Finally, consider the following examples:

(xiv) a. The photograph of John's$_i$
    b. Those photographs
    c. The large photographs

Example (xiv a) contains the construction *[of NP+poss]*. This construction, a PP at the S-structure level, denotes possession (in some sense). Its function is similar to the alternate function of the NP$_{poss}$ constituents in the previous examples. In all three of these examples, the noun *photograph* has a non-predicate function and occurs with no NP arguments. Their F-level representations do not contain a PRED/ARG structure for the noun in question. The F-level representation of (xiv a) is formed by combining the non-predicate representation of *photograph* and the F-structure of the preposition *of*, more or less as shown below:

(ix)   PHOTOGRAPH [OF $\text{NP[i]}_{\text{poss}}$]

The F-level representations of (xiv b and c) are formed by combining the non-predicate representation of *photograph* with the other elements in an analogous way.

We see, then, that the proposed analysis, in which the AR and OD rules can apply to the PRED/ARG structures of such nouns, and the three additional, rather natural, assumptions shown below account for the range of facts considered here:

(xvi) a. NP$_{poss}$ optionally triggers the rule: $\alpha \rightarrow$ poss.

    b. [Of NP+poss] constructions indicating possession may be attached to the PRED/ARG structures or non-predicate representations of nouns of this type.

    c. Nouns can have non-predicate functions, with no relevant PRED/ARG structures, in which case they appear in S-structures with no NP arguments.

Deverbal nominals can also function as non-predicates, in examples like (xvii):

(xvii) a. The destruction was unimaginable

b. Those murders were horrible

[Of NP+poss] constructions can appear in the F-structures of examples containing [+N] predicates as shown below:

(xviii) a. This book about Nixon of Bill's

b. [BOOK   NP[INDEF] NP[i]] [OF NP[j]]
         α   β   poss

12. This variant is discussed in the next section.

13. See Keyser and Roeper (1984).

14. If the relevant S-structures containing one-argument predicates contain no indexed NP constituent, derived F-structures like the following can be produced:

(i)   [φ]PRED Ø

Such structures do not violate WFC I, and are well-formed. In fact, F-structures of this type are the non-lexical analogs of F-structures like (4.21), below, which are assigned to Turkish sentences like (4.22a), which contain verbs and no NP arguments. Therefore, we can allow this possibility at the level of UG and account for the ungrammaticality of English examples like (ii) in some other way:

(ii)   *was walked

Perhaps the ugrammaticality of (ii) is due to the fact that English sentences require an overt subject at S-structure level. Note that examples like the following, which are functionally analogous to such Ø-argument sentences, do occur:

(iii)   There was a lot of walking during that excursion

The contrast between (ii) and (iii) is due to the fact that deverbal nominals like *walking* are members of the set {PRED$_x$ <->

$PRED_y\}_{AR}$. Perhaps the non-predicate F-level representations of nouns of this sort, discussed in footnote 11, are produced by the application of the lexical AR rule.

15. Of course, if non-lexical OD pairs do not occur in any language, some condition on UG is required. I will not pursue this question here.

   In any case, all sentences in which a verb occurs with too few arguments will be odd in the same way as example (4.16). Some examples are shown below:

(i) a. ?Fred went to
     b. ?John said
     c. ?Bill believed

None of these examples can be fully interpreted. So their ungrammaticality is explained by other principles not related to the GAR system itself.

16. In addition, since neither the non-lexical nor the lexical rules of the GAR System can effect a change in the order of SRs from that in the basic F-structures of the relevant predicates, the System cannot relate FS pairs like the following (or any permutation of this type):

(i) $PRED_x$ 1-NP[α] 2-NP[β] 3-NP[γ] <--> $PRED_y$ 1-NP[γ]
        2-NP[β] 3-NP[α]

This explains the longstanding observation that no language relates mirror-image sentence pairs.

   It should be noted at this point that I have not included scrambling rules in this discussion. These rules are formally quite different from the processes discussed here, and do not, in fact have F-level consequences that are of any relevance here. Instead, they relate sentence variants all of which have the same F-level representation. Thus, as discussed in Chapter II, the Polish examples in (ii) all have the same F-structure, which is shown in (iii):

(ii) a. Jan$_i$ widział Marię$_j$
Jan (NOM) saw Maria (ACC)
Jan saw Maria

b. Jan$_i$ Marię$_j$ widział
c. Widział Marię$_j$ Jan$_i$
d. Marię$_j$ widział Jan$_i$

(iii)   WIDZIEC NP[i] NP[j]
$\quad\quad\quad\quad\quad\quad$ α $\quad$ β

17. Finally, in the absence of conditions to the contrary, the GAR System analysis predicts that if two related predicates, PRED$_x$ and PRED$_y$, of the types shown in (i), occur in some language, then a third predicate PRED$_z$, of the type shown in (ii) and related to the other two, will also occur:

(i) a. PRED$_x$ 1-NP[α] 2-NP[β] 3-NP[γ]
    b. PRED$_y$ 1-NP[γ]

(ii)   PRED$_z$ 1-NP[β] 2-NP[γ]

The reason for this is that, as formulated, both the non-lexical and lexical rules of the Generalized Argument Reduction System apply to a single SR or a single x-NP[θ] argument. There is no θ-deletion rule that deletes more than one SR in one application, nor is there an x-NP[θ]-deletion rule that deletes more than one x-NP[θ] argument in a single application. Such triples of related predicates occur in Turkish, as discussed above.

18. The function of WFRs as language-specific values of the parameter associated with the lexical rule of the GAR System is, I believe, a quite natural extension of their function in other theories. These rules, as formulated, are sufficient for defining lexical subclasses (which may ultimately be definable by other criteria). This additional function in the proposed theory involves nothing more than an extended use of what we might term "zero operations". These are WFRs that relate two lexical classes but perform no overt morphological operation. How-

ever, even this sort of WFR is required by most, if not all, current linguistic theories.

19. X-NP[θ] arguments have a feature, [+GR] in the unmarked situation. Thus, lexical rules which have the effect of modifying the S-structure realization of this feature "involve" the relevant term.

20. See Chomsky (1970), Wasow (1977) for related discussion.

Chapter V

The EA System: A reanalysis of wh-movement

1. Introduction

In the standard theory, wh-Movement is a subcase of the general rule, Move-α, by which a wh-constituent is moved from some position in S to the COMP position of the $\bar{S}$ which dominates that S. This is diagrammed in (1.1), below:

(1.1)

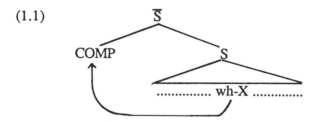

Any adequate theory must contain principles which properly constrain this process, however it is formulated. The most general constraint is that the wh-constituent must be located in a COMP node at the S-structure level, and this COMP node must be higher in the S-structure than the position from which the wh-constituent has been moved. (See Chomsky (1976), (1981), and (1985), for example.) This condition, however, is clearly not sufficient to account for the patterns of wh-Movement (or similar operations). In particular, an adequate theory must explain why the wh-Movement rule cannot apply to the constituents of certain syntactic configurations. Such configurations are generally known as islands, and the literature pertaining to so-called island constraints is vast. However, the primary distinctions among the many proposed analyses lie in the overall nature of the principles which define islands (whether these are formulated in terms of syntactic structure or of function in some sense) and the level of structure at which the principles apply (D-structure, S-structure, or some other level).

The analog of the wh-Movement rule in the proposed theory is the E-Anaphora (EA) rule. This rule applies to syntactic structures to bind a variable, $\underline{x}$, in S to a designated operator, or antecedent, elsewhere in the structure. The application of the EA rule is constrained by the general principles of the theory, in particular, by WFC I, as well as two constraints which apply to structures which contain bound variables. All of these constraints apply at the level of derived F-structure, and the latter two comprise the Generalized EA System of UG.

In Section 2, I formulate the EA rule and discuss its domain. I also demonstrate here that certain misapplications of the rule produce derived F-structures which violate WFC I. This explains the most general constraints on the rule. In Section 3, I discuss the first of the two constraints on bound variables, the Predicate Argument Constraint (PAC). This constraint explains why certain syntactic (S-structure) configurations are islands in certain circumstances, but not islands in other circumstances. In Section 4, I discuss the second constraint, the Single Gap Constraint (SGC), which is, in effect, a constraint on string processing. These two constraints explain the pattern of grammaticality of the central body of data relating to islands. In Section 5, I demonstrate that cross-language variation in the patterns of wh-Movement is attributable to variation of the values of various parameters associated with the constraints. None of the relevant principles are formulated in terms of syntactic configurations, so the theory applies to languages regardless of their general syntactic characteristics.

2. The E-Anaphora Rule

The E-Anaphora (EA) rule applies to the syntactic structures of examples like the following:

(2.1) a. Who_i did Meryl_j dislike
      b. Who_i did Marlon_j believe that Meryl_k disliked

The syntactic structures of these examples before the application of the EA rule are shown in (2.2a and b), respectively:

(2.2) a.

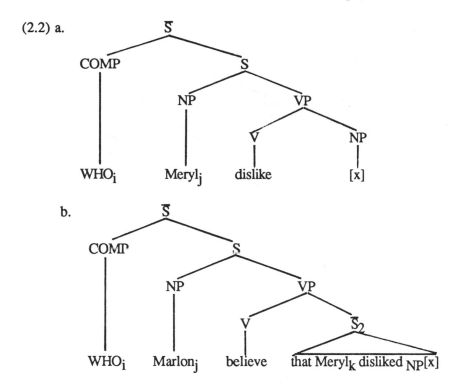

b.

In these structures, the wh-constituents have been inserted directly into the COMP position, and the unbound variables, $\underline{x}$ in each case, have been inserted into the appropriate NP constituent. The EA rule applies to such structures to bind the variable $\underline{x}$ to the wh-constituent. The EA rule is formulated as shown in (2.3):

(2.3)   E-Anaphora Rule: In syntactic structures which contain a variable, $_{XP}[x]$, and a wh-constituent, $_{XP}[[..wh..]_i]$, bind the variable to the wh-constituent.

The EA rule, as formulated in (2.3) is an unbounded unordered operation, and mentions no syntactic configurations other than the XP terms which it directly involves. This rule applies to the structures in (2.2) to produce the structures in (2.4), below, which are the S-structures of examples (2.1a and b):

(2.4) a.

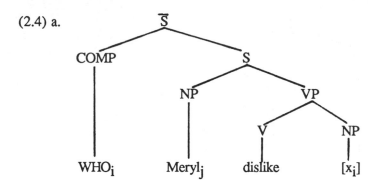

b.

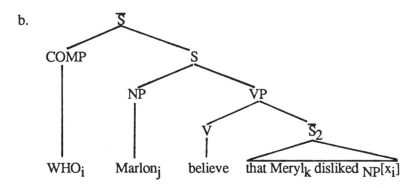

The derived F-structures of these examples are produced from the following bare PRED/ARG structures:

(2.5) a.   (WHO)[DISLIKE   1-NP   2-NP]
     b.   (WHO)[BELIEVE   1-NP   [DISLIKE   1-NP   2-NP]]

These PRED/ARG structures are produced by prefixing the F-structure representation of the wh-antecedent in the COMP of the relevant S-structure to the PRED/ARG structure of the predicate of the matrix clause S.   The Index Insertion rule and the SRA rule apply to the structures in (2.5) to produce (2.6), below:

(2.6) a. $(WHO_i)[DISLIKE \quad NP[j] \quad NP[x_i]]$
                              $\alpha \qquad \beta$

     b. $(WHO_i)[BELIEVE \quad NP[j] \quad [DISLIKE \quad NP[k] \quad NP[x_i]]]$
                              $\alpha \qquad\qquad\qquad \alpha \qquad \beta$

No further operations apply, so these are the derived F-structures of

(2.1). The prefixed elements in such structures do not occupy NP[θ] argument positions, and therefore are not directly assigned an SR. Instead, they are assigned an SR indirectly since they are co-indexed with, and bind, variables, x_i, which occupy NP[θ] argument positions and bear SRs. This is a property of NP_i/x_i pairs.[1]

The following sentence, which contains a wh-constituent in COMP which does not bind a variable elsewhere in the structure, is ungrammatical:

(2.7) *Who_i did the $princess_j$ dislike the $frogs_k$

The S-structure of this example is shown in (2.8):

(2.8)

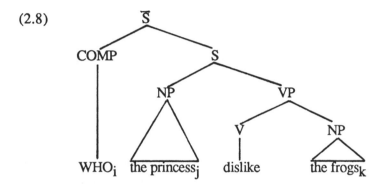

Here, both of the NP constituents in S are lexical NPs and the EA rule cannot apply. The PRED/ARG structure of (2.7), after the application of the Index Insertion rule and the SRA rule, is the following:

(2.9) $(WHO_i)[DISLIKE \quad \underset{\alpha}{NP[j]} \quad \underset{\beta}{NP[k]}]$

This, in fact, is the only derived F-structure that can be produced for example (2.7). In this structure, the prefixed wh-expression, WHO_i, does not bind a variable in an NP[θ] argument position, and is not assigned an SR. Consequently, the structure violates WFC I and is not well-formed. The ungrammaticality of (2.7) is due to the fact that no well-formed derived F-structure can be produced for it.

General principles of the theory, in effect, dictate that wh-constituents must be located in the COMP position in S-structures, and that they must be located higher in the S-structure than the variables that they bind.[2]   The following example, shown with its S-structure, illustrates the first point:

(2.10) a. *Who$_i$ disliked

b.

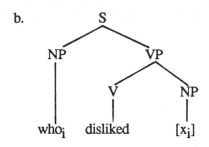

Here, the wh-constituent, *who$_i$*, is located in subject position, and the EA rule has applied to bind the variable x_i to it. The derived F-structure of (2.10a) is shown in (2.11):

(2.11)   DISLIKE $\underset{\alpha}{NP[WHO_i]}$ $\underset{\beta}{NP[x_i]}$

In this structure, WHO$_i$ is directly assigned the SR α, and is indirectly assigned the SR β since it binds the variable, x_i, which bears that SR. Consequently, the derived F-structure in (2.11) violates WFC I, and is not well-formed. This situation arises whenever the wh-constituent occupies an NP[θ] argument position. In fact, no well-formed derived F-structure can be produced for (2.10a), and this explains its ungrammaticality.[3]

Now consider the example in (2.12), below:

(2.12)   *Victoria$_i$ asked who$_j$ Frith$_k$ kissed caterpillars$_m$

The S-structure of this sentence is shown in (2.13):

(2.13)

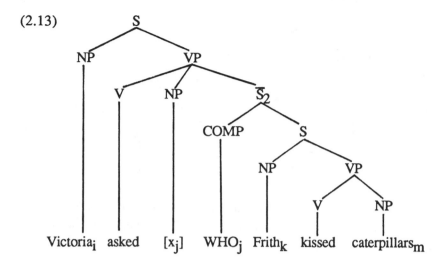

Victoria$_i$ asked [x_j] WHO$_j$ Frith$_k$ kissed caterpillars$_m$

In this structure, the EA rule has applied to bind the variable, $\underline{x}_j$, which is located in the matrix S, to the wh-constituent in the COMP of S$_2$, which is lower in the structure. The derived F-structure of (2.12) appears in (2.14):

(2.14)   ASK $_{NP[i]}$ $_{NP[x_j]}$ [(WHO$_j$)[KISS $_{NP[k]}$ $_{NP[m]}$]]]
$\qquad\qquad\quad \alpha \quad \beta \qquad\qquad\qquad\quad \alpha \quad \beta$

Here, the wh-constituent, WHO$_j$, is prefixed to the PRED/ARG structure of KISS. However, WHO$_j$ does not bind a variable located in this PRED/ARG structure. This substructure is analogous to the ill-formed F-structure in (2.9), above. A quite reasonable way to view the application of WFC I is to require that it apply to all proper substructures of complex derived F-structures. Under this interpretation, Structure (2.14) violates this condition, and is not well-formed. Since no well-formed derived F-structure can be produced for example (2.12), it is ungrammatical.

Next, consider the following example, shown with its syntactic structure prior to the application of the EA rule:

(2.15) a.   Who$_i$ did Johnson$_j$ dislike

b.

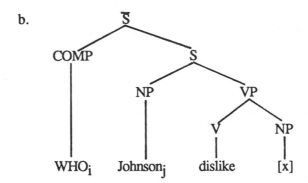

Suppose that the EA rule applies to bind the variable $\underline{x}$ to *Johnson* (the formulation in (2.3) notwithstanding.) The resulting derived F-structure appears in (2.16):

(2.16)   (WHO$_i$)[DISLIKE $\underset{\alpha}{NP[j]}$ $\underset{\beta}{NP[x_j]}$]]

This structure is not well-formed. First of all, it contains a prefixed term, WHO$_i$, which is not assigned an SR. Secondly, the $_{NP}[j]$ argument of DISLIKE is directly assigned the SR α and indirectly assigned the SR β since it binds the variable $\underline{x}_j$ which bears this SR. Therefore the structure violates WFC I. However, if the EA rule applies to bind the variable in (2.15b) to the wh-constituent in COMP, WHO$_i$, the following derived F-structure can be produced for example (2.15a):

(2.17)   (WHO$_i$)[DISLIKE $\underset{\alpha}{NP[j]}$ $\underset{\beta}{NP[x_i]}$]]

This structure is well-formed. This accounts for the grammaticality of example (2.15a) and for its interpretation in which *who* is the object of *dislike*.

These examples demonstrate three things. Firstly, if the constituent which binds a variable, $\underline{x}$, in some S-structure is not located in COMP, no well-formed derived F-structure can be produced from that S-structure. Secondly, if a constituent binds a variable, $\underline{x}$, which is located higher in the S-structure than the constituent which it is bound to, no well-formed derived F-structure can be produced from that S-structure. Thirdly, the EA rule need not be limited to wh-constituents.[4]

In fact, the EA rule can be trivially reformulated to apply to examples like the following, which involve processes which pattern in the same way as wh-questions, but do not contain wh-constituents at the level of S-structure:[5]

(2.18) a. Bullfrogs$_i$ Samantha$_j$ disliked
      b. It was bullfrogs$_i$ that Samantha$_j$ disliked

I assume that such examples have syntactic structures like the following, before the application of the EA rule:[6]

(2.19) a.

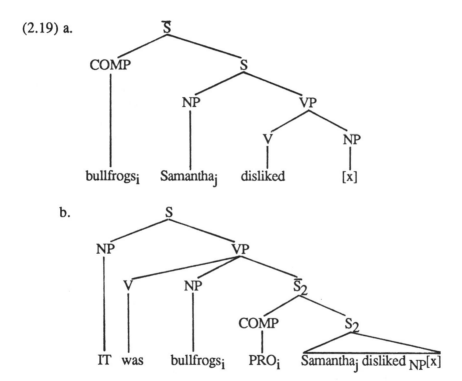

In these structures, the variable, $\underline{x}$ in each case must be bound to an indexed operator elsewhere in the structure. In Structure (2.19a), $\underline{x}$ must be bound to the $_{NP}[i]$ constituent in COMP, and in Structure (2.19b), $\underline{x}$ must be bound to the PRO$_j$ constituent in COMP of S$_2$. The EA rule can be reformulated as shown in (2.20):

(2.20)   <u>E-Anaphora Rule 2</u>: In syntactic structures which contain a variable, $_{XP}[x]$, and a designated indexed constituent, $_{XP}[i]$, bind the variable to the designated constituent.

This rule applies to the structure in (2.19a) to assign the variable x the index i, and to the structure in (2.19b) to assign the variable x the index i. The following derived F-structures are produced from these S-structures:[7]

(2.21) a. $(_{NP}[i])[DISLIKE \underset{\alpha}{NP[j]} \underset{\beta}{NP[x_i]}]$

   b. $BE \underset{\emptyset}{NP[IT]} \underset{\beta}{NP[j]} [(PRO_j)[DISLIKE \underset{\alpha}{NP[k]} \underset{\beta}{NP[x_j]}]]$

These structures are well-formed. The revised EA rule, EA 2, provides the basis for a unified analysis of wh-Movement, topicalization, cleft formation, and other processes which share similar properties.[8]

   We see, then, that WFC I and the principle that assigns the SR of a bound variable to its antecedent explain the most general constraint on the distribution of wh-constituents, and other operators which bind variables, as well as that on the distribution of those bound variables themselves.

3. The Predicate Argument Constraint

In this section, I look at the central body of data which relates to syntactic islands, and demonstrate that the factors which determine the islandhood of syntactic configurations are not purely syntactic ones. Consider first the following examples:

(3.1) a.   *Who did Melvin$_j$ dislike [the people who knew]$_k$
   b.   *What$_i$ did Seamus$_j$ congratulate [the princess who kissed]$_k$
   c.   *What$_i$ did Kingston$_j$ destroy [a book about]$_k$

   The bracketed constituents in these examples are islands. In examples (3.1a and b), these are complex NPs; and in example (3.1c), the bracketed constituent is a non-complex NP. Such examples suggest that S-structure NPs are islands. This generalization first appeared as the Noun Phrase Constraint (NPC) in Horn (1975), and has been accepted, albeit with a quite different explanation, by Chomsky and others

working in the standard theory. (See, for example, Chomsky (1977).)
The NPC, as a constraint on S-structures, appears below:

(3.2)   An S-structure NP constituent cannot properly contain an
         externally bound variable, x_i.

The S-structures of these examples, after the application of the EA rule,
appear in (3.3):

(3.3) a.

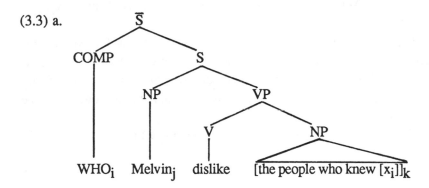

b.

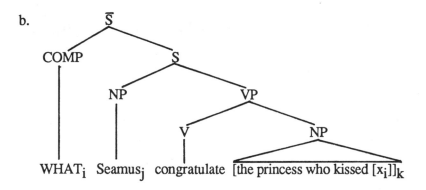

c.

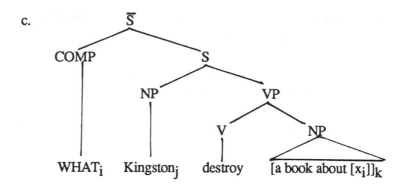

(In these structures, I ignore the internal structures of the NP constituents.) It is easy to see that these S-structures violate the NPC as formulated in (3.2). Each contains an NP constituent of the form: $NP[..[x_i]..]_k$ and the variable x_i is bound to some operator outside of the NP structure.

The derived F-structures of the examples in (3.1) are shown in (3.4), below:

(3.4) a. $(WHO_i)[DISLIKE \underset{\alpha}{NP[j]} \underset{\beta}{NP[...[x_i]...]_k}]$

b. $(WHAT_i)[CONGRATULATE \underset{\alpha}{NP[j]} \underset{\beta}{NP[...[x_i]...]_k}]$

c. $(WHAT_i)[DESTROY \underset{\alpha}{NP[j]} \underset{\beta}{NP[...[x_i]...]_k}]$

The NPC can easily be reformulated so that it applies to the level of derived F-structure. This reformulation is shown in (3.5):

(3.5)   An NP argument in a derived F-structure cannot properly contain an externally bound variable, x_i.

The structures in (3.4) violate this constraint, and are therefore not well-formed. No well-formed derived F-structures can be produced for the examples in (3.1), and this explains their ungrammaticality.

This analysis also explains the ungrammaticality of examples like (3.6b), below:

(3.6) a.   That$_i$ was a bastard of a math test

b. *What$_i$ was that$_j$ a bastard of

The S-structure and derived F-structure of example (3.6b) are shown in (3.7), below:

(3.7) a.

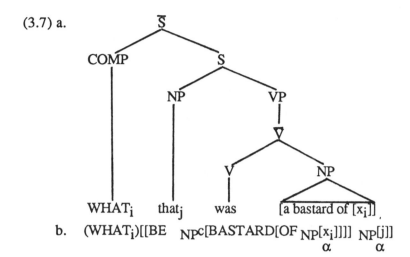

b.   (WHAT$_i$)[[BE $_{NP^c}$[BASTARD[OF $_{NP}$[x$_i$]]]] $_{NP}$[j]]
$\quad\quad\quad\quad\quad\quad\quad\quad\quad\quad\quad\quad\quad\quad$ α $\quad\quad$ α

In the S-structure, the bound variable, x_i, is properly contained in the NP constituent, *a bastard of [x $_i$]*, in the complex predicate, ∇. In the derived F-structure, the F-structure representation of this NP constituent is the NP^c argument of the predicate BE, [BASTARD[OF NP[x_i]]]. This argument properly contains the variable x_i, which is bound to the operator WHAT$_i$ located outside of the NP^c argument itself. Consequently, the derived F-structure violates the NPC as formulated in (3.5), and is not well-formed. No well-formed derived F-structure can be produced for example (3.6b).

The NPC in (3.2), formulated to apply at the level of S-structure, and the NPC in (3.5), formulated to apply at the level of derived F-structure, are equivalent when applied to data like (3.1) and (3.6), for which the F-structure correlates of S-structure NP constituents are NP arguments. Presently, we will see that they make quite different predictions when applied to additional data.

The following examples indicate that APs as well as NPs are islands:

(3.8) a.   Marcello$_i$ is tall for an Italian
   b. *What$_i$ is Marcello$_j$ tall for

(3.9) a. Chadwick$_i$ was stupid for a Rhodes Scholar
      b. *What$_i$ was Chadwick$_j$ stupid for

The S-structures of (3.8b) and (3.9b) appear in (3.10), and their derived F-structures appear in (3.11), below:

(3.10) a.

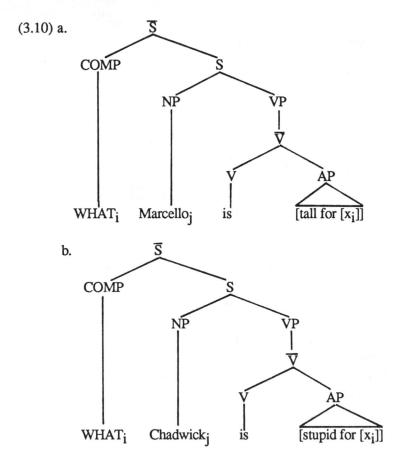

    b.

(3.11) a.   (WHAT$_i$)[[BE $_{AP}$c[TALL[FOR $_{NP}$[x$_i$]]]] $_{NP}$[j]]
                                                    α α

       b.   (WHAT$_i$)[[BE $_{AP}$c[STUPID[FOR $_{NP}$[x$_i$]]]] $_{NP}$[j]]
                                                        α α

In the S-structures of these examples, the AP constituents of the complex predicates, $\overline{V}$, properly contain the bound variables, x_i. In each of the derived F-structures in (3.11), the bound variable is properly contained

in the AP^C argument of the predicate BE. The NPC, as formulated in
(3.5), does not apply to these structures. Therefore, another explanation for the ungrammaticality of examples (3.8b) and (3.9b) is
required. Before I propose an explanation, let us look at the following
examples:

(3.12) a. Everyone$_i$ considered Marcus$_j$ nasty to animals
       b. What$_k$ did everyone$_i$ consider Marcus$_j$ nasty to

(3.13) a. The members$_i$ elected Evelyn$_j$ president of the club
       b. Which club$_k$ did the members$_i$ elect Evelyn$_j$ president of

In the S-structures of examples (3.12b) and (3.13b) the bound variables are properly contained in an AP constituent and an NP constituent,
respectively. These S-structures are shown in (3.14):

(3.14) a.

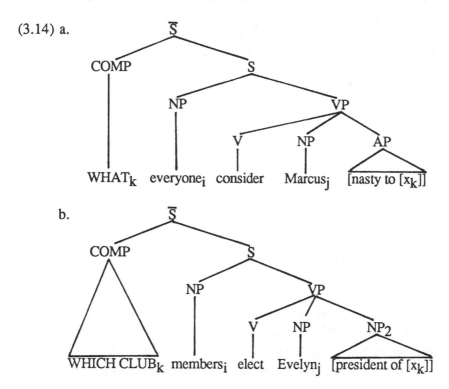

b.

If we compare the S-structures of these examples with the S-structures
in (3.3), (3.7a), and (3.10) of the ungrammatical examples, we see that

there is no significant difference between the two groups. In both groups of S-structures, NP and AP constituents which properly contain externally bound variables occur. However, when the derived F-structures of examples (3.12b) and (3.13b) are compared with those of the ungrammatical examples, a difference emerges.

The derived F-structures of (3.12b) and (3.13b) appear in (3.15), below:

(3.15) a. $(WHAT_k)[CONSIDER \; _{NP}[i] \; [NASTY \; _{NP}[j] \; [TO \; _{NP}[x_k]]]]$
             $\qquad\qquad\qquad\quad \alpha \qquad\qquad \alpha \qquad\qquad \alpha$

        b. $(WH\text{-}club_k)[ELECT \; _{NP}[i] \; _{NP}[j] \; [PRESIDENT \; _{NP}[j][OF$
             $\qquad\qquad\qquad\qquad\quad \alpha \quad\; \beta \qquad\qquad\qquad \alpha$
             $_{NP}[x_k]]]]$
             α

These structures contrast with the derived F-structures of the ungrammatical examples, which appear in (3.4), (3.7b), and (3.11), above. In Structures (3.4a, b, and c), the bound variable is located in a construction of the type shown in (3.16a); in Structure (3.7b), the bound variable is located in a construction of the type shown in (3.16b); and in Structures (3.11a and b), the bound variable is located in a construction of the type shown in (3.16c):

(3.16) a. $_{NP}[...[x_i]...]_k$
             $\;\;\theta$

        b. $_{NP}c[NOUN[...[x_i]...]]$

        c. $_{AP}c[ADJ[...[x_i]...]]$

The NOUN in (3.7b) is BASTARD, and the ADJs in (3.11a and b) are TALL and STUPID, respectively. The construction in (3.16a) is an indexed NP[θ] argument, NP_k. The constructions in (3.16b and c) are the XP^c arguments of the verbal heads of complex predicates. The heads of these XP^c constructions, NOUN and ADJ, are not themselves predicates since they have no NP arguments. Therefore, none of the constructions in (3.16) is a PRED/ARG structure as defined in (3.17):

(3.17)   A PRED/ARG structure is the minimally bracketed structure which contains a predicate and its arguments.

I implicitly adopted this definition in Chapter II, and the statement in (3.17) represents no innovation beyond that discussion.

The XP^c constructions in (3.7b) and (3.11), repeated below, contain the prepositions OF and FOR, which function as predicates and occur with NP arguments:

(3.18) a. $_{NP}c[BASTARD[OF \ _{NP}[x_i]]]$
α

b. $_{AP}c[TALL[FOR \ _{NP}[x_i]]]$
α

c. $_{AP}c[STUPID[FOR \ _{NP}[x_i]]]$
α

According to (3.17), the constructions contained within the brackets which enclose only the prepositions and their NP arguments are PRED/ARG structures. The XP^c constructions, enclosed by the outermost brackets, are not the minimally bracketed constructions which contain the prepositions and their arguments.

In contrast, the bound variables in the structures in (3.15) are located in the PRED/ARG structures of TO and OF, which are themselves located in the PRED/ARG structures of the [+A] and [+N] predicates NASTY and PRESIDENT, respectively. These PRED/ARG structures are in turn located in the PRED/ARG structures of CONSIDER and ELECT. Consequently, at no level of bracketing does a construction which is not the PRED/ARG structure of some predicate properly contain the variable $\underline{x}$.

The following constraint accounts for the ungrammaticality of examples (3.1a, b, and c), (3.6b), (3.8b), and (3.9b), and distinguishes these from the grammatical examples in (3.12b) and (3.13b):

(3.19)   The Predicate Argument Constraint (PAC): Only PRED/ARG structures can properly contain an externally bound variable, $\underline{x}_i$.

The PAC applies at the level of derived F-structure. It is easy to see that the derived F-structures of the ungrammatical examples violate the PAC since, in each case, a construction which is not a PRED/ARG structure properly contains the variable. On the other hand, the derived

F-structures of the grammatical examples do not violate this constraint. Roughly speaking, only PRED/ARG structures which occupy non-NP[θ] argument positions can properly contain externally bound variables. The PRED/ARG structures of matrix predicates occupy non-NP[θ] argument positions by virtue of the fact that they are not embedded in any more inclusive PRED/ARG structure.

The PAC and the functional differences between predicates like *nasty* and *president* on the one hand and *stupid, tall,* and *bastard* on the other explain the contrast between the grammatical examples in (3.12b) and (3.13b) and the ungrammatical ones in (3.21b), (3.22b), (3.23b), and (3.24b), below:

(3.21) a. Everyone$_i$ considered Chadwick$_j$ stupid for a Rhodes Scholar$_k$
       b. *What$_k$ did everyone$_i$ consider Chadwick$_j$ stupid for

(3.22) a. Rhonda$_i$ considered Marcello$_j$ tall for an Italian$_k$
       b. *What$_k$ did Rhonda$_i$ consider Marcello$_j$ tall for

(3.23) a. The class$_i$ considered that$_j$ a bastard of a math test$_k$
       b. *What$_k$ did the class$_i$ consider that$_j$ a bastard of

(3.24) a. They$_i$ elected Myrtle$_j$ bastard of the year$_k$
       b. *Which year$_k$ did they$_i$ elect Myrtle$_j$ bastard of

The S-structures of these examples, which are identical except for the lexical items to those of examples (3.12) and (3.13), are shown below:

(3.25)a.

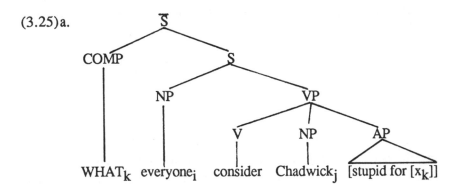

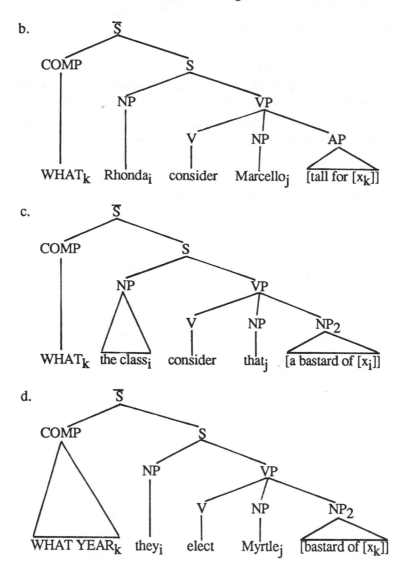

b. [tree diagram]
WHAT$_k$ Rhonda$_i$ consider Marcello$_j$ [tall for [x$_k$]]

c. [tree diagram]
WHAT$_k$ the class$_i$ consider that$_j$ [a bastard of [x$_i$]]

d. [tree diagram]
WHAT YEAR$_k$ they$_i$ elect Myrtle$_j$ [bastard of [x$_k$]]

As discussed in Chapter II, the [+A] predicates *tall* and *stupid* have only single-argument basic F-structures. Consequently, the XP constructions of which they are the heads in these examples must function as XP predicates, which always have single-argument basic F-structures. The [+N] predicate *bastard* is somewhat different. It has both a single-argument basic F-structure and the two-argument basic F-structure shown in (3.26):

(3.26)   BASTARD 1-NP[θ] PP

However, the PP argument in (3.26) must have the preposition TO as its head, as in examples like: *Phil was a bastard to his subordinates.* Because the preposition *of* rather than *to* occurs in examples (3.23b) and (3.24b), the XP construction *bastard of X* can only function as a single-argument XP predicate.[9] The derived F-structures of examples (3.21b), (3.22b), (3.23b) and (3.24b) appear in (3.27):

(3.27) a.   (WHAT$_k$)[CONSIDER $\underset{\alpha}{\text{NP}[i]}$ [[STUPID[FOR $\underset{\alpha}{\text{NP}[x_k]}$]]]

$\underset{\alpha}{\text{NP}[j]}$]]]

b.   (WHAT$_k$)[CONSIDER $\underset{\alpha}{\text{NP}[i]}$ [[TALL[FOR $\underset{\alpha}{\text{NP}[x_k]}$]]]

$\underset{\alpha}{\text{NP}[j]}$]]]

c.   (WHAT$_k$)[CONSIDER $\underset{\alpha}{\text{NP}[i]}$ [[BASTARD[OF $\underset{\alpha}{\text{NP}[x_k]}$]]]

$\underset{\alpha}{\text{NP}[j]}$]]]

d.   (WH-N$_k$)[ELECT $\underset{\alpha}{\text{NP}[i]}$ $\underset{\beta}{\text{NP}[j]}$ [[BASTARD[OF $\underset{\alpha}{\text{NP}[x_k]}$]]]

$\underset{\alpha}{\text{NP}[j]}$]]]

In these structures, the variable, in each case, is properly contained in an XP structure whose head (STUPID in (3.27a), TALL in (3.27b), and BASTARD in (3.27c and d) is not a predicate.   Therefore, these structures are not PRED/ARG structures, even though, as units, they function as predicates, and the derived F-structures violate the PAC. This explains the ungrammaticality of (3.21b), (3.22b), (3.23b), and (3.24b).

The same factors interact to explain the contrast between the ungrammatical examples in (3.6b), (3.8b), and (3.9b) and the grammatical examples in (3.28b) and (3.29b):

(3.28) a.   Gladys$_i$ is president of the club$_j$
     b.   Which club$_j$ is Gladys$_i$ president of

(3.29) a.   Mergatroyd$_i$ is nasty to girls$_j$
     b.   Who$_j$ is Mergatroyd$_i$ nasty to

Both *president* and *nasty* have two-argument basic F-structures as well
as one-argument basic F-structures. The S-structures and derived F-
structures of (3.28b) and (3.29b) are shown in (3.30) and (3.31),
respectively:

(3.30) a.

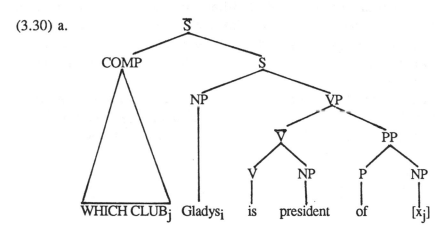

   b.   (WH-club$_j$)[[BE[PRESIDENT]] $_{NP}$[i] [OF $_{NP}$[x$_j$]]]
                                      α   α

(3.31) a.

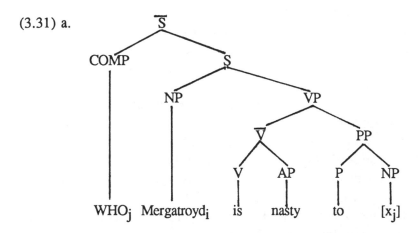

   b.   (WHO$_j$)[[BE[NASTY]] $_{NP}$[i] [TO $_{NP}$[x$_j$]]]
                              α   α

The derived F-structures in (3.30b) and (3.31b) do not violate the PAC.

The bound variables are located in the PRED/ARG structures of the prepositions OF and TO, and these PRED/ARG structures are themselves located in the PRED/ARG structures of the complex predicates [BE[PRESIDENT]] and [BE[NASTY]]. The structures are well-formed and this explains the grammaticality of (3.28b) and (3.29b).

The PAC analysis also explains why the (a) examples in (3.28) and (3.29) are ambiguous, while the (b) ones are not. The (a) examples have two interpretations which differ albeit subtly as pointed out in Chapter II: one which we may think of as the attributive interpretation, and one which we may think of as the action interpretation. These examples can be assigned either of two S-structure types: one which contains the single-argument XP embedded predicate, and one which contains the two-argument X predicate. Consequently, two well-formed derived F-structures can be produced for each example. The ones for (3.29a) which correlate with the two interpretations are shown in (3.32a and b), respectively:

(3.32) a.   [BE[NASTY[TO $NP^{[j]}$]]]] $NP^{[i]}$
                                        α α

b.   [BE[NASTY]] $NP^{[i]}$ [TO $NP^{[j]}$]]
                          α α

As we have seen, the NP argument of TO in a structure like (3.32a) cannot contain an externally bound variable. Only structures like (3.32b) are well-formed when they contain variables in this position. So examples like (3.28b) and (3.29b) are unambiguous and can only have the action interpretation associated with structures like (3.32b).

We see then that the PAC analysis defines the conditions under which various types of syntactic configurations are islands. The NPC, which accounts for the islandhood of S-structure NPs in examples like (3.1), is a special case of this more general constraint. In the balance of this section, I will look at two additional sets of data: (a) data involving sentences in which S-structure VP and S constituents are embedded in NP positions whose F-structure correlates are NP[θ] arguments; and (b) additional data involving $\overline{V}$ predicates. I will demonstrate that the analysis with a minor modification accounts for this extended data base.

As we have seen, PRED/ARG structures which are nested in more inclusive PRED/ARG structures can contain externally bound variables.

Some additional examples are the following, shown with their derived F-structures:

(3.33) a. Who$_k$ did everyone$_i$ believe that Ian$_j$ disliked

  b. (WHO$_k$)[BELIEVE $\underset{\alpha}{NP[i]}$ [DISLIKE $\underset{\alpha}{NP[j]}$ $\underset{\beta}{NP[x_k]}$]]]

(3.34) a. Who$_m$ did Marcus$_i$ say that everyone$_j$ believed that Ian$_k$ disliked

  b. (WHO$_m$)[SAY $\underset{\alpha}{NP[i]}$ [BELIEVE $\underset{\alpha}{NP[j]}$ [DISLIKE $\underset{\alpha}{NP[k]}$ $\underset{\beta}{NP[x_m]}$]]]]

(3.35) a. What$_k$ did Norbert$_i$ force Sophia$_j$ to kiss

  b. (WHAT$_k$)[FORCE $\underset{\alpha}{NP[i]}$ $\underset{\beta}{NP[j]}$ [KISS $\underset{\alpha}{NP[j]}$ $\underset{\beta}{NP[x_k]}$]]]

(3.36) a. Which problem$_k$ did Wolfgang$_i$ make headway$_j$ on

  b. (WH-problem$_k$)[MAKE $\underset{\varsigma}{NP^c[j]}$ $\underset{\alpha}{NP[i]}$ [ON $\underset{\alpha}{NP[x_k]}$]]]

The derived F-structures of these examples do not violate the PAC, and are well-formed. Examples like the following, in contrast, are ungrammatical:

(3.37) a. *Who$_m$ did [that Marlo$_k$ married]$_i$ annoy his mother$_j$
    b. *Who$_k$ would [to marry]$_i$ please Zelma$_j$
    c. *Who$_k$ did Penelope$_i$ realize that [kissing]$_j$ was necessary

Example (3.37a) contains a sentence embedded in the subject, NP$_i$, position. Examples (3.37b and c) contain VP constituents embedded in subject positions, NP$_i$ and NP$_j$, respectively. Examples like these were discussed in Chapter II, Section 4, and Chapter III. In all three examples, the complement S or VP is located in an NP position. The S-structures of these examples are shown below:

(3.38) a.

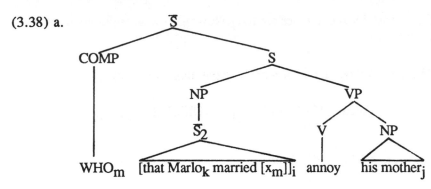

b.

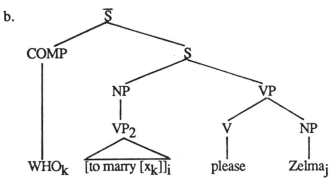

c.

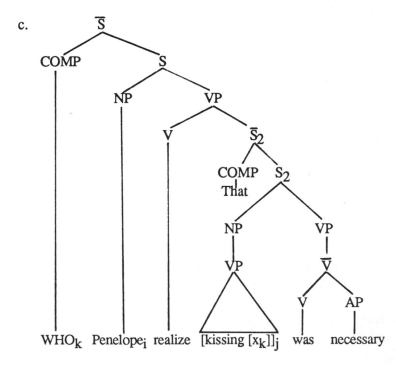

The derived F-structures of these examples appear in (3.39a, b, and c), respectively:

(3.39) a.   (WHO$_m$)[ANNOY $\underset{\alpha}{\text{NP}}$[[MARRY $\underset{\alpha}{\text{NP}}$[k] $\underset{\beta}{\text{NP}}$[x$_m$]]]$_i$ $\underset{\beta}{\text{NP}}$[j]]

   b.   (WHO$_k$)[PLEASE $\underset{\alpha}{\text{NP}}$[[MARRY $\underset{\alpha}{\text{NP}}$[j] $\underset{\beta}{\text{NP}}$[x$_k$]]]$_i$ $\underset{\alpha}{\text{NP}}$[j]]

   c.   (WHO$_k$)[REALIZE $\underset{\alpha}{\text{NP}}$[i] [[BE[NECESSARY]]

      $\underset{\alpha}{\text{NP}}$[[KISSING $\underset{\alpha}{\text{NP}}$[i] $\underset{\beta}{\text{NP}}$[x$_k$]]]$_j$]]

In these derived F-structures, the PRED/ARG structures of MARRY and KISSING are embedded in indexed NP[θ] argument positions. These configurations are of the general type shown in (3.40):

(3.40) $\underset{\theta}{\text{NP}}$[[... [x$_j$]...]]$_i$

The construction enclosed by the innermost brackets in each example is a PRED/ARG structure. The outer brackets enclose the indexed NP[θ] argument itself. As above, the NP[θ] argument is not the minimally bracketed construction which contains the predicate and its arguments, and is not itself a PRED/ARG structure. These NP structures are functionally identical (for the application of the PAC) to the F-structure correlates of complex NPs and non-complex NPs in sentences like (3.1) above, of the type shown in (3.16a). The variables in (3.39) are properly contained in these NP[θ] arguments and are bound to wh-constituents outside of the NP[θ] arguments. Therefore the derived F-structures violate the PAC. This accounts for the ungrammaticality of the examples in (3.37), and the contrast between these and the examples in (3.33) to (3.36).

I return now to examples with complex predicates. As discussed in Chapter II, the XP^c components of $\overline{\text{V}}$ predicates are arguments of the [+V] PRED. Consequently, the PAC analysis predicts that complex predicate structures can contain externally bound variables. The following examples demonstrate that this prediction is correct:[10]

(3.41) a.   How much headway$_i$ did Adolph$_j$ make on the problem$_k$

b.   How many gallons$_i$ did Megan$_j$ drink of that mead$_k$
c.   How nasty$_i$ was Jason$_j$ to girls$_k$
d.   How cruel$_i$ was Arthur$_j$
e.   Which president$_i$ was Lincoln$_j$

The derived F-structures of these examples are shown in (3.42), below:

(3.42) a.   (WH-MUCH HEADWAY$_i$)[[MAKE $_{NP}c[x_i]$] $NP^{[j]}$ [ON

$NP^{[k]}$]]]

b.   (WH-MANY GALLONS$_i$)[[DRINK $_{NP}c[x_i]$] $NP^{[j]}$ [OF

$NP^{[k]}$]]]

c.   (WH-NASTY$_i$)[[BE $_{AP}c[x_i]$] $NP^{[j]}$ [TO $NP^{[k]}$]]]

d.   (WH-CRUEL$_i$)[[BE $_{AP}c[x_i]$] $NP^{[j]}$

e.   (WH-PRESIDENT$_i$)[[BE $_{NP}c[x_i]$] $NP^{[j]}$

The bound variables, x_i in each case, in these structures are located in
substructures of the form [PRED XP^c]. These are PRED/ARG structures, and they are located in the PRED/ARG structures of the complex
predicates. Therefore, these derived F-structures do not violate the
PAC.

In contrast, the following examples are ungrammatical:

(3.43)a.   ?*How nasty$_m$ did everyone$_i$ consider Jason$_j$ to girls$_k$
    b.   ?*How cruel$_k$ did everyone$_i$ consider Arthur$_j$
    c.   ?*Which office$_k$ did they$_i$ elect Lincoln$_j$

The derived F-structures of these examples are shown in (3.44):

(3.44) a.   (WH-NASTY$_m$)[CONSIDER $NP^{[i]}$ [[x_m] $NP^{[j]}$

[TO $NP^{[k]}$]]]]

b. (WH-CRUEL$_k$)[CONSIDER $\underset{\alpha}{NP[i]}$ [[x_k] $\underset{\alpha}{NP[j]}$]]

c. (WH-OFFICE$_k$)[ELECT $\underset{\alpha}{NP[i]}$ $\underset{\beta}{NP[j]}$ [[x_k] $\underset{\alpha}{NP[j]}$]]

In these structures, the bound variables are the terminal elements of the complement predicates themselves rather than arguments of some predicate. These examples suggest that the distribution of bound variables must be restricted to XP arguments. This condition can be incorporated into the PAC, as shown in (3.45):

(3.45) The Predicate Argument Constraint (PAC) 2: Only PRED/ ARG structures can properly contain an externally bound variable, x_i. Bound variables can only appear as the terminal elements of XP arguments of predicates.

The derived F-structures in (3.44) violate the PAC 2, and are therefore not well-formed. This accounts for the ungrammaticality of the sentences in (3.43).

This analysis explains the contrast between the ungrammatical sentences in (3.43) and the following grammatical sentences, which are superficially similar to them:

(3.46) a. How nasty$_m$ did everyone$_i$ consider Jason$_j$ to be to girls$_k$
    b. How cruel$_k$ did everyone$_i$ consider Arthur$_j$ to be
    c. Which office$_k$ did they$_i$ elect Lincoln$_j$ to

The derived F-structures of these sentences are shown below:

(3.47) a. (WH-NASTY$_m$)[CONSIDER $\underset{\alpha}{NP[i]}$ [[BE $\underset{\alpha}{AP^c[x_m]}$]] $\underset{\alpha}{NP[j]}$ [TO $\underset{\alpha}{NP[k]}$]]]

    b. (WH-CRUEL$_k$)[CONSIDER $\underset{\alpha}{NP[i]}$ [[BE $\underset{\alpha}{AP^c[x_k]}$]] $NP[j]$]]

    c. (WH-OFFICE$_k$)[ELECT $\underset{\alpha}{NP[i]}$ $\underset{\beta}{NP[j]}$ [TO $\underset{\alpha}{NP[x_k]}$]]

In these structures, the bound variables occur in XP argument positions,

and the structures do not violate the PAC 2. Consequently, examples
like the ones in (3.46) are grammatical.

4. The Single Gap Constraint

Consider the following ungrammatical sentences:

(4.1) a. *Who$_k$ did Ferdinand$_i$ wonder who$_j$ saw
    b. *What$_k$ did Marian$_i$ ask who$_j$ kissed

In the S-structures of these examples, shown below, the bound variables
are located in the subject and object NP positions in the embedded
complements:

(4.2) a.

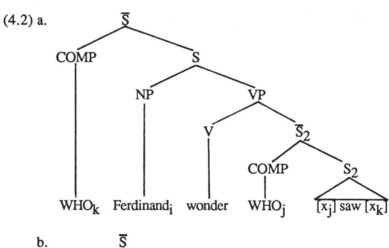

b.

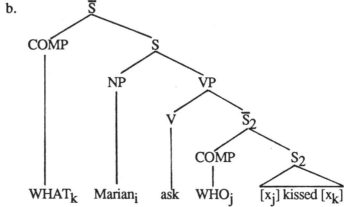

The derived F-structures of these examples appear in (4.3):[11]

(4.3) a. $(WHO_k)[WONDER \underset{\alpha}{NP[i]} [(WHO_j)[SEE \underset{\alpha'}{NP[x_j]} \underset{\beta}{NP[x_k]}]]]$

     b. $(WHAT_k)[ASK \underset{\alpha}{NP[i]} [(WHO_j)[KISS \underset{\alpha'}{NP[x_j]} \underset{\beta}{NP[x_k]}]]]$

In both cases, the PRED/ARG structure of the embedded predicate, SEE in (4.3a) and KISS in (4.3b), contains two variables which are bound to a wh-element outside of that PRED/ARG structure. This distinguishes sentences like (4.1) from the examples in Section 3 and the following, shown with their derived F-structures:

(4.4) a. Who_k did $everyone_i$ think that $Ferdinand_j$ saw

     b. $(WHO_k)[THINK \underset{\alpha}{NP[i]} [SEE \underset{\alpha}{NP[j]} \underset{\beta}{NP[x_k]}]]$

(4.5) a. Who_k did $everyone_i$ think kissed the $frogs_j$

     b. $(WHO_k)[THINK \underset{\alpha}{NP[i]} [KISS \underset{\alpha}{NP[x_k]} \underset{\beta}{NP[j]}]]$

In Structures (4.4b) and (4.5b), the PRED/ARG structures of the embedded predicates, SEE and KISS, respectively, contain a single bound variable. Moreover, the PRED/ARG structure of THINK in each case, which contains the PRED/ARG structure of the embedded predicate, contains only a single bound variable. The following constraint accounts for the ungrammaticality of examples like (4.1) as well as the contrast between these examples and ones like (4.4a) and (4.5a):

(4.6)   <u>The Single Gap Constraint (SGC)</u>: PRED/ARG structures can properly contain only one externally bound variable, x_i.

The derived F-structures in (4.3) violate the SGC, and are therefore not well-formed. The derived F-structures in (4.4b) and (4.5b) do not violate the SGC (or any other constraint) and are therefore well-formed.

     The SGC as formulated in (4.6) correctly permits across-the-board application of the EA rule in examples like the following:

(4.7) a. Who_k did Zelma_i like and Gladys_j hate
   b. Who_j did Philena_i dislike and avoid
   c. Who_j did the street gang_i murder after they_i had robbed

The S-structures of these sentences contain two predicate constructions neither of which is embedded in the other. In (4.7a), these are conjoined clauses, S; in (4.7b), they are conjoined VPs; and in (4.7c), they are a main clause and an adjunct clause introduced by *after*. The PRED/ARG structures of such examples are constructed by adjoining the PRED/ARG structures of the relevant predicates. The derived F-structures of these examples appear in (4.8):

(4.8) a. $(\text{WHO}_k)[[\text{LIKE } \underset{\alpha}{\text{NP}^{[i]}} \underset{\beta}{\text{NP}^{[x_k]}}]\&[\text{HATE } \underset{\alpha}{\text{NP}^{[j]}} \underset{\beta}{\text{NP}^{[x_k]}}]]$

   b. $(\text{WHO}_j)[[\text{DISLIKE } \underset{\alpha}{\text{NP}^{[i]}} \underset{\beta}{\text{NP}^{[x_j]}}]\&[\text{AVOID } \underset{\alpha}{\text{NP}^{[i]}} \underset{\beta}{\text{NP}^{[x_j]}}]]$

   c. $(\text{WHO}_j)[[\text{MURDER } \underset{\alpha}{\text{NP}^{[i]}} \underset{\beta}{\text{NP}^{[x_j]}}][\text{AFTER}[\text{ROB } \underset{\alpha}{\text{NP}^{[i]}}$
   $\underset{\beta}{\text{NP}^{[x_j]}}]]]$

In these structures, neither of the PRED/ARG structures of the predicates is nested in the PRED/ARG structure of the other predicate. In (4.8a), the PRED/ARG structure of LIKE and the PRED/ARG structure of HATE each contain a single bound variable. The same is true of the PRED/ARG structures of DISLIKE and AVOID in (4.8b), and the PRED/ARG structures of MURDER and ROB in (4.8c). Consequently, none of these derived F-structures violates the SGC. They are well-formed, and this explains the grammaticality of the examples in (4.7).[12]

There are, of course, other conditions on across-the-board application of the EA rule. For example, only across-the-board application of the rule results in a grammatical sentence. Examples like the following, in which only one conjunct in the S-structure contains a bound variable, are ungrammatical:

(4.9) a.   *Who did Zelma like and Gladys hate Maurice
   b.   *Who did Philena dislike Fran and avoid

I will not, however, discuss these cases.[13]

Examples like the following are ungrammatical, and contrast with examples like (4.7c):

(4.10)   *Who$_j$ did it$_i$ annoy that everyone$_k$ hated

This example contains an extraposed clause rather than an adjunct clause. Extraposed clauses are located in the VP of the matrix verb at the level of S-structure, and their F-structure correlates occupy a non-NP[θ] argument position in the PRED/ARG structure of the matrix predicate. The derived F-structure of (4.10) is shown below:[14]

(4.11)   (WHO$_j$)[ANNOY $\underset{\alpha}{\text{NP}}$[IT$_i$] $\underset{\beta}{\text{NP}}$[x$_j$] [HATE $\underset{\alpha}{\text{NP}}$[k] $\underset{\beta}{\text{NP}}$[x$_j$]]$_i$]

Here, the PRED/ARG structure of HATE contains a single bound variable. However, the PRED/ARG structure of ANNOY, which includes the PRED/ARG structure of HATE, contains two variables, both of which are bound to a wh-element outside of this PRED/ARG structure. Therefore, Structure (4.11) violates the SGC. This accounts for the ungrammaticality of examples like (4.10).

Examples like the following are analogous to examples like (4.1), and are accounted for in the same way:

(4.12) a. *Which manuscript$_m$ did Marcus$_i$ ask who$_j$ to give to
       b. *Which dried toads$_m$ did the witch$_i$ ask who$_j$ Merlin$_k$
          gave to

The derived F-structures of these examples appear in (4.13), below:

(4.13) a. (WH-N$_m$) [ASK $\underset{\alpha}{\text{NP}}$[i] [(WHO$_j$) [GIVE $\underset{\alpha}{\text{NP}}$[i] $\underset{\beta}{\text{NP}}$[x$_m$]
          [TO $\underset{\alpha}{\text{NP}}$[x$_j$]]]]]

       b. (WH-N$_m$) [ASK $\underset{\alpha}{\text{NP}}$[i] [(WHO$_j$) [GIVE $\underset{\alpha}{\text{NP}}$[k] $\underset{\beta}{\text{NP}}$[x$_m$]
          [TO $\underset{\alpha}{\text{NP}}$[x$_j$]]]]]

In both structures, the PRED/ARG structure of GIVE properly contains two variables, x_m and x_j. Both of these variables are bound to wh-elements outside of the PRED/ARG structure of GIVE. Therefore Structures (4.13a and b) violate the SGC, and are not well-formed. This accounts for the ungrammaticality of examples (4.12a and b). In these structures, the PRED/ARG structure of ASK, which contains the PRED/ARG structure of GIVE, also contains the two variables, x_m and x_j. However, x_j is bound to the WHO_j operator, which is located within the PRED/ARG structure of ASK. Consequently, the PRED/ARG structure of ASK contains only a single variable, x_m, which is bound to a wh-element outside of that PRED/ARG structure.

With this in mind, consider the following examples, which are more acceptable than the ones in (4.12):

(4.14) a.   ?Which manuscripts$_m$ did they$_i$ wonder where$_j$ to buy
b.   ??Which books$_m$ did Gladys$_i$ wonder where$_j$ Murrey$_k$
        bought

In these examples, the wh-operator, *where$_j$* in both cases binds a variable located in an adverbial constituent outside of the VP of which *buy* is the head. The F-structure representations of such adverbials, like the F-structure representations of other adjuncts, are adjoined to the PRED/ARG structures of the relevant predicates rather than embedded in the PRED/ARG structures of those predicates. (See Chapter II for discussion of adjuncts.)

The derived F-structures of (4.14) appear in (4.15), below:

(4.15) a.   (WH-N$_m$) [WONDER $_{NP}[i]$ [(WHERE$_j$) [[BUY $_{NP}[i]$
                                    α α
        $_{NP}[x_m]$]] [ADV$[x_j]$]]]]]
          β

b.   (WH-N$_m$) [WONDER $_{NP}[i]$ [(WHERE$_j$) [[BUY $_{NP}[k]$
                                    α α
        $_{NP}[x_m]$]] [ADV$[x_j]$]]]]]
          β

In these structures, the PRED/ARG structures of BUY contain a single variable, x_m. The variable x_j is located outside of the PRED/ARG structure of BUY in both cases. The PRED/ARG structures of

WONDER contain both of the variables. However, the x_j variables are bound to the WHERE$_j$ operators, which are located in the PRED/ARG structures of WONDER. Only the variable x_m is bound to a wh-operator located outside of the PRED/ARG structures of WONDER. Therefore, (4.15a and b) do not violate the SGC. The acceptability of examples like the following is accounted for in the same way:

(4.16) a.   ?Which manuscript did Marcus ask why he should read
     b.   ??Which currencies was Jones smart enough to know when people should buy
     c.   Which book did Norman ask why to read

These examples have derived F-structures which are analogous to the ones in (4.15), and which do not violate the SGC.

The following examples are slightly different from (4.14) and (4.16):

(4.17) a.   The police$_i$ know how to prevent crimes$_j$
     b.   Which crimes$_j$ do the police$_i$ know how to prevent

(4.18) a.   We$_i$ read where the Russians$_j$ invaded Afghanistan$_k$
     b.   Which country$_k$ did you$_i$ read where the Russians$_j$ invaded

(4.19) a.   We$_i$ wondered whether Barry$_j$ would buy that manuscript$_k$
     b.   Which manuscript$_k$ did you$_i$ wonder whether Barry$_j$ would buy

In these examples, *how, where,* and *whether* are complementizers, like *that,* and do not bind variables elsewhere in the S-structures. The derived F-structures of (4.17b), (4.18b) and (4.19b) are shown in (4.20a, b, and c), respectively:

(4.20) a.   (Wh-N$_j$)[KNOW $\underset{\alpha}{\text{NP}}$[i] [HOW[PREVENT $\underset{\alpha}{\text{NP}}$[i] $\underset{\beta}{\text{NP}}$[$x_k$]]]]

     b.   (WH-N$_k$)[READ $\underset{\alpha}{\text{NP}}$[i] [WHERE[INVADE $\underset{\alpha}{\text{NP}}$[j] $\underset{\beta}{\text{NP}}$[$x_k$]]]]

c. (WH-N$_k$)[WONDER $_{NP}$[i] [WHETHER[BUY $_{NP}$[j]
$\qquad\qquad\qquad\qquad\quad\ \alpha\qquad\qquad\qquad\qquad\qquad\alpha$
$_{NP}$[x$_k$]]]]
$\quad\beta$

It is easy to see that these derived F-structures do not violate the SGC. This accounts for the grammaticality of the relevant examples.[15]

The SGC analysis and general principles of the theory, with a single additional assumption, explain the pattern of grammaticality observed in examples like the following:

(4.21) a. Sonatas$_i$ are easy to play on that violin$_j$
   b. That violin$_i$ is easy to play sonatas$_j$ on

(4.22) a. Which violin$_j$ are the sonatas$_i$ easy to play on
   b. *Which sonatas$_j$ is that violin$_i$ easy to play on

Here, the order of the NP$_i$ and NP$_j$ constituents in statements like (4.21) appears to correlate with the acceptability of the corresponding wh-questions in (4.22). It is possible to assign both of the following S-structure types to examples like (4.21a):

(4.23) a.

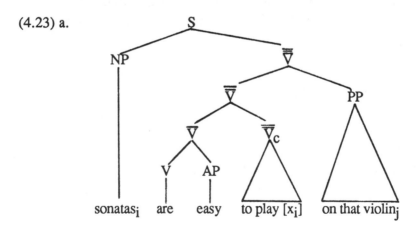

b.

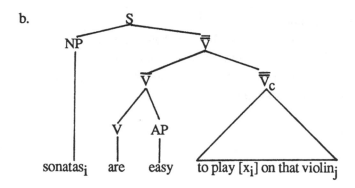

The variable, x_i in each structure, is bound to the $NP[i]$ constituent by the EA rule.

The primary differences between these structures is that in (4.23a), the PP is the sister of $\overline{V}$ in $\overline{\overline{V}}$, while in (4.23b), the PP is a constituent of the $\overline{V}_c$ complement of ∇ in $\overline{V}$. These S-structures contain complex predicates, $\overline{V}$, which consist of [V AP] sequences. These $\underline{\nabla}$ predicates are, in turn, the heads of $\overline{\overline{V}}$ complex predicates which have $\overline{V}_c$ complements.

The derived F-structure produced from the S-structure in (4.23a) is shown in (4.24a), and the derived F-structure produced from the S-structure in (4.23b) is shown in (4.24b):

(4.24) a.   [[BE [EASY]][PLAY $\underset{\alpha}{NP[+I]}$ $\underset{\beta}{NP[x_i]}$]] $\underset{\alpha}{NP[i]}$ [ON $\underset{\alpha}{NP[j]}$]

b.   [[BE [EASY]][PLAY $\underset{\alpha}{NP[+I]}$ $\underset{\beta}{NP[x_i]}$ [ON $\underset{\alpha}{NP[j]}$]]] $\underset{\alpha}{NP[i]}$

In Structure (4.24a), the complex predicate [[BE[EASY]][PLAY ...]] occurs with two external arguments, and in Structure (4.24b), the complex predicate occurs with a single external argument. [+I] represents the feature [+INDEFINITE]. Both of these structures violate WFC I since they contain $NP[i]$ constituents which are directly assigned an SR α, and indirectly assigned the SR β of the variable that they bind. It must therefore be stipulated that bound variables located within complex predicates whose heads are EASY constructions do not transfer their SRs to the operators that bind them. This stipulation is arbitrary. However, it is the only exception to the general properties of NP_i/x_i pairs. With this stipulation, the derived F-structures in (4.24) are, in fact, well-formed.

In contrast, a well-formed derived F-structure can be produced for examples like (4.21b) only if they are assigned S-structures like (4.23b). To see this, first suppose that both S-structure types can be assigned to such examples, as shown below:

(4.25) a.

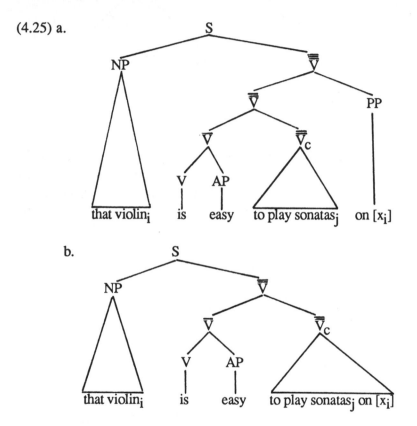

The derived F-structures produced from these S-structures are shown in (4.26a and b), respectively:

(4.26) a.   [[BE [EASY]][PLAY $_{NP[+I]}$ $_{NP[j]}$]] $_{NP[i]}$ [ON $_{NP[x_i]}$]
                              α β α α

b.   [[BE [EASY]][PLAY $_{NP[+I]}$ $_{NP[j]}$ [ON $_{NP[x_i]}$]]] $_{NP[i]}$
                     α β α α

In Structure (4.26a), the bound variable, $\underline{x}_i$, is the argument of the predicate ON, and the operator that binds it, $_{NP[i]}$, is the NP[α]

argument of the complex predicate. Since the variable is not located within the complex EASY predicate itself, the stipulation does not apply to this structure, and it violates WFC I. In (4.26b), the variable, $\underline{x}_i$, is located within the complex EASY predicate, and this structure does not violate WFC I.

Now consider example (4.22a). This is the wh-question which corresponds to the statement in (4.21a). As was the case for (4.21a), either S-structure type in (4.23) can be assigned to it. This is illustrated below:

(4.27) a.

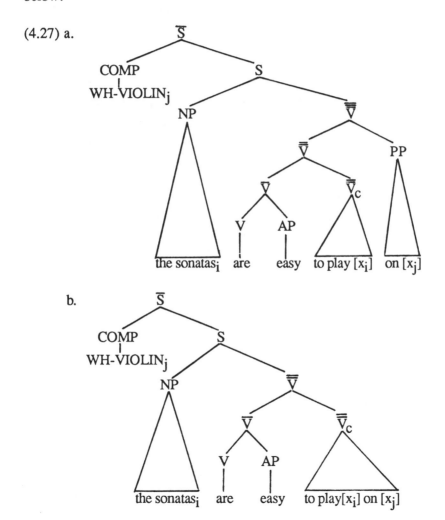

The derived F-structures produced from these S-structures are shown in

(4.28), below:

(4.28)a. (WH-N$_j$)[[[BE[EASY]][PLAY $_{NP}$[+I] $_{NP}$[x$_j$]]] $_{NP}$[i] [ON
α$$β$$α
$_{NP}$[x$_j$]]]
α

b. (WH-N$_j$)[[[BE[EASY]][PLAY $_{NP}$[+I] $_{NP}$[x$_i$] [ON $_{NP}$[x$_j$]]]]
α$$β$$α
$_{NP}$[i]]
α

Structure (4.28a) is well-formed. The PRED/ARG structures of ON and PLAY each contain a single variable, x_j and x_i, respectively. The PRED/ARG structure of the most inclusive complex predicate, [[BE[EASY]][PLAY...]], contains both of these variables. However, only x_j is bound to an operator outside of this PRED/ARG structure. Therefore, this derived F-structure does not violate the SGC.

Structure (4.28b), on the other hand is not well-formed. The PRED/ARG structure of PLAY contains both variables, and both are bound to operators outside of this PRED/ARG structure in violation of the SGC. However, since a well-formed derived F-structure can be produced for it, example (4.22a) is grammatical.

Example (4.22b) is the wh-question counterpart of example (4.21b). As was the case for (4.21b), no well-formed derived F-structure can be produced for this example if it is assigned an S-structure like (4.23a). In this case, however, no well-formed derived F-structure can be produced from an S-structure like (4.23b) either. This S-structure appears in (4.29):

(4.29)

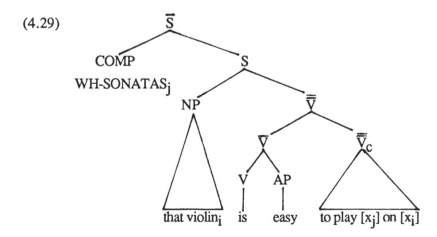

The derived F-structure produced from this S-structure is shown in (4.30), below:

(4.30)   (WH-N$_j$)[[[BE[EASY]][PLAY $_{NP}$[+I] $_{NP}$[x$_j$] [ON $_{NP}$[x$_i$]]]]
$\qquad\qquad\quad$ α$\qquad$ β$\qquad\quad$ α

$\qquad$ $_{NP}$[i]]
$\qquad$ α

This structure violates the SGC. This explains the ungrammaticality of example (4.22b) and the contrast between examples like this and the ones like (4.22a).

It is easy to see that the analysis accounts for sentences like the following, which are further examples of this pattern:

(4.31) a. The trucks are too large to drive through the tunnel
       b. The tunnel is too small to drive those trucks through

(4.32) a. Which tunnel are the trucks too large to drive through
       b. *Which trucks is the tunnel too small to drive through

(4.33) a. Beethoven concertos are good enough to play on that piano
       b. That piano is good enough to play Beethoven concertos on

(4.34) a. Which piano are Beethoven concertos good enough to play on
       b. *Which concertos is that piano good enough to play on

These examples contain TOO+ADJ constructions and ADJ+ENOUGH constructions, which display the same syntactic behavior as EASY constructions.

The SGC, in effect, defines the conditions under which more than a single bound variable can occur in the S-structure of a grammatical sentence. It supplements the PAC, and, like the PAC, applies at the level of derived F-structure.

5. Variation

The EA rule applies to bind the variable $\underline{x}$ to an operator (WH-)X$_i$ in COMP in the configuration in (5.1) regardless of whether the internal structure of S is configurational or non-configurational:

(5.1)

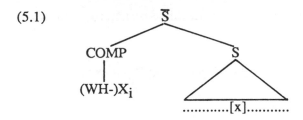

Moreover, as constraints on derived F-structures, the PAC and SGC apply in the same way to all languages. The analysis predicts that the distributional patterns of wh-operators and bound variables are universal. However, while this is true of the general patterns discussed in Section 2, there is nevertheless variation in detail, which is quite striking. Polish and Italian are two languages which differ from English and from each other in interesting ways which reveal the sorts of factors that determine the nature and limits of this variation.

Examples like the following indicate that the PAC applies to Polish and Italian in much the same way as it does to English:

(5.2) a. *Jaki płaszcz$_i$ weszła $_{NP}$[jakaś dziewczyna która
        miała na sobie _]$_j$
        which coat (ACC) came in $_{NP}$[a girl (NOM) who (NOM)
        wore on self (LOC) _]
        *Which coat did a girl who wore come in

      b. *O kim$_k$ on$_i$ zniszczył $_{NP}$[książkę _]$_j$
        About whom (LOC) he (NOM) destroy $_{NP}$[book (ACC) _]
        *About whom did he destroy a book

      c. *Kogo$_k$ Jan$_i$ zniszczył $_{NP}$[zdjęcie _]$_j$
        Whose (GEN) Jan (NOM) destroy $_{NP}$[picture (ACC) _]
        *Of whom/whose did Jan destroy a picture

      d. *W której klasie$_k$ była Maria$_i$ $_{NP}$[najbystrzejszą
        dziewczyną _]$_j$
        In which class (LOC) was Maria (NOM) $_{NP}$[brightest
        girl(INSTR) _]
        *In which class was Maria the brightest girl

(5.3) a. *[Sotto quale albero]$_k$ ha visto Giovanni$_i$ $_{NP}$[l'uomo __]$_j$
　　　　Under which tree　　has seen Giovanni　$_{NP}$[the man __]
　　　　*Under which tree did Giovanni see the man

b. *[Di quale paese]$_k$ ha perduto Guglielmo$_i$ $_{NP}$[un libro __]$_j$
　　　About which country has lost Guglielmo $_{NP}$[a book __]
　　　*About which country did Guglielmo lose a book

c. *Che$_k$ ha visto Luigi$_i$ $_{NP}$[l'uomo chi ha detto __]$_j$
　　　What has seen Luigi $_{NP}$[the man who has said __]
　　　*What did Luigi see the man who said

In the S-structures of both the sentences in (5.2) and the Italian sentences
in (5.3), a bound variable $\underline{x}$, indicated by __ above, occurs within an NP
constituent whose F-structure correlate is an NP[θ] argument of the
relevant predicate. The derived F-structures of (5.2a) and (5.3a) appear
in (5.4), below:

(5.4) a. (JAKI-N$_i$)[WEJŚĆ $\underset{\alpha}{_{NP}[...[x_i]..]_j}$]

b. ([SOTTO[QUALE-N]]$_k$)[VEDERE $\underset{\alpha}{_{NP}[i]}$ $\underset{\beta}{_{NP}[...[x_k]...]_j}$]

These F-structures violate the PAC. The derived F-structures of the
other examples in (5.2) and (5.3) are analogous to these.

　　The similarity of Polish to English extends to sentences like the
following:

(5.5) a. Wybrali Czesława$_i$ $_{NP}$[przewodniczącym klasy]$_j$
　　　　(They) elected Czeslaw (ACC) $_{NP}$[president (INSTR) class
　　　　　　(GEN)]
　　　　They elected Czeslaw president of the class

b. ?*Kim$_j$ wybrali Czesława$_i$
　　　What (INSTR)(they$_k$) elected Czeslaw (ACC)
　　　?*What did they elect Czeslaw

(5.6) a. Czesław$_i$ był $_{NP}$[przewodniczącym klasy]$_j$
Czeslaw (NOM) was $_{NP}$[president (INSTR) class (GEN)]
Czeslaw was president of the class

 b. Kim$_j$ był Czesław$_i$
What (INSTR) was Czeslaw (NOM)
What was Czeslaw

The derived F-structures of (5.5b) and (5.6b) appear in (5.7a and b), respectively:

(5.7) a. (KIM$_j$)[WYBRAĆ $_{NP}$[k] $\underset{\alpha}{_{NP}[i]}$ $\underset{\beta}{}$ [[x$_j$] $\underset{\alpha}{_{NP}[i]}$]]

 b. (KIM$_j$)[[BYĆ $_{NP}$c[x$_j$]] $\underset{\alpha}{_{NP}[i]}$]

In Structure (5.7a), the bound variable is the terminal element of the embedded predicate itself, while in Structure (5.7b), the bound variable is the NP^c argument of the predicate BYĆ. Consequently, Structure (5.7a) violates the PAC and Structure (5.7b) does not.

In spite of these similarities, however, both Polish and Italian wh-questions exhibit significantly different patterns than their English counterparts. Polish sentences like the following are grammatical:

(5.8) a. Jaki$_i$ wykręciłeś $_{NP}$[_ numer]$_j$
which (ACC) (you$_k$) dial $_{NP}$[_ number (ACC)]
Which number did you dial

 b. Których$_i$ oblałeś $_{NP}$[_ studentów]$_j$
which (ACC) (you$_k$) fail $_{NP}$[_ students (ACC)]
Which students did you fail

 c. Czyje$_k$ Jan$_i$ zniszczył $_{NP}$[_ zdjęcie]$_j$
whose (ACC) Jan(NOM) destroy $_{NP}$[_ picture (ACC)]
Whose picture did Jan destroy

In the S-structures of these examples, the bound variables are located in the positions designated as _ within NP constituents whose F-structure correlates are NP[θ] arguments. Examples (5.8a, b, and c) appear to be structurally analogous to the ungrammatical examples in (5.2)

These examples differ from the ones in (5.2) in a crucial way. The wh-constituents in (5.8) are overtly marked to agree with the head noun of the NP which contains the bound variable in case, gender, and number. *Jaki* in (5.8a) is marked as masculine, singular, accusative case, and agrees with the noun *numer*, which is a masculine, singular noun marked for accusative case. Similarly, in (5.8b), *których* is the masculine, plural, accusative case form, and agrees with *studentów*, a masculine, plural noun marked for accusative case; and in (5.8c), *czyje* is a neuter, singular, accusative case form, and agrees with *zdjęcie*, a neuter, singular noun marked for accusative case.

In (5.2a), the NP *jaki płaszcz* is not specially marked to agree with the head noun, *jakaś dziewczyna*, of the NP_j constituent, nor is *jaki płaszcz* marked in any way to indicate that it is to be associated with a relative clause elsewhere in the structure. In (5.2b), the PP, *o kim*, is not marked to agree with the head noun, *książkę*, of the NP_j constituent, and in (5.2d), the PP, *w której klasie*, is not marked to agree with the head noun, *najbystrzejszą dziewczyną*, of the NP_j constituent. Finally, *kogo*, the masculine, singular, genitive form of the interrogative pronoun, is not marked to agree with the head noun, *zdjęcie* (neuter, singular, accusative case), of the NP_k constituent in (5.2c). It appears, then, that the PAC can be overridden just in case the antecedent of the bound variable is marked to agree with the head noun of the NP, or more generally, with the head, or some other element, of the structure which contains the variable that is bound to that antecedent.

The derived F-structures of (5.2c) and (5.8c) are shown in (5.9a and b), respectively:

(5.9) a. $(KOGO_k)[ZNISZCZYĆ \underset{\alpha}{NP[i]} \underset{\beta}{NP[[x_k][j]]}]$

b. $(CZYJE_k\text{-}AGR_n)[ZNISZCZYĆ \underset{\alpha}{NP[i]} \underset{\beta}{NP[[x_k][j\text{-}AGR_n]]}]$

In Structure (5.9b), AGR_n is the cover symbol for the F-structure representation of the overt case and agreement markers which associate constituents like *czyje* with ones like *zdjęcie*. Let us assume that an element which contains an AGR_n marker which matches that of the head of some construction, X, is functionally internal to that construction. In Structure (5.9b), CZYJE-AGR_n is functionally internal to the NP constituent whose head is j-AGR_n. Consequently, the variable, x_k, in this NP constituent is not externally bound.

In Structure (5.9a), KOGO contains no AGR_n marker which associates it with the head of the relevant NP constituent. Consequently, it is functionally external to this constituent, and the variable, x_k, in the NP is externally bound. The derived F-structures of the other examples in (5.2) are analogous to (5.9a), and those of the other examples in (5.8) are analogous to (5.9b), in this respect. The PAC, reformulated as shown below, accounts for the contrast between examples like (5.2) and (5.8):

(5.10)   <u>The Predicate Argument Constraint (PAC) 3</u>: Only PRED/ARG structures can properly contain a variable, x_i, which is bound to a functionally external antecedent. Bound variables can only appear as the terminal elements of XP arguments of predicates.

Derived F-structures like (5.9a) violate this constraint, while derived F-structures like (5.9b) do not.[16]

The PAC 3 also accounts for the contrast between languages like Polish on the one hand and languages like English and Italian on the other. The English and Italian analogs of (5.8c) are ungrammatical. These appear below, with their derived F-structures:

(5.11) a. *$Which_k$ did $Horace_i$ destroy NP[_ picture]$_j$

    b. (WHICH$_k$)[DESTROY NP[i] NP[[x_k][j]]]
                                  α β

(5.12) a. *$Quale_k$ ha perduto $Gianni_i$ NP[_ libro]$_j$

    b. (QUALE$_k$)[PERDERE NP[i] NP[[x_k][j]]]
                                  α β

WHICH$_k$ in Structure (5.11b) and QUALE$_k$ in Structure (5.12b) are functionally external to the N$_j$ argument which properly contains the variable x_k. Therefore these structures violate the PAC 3. No AGR_n

elements occur in either English or Italian, so all external antecedents (in the original sense) are functionally external antecedents, and there are no grammatical counterparts in these languages of examples like (5.8).

The Polish affixes which I have represented as AGR_n are, in fact, morphological GRIs, which also have the function discussed in Chapter II. When morphological GRIs occur on both the head noun and other elements of the NP (such as adjectives), they function as agreement markers as well. The presence or absence of morphological GRIs and their distribution within the language determine the behavior of that language with respect to the PAC.[17]

Let us turn now to the SGC. Polish and Italian sentences like the following suggest that this constraint, as formulated in (4.6), is too strong:

(5.13) a. l'uomo $\bar{S}$[che$_i$ $_S$[mi domando $\bar{S}$ [chi$_j$ $_S$[_ abbia visto _]]]]
       the man [who$_i$ [I wondered [who$_j$ [_ saw _]]]]
       *the man who I wondered who saw

    b. $\bar{S}$ [Che$_k$ $_S$[si domanda $\bar{S}$ [chi$_j$ $_S$[_ abbia visto _]]]]
       who REFLEX (he$_i$) wonder [who [_ saw _]]
       *Who did he wonder who saw

(5.14) a. $\bar{S}$ [Kto$_i$ komu$_j$ $_S$[_ dał _ prezent]]
       who (NOM) whom (DAT) [_ gave _ present (ACC)]
       *Who whom gave a present

    b. $\bar{S}$ [Kto$_i$ co$_j$ $_S$[_ rozumie _]]
       who (NOM) what (ACC) [_ understand _]
       *Who what understands

The derived F-structures of (5.13b) and (5.14b) are shown in (5.15a and b) respectively:

(5.15) a. (CHE$_k$)[DOMANDARSI $_{NP}$[i] [(CHI$_j$)[AVERE VISTO
                                      α
        $_{NP}$[x_j] $_{NP}$[x_k]]]]
          α β

    b. ((KTO$_i$)(CO$_j$))[ROZUMIEĆ $_{NP}$[x_i] $_{NP}$[x_j]]
                                      α β

In Structure (5.15a), the PRED/ARG structure of AVERE VISTO contains two variables, both of which are bound to operators outside of that PRED/ARG structure, and in Structure (5.15b), the same is true of the PRED/ARG structure of ROZUMIEĆ. However, the Polish and Italian examples in (5.13) and (5.14), unlike their English counterparts, are grammatical.

These data can be accounted for by varying the definition of PRED/ARG structure within certain limits from language to language. PRED/ARG structures may be thought of as either including or not including any prefixed elements such as wh-operators. So, for any given language, PRED/ARG structures are defined as either (a) or (b), below:

(5.16) a.   [PRED ... n-NP[θ] ... X ...]
     b.   [(COMP)[PRED ... x-NP[θ] ... X ...]]

For convenience, I will refer to PRED/ARG structures like (5.16a) as P-structures and to PRED/ARG structures like (5.16b) as C-structures. COMP is the cover symbol for any element prefixed to the structure of the PRED. The SGC can be reformulated as shown in (5.17):

(5.17)   The Single Gap Constraint (SGC) 2: X-structures can properly contain only one externally bound variable, x_i.

The parameter X can be assigned the value C or the value P depending on the particular language. I will refer to this as the XSTRUC parameter.

Polish and Italian are classified as C-structure languages, and English is classified as a P-structure language. In Structure (5.15a), the C-structure of AVERE VISTO contains the prefixed term CHI_j. Consequently, only one variable, x_k, is bound to an antecedent outside of that C-structure. In (5.15b), the prefixed terms KTO_i and CO_j are both contained in the C-structure of ROZUMIEĆ, and neither variable is bound to an antecedent outside of that C-structure. These structures do not violate the SGC 2, and this accounts for the grammaticality of (5.13) and (5.14), and the contrast between these examples and their English counterparts. The SGC applies in the same way to all variables, whether or not the variables and their antecedents occur with AGR_n markers.

The analysis predicts that the behavior of both C-structure and P-structure languages is the same with respect to across-the-board phenomena involving coordinate structures and adjunct structures. The C-structure/P-structure distinction is only relevant to nested structures, in which the embedded PRED/ARG structure is an argument in the PRED/ARG structure of a matrix predicate. This prediction appears to be valid. The following (shown with their derived F-structures) are examples of across-the-board phenomena in Polish and Italian, and are analogous to their English counterparts:

(5.18) a. Kogo$_k$ lubił Jan$_i$ a nienawidziła Maria$_j$
   who (ACC) loved Jan (NOM) and hated Maria (NOM)
   Who did Jan love and Maria hate

b. (KOGO$_k$) [[LUBIĆ $_{NP[i]}$ $_{NP[x_k]}$] & [NIENAWIDZIĆ
   $\underset{\alpha}{}$ $\underset{\beta}{}$
   $_{NP[j]}$ $_{NP[x_k]}$]]
   $\underset{\alpha}{}$ $\underset{\beta}{}$

(5.19) a. Chi$_i$ ha visto Giovanni$_j$ ed ha parlato con Luigi$_k$

b. (CHI$_i$)[AVERE VISTO $_{NP[x_i]}$ $_{NP[j]}$] & [AVERE PARLATO
   $\underset{\alpha}{}$ $\underset{\beta}{}$
   $_{NP[x_i]}$ $_{NP[k]}$]]
   $\underset{\alpha}{}$ $\underset{\beta}{}$

Now, consider the following Polish sentences:

(5.20) a. Jan$_i$ myślał $_S$[że Adam$_j$ widział Marię$_k$]
   Jan (NOM) thought [that Adam (NOM) saw Maria (ACC)]
   Jan thought that Adam saw Maria

b. *Kogo$_k$ Jan$_i$ myślał $_S$[że Adam$_j$ widział _]
   who (ACC) Jan (NOM) thought [that Adam (NOM) saw _]
   Who did Jan think that Adam saw

(5.21) a. Czesław$_i$ przypuszczał $_S$[że Maria$_j$ zaprosiła Jana$_k$]
   Czeslaw (NOM) supposed [that Maria (NOM) invited Jan
      (ACC)]
   Czeslaw supposed that Maria invited Jan

b. *Kogo$_k$ Czesław$_i$ przypuszczał $_{\overline{S}}$[że Maria$_j$ zaprosiła _]
whom (ACC) Czeslaw (NOM) supposed [that Maria (NOM)
    invited _]
Who did Czeslaw suppose that Maria invited

(5.22) a. Jan$_i$ powiedział $_{\overline{S}}$[żeby Bolesław$_j$ pocałował Myszkę
    Mickey$_k$]
Jan (NOM) told [that Boleslaw (NOM) kissed Mickey Mouse
    (ACC)]
Jan told Boleslaw to kiss Mickey Mouse

b. *Kogo$_k$ Jan$_i$ powiedział $_{\overline{S}}$[żeby Bolesław (NOM)
    pocałował _]
Whom (ACC) Jan (NOM) told [that Boleslaw (NOM)
    kissed _]
Who did Jan tell Boleslaw to kiss

(5.23) a. Wiesiek$_i$ mówił $_{\overline{S}}$[że Adam$_j$ dał prezent$_k$
    Grzegorzowi$_m$]
Wiesiek (NOM) said [that Adam (NOM) gave present (ACC)
    Grzegorz (DAT)]
Wiesiek said that Adam gave a present to Grzegorz

b. *Komu$_m$ Wiesiek$_i$ mówił $_{\overline{S}}$[że Adam$_j$ dał prezent$_k$ _]
whom (DAT) Wiesiek (NOM) said [that Adam (NOM) gave
    present (ACC) _]
Who did Wiesiek say that Adam gave a present to

In Polish, the EA rule rarely, if ever, applies to bind a variable to an antecedent located outside of the $\overline{S}$ constituent which contains that variable. Explanations for the boundedness of wh-Movement under certain circumstances have appeared in the literature, and some of these can be adapted to the proposed theory.[18] For example, we can account for these facts by assuming that there is a parameter, [BRIDGE], which defines the domain of the EA rule. This parameter is assigned either the value + or the value - depending on the particular language. The value [-BRIDGE] means that the EA rule is limited to a single $\overline{S}$ constituent, and the value [+BRIDGE] means that the EA rule is, in effect, unbounded. Polish is classified as a [-BRIDGE] language, and English and Italian are classified as [+BRIDGE] languages in an analysis of this sort.

The EA rule cannot apply to the syntactic structures of examples (5.20b), (5.21b), (5.22b), and (5.23b). The derived F-structures of (5.20b) and (5.23b) appear in (5.24a and b), respectively:

(5.24) a. $(KOGO_k)[MYŚLEĆ \; _{NP}[i] \; [WIDZIEĆ \; _{NP}[j] \; _{NP}[x]]]$
$\qquad\qquad\qquad\quad \alpha \qquad\qquad\qquad \alpha \qquad \beta$

b. $(KOMU_m)[MÓWIĆ \; _{NP}[i] \; [DAĆ \; _{NP}[j] \; _{NP}[k] \; _{NP}[x]]]$
$\qquad\qquad\qquad\quad \alpha \qquad\qquad \alpha \qquad \beta \qquad \gamma$

In these structures, the prefixed terms, $KOGO_k$ and $KOMU_m$, do not bind a variable in an NP[θ] argument position, and are not assigned an SR. Moreover, both structures contain an unindexed NP[θ] argument, NP[x]. These structures violate WFC I, and are not well-formed. The other examples have analogous structures. This accounts for the ungrammaticality of examples like (5.20b) - (5.23b), and for the contrast between Polish on the one hand and English and Italian on the other.[19]

Finally, let us consider a rather striking contrast between Polish on the one hand and English and Italian on the other. Polish sentences like (5.14), above, and the following suggest that more than one wh-constituent can occur in a single COMP:

(5.25) a. $\bar{S}[Kto_i \; komu_j \; co_k \; _S[\_ \; przyrzekał \_ \_]]$
[who (NOM) whom (DAT) what (ACC) [_ promised _ _]]
*Who whom what promised

b. $Jan_i \; wiedział \; \bar{S}[kto_j \; jaki \; prezent_k \; _S[\_ \; dał \_ \; Adamowi_m]]$
Jan (NOM) knew [who (NOM) which present (ACC) [_ gave_ Adam (DAT)]
*Jan knew who which present gave Adam

The analysis assumed here is the most plausible one for examples like these in the proposed framework. There are two alternatives: (a) only the initial wh-constituent is in COMP and the others have been moved to initial position(s) within the clause S; and (b) none of the wh-constituents are in COMP in Polish sentences of this type. Both of these alternatives suffer from the same weakness: they require an obligatory intra-clausal (S) fronting rule which creates S-structure sequences that are identical to those of wh-questions in COMP-initial languages like English, and which has the same effect as binding a variable to a wh-operator in COMP. If this rule does not apply, examples like the following are produced:

(5.26)   Kto$_i$ rozumie co$_j$
who (NOM) understands what (ACC)
who understands what

The rightmost unfronted wh-constituent, *co*, in this example has only an echo question interpretation. Examples like (5.26) contrast with ones like (5.14) and (5.25), all of which have non-echo question interpretations. The incorporation of such a rule into UG would introduce an undesirable level of duplication and call into question the explanatory power of the supposedly universal bound-variable analysis of wh-questions.

The examples in (5.14) and (5.25) contrast with the following ungrammatical English and Italian sentences:

(5.27)   *$_{\bar{S}}$[who$_i$ what$_j$ $_S$[_ understood _]]

(5.28)   *$_{\bar{S}}$[Chi$_i$ che$_j$ $_S$[_ ha dato _ a Giovanni$_k$]]
[who what [_ gave _ to Giovanni]]
*Who what gave to Giovanni

Polish differs from English and Italian in that it utilizes morphological GRIs and the latter languages do not. As we saw in Chapter II, when NPs occur with morphological GRIs, the Index Insertion rule can apply to insert their indices into the appropriate x-NP[θ] positions in PRED/ARG structures regardless of their positions in the S-structures (or the configurational properties of those S-structures). Thus the Index Insertion rule can apply to the variants in (5.29), below, to produce the PRED/ARG structure in (5.30):

(5.29) a.   Czesław$_i$ dał prezent$_j$ Adamowi$_k$
Czeslaw (NOM) gave present (ACC) Adam (DAT)
Czeslaw gave a present to Adam

　　　b.   Prezent$_j$ Czesław$_i$ Adamowi$_j$ dał
　　　c.   Czesław$_i$ Adamowi$_j$ prezent$_k$ dał
　　　d.   Czesław$_i$ prezent$_k$ dał Adamowi$_j$

(5.30)   [DAĆ $_{NP[i]}$ $_{NP[k]}$ $_{NP[j]}$]
　　　　　　　　α　　β　　γ

Now compare the wh-questions in (5.14) and (5.25) with the variants in (5.29). Both sentence types have the same S-structure sequential patterns (ignoring structural configurations), and the wh-questions are no harder to process than the variants in (5.29b, c, and d). In fact, the operation of the EA rule is analogous to that of the Index Insertion rule. The EA rule associates a constituent in COMP with a variable in some XP position just as the Index Insertion rule associates an S-structure constituent with some x-NP[θ] position in a PRED/ARG structure, and we would expect morphological GRIs to play an analogous role in the operation of both rules. Let us assume, then, that more than one wh-constituent can be inserted into COMP, but that only one wh-constituent per COMP can bind a variable $\underline{x}$ unless the wh-constituents bear a morphological GRI. The syntactic structure of (5.25a), before the application of the EA rule, appears in (5.31):

(5.31)

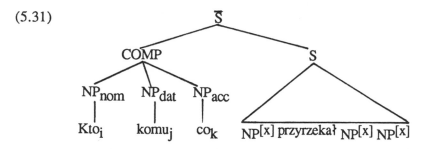

The EA rule can apply to bind each variable $\underline{x}$ with a wh-constituent to produce the S–structure of this example, which is shown below:

(5.32)

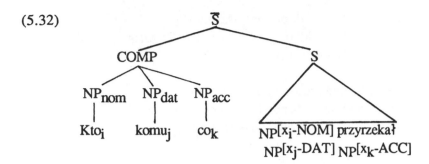

The bound variables in this S-structure are indirectly assigned the GRI features of their antecedents. The derived F-structure shown below is produced from (5.32):

(5.33) $((KTO_i) (KOMU_j) (CO_k))[PRZYRZEKA\acute{C}$
$\quad NP[x_i] \underset{\alpha}{} NP[x_k] \underset{\beta}{} NP[x_j]]\underset{\gamma}{}$

This structure is well-formed. The S-structures and derived F-structures of the other Polish examples are produced in the same way.

The syntactic structure of the English example in (5.27), before the application of the EA rule, is shown below:

(5.34)

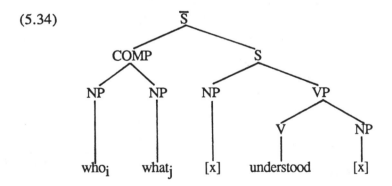

Here, only one wh-constituent, say who_i, can bind a variable, say the $\underline{x}$ in subject position. In this case, the following derived F-structure is produced:

(5.35) $((WHO_i)(WHAT_j))[UNDERSTAND \underset{\alpha}{NP[x_i]} \underset{\beta}{NP[x]}]$

This structure violates WFC I. No well-formed derived F-structure can be produced for example (5.27). The same is true of Italian sentences like (5.28). Consequently, examples of this type are ungrammatical in both languages.

This analysis explains the occurrence of Polish sentences with multiply-filled COMPs, and the difference in this regard between languages like Polish on the one hand and languages like English and Italian on the other. It predicts that the occurrence of morphological GRIs in a language is a necessary, but not sufficient, condition for the occurrence of sentences of this type, which also depends on other factors such as the value of the XSTRUC parameter for that language and its effect on the application of the SGC.

6. The Generalized EA System

The EA system of UG consists of the EA rule, the PAC, and the SGC. These are repeated below:

(6.1) a. <u>The E-Anaphora Rule (EA)</u>: In syntactic structures which contain a variable, $_{XP}[x]$ and a designated indexed constituent, $_{XP}[i]$, bind the variable to the designated constituent.

    b. <u>The Predicate Argument Constraint (PAC)</u>: Only PRED/ARG structures can properly contain a variable, x_i, which is bound to a functionally external antecedent. Bound variables can only appear as the terminal elements of XP arguments of predicates.

    c. <u>The Single Gap Constraint (SGC)</u>: X-structures can properly contain only one externally bound variable, x_i.

The EA rule binds variables to operators elsewhere in the structure by assigning those variables the index of the relevant operator. The PAC and SGC apply at the level of derived F-structure.

The islandhood of an S-structure constituent is determined by the nature of its F-structure correlate. Ignoring details, the combined effect of the PAC and SGC is to limit the occurrence of externally bound variables to one argument per PRED/ARG structure. The distributional patterns of operators and the variables that they bind are determined by universal principles such as WFC I as well as by factors which may vary from language to language. These factors include the presence and distribution of morphological GRIs and the values assigned to the XSTRUC parameter and the BRIDGE parameter. They interact to explain the sorts of differences among languages observed in Section 5. For example, Polish is a C-structure language which utilizes morphological GRIs. Clauses, S, may contain more than one variable bound to an operator outside of the clause, and more than one wh-constituent can occur in a single COMP. This is illustrated by example (5.14b), repeated below:

(5.14) b. $\bar{S}$[kto co $_S$[rozumie]]

Italian is a C-structure language which does not utilize morphological GRIs. Consequently, clauses, S, may contain more than one variable bound to an operator outside of the clause, but only one wh-constituent can occur in a given COMP. Thus examples like (5.13a) are grammatical, while examples like (5.28) are not. Both of these are repeated below:

(5.13) a.   l'uomo che mi domando chi $_S$[abbia visto]

(5.28)   * $\bar{S}$[Chi che $_S$[ha dato a Giovanni]]

Finally, English is a P-structure language which does not utilize morphological GRIs. Consequently, clauses, S, can contain only a single variable bound to an operator outside of the clause, and only one wh-constituent per COMP can occur. This is illustrated by the ungrammaticality of the analogs of the Polish and Italian sentences in (5.13) and (5.14), as shown below:

(6.2)   * the man who I wondered who $_S$[saw]

(5.27)   * $\bar{S}$[who what $_S$[understood]]

Other cross-language differences are accounted for similarly.

The EA rule is sensitive only to the presence or absence of morphological GRIs, and the categories of the variable and antecedent. Moreover, neither of the constraints are formulated in terms of syntactic configurations, so the EA system, like the other systems of UG, applies in the same way to languages regardless of their structural properties.

Notes to Chapter V

1. Unbound variables, represented as $\underline{x}$ here before the application of the EA rule, may be analyzed as [e] nodes which are distinguished from other [e] nodes only after the application of this rule (appropriately reformulated) binding them to an operator. The convention which I have adopted of distinguishing them from [e] nodes as above is a notational variant of this analysis, and I will continue to use it.

2. This does not apply to wh-constituents in echo questions like the following:

  (i) Mildred$_i$ kissed what$_j$

In such examples, the wh-constituent functions as an NP[θ] argument in the relevant derived F-structure, and does not bind a variable elsewhere in the structure.

3. Example (2.10) can also be assigned the following S-structure:

(i)

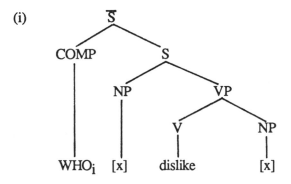

This structure contains two variables, or alternatively, one variable and an $_{NP}$[e] constituent. In either case, the predicate DISLIKE in the derived F-structure produced from (i) occurs with a single indexed NP argument. This structure is shown in (ii), assuming that the variable in the object position is bound to the WHO$_i$ constituent:

(ii)   (WHO$_i$)[DISLIKE $_\beta$NP[x_i]]

This structure cannot be the basis for a complete interpretation of this example.   Since the example can only be partially interpreted, it is unacceptable.

4. Additional cases of potential overgeneration associated with the EA analysis are discussed in Horn (1983a). I briefly discuss three examples here. First of all, consider the following:

(i)   *To whom$_i$ did Malcolm$_j$ give the parchment$_k$ to the monk$_m$

In the S-structure of this example, the PP, *to whom* is located in COMP, and cannot be associated with any other constituent in the structure. The derived F-structure of this example is the following:

(ii)   ([TO $_\alpha$NP[WHOM$_i$]])[GIVE $_\alpha$NP[j] $_\beta$NP[k] [TO $_\alpha$NP[m]]]

In this F-structure, the PP, [TO $_{NP}$WHOM$_i$]] is prefixed to the PRED/ ARG structure of GIVE and does not bind a variable in the argument structure of GIVE. Therefore, it cannot be associated with GIVE in the interpretation of the sentence. In fact, the structure contains two [TO NP] constructions, and its interpretation is redundant.

    Secondly, consider the following example, shown with its S-structure:

(iii) a.   *About what$_i$ did Frederick$_j$ dislike

b.

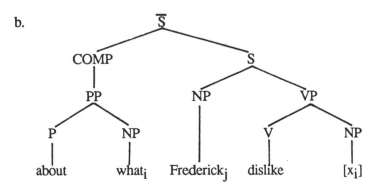

The derived F-structure of this example is shown in (iv):

(iv)   ([ABOUT $_{NP}$[WHAT$_i$]])[DISLIKE $_{NP}$[j] $_{NP}$[x$_i$]]
            α α β

This structure is not well-formed. The preposition ABOUT assigns an SR, α, to the wh-element, WHAT$_i$. This constituent is indirectly assigned a second SR, β, since it binds the $\underline{x_i}$ variable which bears this SR. Consequently, Structure (iv) violates WFC I.

Moreover, the prefixed PP cannot be associated with DISLIKE in the interpretation of the sentence since it does not bind a variable in an argument position of DISLIKE. This accounts for the ungrammaticality of (iii).

Finally, consider example (v), below, shown with its S-structure:

(v) a.   *To whom$_i$ did Malcolm$_j$ give the parchment$_k$ to

b.

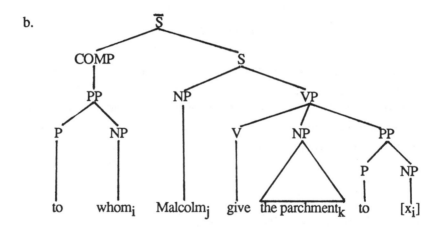

The derived F-structure of this example appears in (vi):

(vi)   ([TO $_{NP}$[WHOM$_i$]])[GIVE $_{NP}$[j] $_{NP}$[k] [TO $_{NP}$[x$_i$]]]
            α 1 α β α 2

In this F-structure, WHOM is directly assigned the SR α_1 by TO, and is indirectly assigned the SR α_2 since it binds the variable $\underline{x_i}$, which bears this SR. Even though α_1 and α_2 are identical, WHOM formally bears two SRs, in violation of WFC I. Consequently, Structure (vi) is not well-formed. Moreover, as in the previous examples, the prefixed constituent does not bind a variable in an argument position of

GIVE and therefore cannot be associated with GIVE in the interpretation of the sentence. This accounts for the ungrammaticality of example (v a).

The general principle that operates in all of these examples is that only elements in argument positions in the PRED/ARG structures of predicates, or prefixed elements which bind variables in these positions can be associated with the predicate in the interpretation of the sentence.

5. The observation that such processes as topicalization are subject to most if not all of the constraints which apply to wh-Movement dates back at least to Ross (1967), and this observation is central to the analysis in Chomsky (1977).

6. The derivation of Structure (2.19b) involves a rule which assigns the index of the focus constituent, NP_j, to a PRO in the COMP of S_2. The analyses assumed here for both topicalized and cleft sentences differ in certain ways from the standard theory analyses of these sentence types, but I will not attempt to defend them since the choice of the particular analyses adopted for these data is not crucial to the overall shape of the proposed theory. See Horn (1978) and (1983a) for discussion of this analysis of topicalization.

7. The dummy IT in structures like (2.21b) is not indexed and does not bear an SR at the level of derived F-structure. (The symbol Ø represents the null SR). Alternatively, such constituents need not be represented at this level at all. The details of the treatment of such dummy constituents are not important to the present discussion.

8. These processes are unified in the standard theory as subcases of wh-Movement. See Chomsky (1977).

9. The two-argument predicate *bastard* occurs in examples like the following:

(i) a. $Phil_i$ was a bastard to his $subordinates_j$
   b. Who_j was $Phil_i$ a bastard to

(ii) a. $Everyone_i$ considered $Phil_j$ a bastard to his $subordinates_k$

b.   Who$_k$ did everyone$_i$ consider Phil$_j$ a bastard to

The derived F-structures of (i)b and (ii)b are shown below:

(iii) a.   (WHO$_j$)[[BE[BASTARD]] NP[i] [TO NP[x$_j$]]]
$\qquad\qquad\qquad\qquad\qquad\quad\alpha\qquad\quad\alpha'$

  b.   (WHO$_k$)[CONSIDER NP[i] [BASTARD NP[j] [TO NP[x$_k$]]]]
$\qquad\qquad\qquad\qquad\alpha\qquad\qquad\qquad\alpha\qquad\qquad\alpha$

These structures are well-formed, and the relevant examples are grammatical. In these examples, *bastard* behaves like *nasty* in examples like (3.12).

10. Other factors, however, appear to govern the application of the EA rule to the XP constituents of $\overline{V}$ predicates. These factors are complex, and may relate to the degree to which the idiomatic expression is frozen, among other things. At any rate, the following examples are ungrammatical, and contrast with those in (3.41):

(i) a.   *What sort of advantage$_i$ did they$_j$ take of Gatsby$_k$
  b.   ?*What sort of president was Jason$_i$ of the club$_k$

The derived F-structures of these examples are shown in (ii):

(ii) a.   (WH-advantage$_i$)[[TAKE NP^c[x$_i$]] NP[j] NP[k]]
$\qquad\qquad\qquad\qquad\qquad\qquad\quad\zeta\qquad\quad\alpha\quad\ \beta$

  b.   (WH-president$_i$)[[BE NP^c[x$_i$]] NP[j] [OF NP[k]]]
$\qquad\qquad\qquad\qquad\qquad\qquad\alpha\qquad\quad\alpha$

These structures do not violate the PAC. Note also the contrast between (i b) and example (3.41e).

11. In these derived F-structures, the order of the bound variables, x_i and x_j, in the complements is not important to the present discussion. The following derived F-structures may also be produced for the examples in (4.1):

(i) a.   (WHO$_k$)[WONDER NP[i] [(WHO$_j$)[SEE NP[x$_k$] NP[x$_j$]]]]
$\qquad\qquad\qquad\qquad\qquad\quad\alpha\qquad\qquad\qquad\qquad\quad\alpha\qquad\ \beta$

b. (WHAT$_k$)[ASK $_{NP}$[i] [(WHO$_j$)[KISS $_{NP}$[x_k] $_{NP}$[x_j]]]]
        α α β

Other independent factors may operate to explain why the interpretations associated with the structures in (4.3) are preferable to those associated with (i) above, even though the sentences in (4.1) are ungrammatical in both senses in English. See Chomsky (1981).

12. Examples (4.7a) and (4.7b) differ at the level of S-structure. The former is a coordinate S structure and the latter contains a coordinate VP structure. The derived F-structures of these examples, in (4.8a and b) respectively, are structurally identical. Those aspects of the interpretations of such sentences which are related to the S-structure differences are derived by rules which have access to the S-structure level. As suggested in Chapter II, both the S-structure level and the level of derived F-structure are available to the semantic interpretation rules. Derived F-structures are the basis for only part of the interpretation.

Sentences like (4.7c) are not coordinate structures and are not, in fact, examples of across-the-board extraction. The rightmost gap, in the object position of *robbed* in the *after*-clause, is a so-called parasitic gap. Examples like these, as discussed, do not violate the SGC, but others such as the following seemingly violate the PAC and/or the SGC:

(i) a. Which girl did you send a picture of _p_ to __
    b. Jason is a man who everyone who knows _p_ dislikes __

In these examples, _p_ represents the parasitic gap and __ represents the "normal" gap.

Parasitic gaps require special treatment in any of the current major frameworks. An analysis along the lines of Engdahl (1983) is compatible with the proposed framework. Essentially, parasitic gaps are not bound variables. Rather, they are null anaphors which are obligatorily interpreted as coreferential with bound variable antecedents. If this is the case, then it is reasonable to assume that the rules and principles which determine the distribution of parasitic gaps, like those which determine the distribution of pronouns when they function as anaphors, apply at the level of S-structure. The primary restriction on the distribution of parasitic gaps seems to be that they do not occur in S-structure configurations which require non-coreference. (See Engdahl (1983) for further discussion.) Certain details remain to be worked out, but it is clear that parasitic gaps are distinct from bound variables and are therefore not subject to the PAC or the SGC. Consequently, sentences like (i) are not counterexamples to the EA analysis.

Finally, consider the following sentence (shown with its derived F-structure):

(ii) a. Who_m did Marvin_i think that Zelma_j liked and Gladys_k hated

b. (WHO_m) [THINK $\underset{\alpha}{\text{NP}[i]}$ [[LIKE $\underset{\alpha}{\text{NP}[j]}$ $\underset{\beta}{\text{NP}[x_m]}$]] & [HATE $\underset{\alpha}{\text{NP}[k]}$ $\underset{\beta}{\text{NP}[x_m]}$]]]]

In Structure (ii b), the PRED/ARG structure of THINK contains two variables (x_m) which are bound to an external wh-element. However, in this case, both variables are bound to the same (single) operator. The contrast between (ii a) and the ungrammatical sentences in (4.1) can be explained by considering multiple variables in coordinate structures bound to the same operator as a single variable for the purpose of the SGC as formulated in (4.6).

13.   The ungrammaticality of examples like (4.9) may be due to a general symmetry condition on coordinate structures which prohibits "unlike" constituents from being conjoined. In the following examples, this condition is violated:

(i) a.   *Horace hit Jake and Matilda, Mergatroyd hit
    b.   *Rufus liked Meryl and who did Gladys like

In example (i a), a topicalized sentence is conjoined with a non-topicalized sentence, and in example (i b), a statement and a question are conjoined. It is not clear, however, how such a symmetry condition might be formulated. Note that examples like the following, in contrast to (i a), are grammatical:

(ii)   Alvin disliked Malcolm, but Elroy, he really despised

Many problems remain to be solved before a hypothesis based on such a condition can be adequately formulated.

14. I assume that the F-structure correlates of extraposed clauses occupy these positions rather than the NP[θ] argument position occupied by the dummy subject IT.

15. Examples like the following also occur:

(i) We heard how the Russians invaded Afghanistan with 50,000 troops

This example contains a manner adverbial, *with 50,000 troops*, and there is no obvious source for *how* as a manner adverbial. This provides further support for the analysis of *how* as a complementizer in examples like (4.17b).

16. Consider the following example, shown with its (partial) derived F-structure:

(i) a. *Czyją$_n$ widziałeś $_{NP}$[człowieka$_j$ [który$_k$ czytał $_{NP}$[—
             książkę$_m$]]]$_o$
        whose (ACC) (you$_i$) saw $_{NP}$[man (ACC)) [who (NOM) read
             $_{NP}$[— book (ACC)]]]
        *Whose did you see the man who read book

   b. (CZYJA$_n$-AGR$_n$)[WIDZIEĆ $_{NP}$[i] $\underset{A}{\underset{\alpha}{NP}}$[[j][(KTÓRY$_k$)

       [CZYTAĆ $\underset{\alpha}{NP}$[x$_k$] $\underset{B}{\underset{\beta}{NP}}$[[x$_n$] [m-AGR$_n$]]]]]$_o$]

In Structure (i b), $\underline{NP}_A$ and $\underline{NP}_B$, which is nested in $\underline{NP}_A$, properly contain the variable x$_n$ which is bound to the operator CZYJA$_n$-AGR$_n$. Neither $\underline{NP}_A$ nor $\underline{NP}_B$ is a PRED/ARG structure. The operator CZYJA$_n$-AGR$_n$ is functionally internal to the $\underline{NP}_B$ structure, whose head, m-AGR$_n$, bears the matching AGR$_n$ marker. However, it is not functionally internal to the $\underline{NP}_A$ structure since no AGR$_n$ marker associates it specifically with this structure (just as no AGR$_n$ marker associates PPs with the NP structures which contain them in examples like (5.2b and d)). If we interpret the PAC 3 as requiring that the operator be functionally internal in this sense to each of the non-PRED/ ARG structures that properly contain the variable bound to it, then Structure (i b) violates this constraint. This explains the ungrammaticality of (i a).

17. Actually, all Polish nouns and adjectives have GRI markers, which are represented at the level of derived F-structure. In these examples, however, I have only indicated these when they can function as agreement markers in the particular example.

In theory, the distribution of the morphological GRIs in a language can be limited to the heads of NPs, in which case they do not have the agreement function, and the theory predicts that such languages will pattern like English rather than Polish with regard to examples like (5.8).

18. See Erteschik (1973), whose terminology I have adopted, and Chomsky (1981).

19. Some additional comments on the [BRIDGE] analysis are perhaps called for. Firstly, it is not the case that in [+BRIDGE] languages, like English, all verbs are bridge verbs. For example, *say* and *think* are bridge verbs while *know, expound* and *snort* are not. The distinction that I wish to make here is the one between languages in which unbounded EA can occur and ones in which it cannot. It is possible, of course, to view this distinction as a difference in degree. That is, some languages have few or no bridge verbs, while others have a large set of bridge verbs. In this case, the feature [BRIDGE] might best be thought of as a feature of individual verbs, and not as a parameter which distinguishes language types. However, in English, the application of wh-Movement to non-bridge verbs generally produces sentences that are not egregiously ungrammatical, such as the following: *?Who did Jason know that Emery disliked; ??Which theory did Anson sniff/snort that he had developed first.* In contrast, the Polish counterparts of sentences like these are clearly ungrammatical. This suggests that there is a distinction between [+BRIDGE] and [-BRIDGE] languages, and [+bridge] and [-bridge] verbs within a language. So [BRIDGE] is a feature of languages as a whole, and [bridge] is a feature of individual lexical items.

Bibliography

Adamko, Jerzy. 1973. Noun objects in Polish and English. *Papers and studies in contrastive linguistics* II (Poznan, Poland: UAM Press): 245 - 254.

Akmajian, Adrian. 1975. More evidence for a NP cycle. *Linguistic Inquiry* 6: 115 - 129.

Anderson, Stephen. 1977. Comments on the paper by Wasow. In: Culicover et al eds. 1977: 361 - 377.

Anderson, Stephen & Paul Kiparsky, eds. 1973. *A festschrift for Morris Halle.* New York: Holt, Rinehart & Winston.

Andrews, Avery. 1978 a. Traces and the Intervention Constraint. Manuscript. Canberra: Australian National University.

Andrews, Avery. 1978 b. Remarks on *to* adjunction. *Linguistic Inquiry* 9: 261 - 278.

Andrews, Avery. 1982 a. The representation of case in Modern Icelandic. In: Bresnan, ed., 1982 a: Chapter 7.

Andrews, Avery. 1982 b. A note on the constituent structure of adverbials and auxiliaries. *Linguistic Inquiry* 13: 313 - 317.

Aronoff, Mark. 1971. Studies in analogical pseudo-syntax 1.1. Manuscript. Cambridge, Mass.: MIT.

Bach, Emmon. 1976. On *On Raising* and more on raising. Manuscript. University of Massachusetts.

Bach, Emmon. 1977 a. Comments on the paper by Chomsky. In: Culicover et al eds. 1977: 133 - 156.

Bach, Emmon. 1977 b. Review of P.M. Postal, *On Raising: One rule of English grammar and its theoretical implications. Language* 52: 621 - 654.

Bach, Emmon. 1980. In defense of passive. *Linguistics & Philosophy* 3: 297 - 341.

Bach, Emmon & George Horn. 1976. Remarks on 'Conditions on transformations'. *Linguistic Inquiry* 7: 265 - 299.

Bartmiński, J. 1973. Czy język polski staje się jezykiem pozycyjnym? [Is Polish becoming a positional language?]. *Język Polski* 53: 81 - 95.

Bird, Charles & Timothy Shopen. 1979. Maninka. In: Shopen ed. 1979 b: 59 - 111.

Borsley, Robert. 1983. A Welsh agreement process and the status of VP and S. In: Gazdar et al eds. 1983: 55 - 65.

Borsley, Robert. 1984. On the nonexistence of VPs. In: Geest, W. de & Y. Putseys eds. 1984: 55-65.

Borsley, Robert. 1986. Prepositional complementizers in Welsh. *Journal of Linguistics* 2: 67 - 84.

Brame, Michael. 1976 a. Alternatives to the tensed S and specified subject constraints. Manuscript. University of Washington.

Brame, Michael. 1976 b. *Conjectures and refutations in syntax and semantics.* New York: Elsevier-North Holland.

Bresnan, Joan. 1976 a. Variables in the theory of transformations. In: Culicover et al eds. 1976: 157 - 196.

Bresnan, Joan. 1976 b. On the form and functioning of transformations. *Linguistic Inquiry* 7: 3 - 40.

Bresnan, Joan. 1978. A realistic transformational grammar. In: Halle et al eds. 1979: 1 - 59.

Bresnan, Joan. 1980. The passive in lexical theory. *Occasional paper no. 7.* Center for Cognitive Science. MIT.

Bresnan, Joan. 1982 a. ed. *The mental representation of grammatical relations.* Cambridge, MA: MIT Press.

Bresnan, Joan. 1982 b. Polyadicity. In: Bresnan ed. 1982 a: Chapter 3.

Bresnan, Joan. 1982 c. Control & complementation. In: Bresnan ed. 1982 a: Chapter 5.

Campbell, Mary Anne et al eds. 1970. *Papers from the 6th Regional Meeting of the Chicago Linguistic Society.* Chicago: University of Chicago.

Cattell, Ray. 1976. Constraints on movement rules. *Language* 52: 18 - 50.

Cattell, Ray. 1978. On extractability from quasi-NPs. *Linguistic Inquiry* 10: 168 - 172.

Chomsky, Noam. 1970. Remarks on nominalization. In: Jacobs & Rosenbaum eds. 1970: 184 - 221.

Chomsky, Noam. 1973. Conditions on transformations. In: Anderson & Kiparsky eds. 1970: 232 - 286.

Chomsky, Noam. 1975. *Reflections on language.* New York: Pantheon.

Chomsky, Noam. 1976. Conditions on rules of grammar. *Linguistic Analysis* 2: 303 - 352.

Chomsky, Noam. 1977 a. On wh-movement. In: Culicover et al eds. 1977: 71 - 132.

Chomsky, Noam. 1977 b. *Essays on form and interpretation.* New York: Elsevier- North Holland.

Chomsky, Noam. 1980. On binding. *Linguistic Inquiry* 11: 1 - 46.

Chomsky, Noam. 1981. *Lectures on government and binding*. Dordrecht: Foris Publications.

Chomsky, Noam. 1982. *Concepts and consequences of the theory of government and binding*. Cambridge, MA: MIT Press.

Chomsky, Noam. 1985. Barriers. Manuscript MIT.

Cole, Peter & Jerrold Sadock eds. 1977. *Syntax and semantics.Vol. 8: Grammatical relations*. New York: Academic Press.

Cole, Peter & O. Hermon. 1981. Subjecthood and islandhood: evidence from Quechua. *Linguistic Inquiry* 12: 1 - 30.

Cooper, Robin. 1979. Binding in wholewheat syntax. Manuscript. University of Wisconsin.

Culicover, Peter, Thomas Wasow & Adrian Akmajian eds. 1977. *Formal Syntax*. New York: Academic Press.

Dixon, Robert. 1972. *The Dyirbal language of North Queensland*. Cambridge University Press.

Emonds, Joseph. 1970. *Root and structure-preserving transformations*. Doctoral dissertation. Cambridge, MA: MIT.

Emonds, Joseph. 1985. *A unified theory of syntactic categories*. Dordrecht: Foris Publications.

Engdahl, Elisabet. 1983. Parasitic gaps. *Linguistics and Philosophy* 6: 5 - 34.

Engdahl, Elisabet & Mark Stein eds. 1979. *Papers presented to Emmon Bach by his students*. Amherst, MA: University of Massachusetts Press.

Erteschik, Naomi. 1973. *On the nature of island constraints*. Doctoral dissertation. Cambridge, MA: MIT.

Fiengo, Robert. 1977. On trace theory. *Linguistic Inquiry* 8: 35 - 61

Fisiak, Jacek, Maria Lipińska-Grzegorek & Tadeusz Zabrocki. 1978. *An introductory English-Polish contrastive grammar*. Warszawa: Panstwowe Wydawnictwo Naukowe.

Freidin, Robert. 1975. The analysis of passives. *Language* 51: 384 - 405.

Gazdar, Gerald, E. Klein & Geoffrey Pullum eds. 1983. *Order, concord, and constituency*. Dordrecht: Foris Publications.

Geest, W. de & Y. Putseys eds. 1984. *Sentential complementation*. Dordrecht: Foris Publications.

Grinder, John. 1970. Super equi-NP-deletion. In: Campbell et al. eds. 1970: 297 - 317.

Haiman, John. 1979. Hua, a Papuan language of New Guinea. In: Shopen ed. 1979a: 35 - 89.

Hale, Kenneth. 1981. On the position of Walbiri in a typology of the base Indiana University Linguistics Club.

Hale, Kenneth. 1983. Warlpiri and the grammar of non-configurational languages. *Natural Language and Linguistic Theory* 1: 5 - 47.

Halle, Morris, Joan Bresnan & G. Miller eds. 1978. *Linguistic theory & psychological reality.* Cambridge, MA: MIT Press.

Hasegawa, Kinsuke. 1968. The passive construction in English. *Language* 44: 230 - 243.

Haviland, John. 1979. How to talk to your brother-in-law in Guugu Yimidhirr. In: Shopen ed. 1979 b: 161 - 239.

Hayes, Bruce. 1976. The semantic nature of the intervention constraint. *Linguistic Inquiry* 7: 371 - 375.

Horn, George Michael. 1974. *The noun phrase constraint.* Doctoral dissertation University of Massachusetts.

Horn, George Michael. 1975. On the nonsentential nature of the POSS-ING construction. *Linguistic Analysis* 1: 333 - 387.

Horn, George Michael. 1977. An analysis of certain reflexive verbs and its implications for the organization of the lexicon. *Studia Anglica Posnaniensia* 9: 17 - 42.

Horn, George Michael. 1979 a. Operations on functional structures. Manuscript University of Newcastle, Australia.

Horn, George Michael. 1979 b. Functional structures and control. In: Engdahl & Stein eds. 1979: 123 - 133.

Horn, George Michael. 1983 a. *Lexical-functional grammar.* Trends in Linguistics, Monograph 21. Berlin: Mouton Publishers.

Horn, George Michael. 1983 b. Argument reduction. *Linguistic Analysis* 12: 339 - 378.

Horn, George Michael. 1985 a. Raising and complementation. *Linguistics* 23: 813 - 850.

Horn, George Michael. 1985 b. Noam Chomsky, *Lectures on Government and Binding. Australian Journal of Linguistics.* 5: 255 - 283.

Horn, George Michael. 1986. The minimal distance principle revisited. In: Kastovsky & Szwedek eds. 1986: 909 - 934.

Horn, George & Tadeusz Zabrocki. 1978. Island constraints in Polish. Paper presented at the *16th Polish-English Contrastive Conference.* Tlen, Poland.

Hornstein, Norbert & David Lightfoot. 1981. *Explanation in linguistics.* London: Longman.

Hornstein, Norbert & David Lightfoot. 1984. Rethinking predication. Manuscript University of Maryland.

Inoue, Kyoko. 1979. Japanese. In Shopen ed. 1979 b: 241 - 300.

Jackendoff, Ray. 1972. *Semantic interpretation in generative grammar*. Cambridge, MA: MIT Press.

Jackendoff, Ray. 1974. Introduction to the X convention. Mimeograph. Cambridge, MA: MIT.

Jackendoff, Ray. 1975. Morphological and semantic regularities in the lexicon. *Language* 51: 639 - 671.

Jackendoff, Ray. 1976. Toward an explanatory semantic representation. *Linguistic Inquiry* 7: 89 - 150.

Jackendoff, Ray. 1977 a. *X syntax: a study of phrase structure*. Linguistic Inquiry Monograph 2. Cambridge, MA: MIT Press.

Jackendoff, Ray. 1977 b. Constraints on phrase structure rules. In: Culicover et al eds. 1977: 249 - 283.

Jacobs, Roderick & Peter Rosenbaum eds. 1970. *Readings in English transformational grammar* Waltham, MA: Ginn & Co.

Jacobson, Polly & Paul Neubauer. 1976. Rule cyclicity: evidence from the intervention constraint. *Linguistic Inquiry* 7: 449 - 461.

Kastovsky, Dieter & Aleksander Szwedek eds. 1986. *Linguistics across historical and geographical boundaries* Berlin: Mouton Publishers.

Keenan, Edward ed. 1975. *Formal semantics of natural language*. London: Cambridge University Press.

Keenan, Edward & Elinor Ochs. 1979. Becoming a competent speaker of Malagasy. In: Shopen ed. 1979b: 113 - 158.

Keyser, Samuel & Thomas Roeper. 1984. On the middle and ergative constructions in English. *Linguistic Inquiry* 15: 381 - 416.

Kuno, Susumu. 1973. Constraints on internal clauses and sentential subjects. *Linguistic Inquiry* 4: 363 - 385.

Kwee, John. 1965. *Indonesian*. New York: David McKay Co..

Lightfoot, David. 1976. On traces and conditions on rules. In: Culicover et al eds. 1976: 207 - 238.

MacDonald, Roderick Ross. 1967. *A students' reference grammar of modern formal Indonesian*. Washington DC: Georgetown University Press.

McCawley, James. 1967. Meaning and the description of languages. Reprinted in McCawley 1973: 99 - 120.

McCawley, James. 1973. *Grammar and meaning*. New York: Academic Press.

McCloskey, John. 1984. Raising, subcategorization, and selection in Modern Irish. *Natural Language and Linguistic Theory* 1: 448 - 485.

Mithun, M. & Wallace Chafe. 1979. Recapturing the Mohawk language. In: Shopen ed. 1979 a: 3 - 33.

Mohanan, K.P. 1982. Grammatical relations and clause structure in Malayalam. In: Bresnan ed. 1982 a, Chapter 5.

Ono, Kiyoharu. 1980. *A study of Japanese complement constructions*. Doctoral dissertation University of Newcastle, Australia.

Ostler, Nicholas. 1977. Remarks on the passive in Old English. Manuscript MIT.

Partee, Barbara. 1975. Deletion and variable binding. In: Keenan ed. 1975: 16 - 34.

Postal, Paul. 1974. *On Raising*. Cambridge, MA: MIT Press.

Pullum, Geoffrey & Robert Borsley. 1980. Comments on the two central claims of 'trace theory'. *Linguistics* 18: 73 - 104.

Radford, Andrew. 1981. *Transformational syntax*. London: Cambridge University Press.

Robson, Roy Anthony. 1972. *On the generation of passive constructions in English.*. Doctoral dissertation University of Texas.

Roeper, Thomas & Muffy Siegal. 1978. A lexical transformation for verbal compounds. *Linguistic Inquiry* 9: 199 - 260.

Rosenbaum, Peter. 1967. *The grammar of English predicate complement constructions*. Cambridge, MA: MIT Press.

Rosenbaum, Peter. 1970. A principle governing deletion in English sentential complements. In: Jacobs & Rosenbaum eds. 1970:

Ross, John. 1967. *Constraints on variables in syntax.*. Doctoral dissertation MIT.

Sag, Ivan. 1977. *Deletion and logical form.*. Doctoral dissertation MIT.

Shopen, Timothy ed. 1979 a. *Languages and their status*. Cambridge, MA: Winthrop.

Shopen, Timothy ed. 1979 b. *Languages and their speakers*. Cambridge, MA: Winthrop.

Soames, Scott & David Perlmutter. 1979. *Syntactic argumentation and the structure of English*. Berkeley, Los Angeles, London: University of California Press.

Stockwell, Robert, Paul Schachter & Barbara Partee. 1973. *The major syntactic structures of English* New York: Holt, Rinehart and Winston.

Warshawsky, Florence. 1965. Reflexivization I, II. Manuscript MIT.

Wasow, Thomas. 1972. *Anaphoric relations in English*. Doctoral dissertation MIT.

Wasow, Thomas. 1977. Transformations and the lexicon. In: Culicover et al eds. 1977: 327 - 360.

Webelhuth, G. 1984. German is configurational. *The Linguistic Review.* 4: 203 - 246.

Williams, Edwin. 1984. Grammatical relations. *Linguistic Inquiry* 15: 639 - 673.

Yallop, Colin. 1982. *Australian aboriginal languages*. London: Andre Deutsch Ltd.

Subject Index

George Horn

Lexical-Functional Grammar

1983. 14,8 x 22,8 cm. IX, 394 pages. Cloth
ISBN 9027931690
(Trends in Linguistics. Studies and Monographs 21)

The analysis outlined in this monograph is formulated in the context of the major developments in linguistic theory stemming from the proposal of the so-called Lexicalist Hypothesis by Chomsky. The most significant product of linguistic research during this period has been the development and expansion of the lexical component and consequent reorganization and reformulation of the rules of the transformational-generative model, in which this component has been assigned many of the tasks formerly associated with the syntactic component.

More recently, various counterproposals to Chomsky's analysis have been suggested. Perhaps the most important of these was developed by Bresnan, the key feature of which is the virtually complete reduction of the syntactic component.

This work is an attempt to extend and reformulate certain of Bresnan's and Chomsky's ideas, combining the basic organization of Chomsky's model, in which lexical and non-lexical operations are clearly distinguished, with a non-syntactic account of bound anaphora, control, and NP movement phenomena. The proposed model provides a framework in which universal generalizations can be captured, and language variation can be accounted for without the complex machinery of Chomsky's current analysis, at the same time maintaining distinctions that are obscured in Bresnan's purely lexical analysis.

mouton de gruyter

Berlin · New York · Amsterdam

LINGUISTICS

an interdisciplinary journal of the language sciences

Editor-in-Chief: Wolfgang Klein

Editorial Board: Bernard Comrie
Östen Dahl
Norbert Dittmar
Flip G. Droste
Gerald Gazdar
Jaap van Marle
Jürgen Weissenborn

LINGUISTICS, which is one of the oldest journals in its field, celebrated its 25th anniversary in 1987. Over the past 25 years, **LINGUISTICS** has published articles by many of the leading figures in the languages sciences, including Anne Cutler, Janet Dean Fodor, Roman Jakobson, Edward Keenan, Shana Poplack, Suzanne Romaine, Pieter M. Seuren, and Arnold Zwicky, and has built up a reputation as an important publication in its area, supporting both practical and theoretical approaches.

LINGUISTICS publishes articles and short notices in the traditional disciplines of linguistics as well as neighboring disciplines that are engaged in the study of natural language.

LINGUISTICS accepts work from other disciplines insofar as it is deemed to be of interest to linguists and other students of natural language; for example, certain studies in logic, artificial intelligence, social interaction, physiology, and neurology would meet this requirement.

LINGUISTICS also publishes occasional Special Issues in any of these fields and welcomes proposals for them.

Special topics to be featured in forthcoming issues include, for example, Linguistic and psychological approaches to morphology, Modality, Chinese syntax, and Syntax and semantics of noun phrases.

mouton de gruyter
Berlin · New York · Amsterdam